Metrics and Models in Software Quality Engineering

Second Edition

Metrics and Models in Software Quality Engineering

Second Edition

Stephen H. Kan

✦ Addison-Wesley

Boston • San Francisco • New York • Toronto • Montreal
London • Munich • Paris • Madrid
Capetown • Sydney • Tokyo • Singapore • Mexico City

The publisher offers discounts on this book when ordered in quantity for bulk purchases and special sales. For more information, please contact:

U.S. Corporate and Government Sales
(800) 382-3419
corpsales@pearsontechgroup.com

For sales outside of the U.S., please contact:

International Sales
international@pearsoned.com

Visit Addison-Wesley on the Web: www.awprofessional.com

Library of Congress Cataloging-in-Publication Data is on file.

ISBN 0-13-398808-2
This product is printed digitally on demand. This book is the paperback version of an original hardcover book.
Fifth printing, October 2005

To my mother, Mui Leong

Contents

Foreword to the Second Edition

For more than 50 years software has been a troublesome discipline. Software's problems are numerous and include cancelations, litigation, cost overruns, schedule overruns, high maintenance costs, and low levels of user satisfaction. The problems with software occur more often than not. My company's research indicates that more than half of large software projects will encounter some kind of delay, overrun, or failure to perform when deployed.

But software does not have to be as troublesome as it has been. Some complex software projects do achieve their delivery schedules and cost targets, and behave properly when used. Throughout my career in software I've been interested in what distinguishes successful software projects from failures and disasters.

It happens that the main factors leading to software success are easily identified when side-by-side comparisons of similar projects are performed, where one set was successful and the other set was troublesome. The successful software projects achieve excellence in software quality control, and they are able to do this because of excellence in software quality measurements.

Although it might be thought that excellent software quality control is expensive, it turns out to yield a very positive return on investment. When canceled software projects and disasters are studied by means of "autopsies," they all have similar patterns: Early phases of troubled projects are handled carelessly without adequate requirements analysis or design reviews. After rushing through the early phases and seeming to be ahead of schedule, problems begin to mount during coding and testing. When testing begins in earnest, serious problems are detected so that schedules and cost targets cannot be achieved. Indeed, some software projects have so many serious problems—termed bugs or defects—that they are canceled without completion.

By contrast, successful projects are more thorough at the start. The requirements are carefully analyzed and the designs are formally inspected. This takes some time and adds upfront costs, but once coding and testing begin, the value of careful quality control allows the projects to move rapidly to a successful conclusion.

Stephen Kan and I both learned the importance of software quality control and good software quality metrics at IBM. Even though Stephen and I worked in different IBM labs during different decades, we have some common viewpoints. We have both been convinced by empirical evidence that without excellent software quality control, large system development is hazardous and likely to fail. We also both know that effective software quality control is built on a foundation of careful measurements using accurate metrics.

Stephen and I both had access to IBM's internal quality data—one of the best and largest collections of software data in the world. But one company's internal information is not sufficient to be convincing unless other organizations replicate the findings. Stephen's excellent book goes beyond IBM; it offers valuable information from many companies and government agencies. He cites studies by Hewlett-Packard, Motorola, NASA, and other organizations that have solved the problems of how to build software successfully.

I first encountered Stephen Kan's *Metrics and Models in Software Quality Engineering* book in 1995 when the first edition was published. I found that the book contained solid research, and that it covered a broad range of topics and very clearly showed the relationships among them.

This new edition keeps all the virtues of the earlier work and adds substantial new information, such as a chapter on measuring quality within the object-oriented paradigm. Stephen Kan's new edition contains an excellent combination of solid scholarship and breadth of coverage. This is the single best book on software quality engineering and metrics that I've encountered.

Capers Jones
Chief Scientist Emeritus
Software Productivity Research, Inc.
(an Artemis company)

Foreword to the First Edition

Quality management and engineering have enjoyed a diversity of applications over the past few years. For example:

☐ A system of teaching hospitals conservatively estimates $17.8 million saved on an investment of $2.5 million in quality management over a five-year time period.

☐ The U.S. Air Force Military Airlift Command improved capacity so much through quality improvement problem solving during the Gulf War that they avoided having to deploy civilian aircraft (thus avoiding the suspension of next-day mail delivery, among other conveniences).

☐ The U.S. Bureau of Labor Statistics reduced the time needed to produce the monthly Consumer Price Index (CPI), compiled by 650 people in five departments, by 33 percent with no loss in accuracy.

☐ The University of Pennsylvania saved more than $60,000 a year from one project focused on reducing mailing costs.

The examples go on and on, from industries such as telecommunications, health care, law, hospitals, government, pharmaceuticals, railways, and schools. The variety of terrains where the seeds of TQM successfully take hold is almost baffling.

As the rest of the world moves headlong into quality improvement at revolutionary rates, the software developers and engineers—consumed in debates over metrics and process models, over methodologies and CASE tools—often lag far behind. Some of the reasons include unique challenges in defining user requirements, the "guru" mentality prevalent in many software organizations, and the relative immaturity of the application of software engineering. Whereas the first two are fascinating topics in their own right, it is the third challenge at which Stephen Kan's book is squarely aimed.

Imagine designing an airplane using a small fraction of the aeronautical engineering knowledge available. Imagine designing an automobile while ignoring mechanical engineering. Imagine running a refinery with no knowledge of chemical process engineering. It is not surprising that the first recommendations from consultants offering credible software quality solutions would be to apply proven software engineering methods first. Just as these methods only slowly find acceptance in software development communities, so also have the methods of quality engineering.

One reason for this slow adoption lies with the relative lack of literature that gives clear descriptions of the fundamentals in these fields while illustrating actual use within leading-edge software development organizations. Stephen Kan's book, *Metrics and Models in Software Quality Engineering,* represents a laudable move to fill this need.

Dr. Kan provides a uniquely comprehensive reference to the field of software quality engineering. He has managed a delightful balance between the technical details needed and practical applications of the models and techniques. This book is peppered with industry examples, not only from Kan's own employer, the Malcolm Baldrige National Quality Award-winning IBM Rochester, but from NEC's Switching Systems Division, Hewlett-Packard, Motorola, NASA Software Engineering Laboratory, and IBM Federal Systems Division. Concepts and theory are illustrated by software industry examples, which make the reading that much richer.

Dr. Joseph Juran, one of the key founders of modern quality management and engineering, describes "life behind the quality dikes." As society becomes more reliant on technology, failures of that technology have increasing adverse impacts. Quality helps to insulate society from these dangers. This role of quality in software development certainly rivals that of business competitiveness, and gives another compelling reason to read, understand, and apply the ideas within this book.

Brian Thomas Eck, Ph.D.
Vice President
Juran Institute, Inc.
Wilton, Connecticut

Preface

Looking at software engineering from a historical perspective, the 1960s and earlier could be viewed as the functional era, the 1970s the schedule era, the 1980s the cost era, and the 1990s and beyond the quality and efficiency era. In the 1960s we learned how to exploit information technology to meet institutional needs and began to link software with the daily operations of institutions. In the 1970s, as the industry was characterized by massive schedule delays and cost overruns, the focus was on planning and control of software projects. Phase-based life-cycle models were introduced, and analysis, like the mythical man-month, emerged. In the 1980s hardware costs continued to decline, and information technology permeated every facet of our institutions and became available to individuals. As competition in the industry became keen and low-cost applications became widely implemented, the importance of productivity in software development increased significantly. Various software engineering cost models were developed and used. In the late 1980s, the importance of quality was also recognized.

The 1990s and beyond is certainly the quality era. With state-of-the-art technology now able to provide abundant functionality, customers demand high quality. Demand for quality is further intensified by the ever-increasing dependence of society on software. Billing errors, large-scale disrupted telephone services, and even missile failures during recent wars can all be traced to the issue of software quality. In this era, quality has been brought to the center of the software development process. From the standpoint of software vendors, quality is no longer an advantage factor in the marketplace; it has become a necessary condition if a company is to compete successfully.

Starting in the mid 1990s two major factors emerged that have proved to have an unprecedented impact on not only software engineering but also on global business environments: business reengineering for efficiency and the Internet. Software development has to be more efficient and the quality level of the delivered products has to be high to meet requirements and to be successful. This is especially the case for mission-critical applications. The adverse impact of poor quality is much more significant and at a much wider scale; the quality "dikes" that software is supposed to provide are never more important. These factors will continue to affect software engineering for many years to come during this new millennium.

Measurement plays a critical role in effective and efficient software development, as well as provides the scientific basis for software engineering that makes it a true engineering discipline. This book describes the software quality engineering metrics and models: quality planning, process improvement and quality control, in-process quality management, product engineering (design and code complexity), reliability estimation and projection, and analysis of customer satisfaction data. Many measurement books take an encyclopedic approach, in which every possible software measurement is included, but this book confines its scope to the metrics and models of software quality. Areas such as cost estimation, productivity, staffing, and performance measurement, for which numerous publications exist, are not covered.

In this edition, seven new chapters have been added, covering in-process metrics for software testing, object-oriented metrics, availability metrics, in-process quality assessment, software project assessment, process improvement dos and don'ts, and measuring software process improvement. The chapter that described the AS/400 software quality management system has been eliminated. Updates and revisions have been made throughout the original chapters, and new sections, figures, and tables have been added.

Two of the new chapters are special contributions from two experts. This is a key feature of the new edition. The chapter on the dos and don'ts of software process improvement is contributed by Patrick O'Toole. A highly regarded process improvement expert and with over 20 years of experience, Patrick brings to this book a perspective on process improvement that I share as a practitioner. That perspective is based on practical experience, is project-centric, and is aligned with the strategic business imperative of the organization. Patrick also brings humor to this otherwise serious subject, making the reading of the chapter so enjoyable. The chapter on measuring software process improvement is a special contribution by Capers Jones. A pioneer in software metrics, productivity research, software quality control, and software assessments, Capers's work is well known nationally and internationally. His data-based and fact-based approach in software assessments and benchmarking studies is unparalleled. Based on experience and data from more than 10,000 projects, he brings to the readers a practical approach to software process improvement and the major quantitative findings related to software process improvement. The value of function point metrics is demonstrated via the analyses and findings. The chapter is a must read for software process professionals who are interested in measuring software process improvement.

Another new feature in this edition is a set of recommendations for small teams and organizations that are starting to implement a metrics program, with minimum resources. These recommendations are shown in the form of box inserts in nine of the chapters. A number of examples in the book are based on small team projects, and many methods and techniques are appropriate for large projects as well as small ones. This set of recommendations is from the perspective of small organizations or teams using a small number of metrics, with the intent to effect improvement in their software development effort.

This book is intended for use by software quality professionals; software project managers; software product managers; software development managers; software engineers; software product assurance personnel; and students in software engineering, management information systems, systems engineering, and quality engineering and management. For teachers, it is intended to provide a basis for a course at the upper-division undergraduate or graduate level. A number of software engineering, computer science, and quality engineering programs in the United States and overseas have used the first edition of this book as a text.

Themes of This Book

This book has several themes. First, balancing theory, techniques, and real-life examples, it provides practical guidelines in the practice of quality engineering in software development. Although equations and formulas are involved, the focus is on the understanding and applications of the metrics and models rather than mathematical derivations. Throughout the book, numerous real-life examples are used from the software development laboratory at IBM Rochester, Minnesota, home of the AS/400 and the IBM eServer iSeries computer systems, and from other companies in the software industry. IBM Rochester won the Malcolm Baldrige National Quality Award in 1990. A number of metrics described in this book were being used at that time, and many have been developed and refined since then. All metrics are substantiated by ample implementation experience. IBM Rochester develops and delivers numerous projects of different sizes and types every year, including very large and complex as well as small ones; and they range from firmware, to operating systems, to middleware, to applications.

Second, I attempt to provide a good coverage of the various types of metrics and models in the emerging field of software quality engineering. In addition to general discussions about metrics and techniques, this book categorizes and covers four types of metrics and models: (1) quality management models; (2) software reliability and projection models; (3) complexity metrics and models; and (4) customer-view metrics, measurements, and models. These metrics and models cover the entire software development process from high-level design to testing and maintenance, as well as all phases of reliability. Furthermore, although this book is not on total quality management (TQM), it is a major consideration in the coverage of metrics. The philosophy of TQM is the linking of product quality and customer satisfaction for the purpose of achieving long-term success. TQM is the reason for including two chapters on customer-view metrics and measurements—availability metrics and customer satisfaction—in addition to the many chapters on product and process metrics. In other discussions in the book, the customer's perspective is included where appropriate.

Third, by linking metrics and models to quality improvement strategies and improvement actions, we attempt to focus on using, not just describing, metrics. A framework for interpreting in-process metrics and assessing in-process quality status—the effort/outcome model—is presented. The direct link between a recommended quality strategy during development and the defect-removal model is shown. Examples of actions tied to specific metrics and analysis are given. Furthermore, to illustrate the metrics, many figures and graphs are used. This is a reflection of the fact that in real-life project and quality management, a clear visual presentation often improves understanding and increases the effectiveness of the metrics.

Fourth, following up on quality and process improvement at a more general level than specific metric discussions, the book continues with chapters that discuss the in-process quality assessment process, a method for conducting software project assessments, practical advice on process improvement dos and don'ts, and quantitative analysis of software process improvement. The common thread underlying these chapters, as with other chapters on metrics and models, is practical experience with industry projects.

Organization of This Book

The following list details the focus of each chapter.

- ☐ *Chapter 1, What Is Software Quality?,* discusses the definition of quality and software quality. The customer's role in the definition is highlighted. Quality attributes and their relationships are discussed. The second part of the chapter covers the definition and framework of TQM and the customer's view of quality, a key focus in this book.

- ☐ *Chapter 2, Software Development Process Models,* reviews various development process models that are used in the software industry. It briefly describes two methods of software process maturity assessment—the SEI process capability maturity model (CMM) (by the Software Engineering Institute) and the SPR assessment method (by the Software Productivity Research, Inc.). It summarizes two bodies of quality management standards—the Malcolm Baldrige National Quality Award assessment discipline and ISO 9000.

☐ *Chapter 3, Fundamentals of Measurement Theory,* examines measurement theory fundamentals, which are very important for the practice of software measurement. The concept of operational definition and its importance in measurement are illustrated with an example. The level of measurement, some basic measures, and the concept of six sigma are discussed. The two key criteria of measurement quality, reliability and validity, and the related issue of measurement errors are examined and their importance is articulated. This chapter also provides a discussion on correlation and addresses the criteria necessary to establish causality based on observational data.

☐ *Chapter 4, Software Quality Metrics Overview,* presents examples of quality metrics for the three categories of metrics associated with the software life cycle: end-product, in-process, and maintenance. It describes the metrics programs of several large software companies and discusses collection of software engineering data.

☐ *Chapter 5, Applying the Seven Basic Quality Tools in Software Development,* describes the application of the basic statistical tools for quality control, known as Ishikawa's seven basic tools, in software development. The potentials and challenges of applying the control chart in software environments are discussed. In addition, a qualitative tool for brainstorming and for displaying complex cause-and-effect relationships—the relations diagram—is discussed.

☐ *Chapter 6, Defect Removal Effectiveness,* is the first of five chapters about the models and metrics that describe the quality dynamics of software development. Through two types of models, quality management models and software reliability and projection models, the quality of software development can be planned, engineered, managed, and projected. This chapter examines the central concept of defect removal effectiveness, its measurements, and its role in quality planning.

☐ *Chapter 7, The Rayleigh Model,* describes the model and its implementation as a reliability and projection model. The Rayleigh Model's use as a quality management model is discussed in Chapter 9.

☐ *Chapter 8, Exponential Distribution and Reliability Growth Models,* discusses the exponential distribution and the major software reliability growth models. These models, like the Rayleigh Model, are used for quality projection before the software is shipped to customers, just before development is complete. The models are also used for maintenance planning, to model the failure pattern or the defect arrival patterns in the field.

☐ *Chapter 9, Quality Management Models,* describes several quality management models that cover the entire development cycle. In-process metrics and reports that support the models are shown and discussed. A framework for interpreting in-process metrics and assessing in-process quality status—the effort/outcome model—is presented.

☐ *Chapter 10, In-Process Metrics for Software Testing,* is a continuation of Chapter 9; it focuses on the metrics for software testing. The effort/outcome model, as it applies to metrics during the testing phase, is elaborated. Candidate metrics for acceptance testing to evaluate vendor-developed software, and the central question of how to know your product is good enough to ship, are also discussed.

☐ *Chapter 11, Complexity Metrics and Models,* discusses the third type of metrics and models in software engineering. While quality management models and reliability and projection models are for project management and quality management, the objective of the complexity metrics and models is for software engineers to be able to improve their design and implementation of software development.

☐ *Chapter 12, Metrics and Lessons Learned for Object-Oriented Projects,* covers design and complexity metrics, productivity metrics, quality and quality management metrics for object-oriented development, and lessons learned from the deployment and implementation of OO projects. The first section can be viewed as a continuation of the discussion on complexity metrics and models; the other sections fall within the framework of quality and project management.

☐ *Chapter 13, Availability Metrics,* discusses system availability and outage metrics, and explores the relationships among availability, reliability, and the traditional defect-rate measurement. Availability metrics and customer satisfaction measurements are the fourth type of metrics and models—customer-oriented metrics.

☐ *Chapter 14, Measuring and Analyzing Customer Satisfaction,* discusses data collection and measurements of customer satisfaction, and techniques and models for the analysis of customer satisfaction data. From Chapter 3 to this chapter, the entire spectrum of metrics and models is covered.

☐ *Chapter 15, Conducting In-Process Quality Assessments,* describes in-process quality assessments as an integrated element of good project quality management. Quality assessments are based on both quantitative indicators, such as those discussed in previous chapters, and qualitative information.

☐ *Chapter 16, Conducting Software Project Assessments,* takes the discussion to yet another level; this chapter proposes a software project assessment method. The focus is at the project level and the discussion is from a practitioner's perspective.

☐ *Chapter 17, Dos and Don'ts of Software Process Improvement* by Patrick O'Toole, offers practical advice for software process improvement professionals. It provides a link to the process maturity discussions in Chapter 2.

☐ *Chapter 18, Using Function Point Metrics to Measure Software Process Improvement* by Capers Jones, discusses the six stages of software process improvement. Based on a large body of empirical data, it examines the costs and effects of process improvement. It shows the results of quantitative analyses with regard to costs, time, schedule, productivity, and quality. It articulates the value of Function Point metrics. It provides a link to the process maturity discussions in Chapter 2.

❑ *Chapter 19, Concluding Remarks,* provides several observations with regard to software measurement in general and software quality metrics and models in particular, and it offers a perspective on the future of software engineering measurement.

❑ In the *Appendix,* a real-life example of a project assessment questionnaire is shown. Per the methods and techniques discussed in Chapter 16, readers can customize the questionnaire for their project assessment efforts.

Suggested Ways to Read This Book

The chapters of this book are organized for reading from beginning to end. Later chapters refer to concepts and discussions in earlier chapters. At the same time, each chapter addresses a separate topic and chapters in some groups are more closely coupled than others. Some readers may choose to read specific topics or decide on different starting points. For example, those who are not interested in quality definitions, process models, and measurement fundamentals discussions can start with Chapter 4, *Software Quality Metrics Overview.* Those who intend to immediately get to the central topics of defect removals, metrics and models for quality planning, and management and projection can start with Chapter 6, *Defect Removal Effectiveness.* In general, I recommend that the chapters be read in groups, as follows.

❑ Chapters 1 through 3
❑ Chapter 4
❑ Chapter 5
❑ Chapters 6 through 10
❑ Chapters 11 and 12
❑ Chapters 13 and 14
❑ Chapters 15 through 18
❑ Chapter 19

Acknowledgments

I would like to thank Terry Larson, Steve Braddish, and Mike Tomashek for their support of this project. I wish to thank the entire iSeries software development team at IBM Rochester, especially the release and project management team and the test teams, who made the many metrics and models described in this book a state of practice instead of just a theoretical discussion. A special thanks is due Diane Manlove and Jerry Parrish for their leadership in the implementation of many of the in-process metrics, and Bob Gintowt for his leadership work, knowledge, and insights on system availability and outage metrics.

Appreciation is due all of my former and present colleagues in software and system quality at IBM Rochester, other IBM divisions, IBM Center for Software Engineering, and IBM Corporate Quality, for the numerous discussions, debates, and insights on the subjects of measurement, quality and process improvement. There are too many individuals and teams to name them all. Among them are: Lionel Craddock, John E. Peterson, Dave Lind, Dr. Sam Huang, Don Mitchell, Judy Wasser, Marijeanne Swift, Duane Miller, Dr. Dave Jacobson, Dick Bhend, Brad Talmo, Brock Peterson, Vern Peterson, Charlie Gilmore, Jim Vlazny, Mary Ann Donovan, Jerry Miller, Mike Tappon, Phil Einspahr, Tami Mena, Peter Bradford, Max Maurer, Roger McKnight, Jack Hickley, Marilyn Moncol, Darrell Moore, Dusan Gasich, Eileen Gottschall, Carl Chamberlin, Paul Hutchings, Gary Davidson, George Stark, Kathleen Coyle, Ram Chillarege, Peter Santhanam, Kathryn Bassin, Beng Chiu, Wanda Sarti, Brent Hodges, Bill Woodworth, and Mike Jesrani. I am grateful to Dave Amundson, Ben Borgen, Dick Sulack, Rod Morlock, Brian Truskowski, Jeff VerHeul, Judy Tenney, Mike Tomashek, and Paul Loftus, from whom I learned a great deal not only about quality and quality management, but also about prudent decision making with regard to business objectives and quality.

A special gratitude is due Capers Jones for his review of this new edition, many excellent suggestions, and his chapter on measuring process improvement. In my early career at IBM I benefitted a great deal from reading Capers' pioneer work on programming productivity, software quality control, and software assessments. Then in 1995, I had the chance to meet him in person in Salt Lake City, where he gave a keynote speech on software measurements at a software technology conference. Now many years later, I continue to learn and benefit from reading his work and from his reviews and suggestions.

My sincere thanks are due Patrick O'Toole for his special contribution of the chapter on the dos and don'ts of software process improvement, amid his very busy schedule. A special thanks is due Steve Hoisington for his review and helpful suggestions of the new materials, and as a former colleague, his passion in quality, his professionalism in quality management, and his long-time influence on the customer view of quality.

Much appreciation is due Dick Hedger, for his review of and help with both the first and second editions, his passion for and expertise in software process improvement, and his continual support over many years. I am thankful to the reviewers for the first edition, Dr. Brian Eck, Dr. Alan Yaung, Professor Wei-Tsek Tsai, and others. They contributed many constructive suggestions.

I thank Debbie Lafferty, Marilyn Rash, Diane Freed, and their Addison-Wesley colleagues for their assistance and guidance during the preparation of this new edition.

Appreciation is due the students at the MSSE program (Masters of Science in Software Engineering) at the University of Minnesota for the past several years. They are software engineering professionals in the industry, with different backgrounds and representing different types of organizations, software, projects, industry segments, and processes. The numerous discussions and exchanges with them influenced my thinking and increased my appreciation of the diversity in software engineering. I wish to thank Professor Mats Heimdahl, who founded and directs the MSSE program, for his vision and successful implementation in bringing industry practices and experiences into the curriculum of a software engineering program.

Finally, a special word of gratitude is due my wife, Teresa, and my sons, Wilbur and Este, for their continual encouragement, patience, and support throughout the entire process. Our discussions of the boys' lawn mowing experiences deepened my appreciation of the approaches to quality and process improvement. I could not have completed this new edition without their support.

Stephen H. Kan, Ph.D.
Rochester, Minnesota

1

What Is Software Quality?

Quality must be defined and measured if improvement is to be achieved. Yet, a major problem in quality engineering and management is that the term *quality* is ambiguous, such that it is commonly misunderstood. The confusion may be attributed to several reasons. First, quality is not a single idea, but rather a multidimensional concept. The dimensions of quality include the entity of interest, the viewpoint on that entity, and the quality attributes of that entity. Second, for any concept there are levels of abstraction; when people talk about quality, one party could be referring to it in its broadest sense, whereas another might be referring to its specific meaning. Third, the term *quality* is a part of our daily language and the popular and professional uses of it may be very different.

In this chapter we discuss the popular views of quality, its formal definitions by quality experts and their implications, the meaning and specific uses of quality in software, and the approach and key elements of total quality management.

1.1 Quality: Popular Views

A popular view of quality is that it is an intangible trait—it can be discussed, felt, and judged, but cannot be weighed or measured. To many people, quality is similar to what a federal judge once commented about obscenity: "I know it when I see it." Terms such as *good quality, bad quality,* and *quality of life* exemplify how people talk about something vague, which they don't intend to define. This view reflects the fact that people perceive and interpret quality in different ways. The implication is that quality cannot be controlled and managed, nor can it be quantified. This view is in vivid contrast to the professional view held in the discipline of quality engineering that quality can, and should, be operationally defined, measured, monitored, managed, and improved.

Another popular view is that quality connotes luxury, class, and taste. Expensive, elaborate, and more complex products are regarded as offering a higher level of quality than their humbler counterparts. Therefore, a Cadillac is a quality car, but a Chevrolet is not, regardless of reliability and repair records; or, a surround-sound hi-fi system is a quality system, but a single-speaker radio is not. According to this view, quality is restricted to a limited class of expensive products with sophisticated functionality and items that have a touch of class. Simple, inexpensive products can hardly be classified as quality products.

1.2 Quality: Professional Views

The misconceptions and vagueness of the popular views do not help the quality improvement effort in the industries. To that end, quality must be described in a workable definition. Crosby (1979) defines quality as "conformance to requirements" and Juran and Gryna (1970) define it as "fitness for use." These two definitions are related and consistent, as we will see later. These definitions of quality have been adopted and used by many quality professionals.

"Conformance to requirements" implies that requirements must be clearly stated such that they cannot be misunderstood. Then, in the development and production process, measurements are taken regularly to determine conformance to those requirements. The nonconformances are regarded as defects—the absence of quality. For example, one requirement (specification) for a certain radio may be that it must be able to receive certain frequencies more than 30 miles away from the source of broadcast. If the radio fails to do so, then it does not meet the quality requirements and should be rejected. By the same token, if a Cadillac conforms to all the requirements of a Cadillac, then it is a quality car. If a Chevrolet conforms to all the requirements of a Chevrolet, then it is also a quality car. The two cars may be very different in style, performance, and economy. But if both measure up to the standards set for them, then both are quality cars.

The "fitness for use" definition takes customers' requirements and expectations into account, which involve whether the products or services fit their uses. Since different customers may use the products in different ways, it means that products must possess multiple elements of fitness for use. According to Juran, each of these elements is a quality characteristic and all of them can be classified into categories known as parameters for fitness for use. The two most important parameters are *quality of design* and *quality of conformance.*

Quality of design in popular terminology is known as grades or models, which are related to the spectrum of purchasing power. The differences between grades are the result of intended or designed differences. Using the example of cars again, all automobiles provide to the user the service of transportation. However, models differ in size, comfort, performance, style, economy, and status. In contrast, quality of conformance is the extent to which the product conforms to the intent of the design. In other words, quality of design can be regarded as the determination of requirements and specifications and quality of conformance is conformance to requirements.

The two definitions of *quality* (conformance to requirements and fitness for use), therefore, are essentially similar. The difference is that the fitness for use concept implies a more significant role for customers' requirements and expectations.

1.2.1 The Role of the Customer

The role of the customer, as it relates to quality, can never be overstated. From a customer's standpoint, quality is the customer's perceived value of the product he or she purchased, based on a variety of variables such as price, performance, reliability, and satisfaction. In Guaspari's book *I Know It When I See It* (1985 p.77), he discusses quality in the customers' context as follows:

> Your customers are in a perfect position to tell you about quality, because that's all they're really buying. They're not buying a product. They're buying your assurances that their expectations for that product will be met.
>
> And you haven't really got anything else to sell them but those assurances. You haven't really got anything else to sell but quality.

From a concept's high-level definition to a product's operational definition, many steps are involved, each of which may be vulnerable to shortcomings. For example, to achieve the state of conformance to requirements, the customers' requirements must be first gathered and analyzed, specifications to meet those requirements must be produced, and the product must be developed and manufactured accordingly. In each phase of the process, errors can occur that will affect the quality of the finished product. The requirements may be erroneous (this is especially the case for software development), the development and manufacturing process may be subject to variables that induce defects, and so forth. From the customer's perspective, satisfaction after the purchase of the product is the ultimate validation that the product conforms to requirements and is fit to use. From the producer's perspective, once requirements are specified, developing and producing the product in accordance with the specifications is the path to achieving quality. Usually, for product quality, the lack of defects and good reliability are the most basic measures.

Because of the two perspectives on quality (customer satisfaction as the ultimate validation of quality and producer's adherence to requirements to achieve quality), the de facto definition of quality consists of two levels. The first is the intrinsic product quality, often operationally limited to the product's defect rate and reliability. This narrow definition is referred to as the "small q" (q for quality). The broader definition of quality includes product quality, process quality, and customer satisfaction, and it is referred to as the "big Q." This two-level approach to the definition of quality is being used in many industries, including the automobile industry, the computer industry (both software and hardware), and the consumer electronics industry.

The two-level concept of quality is supposed to form a closed-loop cycle: customer's wants and needs → requirements and specifications → products designed, developed, and manufactured in accordance with the requirements, and with continuous focus on process improvement → excellent product quality, plus good distribution and service processes → total customer satisfaction. However, this was not always the case in many industries, especially before the late 1980s when the modern quality era began. Product requirements were often generated without customer input, and customer satisfaction was not always a factor in business decision making. Although the final products conformed to requirements, they may not have been what the customers wanted. Therefore, the customers' role should be explicitly stated in the definition of quality: conformance to customers' requirements.

1.3 Software Quality

In software, the narrowest sense of product quality is commonly recognized as lack of "bugs" in the product. It is also the most basic meaning of conformance to requirements, because if the software contains too many functional defects, the basic requirement of providing the desired function is not met. This definition is usually expressed in two ways: defect rate (e.g., number of defects per million lines of source code, per function point, or other unit) and reliability (e.g., number of failures per n hours of operation, mean time to failure, or the probability of failure-free operation in a specified time). Customer satisfaction is usually measured by percent satisfied or nonsatisfied (neutral and dissatisfied) from customer satisfaction surveys. To reduce bias, techniques such as blind surveys (the interviewer does not know the customer and the customer does not know the company the interviewer represents) are usually used. In addition to overall customer satisfaction with the software product, satisfaction toward specific attributes is also gauged. For instance, IBM monitors satisfaction with its software products in levels of CUPRIMDSO (capability [functionality], usability, performance, reliability, installability, maintainability, documentation/information, service, and overall). Hewlett-Packard focuses on FURPS (functionality, usability, reliability, performance, and serviceability). Other companies use similar dimensions of software customer satisfaction. Juran calls such attributes *quality parameters*, or parameters for fitness for use.

To increase overall customer satisfaction as well as satisfaction with various quality attributes, the quality attributes must be taken into account in the planning and design of the software. However, these quality attributes are not always congruous with each other. For example, the higher the functional complexity of the software, the harder it becomes to achieve maintainability. Depending on the type of software and customers, different weighting factors are needed for different quality attributes. For large customers with sophisticated networks and real-time processing, performance and reliability may be the most important attributes. For customers with standalone systems and simple operations, on the other hand, ease of use, installability, and documentation may be more important. Figure 1.1 shows the possible relationships of some quality attributes. Some relationships are mutually supportive, some are negative, and yet others are not clear, depending on the types of customers and applications. For software with a diverse customer set, therefore, setting goals for various quality attributes and to meet customers' requirements is not easy.

In view of these discussions, the updated definition of *quality* (i.e., conformance to customers' requirements) is especially relevant to the software industry. It is not

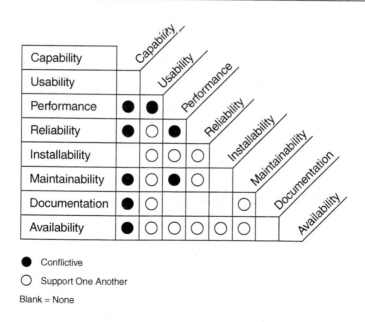

● Conflictive

○ Support One Another

Blank = None

FIGURE 1.1

Interrelationships of Software Attributes—A CUPRIMDA Example surprising that requirements errors constitute one of the major problem categories in software development. According to Jones (1992), 15% or more of all software defects are requirements errors. A development process that does not address requirements quality is bound to produce poor-quality software.

Yet another view of software quality is that of process quality versus end-product quality. From customer requirements to the delivery of software products, the development process is complex and often involves a series of stages, each with feedback paths. In each stage, an intermediate deliverable is produced for an intermediate user—the next stage. Each stage also receives an intermediate deliverable from the preceding stage. Each intermediate deliverable has certain quality attributes that affect the quality of the end product. For instance, Figure 1.2 shows a simplified representation of the most common software development process, the waterfall process.

Intriguingly, if we extend the concept of customer in the definition of quality to include both external and internal customers, the definition also applies to process quality. If each stage of the development process meets the requirements of its intermediate user (the next stage), the end product thus developed and produced will meet the specified requirements. This statement, of course, is an oversimplification of reality, because in each stage numerous factors exist that will affect that stage's ability to fulfill its requirements. To improve quality during development, we need models of

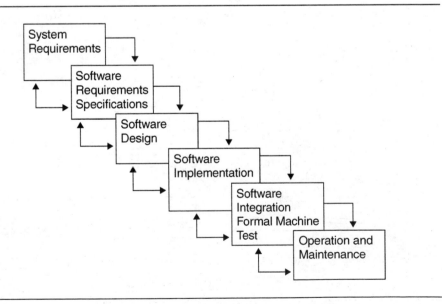

FIGURE 1.2
Simplified Representation of the Waterfall Development Process

the development process, and within the process we need to select and deploy specific methods and approaches, and employ proper tools and technologies. We need measures of the characteristics and quality parameters of the development process and its stages, as well as metrics and models to ensure that the development process is under control and moving toward the product's quality objectives. Quality metrics and models are the focus of this book.

1.4 Total Quality Management

The term *Total quality management* (*TQM*) was originally coined in 1985 by the Naval Air Systems Command to describe its Japanese-style management approach to quality improvement. The term has taken on a number of meanings, depending on who is interpreting it and how they are applying it. In general, however, it represents a style of management aimed at achieving long-term success by linking quality and customer satisfaction. Basic to the approach is the creation of a culture in which all members of the organization participate in the improvement of processes, products, and services. Various specific methods for implementing the TQM philosophy are found in the works of Crosby (1979), Deming (1986), Feigenbaum (1961, 1991), Ishikawa (1985), and Juran and Gryna (1970).

Since the 1980s, many U.S. companies have adopted the TQM approach to quality. The Malcolm Baldrige National Quality Award (MBNQA), established by the U.S. government in 1988, highlights the embracing of such a philosophy and management style. The adoption of ISO 9000 as the quality management standard by the European Community and the acceptance of such standards by the U.S. private sector in recent years further illustrates the importance of the quality philosophy in today's business environments. In the computer and electronic industry, examples of successful TQM implementation include Hewlett-Packard's Total Quality Control (TQC), Motorola's Six Sigma Strategy, and IBM's Market Driven Quality. In fact, Motorola won the first MBNQA award (in 1988) and IBM's AS/400 Division in Rochester, Minnesota, won it in 1990.

Hewlett-Packard's TQC focuses on key areas such as management commitment, leadership, customer focus, total participation, and systematic analysis. Each area has strategies and plans to drive the improvement of quality, efficiency, and responsiveness, with the final objective being to achieve success through customer satisfaction (Shores, 1989). In software development, the Software Quality and Productivity Analysis (SQPA) program (Zimmer, 1989) is one of the approaches to improve quality.

Motorola's Six Sigma strategy focuses on achieving stringent quality levels in order to obtain total customer satisfaction. Cycle time reduction and participative management are among the key initiatives of the strategy (Smith, 1989). Six Sigma is not just a measure of the quality level; inherent in the concept are product design improvements and reductions in process variations (Harry and Lawson, 1992). Six Sigma is applied to product quality as well as everything that can be supported by data and measurement.

"Customer is the final arbiter" is the key theme of IBM's Market Driven Quality strategy. The strategy comprises four initiatives: defect elimination, cycle time reduction, customer and business partner satisfaction, and adherence to the Baldrige assessment discipline.

Despite variations in its implementation, the key elements of a TQM system can be summarized as follows:

- ☐ *Customer focus:* The objective is to achieve total customer satisfaction. Customer focus includes studying customers' wants and needs, gathering customers' requirements, and measuring and managing customers' satisfaction.
- ☐ *Process:* The objective is to reduce process variations and to achieve continuous process improvement. This element includes both the business process and the product development process. Through process improvement, product quality will be enhanced.
- ☐ *Human side of quality:* The objective is to create a companywide quality culture. Focus areas include leadership, management commitment, total participation, employee empowerment, and other social, psychological, and human factors.
- ☐ *Measurement and analysis:* The objective is to drive continuous improvement in all quality parameters by the goal-oriented measurement system.

Furthermore, an organization that practices TQM must have executive leadership, must focus on infrastructure, training, and education, and must do strategic quality planning.

Figure 1.3 is a schematic representation of the key elements of TQM. Clearly, measurement and analysis are the fundamental elements for gauging continuous improvement.

Various organizational frameworks have been proposed to improve quality that can be used to substantiate the TQM philosophy. Specific examples include Plan-Do-Check-Act (Deming, 1986; Shewhart, 1931), Quality Improvement Paradigm/ Experience Factory Organization (Basili, 1985, 1989; Basili and Rombach, 1987, 1988; Basili et al., 1992), Software Engineering Institute (SEI) Capability Maturity Model (Humphrey, 1989; Radice et al., 1985), and Lean Enterprise Management (Womack et al., 1990).

Plan-Do-Check-Act is based on a feedback cycle for optimizing a single process or production line. It uses techniques, such as feedback loops and statistical quality control, to experiment with methods for improvement and to build predictive models

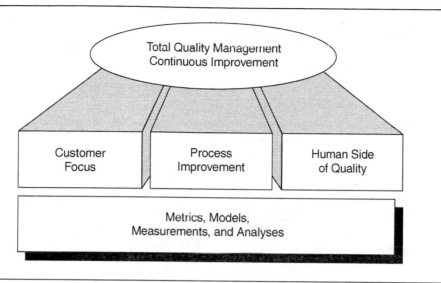

FIGURE 1.3
Key Elements of Total Quality Management

of the product. Basic to the assumption is that a process is repeated multiple times, so that data models can be built that allow one to predict results of the process.

The Quality Improvement Paradigm/Experience Factory Organization aims at building a continually improving organization, based on its evolving goals and an assessment of its status relative to those goals. The approach uses internal assessments against the organization's own goals and status (rather than process areas) and such techniques as Goal/Question/Metric (GQM), model building, and qualitative/quantitative analysis to improve the product through the process. The six fundamental steps of the Quality Improvement Paradigm are (1) characterize the project and its environment, (2) set the goals, (3) choose the appropriate processes, (4) execute the processes, (5) analyze the data, and (6) package the experience for reuse. The Experience Factory Organization separates the product development from the experience packaging activities. Basic to this approach is the need to learn across multiple project developments.

The SEI Capability Maturity Model is a staged process improvement, based on assessment of key process areas, until you reach level 5, which represents a continuous process improvement. The approach is based on organizational and quality management maturity models developed by Likert (1967) and Crosby (1979), respectively. The goal of the approach is to achieve continuous process improvement via defect prevention, technology innovation, and process change management.

As part of the approach, a five-level process maturity model is defined based on repeated assessments of an organization's capability in key process areas. Improvement is achieved by action plans for poor process areas. Basic to this approach is the idea that there are key process areas and attending to them will improve your software development.

Lean Enterprise Management is based on the principle of concentration of production on "value-added" activities and the elimination or reduction of "not-value-added" activities. The approach has been used to improve factory output. The goal is to build software with the minimum necessary set of activities and then to tailor the process to the product's requirements. The approach uses such concepts as technology management, human-centered management, decentralized organization, quality management, supplier and customer integration, and internationalization/regionalization. Basic to this approach is the assumption that the process can be tailored to classes of problems.

1.5 Summary

This chapter discusses the definition of *quality* from both popular and professional views, and describes total quality management (TQM) as it relates to software quality. From the popular view, quality is some type of thing that cannot be quantified: *I know it when I see it.* Quality and grade (or class) are often confused. From the professional view, quality must be defined and measured for improvement and is best defined as "conformance to customers' requirements." In software as well as other industries, the *de facto* operational definition of quality consists of two levels: the intrinsic product quality (small *q*) and customer satisfaction (big *Q*).

The TQM philosophy aims at long-term success by linking quality and customer satisfaction. Despite variations in its implementation, a TQM system comprises four key common elements: (1) customer focus, (2) process improvement, (3) human side of quality, and (4) measurement and analysis.

It is not surprising that the professional definition of *quality* fits perfectly in the TQM context. That definition correlates closely with the first two of the TQM elements (customer focus and process improvement). To achieve good quality, all TQM elements must definitely be addressed, with the aid of some organizational frameworks. In this book, our key focus is on metrics, measurements, and quality models as they relate to software engineering. In the next chapter we discuss various software development models and the process maturity framework.

References

1. Basili, V. R., "Quantitative Evaluation of Software Engineering Methodology," *Proceedings First Pan Pacific Computer Conference*, Melbourne, Australia, September 1985 (also available as Technical Report, TR-1519, Department of Computer Science, University of Maryland, College Park, July 1985).
2. Basili, V. R., "Software Development: A Paradigm for the Future," *Proceedings 13th International Computer Software and Applications Conference (COMPSAC)*, Keynote Address, Orlando, Fl., September 1989.
3. Basili, V. R., and H. D. Rombach, "Tailoring the Software Process to Project Goals and Environments," *Proceedings Ninth International Conference on Software Engineering*, Monterey, Calif.: IEEE Computer Society, March 30–April 2, 1987, pp. 345–357.
4. Basili, V. R., and H. D. Rombach, "The TAME Project: Towards Improvement-Oriented Software Environments," *IEEE Transactions on Software Engineering*, Vol. SE-14, No. 6, June 1988, pp. 758–773.
5. Basili, V. R., G. Caldiera, F. McGarry, R. Pajersky, G. Page, and S. Waligora, "The Software Engineering Laboratory: An Operational Software Experience Factory," *International Conference on Software Engineering*, IEEE Computer Society, May 1992, pp. 370–381.
6. Basili, V. R., and J. D. Musa, "The Future Engineering of Software: A Management Perspective," *IEEE Computer*, 1991, pp. 90–96.
7. Bowen, T. P., "Specification of Software Quality Attributes," RADC-TR-85-37 (3 volumes), *Rome Air Development Center*, February 1985.
8. Crosby, P. B., *Quality Is Free: The Art of Making Quality Certain*, New York: McGraw-Hill, 1979.
9. Deming, W. E., *Out of the Crisis*, Cambridge, Mass.: Massachusetts Institute of Technology, 1986
10. Feigenbaum, A. V., *Total Quality Control: Engineering and Management*, New York: McGraw-Hill, 1961.
11. Feigenbaum, A. V., *Total Quality Control*, New York: McGraw-Hill, 1991.
12. Guaspari, J., *I Know It When I See It: A Modern Fable About Quality*, New York: American Management Association, 1985.
13. Guaspari, J., *Theory Why: In Which the Boss Solves the Riddle of Quality*, New York: American Management Association, 1986.
14. Guaspari, J., *The Customer Connection: Quality for the Rest of Us*, New York: American Management Association, 1988.
15. Harry, M. J., and J. R. Lawson, *Six Sigma Producibility Analysis and Process Characterization*, Reading, Mass.: Addison-Wesley, 1992.
16. Humphrey, W. S., *Managing the Software Process*, Reading, Mass.: Addison-Wesley, 1989.
17. Ishikawa, K., *What Is Total Quality Control? The Japanese Way*, Englewood Cliffs, N.J.: Prentice-Hall, 1985.
18. Jones, C., *Programming Productivity*, New York: McGraw-Hill, 1986.
19. Jones, C., *Applied Software Measurement: Assuring Productivity and Quality*, New York: McGraw-Hill, 1991.
20. Jones, C., "Critical Problems in Software Measurement," Version 1.0, Burlington, Mass.: Software Productivity Research (SPR), August 1992.
21. Juran, J. M., and F. M. Gryna, Jr., *Quality Planning and Analysis: From Product Development Through Use*, New York: McGraw-Hill, 1970.

22. Likert, R., *The Human Organization: Its Management and Value,* New York: McGraw-Hill, 1967.
23. Radice, R. A., J. T. Harding, P. E. Munnis, and R. W. Phillips, "A Programming Process Study," *IBM Systems Journal,* Vol. 24, No. 2, 1985, pp. 91–101.
24. Shewhart, W. A., *Economic Control of Quality of Manufactured Product,* New York: D. Van Nostrand Company, 1931.
25. Shores, D., "TQC: Science, Not Witchcraft," *Quality Progress,* April 1989, pp. 42–45.
26. Smith, W. B., "Six Sigma: TQC, American Style," presented at the National Technological University television series on October 31, 1989.
27. Womack, J. P., D. T. Jones, and D. Ross, *The Machine That Changed the World: Based on the Massachusetts Institute of Technology 5-Million-Dollar, 5-Year Study of the Future of the Automobile,* New York: Rawson Associates, 1990.
28. Zimmer, B., "Software Quality and Productivity at Hewlett-Packard," *Proceedings of the IEEE Computer Software and Applications Conference*, 1989, pp. 628–632.

2

Software Development
Process Models

Software metrics and models cannot be discussed in a vacuum; they must be referenced to the software development process. In this chapter we summarize the major process models being used in the software development community. We start with the waterfall process life-cycle model and then cover the prototyping approach, the spiral model, the iterative development process, and several approaches to the object-oriented development process. Processes pertinent to the improvement of the development process, such as the Cleanroom methodology and the defect prevention process, are also described.

In the last part of the chapter we shift our discussion from specific development processes to the evaluation of development processes and quality management standards. Presented and discussed are the process maturity framework, including the Software Engineering Institute's (SEI) Capability Maturity Model (CMM) and the Software Productivity Research's (SPR) assessment approach, and two bodies of quality standards—the Malcolm Baldrige assessment discipline and ISO 9000—as they relate to software process and quality.

2.1 The Waterfall Development Model

In the 1960s and 1970s software development projects were characterized by massive cost overruns and schedule delays; the focus was on planning and control (Basili and Musa, 1991). The emergence of the waterfall process to help tackle the growing complexity of development projects was a logical event (Boehm, 1976). As Figure 1.2 in Chapter 1 shows, the waterfall process model encourages the development team to specify what the software is supposed to do (gather and define system requirements) before developing the system. It then breaks the complex mission of development into several logical steps (design, code, test, and so forth) with intermediate deliverables that lead to the final product. To ensure proper execution with good-quality deliverables, each step has validation, entry, and exit criteria. This Entry-Task-Validation-Exit (ETVX) paradigm is a key characteristic of the waterfall process and the IBM programming process architecture (Radice et al., 1985).

The divide-and-conquer approach of the waterfall process has several advantages. It enables more accurate tracking of project progress and early identification of possible slippages. It forces the organization that develops the software system to be more structured and manageable. This structural approach is very important for large organizations with large, complex development projects. It demands that the process generate a series of documents that can later be used to test and maintain the system (Davis et al., 1988). The bottom line of this approach is to make large software projects more manageable and delivered on time without cost overrun. Experiences of the past several decades show that the waterfall process is very valuable. Many major developers, especially those who were established early and are involved with systems development, have adopted this process. This group includes commercial corporations, government contractors, and governmental entities. Although a variety of names have been given to each stage in the model, the basic methodologies remain more or less the same. Thus, the system-requirements stages are sometimes called system analysis, customer-requirements gathering and analysis, or user needs analysis; the design stage may be broken down into high-level design and detail-level design; the implementation stage may be called code and debug; and the testing stage may include component-level test, product-level test, and system-level test.

Figure 2.1 shows an implementation of the waterfall process model for a large project. Note that the requirements stage is followed by a stage for architectural design. When the system architecture and design are in place, design and development work for each function begins. This consists of high-level design (HLD), low-level design (LLD), code development, and unit testing (UT). Despite the waterfall concept, parallelism exists because various functions can proceed simultaneously. As shown in the figure, the code development and unit test stages are also implemented

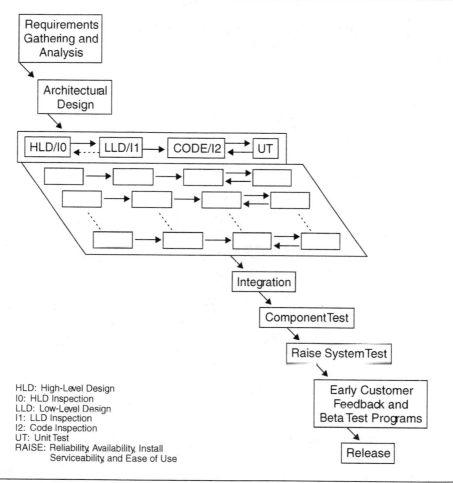

FIGURE 2.1
An Example of the Waterfall Process Model

iteratively. Since UT is an integral part of the implementation stage, it makes little sense to separate it into another formal stage. Before the completion of the HLD, LLD, and code, formal reviews and inspections occur as part of the validation and exit criteria. These inspections are called I0, I1, and I2 inspections, respectively. When the code is completed and unit tested, the subsequent stages are integration, component test, system test, and early customer programs. The final stage is release of the software system to customers.

The following sections describe the objectives of the various stages from high-level design to early customer programs.

High-Level Design

High-level design is the process of defining the externals and internals from the perspective of a component. Its objectives are as follows:

- ☐ Develop the external functions and interfaces, including:
  - external user interfaces
  - application programming interfaces
  - system programming interfaces: intercomponent interfaces and data structures.
- ☐ Design the internal component structure, including intracomponent interfaces and data structures.
- ☐ Ensure all functional requirements are satisfied.
- ☐ Ensure the component fits into the system/product structure.
- ☐ Ensure the component design is complete.
- ☐ Ensure the external functions can be accomplished—"doability" of requirements.

Low-Level Design

Low-level design is the process of transforming the HLD into more detailed designs from the perspective of a part (modules, macros, includes, and so forth). Its objectives are as follows:

- ☐ Finalize the design of components and parts (modules, macros, includes) within a system or product.
- ☐ Complete the component test plans.
- ☐ Give feedback about HLD and verify changes in HLD.

Code Stage

The coding portion of the process results in the transformation of a function's LLD to completely coded parts. The objectives of this stage are as follows:

- ☐ Code parts (modules, macros, includes, messages, etc.).
- ☐ Code component test cases.
- ☐ Verify changes in HLD and LLD.

Unit Test

The unit test is the first test of an executable module. Its objectives are as follows:

- ☐ Verify the code against the component's
  - high-level design and
  - low-level design.

☐ Execute all new and changed code to ensure
- all branches are executed in all directions,
- logic is correct, and
- data paths are verified.

☐ Exercise all error messages, return codes, and response options.

☐ Give feedback about code, LLD, and HLD.

The level of unit test is for verification of limits, internal interfaces, and logic and data paths in a module, macro, or executable include. Unit testing is performed on nonintegrated code and may require scaffold code to construct the proper environment.

Component Test

Component tests evaluate the combined software parts that make up a component after they have been integrated into the system library. The objectives of this test are as follows:

☐ Test external user interfaces against the component's design documentation—user requirements.

☐ Test intercomponent interfaces against the component's design documentation.

☐ Test application program interfaces against the component's design documentation.

☐ Test function against the component's design documentation.

☐ Test intracomponent interfaces (module level) against the component's design documentation.

☐ Test error recovery and messages against the component's design documentation.

☐ Verify that component drivers are functionally complete and at the acceptable quality level.

☐ Test the shared paths (multitasking) and shared resources (files, locks, queues, etc.) against the component's design documentation.

☐ Test ported and unchanged functions against the component's design documentation.

System-Level Test

The system-level test phase comprises the following tests:

☐ System test

☐ System regression test

☐ System performance measurement test

☐ Usability tests

The system test follows the component tests and precedes system regression tests. The system performance test usually begins shortly after system testing starts and proceeds throughout the system-level test phase. Usability tests occur throughout the development process (i.e., prototyping during design stages, formal usability testing during system test period).

- ☐ System test objectives
  - Ensure software products function correctly when executed concurrently and in stressful system environments.
  - Verify overall system stability when development activity has been completed for all products.
- ☐ System regression test objective
  - Verify that the final programming package is ready to be shipped to external customers.
  - Make sure original functions work correctly after functions were added to the system.
- ☐ System performance measurement test objectives
  - Validate the performance of the system.
  - Verify performance specifications.
  - Provide performance information to marketing.
  - Establish base performance measurements for future releases.
- ☐ Usability tests objective
  - Verify that the system contains the usability characteristics required for the intended user tasks and user environment.

Early Customer Programs

The early customer programs (ECP) include testing of the following support structures to verify their readiness:

- ☐ Service structures
- ☐ Development fix support
- ☐ Electronic customer support
- ☐ Market support
- ☐ Ordering, manufacturing, and distribution

In addition to these objectives, a side benefit of having production systems installed in a customer's environment for the ECP is the opportunity to gather customers' feedback so developers can evaluate features and improve them for future releases. Collections of such data or user opinion include:

- ☐ Product feedback: functions offered, ease of use, and quality of online documentation

☐ Installability of hardware and software
☐ Reliability
☐ Performance (measure throughput under the customer's typical load)
☐ System connectivity
☐ Customer acceptance

As the preceding lists illustrate, the waterfall process model is a disciplined approach to software development. It is most appropriate for systems development characterized by a high degree of complexity and interdependency. Although expressed as a cascading waterfall, parallelism and some amount of iteration among process phases often exist in actual implementation. During this process, the focus should be on the intermediate deliverables (e.g., design document, interface rules, test plans, and test cases) rather than on the sequence of activities for each development phase. In other words, it should be entity-based instead of step-by-step based. Otherwise the process could become too rigid to be efficient and effective.

2.2 The Prototyping Approach

The first step in the waterfall model is the gathering and analysis of customers' requirements. When the requirements are defined, the design and development work begins. The model assumes that requirements are known, and that once requirements are defined, they will not change or any change will be insignificant. This may well be the case for system development in which the system's purpose and architecture are thoroughly investigated. However, if requirements change significantly between the time the system's specifications are finalized and when the product's development is complete, the waterfall may not be the best model to deal with the resulting problems. Sometimes the requirements are not even known. In the past, various software process models have been proposed to deal with customer feedback on the product to ensure that it satisfied the requirements. Each of these models provides some form of prototyping, of either a part or all of the system. Some of them build prototypes to be thrown away; others evolve the prototype over time, based on customer needs.

A prototype is a partial implementation of the product expressed either logically or physically with all external interfaces presented. The potential customers use the prototype and provide feedback to the development team before full-scale development begins. *Seeing is believing*, and that is really what prototyping intends to achieve. By using this approach, the customers and the development team can clarify requirements and their interpretation.

As Figure 2.2 shows, the prototyping approach usually involves the following steps:

1. Gather and analyze requirements.
2. Do a quick design.
3. Build a prototype.
4. Customers evaluate the prototype.
5. Refine the design and prototype.
6. If customers are not satisfied with the prototype, loop back to step 5.
7. If customers are satisfied, begin full-scale product development.

The critical factor for success of the prototyping approach is quick turnaround in designing and building the prototypes. Several technologies can be used to achieve such an objective. Reusable software parts could make the design and implementation of prototypes easier. Formal specification languages could facilitate the generation of executable code (e.g., the Z notation and the Input/Output Requirements Language (IORL) (Smith and Wood, 1989; Wing, 1990)). Fourth-generation lan-

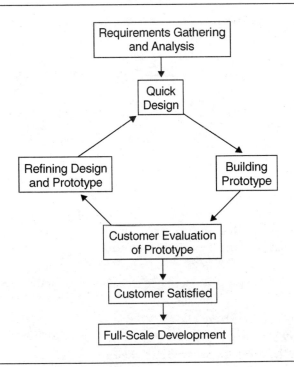

FIGURE 2.2
The Prototyping Approach

guages and technologies could be extremely useful for prototyping in the graphical user interface (GUI) domain. These technologies are still emerging, however, and are used in varying degrees depending on the specific characteristics of the projects.

The prototyping approach is most applicable to small tasks or at the subsystem level. Prototyping a complete system is difficult. Another difficulty with this approach is knowing when to stop iterating. In practice, the method of *time boxing* is being used. This method involves setting arbitrary time limits (e.g., three weeks) for each activity in the iteration cycle and for the entire iteration and then assessing progress at these checkpoints.

Rapid Throwaway Prototyping

The rapid throwaway prototyping approach of software development, made popular by Gomaa and Scott (1981), is now used widely in the industry, especially in application development. It is usually used with high-risk items or with parts of the system that the development team does not understand thoroughly. In this approach, "quick and dirty" prototypes are built, verified with customers, and thrown away until a satisfactory prototype is reached, at which time full-scale development begins.

Evolutionary Prototyping

In the evolutionary prototyping approach, a prototype is built based on some known requirements and understanding. The prototype is then refined and evolved instead of thrown away. Whereas throwaway prototypes are usually used with the aspects of the system that are poorly understood, evolutionary prototypes are likely to be used with aspects of the system that are well understood and thus build on the development team's strengths. These prototypes are also based on prioritized requirements, sometimes referred to as "chunking" in application development (Hough, 1993). For complex applications, it is not reasonable or economical to expect the prototypes to be developed and thrown away rapidly.

2.3 The Spiral Model

The spiral model of software development and enhancement, developed by Boehm (1988), is based on experience with various refinements of the waterfall model as applied to large government software projects. Relying heavily on prototyping and risk management, it is much more flexible than the waterfall model. The most comprehensive application of the model is the development of the TRW Software Productivity System (TRW-SPS) as described by Boehm. The spiral concept and the risk management focus have gained acceptance in software engineering and project management in recent years.

Figure 2.3 shows Boehm's spiral model. The underlying concept of the model is that each portion of the product and each level of elaboration involves the same sequence of steps (cycle). Starting at the center of the spiral, one can see that each development phase (concept of operation, software requirements, product design, detailed design, and implementation) involves one cycle of the spiral. The radial

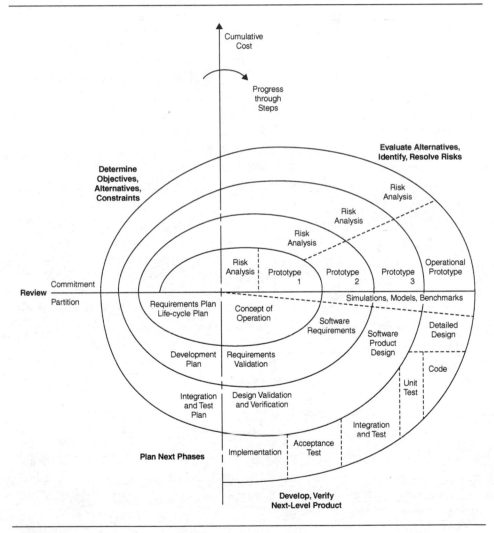

FIGURE 2.3
Spiral Model of the Software Process

dimension in Figure 2.3 represents the cumulative cost incurred in accomplishing the steps. The angular dimension represents the progress made in completing each cycle of the spiral. As indicated by the quadrants in the figure, the first step of each cycle of the spiral is to identify the objectives of the portion of the product being elaborated, the alternative means of implementation of this portion of the product, and the constraints imposed on the application of the alternatives. The next step is to evaluate the alternatives relative to the objectives and constraints, to identify the associated risks, and to resolve them. Risk analysis and the risk-driven approach, therefore, are key characteristics of the spiral model, in contrast to the document-driven approach of the waterfall model.

In this risk-driven approach, prototyping is an important tool. Usually prototyping is applied to the elements of the system or the alternatives that present the higher risks. Unsatisfactory prototypes can be thrown away; when an operational prototype is in place, implementation can begin. In addition to prototyping, the spiral model uses simulations, models, and benchmarks in order to reach the best alternative. Finally, as indicated in the illustration, an important feature of the spiral model, as with other models, is that each cycle ends with a review involving the key members or organizations concerned with the product.

For software projects with incremental development or with components to be developed by separate organizations or individuals, a series of spiral cycles can be used, one for each increment or component. A third dimension could be added to Figure 2.3 to represent the model better.

Boehm (1988) provides a candid discussion of the advantages and disadvantages of the spiral model. Its advantages are as follows:

☐ Its range of options accommodates the good features of existing software process models, whereas its risk-driven approach avoids many of their difficulties. This is the primary advantage. Boehm also discusses the primary conditions under which this model becomes equivalent to other process models such as the waterfall model and the evolutionary prototype model.

☐ It focuses early attention on options involving the reuse of existing software. These options are encouraged because early identification and evaluation of alternatives is a key step in each spiral cycle. This model accommodates preparation for life-cycle evolution, growth, and changes of the software product.

☐ It provides a mechanism for incorporating software quality objectives into software product development.

☐ It focuses on eliminating errors and unattractive alternatives early.

☐ It does not involve separate approaches for software development and software enhancement.

☐ It provides a viable framework for integrating hardware-software system development. The risk-driven approach can be applied to both hardware and software.

On the other hand, difficulties with the spiral model include the following:

☐ *Matching to contract software:* Contract software relies heavily on control, checkpoint, and intermediate deliverables for which the waterfall model is good. The spiral model has a great deal of flexibility and freedom and is, therefore, more suitable for internal software development. The challenge is how to achieve the flexibility and freedom prescribed by the spiral model without losing accountability and control for contract software.

☐ *Relying on risk management expertise:* The risk-driven approach is the backbone of the model. The risk-driven specification addresses high-risk elements in great detail and leaves low-risk elements to be elaborated in later stages. However, an inexperienced team may also produce a specification just the opposite: a great deal of detail for the well-understood, low-risk elements and little elaboration of the poorly understood, high-risk elements. In such a case, the project may fail and the failure may be discovered only after major resources have been invested. Another concern is that a risk-driven specification is people dependent. In the case where a design produced by an expert is to be implemented by nonexperts, the expert must furnish additional documentation.

☐ *Need for further elaboration of spiral steps:* The spiral model describes a flexible and dynamic process model that can be used to its fullest advantage by experienced developers. For nonexperts and especially for large-scale projects, however, the steps in the spiral must be elaborated and more specifically defined so that consistency, tracking, and control can be achieved. Such elaboration and control are especially important in the area of risk analysis and risk management.

2.4 The Iterative Development Process Model

The iterative enhancement (IE) approach (Basili and Turner, 1975), or the iterative development process (IDP), was defined to begin with a subset of the requirements and develop a subset of the product that satisfies the essential needs of the users, provides a vehicle for analysis and training for the customers, and provides a learning experience for the developer. Based on the analysis of each intermediate product, the design and the requirements are modified over a series of iterations to provide a system to the users that meets evolving customer needs with improved design based on feedback and learning.

The IDP model combines prototyping with the strength of the classical waterfall model. Other methods such as domain analysis and risk analysis can also be incorporated into the IDP model. The model has much in common with the spiral model, especially with regard to prototyping and risk management. Indeed, the spiral model can be regarded as a specific IDP model, while the term *IDP* is a general rubric under which various forms of the model can exist. The model also provides a framework for many modern systems and software engineering methods and techniques such as reuse, object-oriented development, and rapid prototyping.

Figure 2.4 shows an example of the iterative development process model used by IBM Owego, New York. With the purpose of "building a system by evolving an architectural prototype through a series of executable versions, with each successive

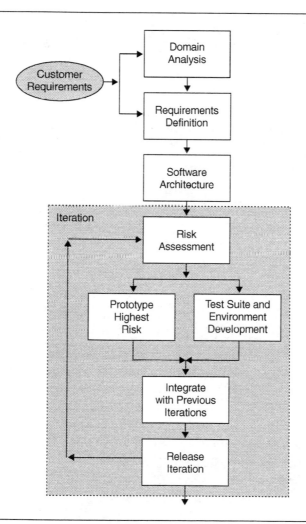

FIGURE 2.4

An Example of the Iterative Development Process Model

Source: P. H. Luckey, R. M. Pittman, and A. Q. LeVan, 1992, "Iterative Development Process with Proposed Applications," IBM Federal Sector Division, Route 17C, Owego, NY 13827.

iteration incorporating experience and more system functionality," the example implementation contains eight major steps (Luckey et al., 1992):

1. Domain analysis
2. Requirements definition
3. Software architecture
4. Risk analysis
5. Prototype
6. Test suite and environment development
7. Integration with previous iterations
8. Release of iteration

As illustrated in the figure, the iteration process involves the last five steps; domain analysis, requirements definition, and software architecture are preiteration steps, which are similar to those in the waterfall model. During the five iteration steps, the following activities occur:

- ☐ Analyze or review the system requirements.
- ☐ Design or revise the solution that best satisfies the requirements.
- ☐ Identify the highest risks for the project and prioritize them. Mitigate the highest priority risk via prototyping, leaving lower risks for subsequent iterations.
- ☐ Define and schedule or revise the next few iterations.
- ☐ Develop the iteration test suite and supporting test environment.
- ☐ Implement the portion of the design that is minimally required to satisfy the current iteration.
- ☐ Integrate the software in test environments and perform regression testing.
- ☐ Update documents for release with the iteration.
- ☐ Release the iteration.

Note that test suite development along with design and development is extremely important for the verification of the function and quality of each iteration. Yet in practice this activity is not always emphasized appropriately.

The development of IBM's OS/2 2.0 operating system is a combination of the iterative development process and the small team approach. Different from the last example to some extent, the OS/2 2.0 iterative development process involved large-scale early customer feedback instead of just prototyping. The iterative part of the process involved the loop of subsystem design → subsystem code and test → system integration → customer feedback → subsystem design. Specifically, the waterfall process involved the steps of market requirements, design, code and test, and system certification. The iterative process went from initial market requirements to the iterative loop, then to system certification. Within the one-year development cycle, there were five iterations, each with increased functionality, before completion of the system. For each iteration, the customer feedback involved a beta test of the available functions, a formal customer satisfaction survey, and feedback from various vehicles such as electronic messages on Prodigy, IBM internal e-mail conferences, customer visits, technical seminars, and internal and public bulletin boards. Feedback from various channels was also statistically verified and validated by the formal customer satisfaction surveys. More than 30,000 customers and 100,000 users were involved in the iteration feedback process. Supporting the iterative process was the small team approach in which each team assumed full responsibility for a particular function of the system. Each team owned its project, functionality, quality, and customer satisfaction, and was held completely responsible. Cross-functional system teams also provided support and services to make the subsystem teams successful and to help resolve cross-subsystem concerns (Jenkins, 1992).

The OS/2 2.0 development process and approach, although it may not be universally applicable to other products and systems, was apparently a success as attested by customers' acceptance of the product and positive responses.

2.5 The Object-Oriented Development Process

The object-oriented (OO) approach to design and programming, which was introduced in the 1980s, represents a major paradigm shift in software development. This approach will continue to have a major effect in software for many years. Different from traditional programming, which separates data and control, object-oriented programming is based on objects, each of which is a set of defined data and a set of operations (methods) that can be performed on that data. Like the paradigm of structural design and functional decomposition, the object-oriented approach has become a major cornerstone of software engineering. In the early days of OO technology deployment (from late 1980s to mid 1990s), much of the OO literature concerned analysis and design methods; there was little information about OO development processes. In recent years the object-oriented technology has been widely accepted and object-oriented development is now so pervasive that there is no longer a question of its viability.

Branson and Herness (1992) proposed an OO development process for large-scale projects that centers on an eight-step methodology supported by a mechanism for tracking, a series of inspections, a set of technologies, and rules for prototyping and testing.

The eight-step process is divided into three logical phases:

1. *The analysis phase* focuses on obtaining and representing customers' requirements in a concise manner, to visualize an essential system that represents the users' requirements regardless of which implementation platform (hardware or software environment) is developed.

2. *The design phase* involves modifying the essential system so that it can be imple-
    mented on a given set of hardware and software. Essential classes and incarnation
    classes are combined and refined into the evolving class hierarchy. The objectives
    of class synthesis are to optimize reuse and to create reusable classes.

3. *The implementation phase* takes the defined classes to completion.

The eight steps of the process are summarized as follows:

1. *Model the essential system:* The essential system describes those aspects of the
    system required for it to achieve its purpose, regardless of the target hardware
    and software environment. It is composed of essential activities and essential
    data. This step has five substeps:
    □ Create the user view.
    □ Model essential activities.
    □ Define solution data.
    □ Refine the essential model.
    □ Construct a detailed analysis.
    This step focuses on the user requirements. Requirements are analyzed, dis-
    sected, refined, combined, and organized into an essential logical model of the
    system. This model is based on the perfect technology premise.

2. *Derive candidate-essential classes:* This step uses a technique known as
    "carving" to identify candidate-essential classes and methods from the essen-
    tial model of the whole system. A complete set of data-flow diagrams, along
    with supporting process specifications and data dictionary entries, is the basis
    for class and method selection. Candidate classes and methods are found in
    external entities, data stores, input flows, and process specifications.

3. *Constrain the essential model:* The essential model is modified to work within
    the constraints of the target implementation environment. Essential activities
    and essential data are allocated to the various processors and containers (data
    repositories). Activities are added to the system as needed, based on limitations
    in the target implementation environment. The essential model, when aug-
    mented with the activities needed to support the target environment, is referred
    to as the incarnation model.

4. *Derive additional classes:* Additional candidate classes and methods specific to
    the implementation environment are selected based on the activities added
    while constraining the essential model. These classes supply interfaces to the
    essential classes at a consistent level.

5. *Synthesize classes:* The candidate-essential classes and the candidate-additional
    classes are refined and organized into a hierarchy. Common attributes and oper-
    ations are extracted to produce superclasses and subclasses. Final classes are
    selected to maximize reuse through inheritance and importation.

6. *Define interfaces:* The interfaces, object-type declarations, and class definitions
    are written based on the documented synthesized classes.

7. *Complete the design:* The design of the implementation module is completed. The implementation module comprises several methods, each of which provides a single cohesive function. Logic, system interaction, and method invocations to other classes are used to accomplish the complete design for each method in a class. Referential integrity constraints specified in the essential model (using the data model diagrams and data dictionary) are now reflected in the class design.

8. *Implement the solution:* The implementation of the classes is coded and unit tested.

The analysis phase of the process consists of steps 1 and 2, the design phase consists of steps 3 through 6, and the implementation phase consists of steps 7 and 8. Several iterations are expected during analysis and design. Prototyping may also be used to validate the essential model and to assist in selecting the appropriate incarnation. Furthermore, the process calls for several reviews and checkpoints to enhance the control of the project. The reviews include the following:

☐ Requirements review after the second substep of step 1 (model essential system)
☐ External structure and design review after the fourth substep (refined model) of step 1
☐ Class analysis verification review after step 5
☐ Class externals review after step 6
☐ Code inspection after step 8 code is complete

In addition to methodology, requirements, design, analysis, implementation, prototyping, and verification, Branson and Herness (1993) assert that the object-oriented development process architecture must also address elements such as reuse, CASE tools, integration, build and test, and project management. The Branson and Herness process model, based on their object-oriented experience at IBM Rochester, represents one attempt to deploy the object-oriented technology in large organizations. It is certain that many more variations will emerge before a commonly recognized OOP model is reached.

Finally, the element of reuse merits more discussion from the process perspective, even in this brief section. Design and code reuse gives object-oriented development significant advantages in quality and productivity. However, reuse is not automatically achieved simply by using object-oriented development. Object-oriented development provides a large potential source of reusable components, which must be generalized to become usable in new development environments. In terms of development life cycle, generalization for reuse is typically considered an "add-on" at the end of the project. However, generalization activities take time and resources. Therefore, *developing with reuse* is what every object-oriented project is aiming for, but *developing for reuse* is difficult to accomplish. This reuse paradox explains the reality that there are no significant amounts of business-level reusable code despite the promises OO technology offers, although there are many general-purpose reusable libraries. Therefore, organizations that intend to leverage the reuse advantage of OO development must deal with this issue in their development process.

Henderson-Sellers and Pant (1993) propose a two-library model for the generalization activities for reusable parts. The model addresses the problem of costing and is quite promising. The first step is to put "on hold" project-specific classes from the current project by placing them in a library of potentially reusable components (LPRC). Thus the only cost to the current project is the identification of these classes. The second library, the library of generalized components (LGC), is the high-quality company resource. At the beginning of each new project, an early phase in the development process is an assessment of classes that reside in the LPRC and LGC libraries in terms of their reuse value for the project. If of value, additional spending on generalization is made and potential parts in LPRC can undergo the generalization process and quality checks and be placed in LGC. Because the reusable parts are to benefit the new project, it is reasonable to allocate the cost of generalization to the customer, for whom it will be a savings.

As the preceding discussion illustrates, it may take significant research, experience, and ingenuity to piece together the key elements of an object-oriented development process and for it to mature. In 1997, the Unified Software Development Process, which was developed by Jacobson, Booch, and Rumbaugh (1997) and is owned by the Rational Software Corporation, was published. The process relies on the Unified Modeling Language (UML) for its visual modeling standard. It is use-case driven, architecture-centric, iterative, and incremental. Use cases are the key components that drive this process model. A use case can be defined as a piece of functionality that gives a user a result of a value. All the use cases developed can be combined into a use-case model, which describes the complete functionality of the system. The use-case model is analogous to the functional specification in a traditional software development process model. Use cases are developed with the users and are modeled in UML. These represent the requirements for the software and are used throughout the process model. The Unified Process is also described as architecture-centric. This architecture is a view of the whole design with important characterisitcs made visible by leaving details out. It works hand in hand with the use cases. Subsystems, classes, and components are expressed in the architecture and are also modeled in UML. Last, the Unified Process is iterative and incremental. Iterations represent steps in a workflow, and increments show growth in functionality of the product. The core workflows for iterative development are:

- ☐ Requirements
- ☐ Analysis

- ☐ Design
- ☐ Implementation
- ☐ Test

The Unified Process consists of cycles. Each cycle results in a new release of the system, and each release is a deliverable product. Each cycle has four phases: inception, elaboration, construction, and transition. A number of iterations occur in each phase, and the five core workflows take place over the four phases.

During inception, a good idea for a software product is developed and the project is kicked off. A simplified use-case model is created and project risks are prioritized. Next, during the elaboration phase, product use cases are specified in detail and the system architecture is designed. The project manager begins planning for resources and estimating activities. All views of the system are delivered, including the use-case model, the design model, and the implementation model. These models are developed using UML and held under configuration management. Once this phase is complete, the construction phase begins. From here the architecture design grows into a full system. Code is developed and the software is tested. Then the software is assessed to determine if the product meets the users' needs so that some customers can take early delivery. Finally, the transition phase begins with beta testing. In this phase, defects are tracked and fixed and the software is transitioned to a maintenance team.

One very controversial OO process that has gained recognition and generated vigorous debates among software engineers is Extreme Programming (XP) proposed by Kent Beck (2000). This lightweight, iterative and incremental process has four cornerstone values: communication, simplicity, feedback, and courage. With this foundation, XP advocates the following practices:

- ☐ *The Planning Game:* Development teams estimate time, risk, and story order. The customer defines scope, release dates, and priority.
- ☐ *System metaphor:* A metaphor describes how the system works.
- ☐ *Simple design:* Designs are minimal, just enough to pass the tests that bound the scope.
- ☐ *Pair programming:* All design and coding is done by two people at one workstation. This spreads knowledge better and uses constant peer reviews.
- ☐ *Unit testing and acceptance testing:* Unit tests are written before code to give a clear intent of the code and provide a complete library of tests.
- ☐ *Refactoring:* Code is refactored before and after implementing a feature to help keep the code clean.
- ☐ *Collective code ownership:* By switching teams and seeing all pieces of the code, all developers are able to fix broken pieces.
- ☐ *Continuous integration:* The more code is integrated, the more likely it is to keep running without big hang-ups.

    ☐ *On-site customer:* An onsite customer is considered part of the team and is responsible for domain expertise and acceptance testing.

    ☐ *40-hour week:* Stipulating a 40-hour week ensures that developers are always alert.

    ☐ *Small releases:* Releases are small but contain useful functionality.

    ☐ *Coding standard:* Coding standards are defined by the team and are adhered to.

According to Beck, because these practices balance and reinforce one another, implementing all of them in concert is what makes XP extreme. With these practices, a software engineering team can "embrace changes." Unlike other evolutionary process models, XP discourages preliminary requirements gathering, extensive analysis, and design modeling. Instead, it intentionally limits planning for future flexibility, promoting a "You Aren't Gonna Need It" (YANGI) philosophy that emphasizes fewer classes and reduced documentation. It appears that the XP philosophy and practices may be more applicable to small projects. For large and complex software development, some XP principles become harder to implement and may even run against traditional wisdom that is built upon successful projects. Beck stipulates that to date XP efforts have worked best with teams of ten or fewer members.

2.6 The Cleanroom Methodology

Cleanroom Software Engineering approaches software development as an engineering process with mathematical foundations rather than a trial-and-error programming process (Linger and Hausler, 1992). The Cleanroom process employs theory-based technologies such as box structure specification of user function and system object architecture, function-theoretic design and correctness verification, and statistical usage testing for quality certification. Cleanroom management is based on incremental development and certification of a pipeline of user-function increments that accumulate into the final product. Cleanroom operations are carried out by small, independent development and certification (test) teams, with teams of teams for large projects (Linger, 1993). Figure 2.5 shows the full implementation of the Cleanroom process (Linger, 1993).

    The Cleanroom process emphasizes the importance of the development team having intellectual control over the project. The bases of the process are proof of correctness (of design and code) and formal quality certification via statistical testing. Perhaps the most controversial aspect of Cleanroom is that team verification of correctness takes the place of individual unit testing. Once the code is developed, it is subject to statistical testing for quality assessment. Proponents argue that the intellectual control of a project afforded by team verification of correctness is the basis

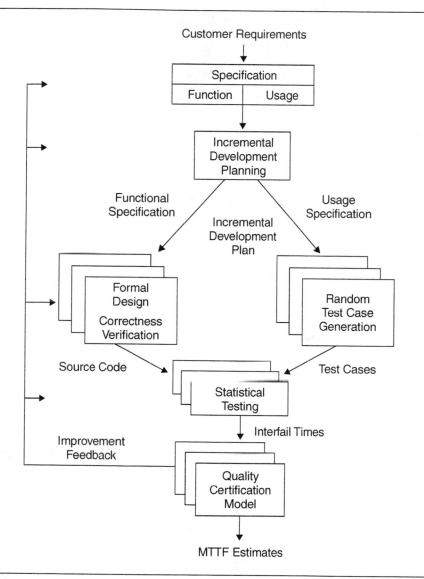

FIGURE 2.5
The Cleanroom Process

From "Cleanroom Software Engineering for Zero-Defect Software," by R. C. Linger. *Proceedings Fifteenth International Conference on Software Engineering,* May 17–21. © 1993 IEEE. Reprinted with permission.

for prohibition of unit testing. This elimination also motivates tremendous determination by developers that the code they deliver for independent testing be error-free on first execution (Hausler and Trammell, 1993).

The Cleanroom process proclaims that statistical testing can replace coverage and path testing. In Cleanroom, all testing is based on anticipated customer usage. Test cases are designed to rehearse the more frequently used functions. Therefore, errors that are likely to cause frequent failures to the users are likely to be found first. In terms of measurement, software quality is certified in terms of mean time to failure (MTTF).

The Cleanroom process represents one of the formal approaches in software development that have begun to see application in industry. Other examples of formal approaches include the Vienna Development Method (VDM) and the Z notation (Smith and Wood, 1989; Wing, 1990). It appears that Z and VDM have been used primarily by developers in the United Kingdom and Europe; Cleanroom projects are conducted mostly in the United States.

Since the pilot projects in 1987 and 1988, a number of projects have been completed using the Cleanroom process. As reported by Linger (1993), the average defect rate in first-time execution was 2.9 defects per thousand lines of code (KLOC), which is significantly better than the industry average.

The adoption of Cleanroom thus far is mostly confined to small projects. Like other formal methods, the questions about its ability to be scaled up to large projects and the mathematical training required have been asked by many developers and project managers. Also, as discussed previously, the prohibition of unit testing is perhaps the most controversial concern. Whether statistical testing could completely replace range/limit testing and path testing remains a key question in many developers' minds. This is especially true when the software system is complex or when the system is a common-purpose system where a typical customer usage profile is itself in question. Not surprisingly, some Cleanroom projects do not preclude the traditional methods (such as unit test and limit test) while adopting Cleanroom's formal approaches. Hausler and Trammell (1993) even proposed a phased implementation approach in order to facilitate the acceptance of Cleanroom. The phased implementation framework includes three stages:

1. *Introductory implementation* involves the implementation of Cleanroom principles without the full formality of the methodology (e.g., box structure, statistical testing, and certification of reliability).
2. *Full implementation* involves the complete use of Cleanroom's formal methods (as illustrated in Figure 2.5).
3. *Advanced implementation* optimizes the process for the local environment (e.g., the use of an automated code generator, Markov modeling and analysis of system usage, and certification using a locally validated reliability model).

In their recent work, the Cleanroom experts elaborate in detail the development and certification process (Prowell et al., 1999). They also show that the Cleanroom software process is compatible with the Software Engineering Institute's capability maturity model (CMM).

2.7 The Defect Prevention Process

The defect prevention process (DPP) is not itself a software development process. Rather, it is a process to continually improve the development process. It originated in the software development environment and thus far has been implemented mostly in software development organizations. Because we would be remiss if we did not discuss this process while discussing software development processes, this chapter includes a brief discussion of DPP.

The DPP was modeled on techniques used in Japan for decades and is in agreement with Deming's principles. It is based on three simple steps:

1. Analyze defects or errors to trace the root causes.
2. Suggest preventive actions to eliminate the defect root causes.
3. Implement the preventive actions.

The formal process, first used at the IBM Communications Programming Laboratory at Research Triangle Park, North Carolina (Jones, 1985; Mays et al., 1990), consists of the following four key elements:

1. *Causal analysis meetings:* These are usually two-hour brainstorming sessions conducted by technical teams at the end of each stage of the development process. Developers analyze defects that occurred in the stage, trace the root causes of errors, and suggest possible actions to prevent similar errors from recurring. Methods for removing similar defects in a current product are also discussed. Team members discuss overall defect trends that may emerge from their analysis of this stage, particularly what went wrong and what went right, and examine suggestions for improvement. After the meeting, the causal analysis leader records the data (defects, causes, and suggested actions) in an action database for subsequent reporting and tracking. To allow participants at this meeting to express their thoughts and feelings on why defects occurred without fear of jeopardizing their careers, managers do not attend this meeting.

2. *Action team:* The action team is responsible for screening, prioritizing, and implementing suggested actions from causal analysis meetings. Each member has a percentage of time allotted for this task. Each action team has a coordinator and a management representative (the action team manager). The team uses reports from

the action database to guide its meetings. The action team is the engine of the process. Other than action implementation, the team is involved in feedback to the organization, reports to management on the status of its activities, publishing success stories, and taking the lead in various aspects of the process. The action team relieves the programmers of having to implement their own suggestions, especially actions that have a broad scope of influence and require substantial resources. Of course, existence of the action team does not preclude action implemented by others. In fact, technical teams are encouraged to take improvement actions, especially those that pertain to their specific areas.

3. *Stage kickoff meetings:* The technical teams conduct these meetings at the beginning of each development stage. The emphasis is on the technical aspect of the development process and on quality: What is the right process? How do we do things more effectively? What are the tools and methods that can help? What are the common errors to avoid? What improvements and actions had been implemented? The meetings thus serve two main purposes: as a primary feedback mechanism of the defect prevention process and as a preventive measure.

4. *Action tracking and data collection:* To prevent suggestions from being lost over time, to aid action implementation, and to enhance communications among groups, an action database tool is needed to track action status.

Figure 2.6 shows this process schematically.

Different from postmortem analysis, the DPP is a real-time process, integrated into every stage of the development process. Rather than wait for a postmortem on the project, which has frequently been the case, DPP is incorporated into every subprocess and phase of that project. This approach ensures that meaningful discussion takes place when it is fresh in everyone's mind. It focuses on defect-related actions and process-oriented preventive actions, which is very important. Through the action teams and action tracking tools and methodology, DPP provides a systematic, objective, data-based mechanism for action implementation. It is a bottoms-up approach; causal analysis meetings are conducted by developers without management interference. However, the process requires management support and direct participation via the action teams.

Many divisions of IBM have had successful experiences with DPP and causal analysis. DPP was successful at IBM in Raleigh, North Carolina, on several software products. For example, IBM's Network Communications Program had a 54% reduction in error injection during development and a 60% reduction in field defects after DPP was implemented. Also, IBM in Houston, Texas, developed the space shuttle onboard software control system with DPP and achieved zero defects since the late 1980s. Causal analysis of defects along with actions aimed at eliminating the cause of defects are credited as the key factors in these successes (Mays et al., 1990).

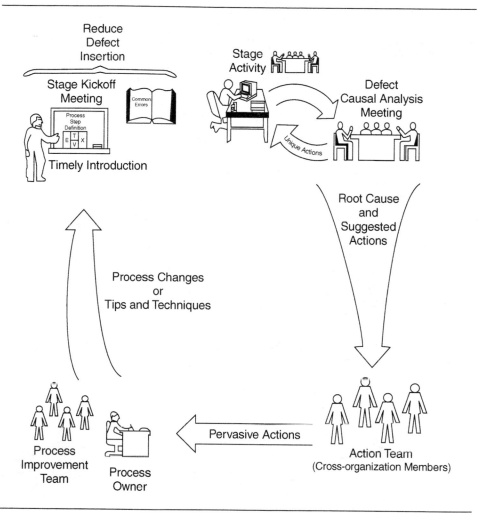

FIGURE 2.6
Defect Prevention Process

Indeed, the element of defect prevention has been incorporated as one of the "imperatives" of the software development process at IBM. Other companies, especially those in the software industry, have also begun to implement the process.

DPP can be applied to any development process—waterfall, prototyping, iterative, spiral, Cleanroom, or others. As long as the defects are recorded, causal analysis can be performed and preventive actions mapped and implemented. For example, the middle of the waterfall process includes designing, coding, and testing. After incorporating DPP at each stage, the process will look like Figure 2.7. The important role

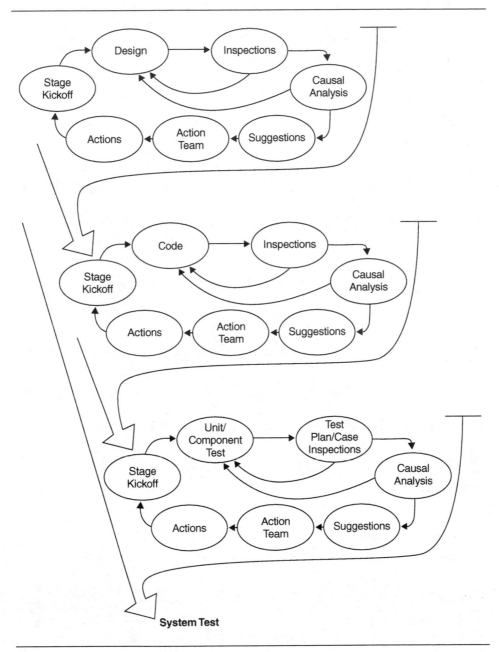

FIGURE 2.7
Applying the Defect Prevention Process to the Middle Segment of the
Waterfall Model

of DPP in software process improvement is widely recognized by the software community. In the SEI (Software Engineering Institute) software process maturity assessment model (Humphrey, 1989), the element of defect prevention is necessary for a process to achieve the highest maturity level—level 5. The SEI maturity model is discussed in more detail in the next section.

Finally, although the defect prevention process has been implemented primarily in software development environments, it can be applied to any product or industry. Indeed, the international quality standard ISO 9000 has a major element of corrective action; DPP is often an effective vehicle employed by companies to address this element when they implement the ISO 9000 registration process. ISO 9000 is also covered in the next section on process maturity assessment and quality standards.

2.8 Process Maturity Framework and Quality Standards

Regardless of which process is used, the degree to which it is implemented varies from organization to organization and even from project to project. Indeed, given the framework of a certain process model, the development team usually defines its specifics such as implementation procedures, methods and tools, metrics and measurements, and so forth. Whereas certain process models are better for certain types of projects under certain environments, the success of a project depends heavily on the implementation maturity, regardless of the process model. In addition to the process model, questions related to the overall quality management system of the company are important to the outcome of the software projects.

This section discusses frameworks to assess the process maturity of an organization or a project. They include the SEI and the Software Productivity Research (SPR) process maturity assessment methods, the Malcolm Baldrige discipline and assessment processes, and the ISO 9000 registration process. Although the SEI and SPR methods are specific to software processes, the latter two frameworks are quality process and quality management standards that apply to all industries.

2.8.1 The SEI Process Capability Maturity Model

The Software Engineering Institute at the Carnegie-Mellon University developed the Process Capability Maturity Model (CMM), a framework for software development (Humphrey, 1989). The CMM includes five levels of process maturity (Humphrey, 1989, p. 56):

Level 1: Initial

Characteristics: Chaotic—unpredictable cost, schedule, and quality performance.

Level 2: Repeatable

Characteristics: Intuitive—cost and quality highly variable, reasonable control of schedules, informal and ad hoc methods and procedures. The key elements, or key process areas (KPA), to achieve level 2 maturity follow:

- ☐ Requirements management
- ☐ Software project planning and oversight
- ☐ Software subcontract management
- ☐ Software quality assurance
- ☐ Software configuration management

Level 3: Defined

Characteristics: Qualitative—reliable costs and schedules, improving but un-predictable quality performance. The key elements to achieve this level of maturity follow:

- ☐ Organizational process improvement
- ☐ Organizational process definition
- ☐ Training program
- ☐ Integrated software management
- ☐ Software product engineering
- ☐ Intergroup coordination
- ☐ Peer reviews

Level 4: Managed

Characteristics: Quantitative—reasonable statistical control over product quality. The key elements to achieve this level of maturity follow:

- ☐ Process measurement and analysis
- ☐ Quality management

Level 5: Optimizing

Characteristics: Quantitative basis for continued capital investment in process automation and improvement. The key elements to achieve this highest level of maturity follow:

- ☐ Defect prevention
- ☐ Technology innovation
- ☐ Process change management

The SEI maturity assessment framework has been used by government agencies and software companies. It is meant to be used with an assessment methodology and a management system. The assessment methodology relies on a questionnaire (85 items in version 1 and 124 items in version 1.1), with yes or no answers. For each question, the SEI maturity level that the question is associated with is indicated. Special questions are designated as key to each maturity level. To be qualified for a certain level, 90% of the key questions and 80% of all questions for that level must be answered yes. The maturity levels are hierarchical. Level 2 must be attained before the calculation for level 3 or higher is accepted. Levels 2 and 3 must be attained before level 4 calculation is accepted, and so forth. If an organization has more than one project, its ranking is determined by answering the questionnaire with a composite viewpoint—specifically, the answer to each question should be substantially true across the organization.

It is interesting to note that pervasive use of software metrics and models is a key characteristic of level 4 maturity, and for level 5 the element of defect prevention is key. Following is a list of metrics-related topics addressed by the questionnaire.

- Profiles of software size maintained for each software configuration item over time
- Statistics on software design errors
- Statistics on software code and test errors
- Projection of design errors and comparison between projected and actual numbers
- Projection of test errors and comparison between projected and actual numbers
- Measurement of design review coverage
- Measurement of test coverage
- Tracking of design review actions to closure
- Tracking of testing defects to closure
- Database for process metrics data across all projects
- Analysis of review data gathered during design reviews
- Analysis of data already gathered to determine the likely distribution and characteristics of the errors in the remainder of the project
- Analysis of errors to determine their process-related causes
- Analysis of review efficiency for each project

Several questions on defect prevention address the following topics:

- Mechanism for error cause analysis
- Analysis of error causes to determine the process changes required for error prevention
- Mechanism for initiating error-prevention actions

The SEI maturity assessment has been conducted on many projects, carried out by SEI or by the organizations themselves in the form of self-assessment. As of April

1996, based on assessments of 477 organizations by SEI, 68.8% were at level 1, 18% were at level 2, 11.3% were at level 3, 1.5% were at level 4, and only 0.4% were at level 5 (Humphrey, 2000). As of March 2000, based on more recent assessments of 870 organizations since 1995, the percentage distribution by level was: level 1, 39.3%; level 2, 36.3%; level 3, 17.7%; level 4, 4.8%; level 5, 1.8% (Humphrey, 2000). The data indicate that the maturity profile of software organizations is improving.

The SEI maturity assessment framework applies to the organizational or project level. At the individual level and team level, Humphrey developed the Personal Software Processs (PSP) and Team Software Processs (TSP) (Humphrey, 1995, 1997, 2000 a,b). The PSP shows software engineers how to plan and track their work, and good and consistent practices that lead to high-quality software. Time management, good software engineering practices, data tracking, and analysis at the individual level are among the focus areas of PSP. The TSP is built on the PSP and addresses how to apply similar engineering discipline to the full range of a team's software tasks. The PSP and TSP can be viewed as the individual and team versions of the capability maturity model (CMM), respectively. Per Humphrey's guidelines, PSP introduction should follow organizational process improvement and should generally be deferred until the organization is working on achieving at least CMM level 2 (Humphrey, 1995).

Since the early 1990s, a number of capability maturity models have been developed for different disciplines. The Capability Maturity Model Integration[sm] (CMMI[sm]) was developed by integrating practices from four CMMs: for software engineering, for systems engineering, for integrated product and process development (IPPD), and for acquisition. It was released in late 2001 (Software Engineering Institute, 2001a, 2001b). Organizations that want to pursue process improvement across disciplines can now rely on a consistent model. The CMMI has two representations, the staged representation and the continuous representation. The staged representation of the CMMI provides five levels of process maturity.

Maturity Level 1: Initial

Processes are ad hoc and chaotic.

Maturity Level 2: Managed

Focuses on basic project management. The process areas (PAs) are:

☐ Requirements management
☐ Project planning
☐ Project monitoring and control
☐ Supplier agreement management
☐ Measurement and analysis
☐ Process and product quality assurance
☐ Configuration management

Maturity Level 3: Defined

Focuses on process standardization. The process areas are:

- ☐ Requirements development
- ☐ Technical solution
- ☐ Product integration
- ☐ Verification
- ☐ Validation
- ☐ Organizational process focus
- ☐ Organizational process definition
- ☐ Organizational training
- ☐ Integrated project management
- ☐ Integrated supplier management
- ☐ Risk management
- ☐ Decision analysis and resolution
- ☐ Organizational environment for integration (IPPD)
- ☐ Integrated teaming (IPPD)

Level 4: Quantitatively Managed

Focuses on quantitative management. The process areas are:

- ☐ Organizational process performance
- ☐ Quantitative project management

Level 5: Optimizing

Focuses on continuous process improvement. The process areas are:

- ☐ Organizational innovation and deployment
- ☐ Causal analysis and resolution

The continuous representation of the CMMI is used to describe the capability level of individual process areas. The capability levels are as follows:

- ☐ Capability Level 0: Incomplete
- ☐ Capability Level 1: Performed
- ☐ Capability Level 2: Managed
- ☐ Capability Level 3: Defined
- ☐ Capability Level 4: Quantitatively Managed
- ☐ Capability Level 5: Optimizing

The two representations of the CMMI take different approaches to process improvement. One focuses on the organization as a whole and provides a road map for the organization to understand and improve its processes through successive stages. The other approach focuses on individual processes and allows the organization to focus on processes that require personnel with more or different capability. The rules for moving from one representation into the other have been defined. Therefore, a choice of one representation does not preclude the use of another at a later time.

2.8.2 The SPR Assessment

Software Productivity Research, Inc. (SPR), developed the SPR assessment method at about the same time (Jones, 1986) the SEI process maturity model was developed. There is a large degree of similarity and some substantial differences between the SEI and SPR methods (Jones, 1992). Some leading U.S. software developers use both methods concurrently. While SEI's questions focus on software organization structure and software process, SPR's questions cover both strategic corporate issues and tactical project issues that affect quality, productivity, and user satisfaction. The number of questions in the SPR questionnaire is about 400. Furthermore, the SPR questions are linked-multiple-choice questions with a five-point Likert scale for responses, whereas the SEI method uses a binary (yes/no) scale. The overall process assessment outcome by the SPR method is also expressed in the same five-point scale:

1. Excellent
2. Good
3. Average
4. Below average
5. Poor

Different from SEI's five maturity levels, which have defined criteria, the SPR questions are structured so that a rating of "3" is the approximate average for the topic being explored. SPR has also developed an automated software tool (CHECKPOINT) for assessment and for resource planning and quality projection. In addition, the SPR method collects quantitative productivity and quality data from each project assessed. This is one of the differences between the SPR and SEI assessment methods.

With regard to software quality and metrics, topics such as the following are addressed by the SPR questions:

☐ Quality and productivity measurements
☐ Pretest defect removal experience among programmers
☐ Testing defect removal experience among programmers

- ☐ Project quality and reliability targets
- ☐ Pretest defect removal at the project level
- ☐ Project testing defect removal
- ☐ Postrelease defect removal

Findings of the SPR assessments are often divided into five major themes (Jones, 2000):

- ☐ Findings about the projects or software products assessed
- ☐ Findings about the software technologies used
- ☐ Findings about the software processes used
- ☐ Findings about the ergonomics and work environments for staff
- ☐ Findings about personnel and training for management and staff

According to Jones (2000), as of 2000, SPR has performed assessments and benchmarks for nearly 350 corporations and 50 government organizations, with the number of sites assessed in excess of 600. The percent distributions of these assessments by the five assessment scales are excellent, 3.0%; above average, 18.0%; average, 54.0%; below average, 22.0%; poor, 3.0%.

2.8.3 The Malcolm Baldrige Assessment

The Malcolm Baldrige National Quality Award (MBNQA) is the most prestigious quality award in the United States. Established in 1988 by the U.S. Department of Commerce (and named after Secretary Malcolm Baldrige), the award is given annually to recognize U.S. companies that excel in quality management and quality achievement. The examination criteria are divided into seven categories that contain twenty-eight examination items:

- ☐ Leadership
- ☐ Information and analysis
- ☐ Strategic quality planning
- ☐ Human resource utilization
- ☐ Quality assurance of products and services
- ☐ Quality results
- ☐ Customer satisfaction

The system for scoring the examination items is based on three evaluation dimensions: approach, deployment, and results. Each item requires information relating to at least one of these dimensions. *Approach* refers to the methods the company is using to achieve the purposes addressed in the examination item. *Deployment* refers to the extent to which the approach is applied. *Results* refers to the outcomes and effects of achieving the purposes addressed and applied.

The purpose of the Malcolm Baldrige assessment approach (the examination items and their assessment) is fivefold:

1. Elevate quality standards and expectations in the United States.
2. Facilitate communication and sharing among and within organizations of all types based on a common understanding of key quality requirements.
3. Serve as a working tool for planning, training, assessment, and other uses.
4. Provide the basis for making the award.
5. Provide feedback to the applicants.

There are 1,000 points available in the award criteria. Each examination item is given a percentage score (ranging from 0% to 100%). A candidate for the Baldrige award should be scoring above 70%. This would generally translate as follows:

☐ For an approach examination item, continuous refinement of approaches are in place and a majority of them are linked to each other.
☐ For a deployment examination item, deployment has reached all of the company's major business areas as well as many support areas.
☐ For a results examination item, the company's results in many of its major areas are among the highest in the industry. There should be evidence that the results are caused by the approach.

While score is important, the most valuable output from an assessment is the feedback, which consists of the observed strengths and (most significant) the areas for improvement. It is not unusual for even the higher scoring enterprises to receive hundreds of improvement suggestions. By focusing on and eliminating the high-priority weaknesses, the company can be assured of continuous improvement.

To be the MBNQA winner, the four basic elements of the award criteria must be evident:

1. *Driver:* The leadership of the senior executive management team.
2. *System:* The set of well-defined and well-designed processes for meeting the company's quality and performance requirements.
3. *Measure of progress:* The results of the company's in-process quality measurements (aimed at improving customer value and company performance).
4. *Goal:* The basic aim of the quality process is the delivery of continuously improving value to customers.

Many U.S. companies have adopted the Malcolm Baldrige assessment and its discipline as the basis for their in-company quality programs. In 1992, the European

Foundation for Quality Management published the European Quality Award, which is awarded to the most successful proponents of total quality management in Western Europe. Its criteria are similar to those of the Baldrige award (i.e., 1,000 maximum points; the areas of approach, deployment, results are scoring dimensions). Although there are nine categories (versus Baldrige's seven), they cover similar examination areas. In 1998, the seven MBNQA categories were reorganized as: Leadership, Strategic Planning, Customer and Market Focus, Information and Analysis, Human Resource Focus, Process Management, and Business Results. Many U.S. states have established quality award programs modeled on the Malcolm Baldrige National Quality Award.

Unlike the SEI and SPR assessments, which focus on software organizations, projects, and processes, the MBNQA and the European Quality Award encompass a much broader scope. They are quality standards for overall quality management, regardless of industry. Indeed, the MBNQA covers three broad categories: manufacturing, service, and small business.

2.8.4 ISO 9000

ISO 9000, a set of standards and guidelines for a quality assurance management system, represents another body of quality standards. It was established by the International Organization for Standardization and has been adopted by the European Community. Many European Community companies are ISO 9000 registered. To position their products to compete better in the European market, many U.S. companies are working to have their development and manufacturing processes registered. To obtain ISO registration, a formal audit of twenty elements is involved and the outcome has to be positive. Guidelines for the application of the twenty elements to the development, supply, and maintenance of software are specified in ISO 9000-3. The twenty elements are as follows:

1. Management responsibility
2. Quality system
3. Contract review
4. Design control
5. Document control
6. Purchasing
7. Purchaser-supplied product
8. Product identification and traceability
9. Process control
10. Inspection and testing
11. Inspection, measuring, and test equipment
12. Inspection and test status
13. Control of nonconforming product

14. Corrective action
15. Handling, storage, packaging, and delivery
16. Quality records
17. Internal quality audits
18. Training
19. Servicing
20. Statistical techniques

Many firms and companies pursue ISO 9000 registration, and many companies fail the first audit. The number of initial failures ranges from 60% to 70%. This interesting statistic is probably explained by the complexity of the standards, their bureaucratic nature, the opportunity for omissions, and a lack of familiarity with the requirements.

From the software standpoint, corrective actions and document control are the areas of most nonconformance. As discussed earlier, the defect prevention process is a good vehicle to address the element of corrective action. It is important, however, to make sure that the process is fully implemented throughout the entire organization. If an organization does not implement the DPP, a process for corrective action must be established to meet the ISO requirements.

With regard to document control, ISO 9000 has very strong requirements, as the following examples demonstrate:

☐ *Must be adequate for purpose:* The document must allow a properly trained person to adequately perform the described duties.

☐ *Owner must be identified:* The owner may be a person or department. The owner is not necessarily the author.

☐ *Properly approved before issued:* Qualified approvers must be identified by the organization's title and the approver's name before the document is distributed.

☐ *Distribution must be controlled:* Control may consist of:
- Keeping a master hard copy with distribution on demand
- Maintaining a distribution record
- Having documents reside online available to all authorized users, with the following control statement, "Master document is the online version."

☐ *Version identified:* The version must be identified clearly by a version level or a date.

☐ *Pages numbered:* All pages must be numbered to ensure sections are not missing.

☐ *Total pages indicated:* The total number of pages must be indicated, at least on the title page.

☐ *Promptly destroyed when obsolete:* When a controlled document is revised or replaced, all copies of it must be recalled or destroyed. Individuals who receive controlled documents are responsible for prompt disposition of superseded documents.

From our perspective, the more interesting requirements address software metrics, which are listed under the element of statistical techniques. The requirements address both product metrics and process metrics.

1. *Product metrics:* Measurements should be used for the following purposes:
   - To collect data and report metric values on a regular basis
   - To identify the current level of performance on each metric
   - To take remedial action if metric levels grow worse or exceed established target levels
   - To establish specific improvement goals in terms of the metrics

   At a minimum, some metrics should be used that represent
   - Reported field failures
   - Defects from customer viewpoint

   Selected metrics should be described such that results are comparable.

2. *Process metrics*
   - Ask if in-process quality objectives are being met.
   - Address how well development process is being carried out with checkpoints.
   - Address how effective the development process is at reducing the probability that faults are introduced or go undetected.

The MBNQA criteria and the ISO 9000 quality assurance system can complement each other as an enterprise pursues quality. However, note that Baldrige is a nonprescriptive assessment tool that illuminates improvement items; ISO 9000 registration requires passing an audit. Furthermore, while the Malcolm Baldrige assessment focuses on both process and results, the ISO 9000 audit focuses on a quality management system and process control. Simply put, ISO 9000 can be described as "say what you do, do what you say, and prove it." But ISO 9000 does not examine the quality results and customer satisfaction, to which the MBNQA is heavily tilted. The two sets of standards are thus complementary. Development organizations that adopt them will have more rigorous processes. Figure 2.8 shows a comparison of ISO 9000 and the Baldrige scoring system. For the Baldrige system, the length of the arrow for each category is in proportion to the maximum score for that category. For ISO 9000, the lengths of the arrows are based on the perceived strength of focus from the IBM Rochester ISO 9000 audit experience, initial registration audit in 1992 and subsequent yearly surveillance audits. As can be seen, if the strengths of ISO 9000 (process quality and process implementation) are combined with the strengths of the Baldrige discipline (quality results, customer focus and satisfaction, and broader issues such as leadership and human resource development), the resulting quality system will have both broad-based coverage and deep penetration.

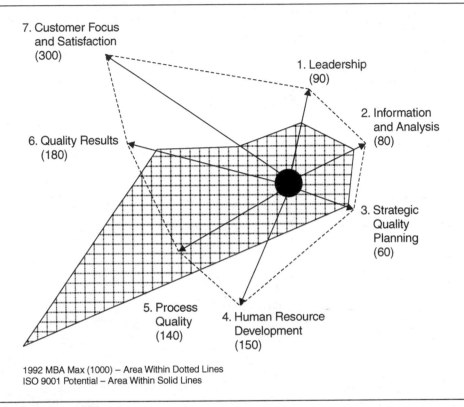

1992 MBA Max (1000) – Area Within Dotted Lines
ISO 9001 Potential – Area Within Solid Lines

FIGURE 2.8
Malcolm Baldrige Assessment and ISO 9000: A Comparison Based on the
Baldrige Scoring

The Baldrige/ISO synergism comes from the following:

☐ The formal ISO documentation requirements (e.g., quality record) facilitate
addressing the Baldrige examination items.
☐ The formal ISO validation requirements (i.e., internal assessments, external
audits, and periodic surveillance) assist completeness and thoroughness.
☐ The heavy ISO emphasis on corrective action contributes to the company's
continuous improvement program.
☐ The audit process itself results in additional focus on many of the Baldrige
examination areas.

In recent years, the ISO technical committee responsible for ISO 9000 family of
quality standards has undertaken a major project to update the standards and to make
them more user-friendly. ISO 9001:2000 contains the first major changes to the stan-

dards since their initial issue. Some of the major changes include the following (British Standards Institution, 2001; Cianfrani, Tsiakals, and West, 2001):

- ☐ Use of a process approach and new structure for standards built around a process model that considers all work in terms of inputs and outputs
- ☐ Shift of emphasis from preparing documented procedures to describe the system to developing and managing a family of effective processes
- ☐ Greater emphasis on role of top management
- ☐ Increased emphasis on the customer, including understanding needs, meeting requirements, and measuring customer satisfaction
- ☐ Emphasis on setting measurable objectives and on measuring product and process performance
- ☐ Introduction of requirements for analysis and the use of data to define opportunity for improvement
- ☐ Formalization of the concept of continual improvement of the quality management system
- ☐ Use of wording that is easily understood in all product sectors, not just hardware
- ☐ Provisions via the application clause to adapt ISO 9001:2000 to all sizes and kinds of organizations and to all sectors of the marketplace

From these changes, it appears ISO 9000 is moving closer to the MBNQA criteria while maintaining a strong process improvement focus.

2.9 Summary

This chapter

- ☐ Describes the major process models and approaches in software development— the waterfall process, the prototyping approach, the spiral model, the iterative process, the object-oriented process, the Cleanroom methodology, and the defect prevention process.
- ☐ Discusses two methods of process maturity assessment—the SEI process capability maturity model and the SPR assessment method.
- ☐ Summarizes two bodies of quality management standards—the Malcolm Baldrige National Quality Award assessment discipline and ISO 9000.

The waterfall process is time-tested and is most suitable for the development of complex system software with numerous interdependencies. This process yields clearly defined intermediate deliverables and enables strong project control.

The prototyping approach enables the development team and the customers to clarify the requirements and their interpretation early in the development cycle. It is not a process per se; it can be used with various process models. It has become widely used in application development. It can also be used with subsystems of systems software when external interfaces are involved.

The iterative process and the spiral model have seen wide use in recent years, especially in application development. Coupled with risk management and prototyping, these new processes increase the likelihood that the final product will satisfy user requirements and facilitate the reduction of cycle time.

In terms of the object-oriented development process, the Unified Process is the most well known process among the object-oriented community. The light-weight Extreme Programming process is one of the more controversial processes.

The Cleanroom approach can be regarded as a process as well as a methodology. As a process, it is well defined. As a methodology, it can be used with other processes such as the waterfall and even object-oriented development. Since the early experimental projects in the late 1980s, the Cleanroom approach has seen increased use in recent years.

The defect prevention process is aimed at process development. When integrated with the development process, it facilitates process maturity because it enables the process to fine-tune itself through the closed-loop learning process. It can be applied to software development as well as to other industries.

Whereas the process models deal with software development, the SEI and SPR maturity models deal with the maturity of the organization's development process, regardless of the process model being used. They entail defining a set of ideal criteria and measuring the processes of organizations against these ideals. This concept has become very popular in the last decade and provides a mechanism for companies to be related with regard to process. The Malcolm Baldrige assessment and ISO 9000 are bodies of quality standards of an even broader scope. They pertain to the quality assurance management system at the company level regardless of industry. In sum, the specific development process being used, the maturity level of the process, and the company's quality management system are all important factors that affect the quality of a software project.

In the next chapter we focus on some aspects of measurement theory that will set the stage for our discussions of software metrics.

References

1. *American Programmer,* "An Interview with Watts Humphrey," September 1990, pp. 8–9.
2. Basili, V. R., and J. D. Musa, "The Future Engineering of Software: A Management Perspective," *IEEE Computer,* 1991, pp. 90–96.
3. Basili, V. R., and A. J. Turner, "Iterative Enhancement: A Practical Technique for Software Development," *IEEE Transactions on Software Engineering,* Vol. SE-1, No. 4, December 1975, pp. 390–396.
4. Beck, K., *Extreme Programming Explained,* Boston: Addison-Wesley, 2000.

5.   Boehm, B. W., "Software Engineering," *IEEE Transactions on Computer,* Vol. C-25, December 1976, pp. 1226–1241.

6.   Boehm, B. W., "A Spiral Model of Software Development and Enhancement," *IEEE Computer,* May 1988, pp. 61–72.

7.   Booch, G., *Object-Oriented Design with Applications,* Redwood City, Calif.: Benjamin/ Cummings, 1991.

8.   Branson, M. J., and E. N. Herness, "Process for Building Object-Oriented Systems from Essential and Constrained System Models: Overview," *Proceedings of the Fourth Worldwide MDQ Productivity and Process Tools Symposium: Volume 1 of 2,* Thornwood, N.Y.: International Business Machines Corp., March 1992, pp. 577–598.

9.   Branson, M. J., and E. N. Herness, "The Object-Oriented Development Process," *Object Magazine,* Vol. 3, No. 4, Nov.–Dec. 1993, pp. 66–70.

10. British Standards Institution (BSI), *The TickIT Guide, Using ISO9001:2000 for Software Quality Management System Construction, Certification and Continual Improvement,* London: BSI DISC TickIT Office, 2001.

11. Cianfrani, C. A., J. J. Tsiakals, and J. E. West, *ISO 9001:2000 Explained,* 2nd ed., Milwaukee, Wisconsin: ASQ Quality Press, 2001.

12. Coad, P., and E. Yourdon, *Object-Oriented Analysis,* Englewood Cliffs, N.J.: Yourdon Press, 1990.

13. Davis, A. M., E. H. Bersoff, and E. R. Comer, "A Strategy for Comparing Alternative Software Development Life Cycle Models," *IEEE Transactions on Software Engineering,* Vol. 14, No. 10, October 1988, pp. 1453–1461.

14. Gomaa, H., and D. Scott, "Prototyping as a Tool in the Specification of User Requirements," *Proceedings 5th IEEE International Conference on Software Engineering,* March 1981, pp. 333–342.

15. Hausler, P. A., and C. J. Trammell, "Adopting Cleanroom Software Engineering with a Phased Approach," IBM Cleanroom Software Technology Center, Gaithersburg, Md., February 1993.

16. Henderson-Sellers, B., and Y. R. Pant, "Adopting the Reuse Mindset Throughout the Lifecycle: When Should We Generalize Classes to Make Them Reusable?" *Object Magazine,* Vol. 3, No. 4, Nov.–Dec. 1993, pp. 73–75.

17. Hough, D., "Rapid Delivery: An Evolutionary Approach for Application Development," *IBM Systems Journal,* Vol. 32, No. 3, 1993, pp. 397–419.

18. Humphrey, W. S., *Managing the Software Process,* Reading, Mass.: Addison-Wesley, 1989.

19. Humphrey, W. S., *A Discipline for Software Engineering,* Reading, Mass.: Addison-Wesley, 1995.

20. Humphrey, W. S., *Introduction to the Personal Software Process^{sm},* Reading, Mass.: Addison-Wesley, 1997.

21. Humphrey, W. S., *Introduction to the Team Software Process^{sm},* Reading, Mass.: Addison-Wesley, 2000a.

22. Humphrey, W. S., *Team Software Process Executive Seminar,* presented to IBM, Austin, Texas, July 25, 2000b.

23. Jacobson, I., G. Booch, and J. Rumbaugh, *The Unified Software Development Process,* Reading, Mass.: Addison-Wesley, 1998.

24. Jenkins, P., IBM Boca Raton, Fl., personal communication, 1992.

25. Jones, Capers, *Software Assessments, Benchmarks, and Best Practices,* Boston: Addison-Wesley, 2000.

26. Jones, C., *Programming Productivity,* New York: McGraw-Hill, 1986.

27. Jones, C., *Applied Software Measurement: Assuring Productivity and Quality,* New York: McGraw-Hill, 1991.

28. Jones, C., "Critical Problems in Software Measurement," Version 1.0, Burlington, Mass.: Software Productivity Research (SPR), August 1992.

29. Jones, C. L., "A Process-Integrated Approach to Defect Prevention," *IBM Systems Journal,* Vol. 24, No. 2, 1985, pp. 150–167.

30. Leishman, T., "Extreme Methodologies for an Extreme World," *CrossTalk, The Journal of Defense Software Engineering,* Vol. 14, No. 6, June 2001, pp.15–18.

31. Linger, R. C., "Cleanroom Software Engineering for Zero-Defect Software," *Proceedings 15th International Conference on Software Engineering,* May 17–21, 1993, IEEE Computer Society Press.

32. Linger, R. C., and P. A. Hausler, "The Journey to Zero Defects with Cleanroom Software Engineering," *Creativity!,* IBM Corporation, September 1992.

33. Luckey, P. H., R. M. Pittman, and A. Q. LeVan, "Iterative Development Process with Proposed Applications," Technical Report, IBM Owego, New York, 1992.

34. Mays, Robert G., C. L. Jones, G. J. Holloway, and D. P. Studinski, "Experiences with Defect Prevention," *IBM Systems Journal,* Vol. 29, No. 1, 1990, pp. 4–32.

35. McMenamin, S. M., and J. F. Palmer, *Essential Systems Analysis,* Englewood Cliffs, N.J.: Yourdon Press, 1984.

36. Meyer, B., *Object-Oriented Software Construction,* Englewood Cliffs, N.J.: Prentice-Hall, 1988.

37. Phillips, M., "CMMI Version 1.1: What Has Changed?" *CrossTalk, The Journal of Defense Software Engineering,* Vol. 15, No. 2, February 2002, pp. 4–6.

38. Prowell, S., C. J. Trammell, R. C. Linger, and J. H. Poore, *Cleanroom Software Engineering, Technology and Process,* Reading, Mass.: Addison-Wesley, 1999.

39. Radice, R. A., N. K. Roth, A. C. O'Hara, Jr., and W. A. Ciarfella, "A Programming Process Architecture," *IBM Systems Journal,* Vol. 24, No. 2, 1985, pp. 79–90.

40. Smith, D. J., and K. B. Wood, *Engineering Quality Software: A Review of Current Practices, Standards and Guidelines Including New Methods and Development Tools,* 2nd ed., New York: Elsevier Applied Science, 1989.

41. Software Engineering Institute, Capability Maturity Model Integration (CMMI), Version 1.1, CMMI for Systems Engineering and Software Engineering (CMMI-SE/SW, V1.1), Continuous Representation, Carnegie Mellon University, CMU/SEI-2002-TR-001, December 2001.

42. Software Engineering Institute, Capability Maturity Model Integration (CMMI), Version 1.1, CMMI for Systems Engineering and Software Engineering (CMMI-SE/SW, V1.1), Staged Representation, Carnegie Mellon University, CMU/SEI-2002-TR-002, December 2001.

43. Wing, J. M., "A Specifier's Introduction to Formal Methods," *Computer,* Vol. 23, No. 9, September 1990, pp. 8–24.

3

Fundamentals of
Measurement Theory

This chapter discusses the fundamentals of measurement theory. We outline the relationships among theoretical concepts, definitions, and measurement, and describe some basic measures that are used frequently. It is important to distinguish the levels of the conceptualization process, from abstract concepts, to definitions that are used operationally, to actual measurements. Depending on the concept and the operational definition derived from it, different levels of measurement may be applied: nominal scale, ordinal scale, interval scale, and ratio scale. It is also beneficial to spell out the explicit differences among some basic measures such as ratio, proportion, percentage, and rate. Significant amounts of wasted effort and resources can be avoided if these fundamental measurements are well understood.

We then focus on measurement quality. We discuss the most important issues in measurement quality, namely, reliability and validity, and their relationships with measurement errors. We then discuss the role of correlation in observational studies and the criteria for causality.

3.1 Definition, Operational Definition, and Measurement

It is undisputed that measurement is crucial to the progress of all sciences. Scientific progress is made through observations and generalizations based on data and measurements, the derivation of theories as a result, and in turn the confirmation or refutation of theories via hypothesis testing based on further empirical data. As an example, consider the proposition "the more rigorously the front end of the software development process is executed, the better the quality at the back end." To confirm or refute this proposition, we first need to define the key concepts. For example, we define "the software development process" and distinguish the process steps and activities of the front end from those of the back end. Assume that after the requirements-gathering process, our development process consists of the following phases:

- ☐ Design
- ☐ Design reviews and inspections
- ☐ Code
- ☐ Code inspection
- ☐ Debug and development tests
- ☐ Integration of components and modules to form the product
- ☐ Formal machine testing
- ☐ Early customer programs

Integration is the development phase during which various parts and components are integrated to form one complete software product. Usually after integration the product is under formal change control. Specifically, after integration every change of the software must have a specific reason (e.g., to fix a bug uncovered during testing) and must be documented and tracked. Therefore, we may want to use integration as the cutoff point: The design, coding, debugging, and integration phases are classified as the front end of the development process and the formal machine testing and early customer trials constitute the back end.

We then define rigorous implementation both in the general sense and in specific terms as they relate to the front end of the development process. Assuming the development process has been formally documented, we may define rigorous implementation as total adherence to the process: Whatever is described in the process documentation that needs to be executed, we execute. However, this general definition is not sufficient for our purpose, which is to gather data to test our proposition. We need to specify the indicator(s) of the definition and to make it (them) operational. For example, suppose the process documentation says all designs and code should be inspected. One operational definition of rigorous implementation may be inspection coverage expressed in terms of the percentage of the estimated lines of code (LOC) or of the function points (FP) that are actually inspected. Another indicator of good reviews and inspections could be the scoring of each inspection by the inspectors at the end of the inspection, based on a set of criteria. We may want to operationally use a five-point Likert scale to denote the degree of effectiveness (e.g.,

5 = very effective, 4 = effective, 3 = somewhat effective, 2 = not effective, 1 = poor inspection). There may also be other indicators.

In addition to design, design reviews, code implementation, and code inspections, development testing is part of our definition of the front end of the development process. We also need to operationally define "rigorous execution" of this test. Two indicators that could be used are the percent coverage in terms of instructions executed (as measured by some test coverage measurement tools) and the defect rate expressed in terms of number of defects removed per thousand lines of source code (KLOC) or per function point.

Likewise, we need to operationally define "quality at the back end" and decide which measurement indicators to use. For the sake of simplicity let us use defects found per KLOC (or defects per function point) during formal machine testing as the indicator of back-end quality. From these metrics, we can formulate several testable hypotheses such as the following:

- For software projects, the higher the percentage of the designs and code that are inspected, the lower the defect rate at the later phase of formal machine testing.
- The more effective the design reviews and the code inspections as scored by the inspection team, the lower the defect rate at the later phase of formal machine testing.
- The more thorough the development testing (in terms of test coverage) before integration, the lower the defect rate at the formal machine testing phase.

With the hypotheses formulated, we can set out to gather data and test the hypotheses. We also need to determine the unit of analysis for our measurement and data. In this case, it could be at the project level or at the component level of a large project. If we are able to collect a number of data points that form a reasonable sample size (e.g., 35 projects or components), we can perform statistical analysis to test the hypotheses. We can classify projects or components into several groups according to the independent variable of each hypothesis, then compare the outcome of the dependent variable (defect rate during formal machine testing) across the groups. We can conduct simple correlation analysis, or we can perform more sophisticated statistical analyses. If the hypotheses are substantiated by the data, we confirm the proposition. If they are rejected, we refute the proposition. If we have doubts or unanswered questions during the process (e.g., Are our indicators valid? Are our data reliable? Are there other variables we need to control when we conduct the analysis for hypothesis testing?), then perhaps more research is needed. However, if the hypothesis(es) or the proposition is confirmed, we can use the knowledge thus gained and act accordingly to improve our software development quality.

The example demonstrates the importance of measurement and data. Measurement and data really drive the progress of science and engineering. Without empirical verification by data and measurement, theories and propositions remain abstract. The example also illustrates that from theory to testable hypothesis, and likewise from concepts to measurement, there are several steps with levels of abstraction. Simply put, a theory consists of one or more propositional statements that describe the relationships among concepts—usually expressed in terms of cause and effect. From each proposition, one or more empirical hypotheses can be derived. The concepts are then formally defined and operationalized. The operationalization process produces metrics and indicators for which data can be collected. The hypotheses thus can be tested empirically. A hierarchy from theory to hypothesis and from concept to measurement indicators is illustrated in Figure 3.1.

The building blocks of theory are concepts and definitions. In a theoretical definition a concept is defined in terms of other concepts that are already well understood. In the deductive logic system, certain concepts would be taken as undefined; they are the primitives. All other concepts would be defined in terms of the primitive concepts. For example, the concepts of point and line may be used as undefined and the concepts of triangle or rectangle can then be defined based on these primitives.

Operational definitions, in contrast, are definitions that spell out the metrics and the procedures to be used to obtain data. An operational definition of "body weight" would indicate how the weight of a person is to be measured, the instrument to be used, and the measurement unit to record the results. An operational definition of

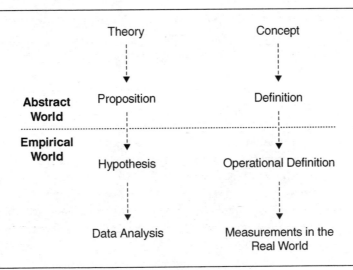

FIGURE 3.1
Abstraction Hierarchy

"software product defect rate" would indicate the formula for defect rate, the defect to be measured (numerator), the denominator (e.g., lines of code count, function point), how to measure, and so forth.

3.2 Level of Measurement

We have seen that from theory to empirical hypothesis and from theoretically defined concepts to operational definitions, the process is by no means direct. As the example illustrates, when we operationalize a definition and derive measurement indicators, we must consider the scale of measurement. For instance, to measure the quality of software inspection we may use a five-point scale to score the inspection effectiveness or we may use percentage to indicate the inspection coverage. For some cases, more than one measurement scale is applicable; for others, the nature of the concept and the resultant operational definition can be measured only with a certain scale. In this section, we briefly discuss the four levels of measurement: nominal scale, ordinal scale, interval scale, and ratio scale.

Nominal Scale

The most simple operation in science and the lowest level of measurement is classification. In classifying we attempt to sort elements into categories with respect to a certain attribute. For example, if the attribute of interest is religion, we may classify the subjects of the study into Catholics, Protestants, Jews, Buddhists, and so on. If we classify software products by the development process models through which the products were developed, then we may have categories such as waterfall development process, spiral development process, iterative development process, object-oriented programming process, and others. In a nominal scale, the two key requirements for the categories are jointly exhaustive and mutually exclusive. Mutually exclusive means a subject can be classified into one and only one category. Jointly exhaustive means that all categories together should cover all possible categories of the attribute. If the attribute has more categories than we are interested in, an "other" category is needed to make the categories jointly exhaustive.

In a nominal scale, the names of the categories and their sequence bear no assumptions about relationships among categories. For instance, we place the waterfall development process in front of spiral development process, but we do not imply that one is "better than" or "greater than" the other. As long as the requirements of mutually exclusive and jointly exhaustive are met, we have the minimal conditions necessary for the application of statistical analysis. For example, we may want to compare the values of interested attributes such as defect rate, cycle time, and requirements defects across the different categories of software products.

Ordinal Scale

Ordinal scale refers to the measurement operations through which the subjects can be compared in order. For example, we may classify families according to socio-economic status: upper class, middle class, and lower class. We may classify software development projects according to the SEI maturity levels or according to a process rigor scale: totally adheres to process, somewhat adheres to process, does not adhere to process. Our earlier example of inspection effectiveness scoring is an ordinal scale.

The ordinal measurement scale is at a higher level than the nominal scale in the measurement hierarchy. Through it we are able not only to group subjects into categories, but also to order the categories. An ordinal scale is asymmetric in the sense that if $A > B$ is true then $B > A$ is false. It has the transitivity property in that if $A > B$ and $B > C$, then $A > C$.

We must recognize that an ordinal scale offers no information about the magnitude of the differences between elements. For instance, for the process rigor scale we know only that "totally adheres to process" is better than "somewhat adheres to process" in terms of the quality outcome of the software product, and "somewhat adheres to process" is better than "does not adhere to process." However, we cannot say that the difference between the former pair of categories is the same as that between the latter pair. In customer satisfaction surveys of software products, the five-point Likert scale is often used with 1 = completely dissatisfied, 2 = somewhat dissatisfied, 3 = neutral, 4 = satisfied, and 5 = completely satisfied. We know only $5 > 4$, $4 > 3$, and $5 > 2$, and so forth, but we cannot say how much greater 5 is than 4. Nor can we say that the difference between categories 5 and 4 is equal to that between categories 3 and 2. Indeed, to move customers from satisfied (4) to very satisfied (5) versus from dissatisfied (2) to neutral (3), may require very different actions and types of improvements.

Therefore, when we translate order relations into mathematical operations, we cannot use operations such as addition, subtraction, multiplication, and division. We can use "greater than" and "less than." However, in real-world application for some specific types of ordinal scales (such as the Likert five-point, seven-point, or ten-point scales), the assumption of equal distance is often made and operations such as averaging are applied to these scales. In such cases, we should be aware that the measurement assumption is deviated, and then use extreme caution when interpreting the results of data analysis.

Interval and Ratio Scales

An interval scale indicates the exact differences between measurement points. The mathematical operations of addition and subtraction can be applied to interval scale data. For instance, assuming products A, B, and C are developed in the same language, if the defect rate of software product A is 5 defects per KLOC and product B's rate is 3.5 defects per KLOC, then we can say product A's defect level is 1.5 defects per KLOC higher than product B's defect level. An interval scale of measurement requires a well-defined unit of measurement that can be agreed on as a common standard and that is repeatable. Given a unit of measurement, it is possible to say that the difference between two scores is 15 units or that one difference is the same as a second. Assuming product C's defect rate is 2 defects per KLOC, we can thus say the difference in defect rate between products A and B is the same as that between B and C.

When an absolute or nonarbitrary zero point can be located on an interval scale, it becomes a ratio scale. Ratio scale is the highest level of measurement and all mathematical operations can be applied to it, including division and multiplication. For example, we can say that product A's defect rate is twice as much as product C's because when the defect rate is zero, that means not a single defect exists in the product. Had the zero point been arbitrary, the statement would have been illegitimate. A good example of an interval scale with an arbitrary zero point is the traditional temperature measurement (Fahrenheit and centigrade scales). Thus we say that the difference between the average summer temperature (80°F) and the average winter temperature (16°F) is 64°F, but we do not say that 80°F is five times as hot as 16°F. Fahrenheit and centigrade temperature scales are interval, not ratio, scales. For this reason, scientists developed the absolute temperature scale (a ratio scale) for use in scientific activities.

Except for a few notable examples, for all practical purposes almost all interval measurement scales are also ratio scales. When the size of the unit is established, it is usually possible to conceive of a zero unit.

For interval and ratio scales, the measurement can be expressed in both integer and noninteger data. Integer data are usually given in terms of frequency counts (e.g., the number of defects customers will encounter for a software product over a specified time length).

We should note that the measurement scales are hierarchical. Each higher-level scale possesses all properties of the lower ones. The higher the level of measurement, the more powerful analysis can be applied to the data. Therefore, in our operationalization process we should devise metrics that can take advantage of the highest level of measurement allowed by the nature of the concept and its definition. A higher-level measurement can always be reduced to a lower one, but not vice versa. For example, in our defect measurement we can always make various types of comparisons if the scale is in terms of actual defect rate. However, if the scale is in terms of excellent, good, average, worse than average, and poor, as compared to an industrial standard, then our ability to perform additional analysis of the data is limited.

3.3 Some Basic Measures

Regardless of the measurement scale, when the data are gathered we need to analyze them to extract meaningful information. Various measures and statistics are available for summarizing the raw data and for making comparisons across groups. In this section we discuss some basic measures such as ratio, proportion, percentage, and rate, which are frequently used in our daily lives as well as in various activities associated with software development and software quality. These basic measures, while seemingly easy, are often misused. There are also numerous sophisticated statistical techniques and methodologies that can be employed in data analysis. However, such topics are not within the scope of this discussion.

Ratio

A ratio results from dividing one quantity by another. The numerator and denominator are from two distinct populations and are mutually exclusive. For example, in demography, sex ratio is defined as

$$\frac{\text{Number of males}}{\text{Number of females}} \times 100\%$$

If the ratio is less than 100, there are more females than males; otherwise there are more males than females.

Ratios are also used in software metrics. The most often used, perhaps, is the ratio of number of people in an independent test organization to the number of those in the development group. The test/development head-count ratio could range from 1:1 to 1:10 depending on the management approach to the software development process. For the large-ratio (e.g., 1:10) organizations, the development group usually is responsible for the complete development (including extensive development tests) of the product, and the test group conducts system-level testing in terms of customer environment verifications. For the small-ratio organizations, the independent group takes the major responsibility for testing (after debugging and code integration) and quality assurance.

Proportion

Proportion is different from ratio in that the numerator in a proportion is a part of the denominator:

$$p = \frac{a}{a+b}$$

Proportion also differs from ratio in that ratio is best used for two groups, whereas proportion is used for multiple categories (or populations) of one group. In other words, the denominator in the preceding formula can be more than just $a + b$. If

$$a + b + c + d + e = N$$

then we have

$$\frac{a}{N} + \frac{b}{N} + \frac{c}{N} + \frac{d}{N} + \frac{e}{N} = 1$$

When the numerator and the denominator are integers and represent counts of certain events, then p is also referred to as a relative frequency. For example, the following gives the proportion of satisfied customers of the total customer set:

$$\frac{\text{Number of satisfied customers}}{\text{Total number of customers of a software product}}$$

The numerator and the denominator in a proportion need not be integers. They can be frequency counts as well as measurement units on a continuous scale (e.g., height in inches, weight in pounds). When the measurement unit is not integer, proportions are called fractions.

Percentage

A proportion or a fraction becomes a percentage when it is expressed in terms of per hundred units (the denominator is normalized to 100). The word *percent* means per hundred. A proportion p is therefore equal to $100p$ percent ($100p\%$).

Percentages are frequently used to report results, and as such are frequently misused. First, because percentages represent relative frequencies, it is important that enough contextual information be given, especially the total number of cases, so that the readers can interpret the information correctly. Jones (1992) observes that many reports and presentations in the software industry are careless in using percentages and ratios. He cites the example:

> Requirements bugs were 15% of the total, design bugs were 25% of the total, coding bugs were 50% of the total, and other bugs made up 10% of the total.

Had the results been stated as follows, it would have been much more informative:

> The project consists of 8 thousand lines of code (KLOC). During its development a total of 200 defects were detected and removed, giving a defect removal

rate of 25 defects per KLOC. Of the 200 defects, requirements bugs constituted 15%, design bugs 25%, coding bugs 50%, and other bugs made up 10%.

A second important rule of thumb is that the total number of cases must be sufficiently large enough to use percentages. Percentages computed from a small total are not stable; they also convey an impression that a large number of cases are involved. Some writers recommend that the minimum number of cases for which percentages should be calculated is 50. We recommend that, depending on the number of categories, the minimum number be 30, the smallest sample size required for parametric statistics. If the number of cases is too small, then absolute numbers, instead of percentages, should be used. For instance,

Of the total 20 defects for the entire project of 2 KLOC, there were 3 requirements bugs, 5 design bugs, 10 coding bugs, and 2 others.

When results in percentages appear in table format, usually both the percentages and actual numbers are shown when there is only one variable. When there are more than two groups, such as the example in Table 3.1, it is better just to show the percentages and the total number of cases (N) for each group. With percentages and N known, one can always reconstruct the frequency distributions. The total of 100.0% should always be shown so that it is clear how the percentages are computed. In a two-way table, the direction in which the percentages are computed depends on the purpose of the comparison. For instance, the percentages in Table 3.1 are computed vertically (the total of each column is 100.0%), and the purpose is to compare the defect-type profile across projects (e.g., project B proportionally has more requirements defects than project A).

In Table 3.2, the percentages are computed horizontally. The purpose here is to compare the distribution of defects across projects for each type of defect. The inter-

TABLE 3.1
Percentage Distributions of Defect Type by Project

Type of Defect	Project A (%)	Project B (%)	Project C (%)
Requirements	15.0	41.0	20.3
Design	25.0	21.8	22.7
Code	50.0	28.6	36.7
Others	10.0	8.6	20.3
Total	100.0	100.0	100.0
(N)	(200)	(105)	(128)

TABLE 3.2
Percentage Distributions of Defects Across Project by Defect Type

	Project				
Type of Defect	A	B	C	Total	(N)
Requirements (%)	30.3	43.4	26.3	100.0	(99)
Design (%)	49.0	22.5	28.5	100.0	(102)
Code (%)	56.5	16.9	26.6	100.0	(177)
Others (%)	36.4	16.4	47.2	100.0	(55)

pretations of the two tables differ. Therefore, it is important to carefully examine percentage tables to determine exactly how the percentages are calculated.

Rate

Ratios, proportions, and percentages are static summary measures. They provide a cross-sectional view of the phenomena of interest at a specific time. The concept of *rate* is associated with the dynamics (change) of the phenomena of interest; generally it can be defined as a measure of change in one quantity (y) per unit of another quantity (x) on which the former (y) depends. Usually the x variable is time. It is important that the time unit always be specified when describing a rate associated with time. For instance, in demography the crude birth rate (CBR) is defined as:

$$\text{Crude birth rate} = \frac{B}{P} \times K$$

where B is the number of live births in a given calendar year, P is the mid-year population, and K is a constant, usually 1,000.

The concept of *exposure to risk* is also central to the definition of rate, which distinguishes rate from proportion. Simply stated, all elements or subjects in the denominator have to be at risk of becoming or producing the elements or subjects in the numerator. If we take a second look at the crude birth rate formula, we will note that the denominator is mid-year population and we know that not the entire population is subject to the risk of giving birth. Therefore, the operational definition of CBR is not in compliance with the concept of population at risk, and for this reason, it is a "crude" rate. A better measurement is the general fertility rate, in which the denominator is the number of women of childbearing age, usually defined as ages 15 to 44. In addition, there are other more refined measurements for birth rate.

In literature about quality, the risk exposure concept is defined as opportunities for error (OFE). The numerator is the number of defects of interest. Therefore,

$$\text{Defect rate} = \frac{\text{Number of defects}}{\text{OFE}} \times K$$

In software, *defect rate* is usually defined as the number of defects per thousand source lines of code (KLOC or KSLOC) in a given time unit (e.g., one year after the general availability of the product in the marketplace, or for the entire life of the product). Note that this metric, defects per KLOC, is also a crude measure. First, the opportunity for error is not known. Second, while any line of source code may be subject to error, a defect may involve many source lines. Therefore, the metric is only a proxy measure of defect rate, even assuming no other problems. Such limitations should be taken into account when analyzing results or interpreting data pertaining to software quality.

Six Sigma

The term *six sigma* represents a stringent level of quality. It is a specific defect rate: 3.4 defective parts per million (ppm). It was made known in the industry by Motorola, Inc., in the late 1980s when Motorola won the first Malcolm Baldrige National Quality Award (MBNQA). Six sigma has become an industry standard as an ultimate quality goal.

Sigma (σ) is the Greek symbol for standard deviation. As Figure 3.2 indicates, the areas under the curve of normal distribution defined by standard deviations are constants in terms of percentages, regardless of the distribution parameters. The area under the curve as defined by plus and minus one standard deviation (sigma) from the mean is 68.26%. The area defined by plus/minus two standard deviations is 95.44%, and so forth. The area defined by plus/minus six sigma is 99.9999998%. The area outside the six sigma area is thus 100% −99.9999998% = 0.0000002%.

If we take the area within the six sigma limit as the percentage of defect-free parts and the area outside the limit as the percentage of defective parts, we find that six sigma is equal to 2 defectives per billion parts or 0.002 defective parts per million. The interpretation of defect rate as it relates to the normal distribution will be clearer if we include the specification limits in the discussion, as shown in the top panel of Figure 3.3. Given the specification limits (which were derived from customers' requirements), our purpose is to produce parts or products within the limits. Parts or products outside the specification limits do not conform to requirements. If we can reduce the variations in the production process so that the six sigma (standard deviations) variation of the production process is within the specification limits, then we will have six sigma quality level.

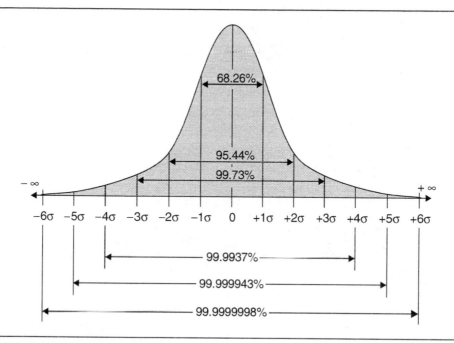

FIGURE 3.2
Areas Under the Normal Curve

The six sigma value of 0.002 ppm is from the statistical normal distribution. It assumes that each execution of the production process will produce the exact distribution of parts or products centered with regard to the specification limits. In reality, however, process shifts and drifts always result from variations in process execution. The maximum process shifts as indicated by research (Harry, 1989) is 1.5 sigma. If we account for this 1.5-sigma shift in the production process, we will get the value of 3.4 ppm. Such shifting is illustrated in the two lower panels of Figure 3.3. Given fixed specification limits, the distribution of the production process may shift to the left or to the right. When the shift is 1.5 sigma, the area outside the specification limit on one end is 3.4 ppm, and on the other it is nearly zero.

The six sigma definition accounting for the 1.5-sigma shift (3.4 ppm) proposed and used by Motorola (Harry, 1989) has become the industry standard in terms of six sigma–level quality (versus the normal distribution's six sigma of 0.002 ppm). Furthermore, when the production distribution shifts 1.5 sigma, the intersection points of the normal curve and the specification limits become 4.5 sigma at one end and 7.5 sigma at the other. Since for all practical purposes, the area outside 7.5 sigma is zero, one may say that the Motorola Six Sigma is equal to the one-tailed 4.5 sigma of the centered normal distribution.

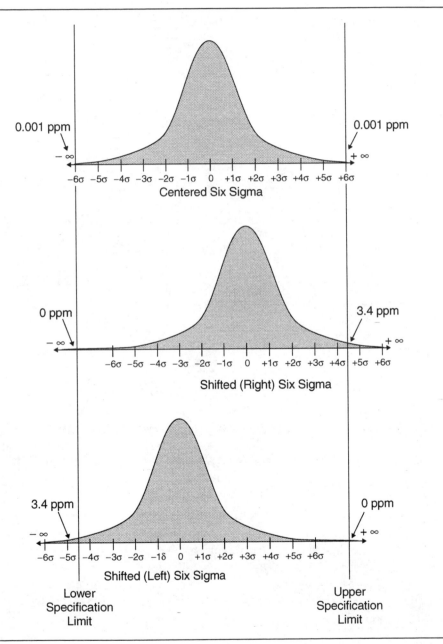

FIGURE 3.3
Specification Limits, Centered Six Sigma, and Shifted (1.5 Sigma) Six Sigma

The subtle difference between the centered six sigma and the shifted six sigma may imply something significant. The former is practically equivalent to zero defects, which may invite the debate whether it is feasible to achieve such a goal. The shifted six sigma, while remaining at a very stringent level, does contain a sense of reality. As an example to illustrate the difference, assume we are to clean a house of 1500 sq. ft. By centered six sigma, the area that we allow not to be clean enough is about the area of the head of a pin. By shifted six sigma, the area is about the size of the bottom of a soft drink can. Table 3.3 shows the defect rates by sigma level with and without the 1.5-sigma shift. The defect rates are expressed in terms of defective parts per million (DPPM).

So far our discussion of six sigma has centered on the fact that it is a specific defect rate. Its concept, however, is much richer than that. As we touched on in the discussion, in order to reach six sigma, we have to improve the process. Specifically, we must reduce process variations so that the six sigma variation is still within the specification limits. The notion of process improvement/process variation reduction is, therefore, an inherent part of the concept. Another notion is that of product design and product engineering. If failure tolerance is incorporated into the design of the product, it is a lot easier to make the finished product meet the specifications and, therefore, easier to achieve six sigma quality. The concept of process variation reduction also involves the theory and elaboration of process capability. For details, see Harry and Lawson (1992) and other Motorola literature on the subject (e.g, Smith, 1989). In recent years, the concept and approach of six sigma has been expanded and applied to the improvement of management systems and total quality management. In their recent work, Harry and Schroeder (2000) discuss this expanded approach and its successful applications in several well-known corporations. In *Customer-Centered Six Sigma,* Naumann and Hoisington (2001) discuss the approach and

TABLE 3.3
DPPM by Sigma Level with and without Process Shift

Sigma	DPPM (Centered)	DPPM (with 1.5-Sigma Shift)
2	45,500	308,733
3	2,200	66,810
3.5	466	22,700
4	63	6,210
4.5	6.8	1,350
5	0.57	233
5.5	0.038	32
6	0.002	3.4

methods to link six sigma quality and process improvement with customer satisfaction, customer loyalty, and financial results.

In software, a defect is a binary variable (the program either works or does not), and it is difficult to relate to continuous distributions such as the normal distribution. However, for discrete distributions there is an equivalent approximation to the six sigma calculation in statistical theory. Moreover, the notions of process improvement and tolerance design cannot be more applicable. In the software industry, six sigma in terms of defect level is defined as 3.4 defects per million lines of code of the software product over its life. Interestingly, the original reason for using the sigma scale to measure quality was to facilitate comparisons across products or organizations. However, in reality this is not the case because the operational definition differs across organizations. For instance, the lines of code in the denominator are taken as the count of shipped source instructions by the International Business Machine Corporation regardless of the language type used to develop the software. Motorola, on the other hand, operationalized the denominator as Assembler language–equivalent instructions. In other words, the normalized lines of code (to Assembler language) is used. To achieve the normalization, the ratios of high-level language to Assembler by Jones (1986) were used. The difference between the two operational definitions can be orders of magnitude. For example, according to Jones's conversion table, one line of PL/I code is equivalent to four lines of Assembler statements, and one line of Smalltalk is equivalent to 15 lines of Assembler.

3.4 Reliability and Validity

Recall that concepts and definitions have to be operationally defined before measurements can be taken. Assuming operational definitions are derived and measurements are taken, the logical question to ask is, how good are the operational metrics and the measurement data? Do they really accomplish their task—measuring the concept that we want to measure and doing so with good quality? Of the many criteria of measurement quality, reliability and validity are the two most important.

Reliability refers to the consistency of a number of measurements taken using the same measurement method on the same subject. If repeated measurements are highly consistent or even identical, then the measurement method or the operational definition has a high degree of reliability. If the variations among repeated measurements are large, then reliability is low. For example, if an operational definition of a body height measurement of children (e.g., between ages 3 and 12) includes specifications of the time of the day to take measurements, the specific scale to use, who takes the measurements (e.g., trained pediatric nurses), whether the measurements should be taken barefooted, and so on, it is likely that reliable data will be obtained. If the operational definition is very vague in terms of these considerations, the data reliability may be low. Measurements taken in the early morning may be greater than those taken in the late afternoon because children's bodies tend to be more stretched after a good night's sleep and become somewhat compacted after a tiring day. Other factors that can contribute to the variations of the measurement data include different scales, trained or untrained personnel, with or without shoes on, and so on.

The measurement of any phenomenon contains a certain amount of chance error. The goal of error-free measurement, although laudable and widely recognized, is never attained in any discipline of scientific investigation. The amount of measurement error may be large or small, but it is universally present. The goal, of course, is to achieve the best possible reliability. Reliability can be expressed in terms of the size of the standard deviations of the repeated measurements. When variables are compared, usually the index of variation (IV) is used. IV is simply a ratio of the standard deviation to the mean:

$$IV = \frac{\text{Standard deviation}}{\text{Mean}}$$

The smaller the IV, the more reliable the measurements.

Validity refers to whether the measurement or metric really measures what we intend it to measure. In other words, it refers to the extent to which an empirical measure reflects the real meaning of the concept under consideration. In cases where the measurement involves no higher level of abstraction, for example, the measurements of body height and weight, validity is simply accuracy. However, validity is different from reliability. Measurements that are reliable are not necessarily valid, and vice versa. For example, a new bathroom scale for body weight may give identical results upon five consecutive measurements (e.g., 160 lb.) and therefore it is reliable. However, the measurements may not be valid; they would not reflect the person's body weight if the offset of the scale were at 10 lb. instead of at zero.

For abstract concepts, validity can be a very difficult issue. For instance, the use of church attendance for measuring religiousness in a community may have low validity because religious persons may or may not go to church and may or may not go regularly. Often, it is difficult to recognize that a certain metric is invalid in measuring a concept; it is even more difficult to improve it or to invent a new metric.

Researchers tend to classify validity into several types. The type of validity we have discussed so far is *construct validity,* which refers to the validity of the operational measurement or metric representing the theoretical construct. In addition, there are *criterion-related validity* and *content validity*. Criterion-related validity is also referred to as predictive validity. For example, the validity of a written driver's test is determined by the relationship between the scores people get on the test and how well they drive. Predictive validity is also applicable to modeling, which we will discuss in later chapters on software reliability models. Content validity refers to the degree to which a measure covers the range of meanings included in the concept. For instance, a test of mathematical ability for elementary pupils cannot be limited to addition, but would also need to cover subtraction, multiplication, division, and so forth.

Given a theoretical construct, the purpose of measurement is to measure the construct validly and reliably. Figure 3.4 graphically portrays the difference between validity and reliability. If the purpose of the measurement is to hit the center of the target, we see that reliability looks like a tight pattern regardless of where it hits, because reliability is a function of consistency. Validity, on the other hand, is a function of shots being arranged around the bull's eye. In statistical terms, if the expected value (or the mean) is the bull's eye, then it is valid; if the variations are small relative to the entire target, then it is reliable.

Note that there is some tension between validity and reliability. For the data to be reliable, the measurement must be specifically defined. In such an endeavor, the risk of being unable to represent the theoretical concept validly may be high. On the other hand, for the definition to have good validity, it may be quite difficult to define the measurements precisely. For example, the measurement of church attendance may be quite reliable because it is specific and observable. However, it may not be valid to represent the concept of religiousness. On the other hand, to derive valid measurements of religiousness is quite difficult. In the real world of measurements and metrics, it is not uncommon for a certain tradeoff or balance to be made between validity and reliability.

Validity and reliability issues come to the fore when we try to use metrics and measurements to represent abstract theoretical constructs. In traditional quality engi-

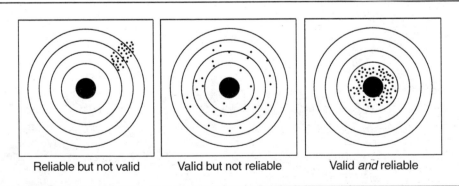

| Reliable but not valid | Valid but not reliable | Valid *and* reliable |

FIGURE 3.4
An Analogy to Validity and Reliability

neering where measurements are frequently physical and usually do not involve abstract concepts, the counterparts of validity and reliability are termed *accuracy* and *precision* (Juran and Gryna, 1970). Much confusion surrounds these two terms despite their having distinctly different meanings. If we want a much higher degree of precision in measurement (e.g., accuracy up to three digits after the decimal point when measuring height), then our chance of getting all measurements accurate may be reduced. In contrast, if accuracy is required only at the level of integer inch (less precise), then it is a lot easier to meet the accuracy requirement.

Reliability and validity are the two most important issues of measurement quality. These two issues should be well thought-through before a metric is proposed, used, and analyzed. In addition, other attributes for software metrics are desirable. For instance, the draft of the IEEE standard for a software quality metrics methodology includes factors such as correlation, tracking, consistency, predictability, and discriminative power (Schneidewind, 1991).

3.5 Measurement Errors

In this section we discuss validity and reliability in the context of measurement error. There are two types of measurement error: *systematic* and *random*. Systematic measurement error is associated with validity; random error is associated with reliability. Let us revisit our example about the bathroom weight scale with an offset of 10 lb. Each time a person uses the scale, he will get a measurement that is 10 lb. more than his actual body weight, in addition to the slight variations among measurements. Therefore, the expected value of the measurements from the scale does not equal the true value because of the systematic deviation of 10 lb. In simple formula:

Measurement from the scale = True body weight + 10 lb. + Random variations

In a general case:

$$M = T + s + e$$

where M is the observed/measured score, T is the true score, s is systematic error, and e is random error.

The presence of s (systematic error) makes the measurement invalid. Now let us assume the measurement is valid and the s term is not in the equation. We have the following:

$$M = T + e$$

The equation still states that any observed score is not equal to the true score because of random disturbance—the random error e. These disturbances mean that on one measurement, a person's score may be higher than his true score and on another occasion the measurement may be lower than the true score. However, since the disturbances are random, it means that the positive errors are just as likely to occur as the negative errors and these errors are expected to cancel each other. In other words, the average of these errors in the long run, or the expected value of e, is zero: $E(e) = 0$. Furthermore, from statistical theory about random error, we can also assume the following:

☐ The correlation between the true score and the error term is zero.
☐ There is no serial correlation between the true score and the error term.
☐ The correlation between errors on distinct measurements is zero.

From these assumptions, we find that the expected value of the observed scores is equal to the true score:

$$
\begin{aligned}
E(M) &= E(T) + E(e) \\
&= E(T) + 0 \\
&= E(T) \\
&= T
\end{aligned}
$$

The question now is to assess the impact of e on the reliability of the measurements (observed scores). Intuitively, the smaller the variations of the error term, the more reliable the measurements. This intuition can be observed in Figure 3.4 as well as expressed in statistical terms:

$$M = T + e$$
$$\text{var}(M) = \text{var}(T) + \text{var}(e) \quad \text{(var represents variance.}$$

This relationship is due to the assumptions on error terms.)

$$
\begin{aligned}
\text{Reliability} = \rho_m &= \text{var}(T)/\text{var}(M) \\
&= [\text{var}(M) - \text{var}(e)]/\text{var}(M) \\
&= 1 - [\text{var}(e)/\text{var}(M)]
\end{aligned}
$$

Therefore, the reliability of a metric varies between 0 and 1. In general, the larger the error variance relative to the variance of the observed score, the poorer the reliability. If all variance of the observed scores is a result of random errors, then the reliability is zero $[1 - (1/1) = 0]$.

3.5.1 Assessing Reliability

Thus far we have discussed the concept and meaning of validity and reliability and their interpretation in the context of measurement errors. Validity is associated with systematic error and the only way to eliminate systematic error is through better understanding of the concept we try to measure, and through deductive logic and reasoning to derive better definitions. Reliability is associated with random error. To reduce random error, we need good operational definitions, and based on them, good execution of measurement operations and data collection. In this section, we discuss how to assess the reliability of empirical measurements.

There are several ways to assess the reliability of empirical measurements including the test/retest method, the alternative-form method, the split-halves method, and the internal consistency method (Carmines and Zeller, 1979). Because our purpose is to illustrate how to use our understanding of reliability to interpret software metrics rather than in-depth statistical examination of the subject, we take the easiest method, the retest method. The retest method is simply taking a second measurement of the subjects some time after the first measurement is taken and then computing the correlation between the first and the second measurements. For instance, to evaluate the reliability of a blood pressure machine, we would measure the blood pressures of a group of people and, after everyone has been measured, we would take another set of measurements. The second measurement could be taken one day later at the same time of day, or we could simply take two measurements at one time. Either way, each person will have two scores. For the sake of simplicity, let us confine ourselves to just one measurement, either the systolic or the diastolic score. We then calculate the correlation between the first and second score and the correlation coefficient is the reliability of the blood pressure machine. A schematic representation of the test/retest method for estimating reliability is shown in Figure 3.5.

The equations for the two tests can be represented as follows:

$$M_1 = T + e_1$$
$$M_2 = T + e_2$$

From the assumptions about the error terms, as we briefly stated before, it can be shown that

$$\rho_m = p_{m1m2} = \text{var}(T)/\text{var}(M)$$

in which ρ_m is the reliability measure.

As an example in software metrics, let us assess the reliability of the reported number of defects found at design inspection. Assume that the inspection is formal; that is, an inspection meeting was held and the participants include the design owner,

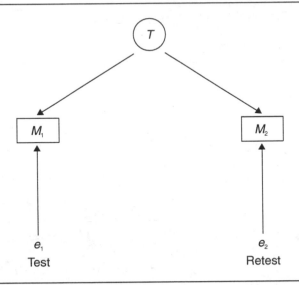

FIGURE 3.5
Test/Retest Method for Estimating Reliability

the inspection moderator, and the inspectors. At the meeting, each defect is acknowledged by the whole group and the record keeping is done by the moderator. The test/retest method may involve two record keepers and, at the end of the inspection, each turns in his recorded number of defects. If this method is applied to a series of inspections in a development organization, we will have two reports for each inspection over a sample of inspections. We then calculate the correlation between the two series of reported numbers and we can estimate the reliability of the reported inspection defects.

3.5.2 Correction for Attenuation

One of the important uses of reliability assessment is to adjust or correct correlations for unreliability that result from random errors in measurements. Correlation is perhaps one of the most important methods in software engineering and other disciplines for analyzing relationships between metrics. For us to substantiate or refute a hypothesis, we have to gather data for both the independent and the dependent variables and examine the correlation of the data. Let us revisit our hypothesis testing example at the beginning of this chapter: The more effective the design reviews and the code inspections as scored by the inspection team, the lower the defect rate encountered at the later phase of formal machine testing.

As mentioned, we first need to operationally define the independent variable (inspection effectiveness) and the dependent variable (defect rate during formal machine testing). Then we gather data on a sample of components or projects and calculate the correlation between the independent variable and dependent variable. However, because of random errors in the data, the resultant correlation often is lower than the true correlation. With knowledge about the estimate of the reliability of the variables of interest, we can adjust the observed correlation to get a more accurate picture of the relationship under consideration. In software development, we observed that a key reason for some theoretically sound hypotheses not being supported by actual project data is that the operational definitions of the metrics are poor and there are too many noises in the data.

Given the observed correlation and the reliability estimates of the two variables, the formula for correction for attenuation (Carmines and Zeller, 1979) is as follows:

$$\rho(x_t y_t) = \rho(x_i y_i) / \sqrt{\rho_{xx'} \rho_{yy'}}$$

where
$\rho(x_t y_t)$ is the correlation corrected for attenuation, in other words, the
      estimated true correlation
$\rho(x_i y_i)$ is the observed correlation, calculated from the observed data
$\rho_{xx'}$ is the estimated reliability of the X variable
$\rho_{yy'}$ is the estimated reliability of the Y variable

For example, if the observed correlation between two variables was 0.2 and the reliability estimates were 0.5 and 0.7, respectively, for X and Y, then the correlation corrected for attenuation would be

$$\rho(x_t y_t) = 0.2 / \sqrt{0.5 \times 0.7}$$
$$= 0.34$$

This means that the correlation between X and Y would be 0.34 if both were measured perfectly without error.

3.6 Be Careful with Correlation

Correlation is probably the most widely used statistical method to assess relationships among observational data (versus experimental data). However, caution must be exercised when using correlation; otherwise, the true relationship under investigation may be disguised or misrepresented. There are several points about correlation that one has to know before using it. First, although there are special types of nonlinear correlation analysis available in statistical literature, most of the time when one mentions correlation, it means linear correlation. Indeed, the most well-known Pearson correlation coefficient assumes a linear relationship. Therefore, if a correlation coefficient between two variables is weak, it simply means there is no linear relationship between the two variables. It doesn't mean there is no relationship of any kind.

Let us look at the five types of relationship shown in Figure 3.6. Panel A represents a positive linear relationship and panel B a negative linear relationship. Panel C shows a curvilinear convex relationship, and panel D a concave relationship. In panel E, a cyclical relationship (such as the Fourier series representing frequency waves) is shown. Because correlation assumes linear relationships, when the correlation coefficients (Pearson) for the five relationships are calculated, the results accurately show that panels A and B have significant correlation. However, the correlation coefficients for the other three relationships will be very weak or will show no relationship at all. For this reason, it is highly recommended that when we use correlation we always look at the scattergrams. If the scattergram shows a particular type of nonlinear relationship, then we need to pursue analyses or coefficients other than linear correlation.

Second, if the data contain noise (due to unreliability in measurement) or if the range of the data points is large, the correlation coefficient (Pearson) will probably show no relationship. In such a situation, we recommend using the rank-order correlation method, such as Spearman's rank-order correlation. The Pearson correlation (the correlation we usually refer to) requires interval scale data, whereas rank-order correlation requires only ordinal data. If there is too much noise in the interval data, the Pearson correlation coefficient thus calculated will be greatly attenuated. As discussed in the last section, if we know the reliability of the variables involved, we can adjust the resultant correlation. However, if we have no knowledge about the reliability of the variables, rank-order correlation will be more likely to detect the underlying relationship. Specifically, if the noises of the data did not affect the original ordering of the data points, then rank-order correlation will be more successful in representing the true relationship. Since both Pearson's correlation and Spearman's rank-order correlation are covered in basic statistics textbooks and are available in most statistical software packages, we need not get into the calculation details here.

Third, the method of linear correlation (least-squares method) is very vulnerable to extreme values. If there are a few extreme outliers in the sample, the correlation coefficient may be seriously affected. For example, Figure 3.7 shows a moderately negative relationship between X and Y. However, because there are three extreme outliers at the northeast coordinates, the correlation coefficient will become positive. This outlier susceptibility reinforces the point that when correlation is used, one should also look at the scatter diagram of the data.

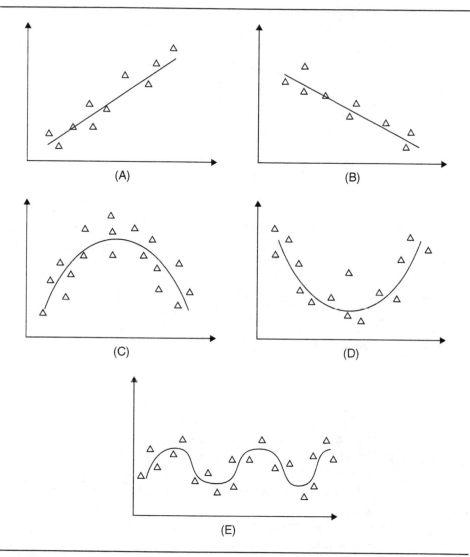

FIGURE 3.6
Five Types of Relationship Between Two Variables

Finally, although a significant correlation demonstrates that an association exists between two variables, it does not automatically imply a cause-and-effect relationship. Although an element of causality, correlation alone is inadequate to show the existence of causality. In the next section, we discuss the criteria for establishing causality.

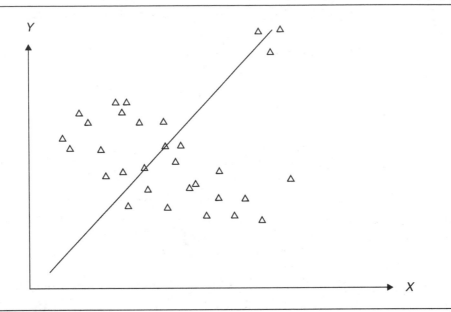

FIGURE 3.7
Effect of Outliers on Correlation

3.7 Criteria for Causality

The isolation of cause and effect in controlled experiments is relatively easy. For example, a headache medicine was administered to a sample of subjects who were having headaches. A placebo was administered to another group with headaches (who were statistically not different from the first group). If after a certain time of taking the headache medicine and the placebo, the headaches of the first group were reduced or disappeared, while headaches persisted among the second group, then the curing effect of the headache medicine is clear.

For analysis with observational data, the task is much more difficult. Researchers (e.g., Babbie, 1986) have identified three criteria:

1. The first requirement in a causal relationship between two variables is that the cause precede the effect in time or as shown clearly in logic.
2. The second requirement in a causal relationship is that the two variables be empirically correlated with one another.
3. The third requirement for a causal relationship is that the observed empirical correlation between two variables be not the result of a spurious relationship.

The first and second requirements simply state that in addition to empirical correlation, the relationship has to be examined in terms of sequence of occurrence or deductive logic. Correlation is a statistical tool and could be misused without the guidance of a logic system. For instance, it is possible to correlate the outcome of a Super Bowl (National Football League versus American Football League) to some interesting artifacts such as fashion (length of skirt, popular color, and so forth) and weather. However, logic tells us that coincidence or spurious association cannot substantiate causation.

The third requirement is a difficult one. There are several types of spurious relationships, as Figure 3.8 shows, and sometimes it may be a formidable task to show that the observed correlation is not due to a spurious relationship. For this reason, it is much more difficult to prove causality in observational data than in experimental data. Nonetheless, examining for spurious relationships is necessary for scientific reasoning; as a result, findings from the data will be of higher quality.

In Figure 3.8, case A is the typical spurious relationship between X and Y in which X and Y have a common cause Z. Case B is a case of the *intervening variable*, in which the real cause of Y is an intervening variable Z instead of X. In the strict sense, X is not a direct cause of Y. However, since X causes Z and Z in turn causes Y, one could claim causality if the sequence is not too indirect. Case C is similar to case A. However, instead of X and Y having a common cause as in case B, both X and Y are indicators (operational definitions) of the same concept C. It is logical that there is a correlation between them, but causality should not be inferred.

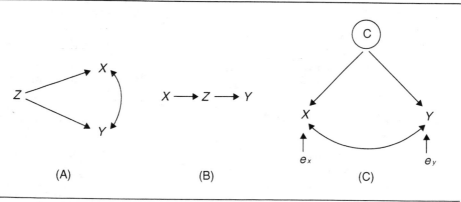

FIGURE 3.8
Spurious Relationships

An example of the spurious causal relationship due to two indicators measuring the same concept is Halstead's (1977) software science formula for program length:

$$N = n_1 \times \log_2 n_1 + n_2 \times \log_2 n_2$$

where
N = estimated program length
n_1 = number of unique operators
n_2 = number of unique operands

Researchers have reported high correlations between actual program length (actual lines of code count) and the predicted length based on the formula, sometimes as high as 0.95 (Fitzsimmons and Love, 1978). However, as Card and Agresti (1987) show, both the formula and actual program length are functions of n_1 and n_2, so correlation exists by definition. In other words, both the formula and the actual lines of code counts are operational measurements of the concept of program length. One has to conduct an actual n_1 and n_2 count for the formula to work. However, n_1 and n_2 counts are not available until the program is complete or almost complete. Therefore, the relationship is not a cause-and-effect relationship and the usefulness of the formula's predictability is limited.

3.8 Summary

Measurement is related to the concept or entity of interest and the operational definition of the concept. Depending on the operational definition, different levels of measurement can be applied: nominal scale, ordinal scale, interval scale, and ratio scale. The measurement scales are hierarchical; each scale possesses all properties of scales at lower levels.

Basic measures such as ratio, proportion, percentage, and rate all have specific purposes. Care should be exercised to avoid misuse. The concept of six sigma not only represents a stringent level of quality, it also includes the notions of process-variation reduction and product-design improvement. Its definition as used in the industry (shifted six sigma) is different from the statistical definition based on normal distribution (centered six sigma). Although meant for comparisons across different measurement units, in software the sigma levels cannot be compared across companies because of differences in operational definitions.

Validity and reliability are the two most important criteria of measurement quality. Validity refers to whether the metric really measures what it is intended to. Reliability refers to the consistency of measurements of the metric and measurement method. Validity is associated with systematic measurement errors and reliability with random measurement errors. Unreliability of measurements leads to an attenuation of correlation between two variables. When the measurement reliabilities of the variables are known, correction for such attenuation can be made.

Correlation is widely used with observational data, including software measurements. Correlation alone, however, cannot establish causality. To establish a cause-and-effect relationship based on observational data, three criteria must be met: (1) the cause precedes the effect in time or logically, (2) significant correlation exists, and (3) the observed correlation is not caused by a spurious relationship.

Measurement is the key to making software development a true engineering discipline. To improve the practice of software measurement, it is important to understand the fundamentals of measurement theory.

References

1. Babbie, E., *The Practice of Social Research*, 4th ed., Belmont, Calif.: Wadsworth, 1986.
2. Card, D. N., and W. W. Agresti, "Resolving the Software Science Anomaly," *Journal of Systems and Software*, Vol. 7, March 1987, pp. 29–35.
3. Carmines, E. G., and R. A. Zeller, *Reliability and Validity Assessment*, Beverly Hills, Calif.: Sage, 1979.
4. Fitzsimmons, A., and T. Love, "A Review and Evaluation of Software Science," *ACM Computing Surveys*, Vol. 10, No. 1, March 1978, pp. 3–18.
5. Halstead, M. H., *Elements of Software Science*, New York: Elsevier, 1977.
6. Harry, M. J., "The Nature of Six Sigma Quality," Government Electronics Group, Motorola, Inc., Schaumburg, Il. 1989.
7. Harry, M. J., and J. R. Lawson, *Six Sigma Producibility Analysis and Process Characterization*, Reading, Mass.: Addison-Wesley, 1992.
8. Harry, M. J., and R. Schroeder, *Six Sigma: The Breakthrough Management Strategy Revolutionizing the World's Top Corporations*, Milwaukee, Wisc.: ASQ Quality Press, 2000.
9. Information obtained from Motorola when the author was a member of a software benchmarking team at Motorola, Schaumburg, Il., February 9, 1990.
10. Jones, C., *Applied Software Measurement: Assuring Productivity and Quality*, New York: McGraw-Hill, 1986.
11. Jones, C., "Critical Problems in Software Measurement," Version 1.0, Burlington, Mass.: Software Productivity Research (SPR), August 1992.
12. Juran, J. M., and F. M. Gryna, Jr., *Quality Planning and Analysis: From Product Development Through Use*, New York: McGraw-Hill, 1970.
13. Naumann, E., and S. H. Hoisington, *Customer-Centered Six Sigma, Linking Customers, Process Improvement, and Financial Results*, Milwaukee, Wisc.: ASQ Quality Press, 2001.
14. Schneidewind, N. F., "Report on IEEE Standard for a Software Quality Metrics Methodology (Draft) P1061, with Discussion of Metrics Validation," *Proceedings IEEE Fourth Software Engineering Standards Application Workshop*, 1991, pp. 155–157.
15. Smith, W. B., "Six Sigma: TQC, American Style," presented at the National Technological University television series, October 31, 1989.

4

Software Quality Metrics Overview

Software metrics can be classified into three categories: product metrics, process metrics, and project metrics. Product metrics describe the characteristics of the product such as size, complexity, design features, performance, and quality level. Process metrics can be used to improve software development and maintenance. Examples include the effectiveness of defect removal during development, the pattern of testing defect arrival, and the response time of the fix process. Project metrics describe the project characteristics and execution. Examples include the number of software developers, the staffing pattern over the life cycle of the software, cost, schedule, and productivity. Some metrics belong to multiple categories. For example, the in-process quality metrics of a project are both process metrics and project metrics.

Software quality metrics are a subset of software metrics that focus on the quality aspects of the product, process, and project. In general, software quality metrics are more closely associated with process and product metrics than with project metrics. Nonetheless, the project parameters such as the number of developers and their skill levels, the schedule, the size, and the organization structure certainly affect the quality of the product. Software quality metrics can be divided further into end-product quality metrics and in-process quality metrics. The essence of software quality engineering is to investigate the relationships among in-process metrics, project characteristics, and end-product quality, and, based on the findings, to engineer improvements in both process and product quality. Moreover, we should view quality from the entire software life-cycle perspective and, in this regard, we should include metrics that measure the quality level of the maintenance process as another category of software quality metrics. In this chapter we discuss several metrics in each of three groups of software quality metrics: product quality, in-process quality, and maintenance quality. In the last sections we also describe the key metrics used by several major software developers and discuss software metrics data collection.

4.1 Product Quality Metrics

As discussed in Chapter 1, the de facto definition of software quality consists of two levels: intrinsic product quality and customer satisfaction. The metrics we discuss here cover both levels:

- ☐ Mean time to failure
- ☐ Defect density
- ☐ Customer problems
- ☐ Customer satisfaction.

Intrinsic product quality is usually measured by the number of "bugs" (functional defects) in the software or by how long the software can run before encountering a "crash." In operational definitions, the two metrics are defect density (rate) and mean time to failure (MTTF). The MTTF metric is most often used with safety-critical systems such as the airline traffic control systems, avionics, and weapons. For instance, the U.S. government mandates that its air traffic control system cannot be unavailable for more than three seconds per year. In civilian airliners, the probability of certain catastrophic failures must be no worse than 10^{-9} per hour (Littlewood and Strigini, 1992). The defect density metric, in contrast, is used in many commercial software systems.

The two metrics are correlated but are different enough to merit close attention. First, one measures the *time* between failures, the other measures the *defects* relative to the software size (lines of code, function points, etc.). Second, although it is difficult to separate defects and failures in actual measurements and data tracking, failures and defects (or faults) have different meanings. According to the IEEE/ American National Standards Institute (ANSI) standard (982.2):

- ☐ An error is a human mistake that results in incorrect software.
- ☐ The resulting fault is an accidental condition that causes a unit of the system to fail to function as required.
- ☐ A defect is an anomaly in a product.
- ☐ A failure occurs when a functional unit of a software-related system can no longer perform its required function or cannot perform it within specified limits.

From these definitions, the difference between a fault and a defect is unclear. For practical purposes, there is no difference between the two terms. Indeed, in many development organizations the two terms are used synonymously. In this book we also use the two terms interchangeably.

Simply put, when an error occurs during the development process, a fault or a defect is injected in the software. In operational mode, failures are caused by faults or defects, or failures are materializations of faults. Sometimes a fault causes more than one failure situation and, on the other hand, some faults do not materialize until the software has been executed for a long time with some particular scenarios. Therefore, defect and failure do not have a one-to-one correspondence.

Third, the defects that cause higher failure rates are usually discovered and removed early. The probability of failure associated with a latent defect is called its size, or "bug size." For special-purpose software systems such as the air traffic control systems or the space shuttle control systems, the operations profile and scenarios are better defined and, therefore, the time to failure metric is appropriate. For general-purpose computer systems or commercial-use software, for which there is no typical user profile of the software, the MTTF metric is more difficult to implement and may not be representative of all customers.

Fourth, gathering data about time between failures is very expensive. It requires recording the occurrence time of each software failure. It is sometimes quite difficult to record the time for all the failures observed during testing or operation. To be useful, time between failures data also requires a high degree of accuracy. This is perhaps the reason the MTTF metric is not widely used by commercial developers.

Finally, the defect rate metric (or the volume of defects) has another appeal to commercial software development organizations. The defect rate of a product or the expected number of defects over a certain time period is important for cost and resource estimates of the maintenance phase of the software life cycle.

Regardless of their differences and similarities, MTTF and defect density are the two key metrics for intrinsic product quality. Accordingly, there are two main types of software reliability growth models—the time between failures models and the defect count (defect rate) models. We discuss the two types of models and provide several examples of each type in Chapter 8.

4.1.1 The Defect Density Metric

Although seemingly straightforward, comparing the defect rates of software products involves many issues. In this section we try to articulate the major points. To define a rate, we first have to operationalize the numerator and the denominator, and specify the time frame. As discussed in Chapter 3, the general concept of defect rate is the number of defects over the opportunities for error (OFE) during a specific time frame. We have just discussed the definitions of software defect and failure. Because

failures are defects materialized, we can use the number of unique causes of observed failures to approximate the number of defects in the software. The denominator is the size of the software, usually expressed in thousand lines of code (KLOC) or
in the number of function points. In terms of time frames, various operational definitions are used for the life of product (LOP), ranging from one year to many years
after the software product's release to the general market. In our experience with
operating systems, usually more than 95% of the defects are found within four years
of the software's release. For application software, most defects are normally found
within two years of its release.

Lines of Code

The lines of code (LOC) metric is anything but simple. The major problem comes
from the ambiguity of the operational definition, the actual counting. In the early
days of Assembler programming, in which one physical line was the same as one
instruction, the LOC definition was clear. With the availability of high-level languages the one-to-one correspondence broke down. Differences between physical
lines and instruction statements (or logical lines of code) and differences among languages contribute to the huge variations in counting LOCs. Even within the same
language, the methods and algorithms used by different counting tools can cause significant differences in the final counts. Jones (1986) describes several variations:

- ☐ Count only executable lines.
- ☐ Count executable lines plus data definitions.
- ☐ Count executable lines, data definitions, and comments.
- ☐ Count executable lines, data definitions, comments, and job control language.
- ☐ Count lines as physical lines on an input screen.
- ☐ Count lines as terminated by logical delimiters.

To illustrate the variations in LOC count practices, let us look at a few examples
by authors of software metrics. In Boehm's well-known book *Software Engineering
Economics* (1981), the LOC counting method counts lines as physical lines and
includes executable lines, data definitions, and comments. In *Software Engineering
Metrics and Models* by Conte et al. (1986), LOC is defined as follows:

> A line of code is any line of program text that is not a comment or blank line,
> regardless of the number of statements or fragments of statements on the line.
> This specifically includes all lines containing program headers, declarations,
> and executable and non-executable statements. (p. 35)

Thus their method is to count physical lines including prologues and data definitions (declarations) but not comments. In *Programming Productivity* by Jones

(1986), the source instruction (or logical lines of code) method is used. The method used by IBM Rochester is also to count source instructions including executable lines and data definitions but excluding comments and program prologues.

The resultant differences in program size between counting physical lines and counting instruction statements are difficult to assess. It is not even known which method will result in a larger number. In some languages such as BASIC, PASCAL, and C, several instruction statements can be entered on one physical line. On the other hand, instruction statements and data declarations might span several physical lines, especially when the programming style aims for easy maintenance, which is not necessarily done by the original code owner. Languages that have a fixed column format such as FORTRAN may have the physical-lines-to-source-instructions ratio closest to one. According to Jones (1992), the difference between counts of physical lines and counts including instruction statements can be as large as 500%; and the average difference is about 200%, with logical statements outnumbering physical lines. In contrast, for COBOL the difference is about 200% in the opposite direction, with physical lines outnumbering instruction statements.

There are strengths and weaknesses of physical LOC and logical LOC (Jones, 2000). In general, logical statements are a somewhat more rational choice for quality data. When any data on size of program products and their quality are presented, the method for LOC counting should be described. At the minimum, in any publication of quality when LOC data is involved, the author should state whether the LOC counting method is based on physical LOC or logical LOC.

Furthermore, as discussed in Chapter 3, some companies may use the straight LOC count (whatever LOC counting method is used) as the denominator for calculating defect rate, whereas others may use the normalized count (normalized to Assembler-equivalent LOC based on some conversion ratios) for the denominator. Therefore, industrywide standards should include the conversion ratios from high-level language to Assembler. So far, very little research on this topic has been published. The conversion ratios published by Jones (1986) are the most well known in the industry. As more and more high-level languages become available for software development, more research will be needed in this area.

When straight LOC count data is used, size and defect rate comparisons across languages are often invalid. Extreme caution should be exercised when comparing the defect rates of two products if the operational definitions (counting) of LOC, defects, and time frame are not identical. Indeed, we do not recommend such comparisons. We recommend comparison against one's own history for the sake of measuring improvement over time.

Note: The LOC discussions in this section are in the context of defect rate calculation. For productivity studies, the problems with using LOC are more severe. A basic problem is that the amount of LOC in a softare program is negatively correlated with design efficiency. The purpose of software is to provide certain functionality for solving some specific problems or to perform certain tasks. Efficient design provides the functionality with lower implementation effort and fewer LOCs. Therefore, using LOC data to measure software productivity is like using the weight of an airplane to measure its speed and capability. In addition to the level of languages issue, LOC data do not reflect noncoding work such as the creation of requirements, specifications, and user manuals. The LOC results are so misleading in productivity studies that Jones states "using lines of code for productivity studies involving multiple languages and full life cycle activities should be viewed as professional malpractice" (2000, p. 72). For detailed discussions of LOC and function point metrics, see Jones's work (1986, 1992, 1994, 1997, 2000).

When a software product is released to the market for the first time, and when a certain LOC count method is specified, it is relatively easy to state its quality level (projected or actual). For example, statements such as the following can be made: "This product has a total of 50 KLOC; the latent defect rate for this product during the next four years is 2.0 defects per KLOC." However, when enhancements are made and subsequent versions of the product are released, the situation becomes more complicated. One needs to measure the quality of the entire product as well as the portion of the product that is new. The latter is the measurement of true development quality—the defect rate of the new and changed code. Although the defect rate for the entire product will improve from release to release due to aging, the defect rate of the new and changed code will not improve unless there is real improvement in the development process. To calculate defect rate for the new and changed code, the following must be available:

- ☐ *LOC count:* The entire software product as well as the new and changed code of the release must be available.
- ☐ *Defect tracking:* Defects must be tracked to the release origin—the portion of the code that contains the defects and at what release the portion was added, changed, or enhanced. When calculating the defect rate of the entire product, all defects are used; when calculating the defect rate for the new and changed code, only defects of the release origin of the new and changed code are included.

These tasks are enabled by the practice of change flagging. Specifically, when a new function is added or an enhancement is made to an existing function, the new and changed lines of code are flagged with a specific identification (ID) number through the use of comments. The ID is linked to the requirements number, which is usually described briefly in the module's prologue. Therefore, any changes in the program modules can be linked to a certain requirement. This linkage procedure is part of the software configuration management mechanism and is usually practiced by organizations that have an established process. If the change-flagging IDs and requirements

IDs are further linked to the release number of the product, the LOC counting tools can use the linkages to count the new and changed code in new releases. The change-flagging practice is also important to the developers who deal with problem determination and maintenance. When a defect is reported and the fault zone determined, the developer can determine in which function or enhancement pertaining to what requirements at what release origin the defect was injected.

The new and changed LOC counts can also be obtained via the delta-library method. By comparing program modules in the original library with the new versions in the current release library, the LOC count tools can determine the amount of new and changed code for the new release. This method does not involve the change-flagging method. However, change flagging remains very important for maintenance. In many software development environments, tools for automatic change flagging are also available.

Example: Lines of Code Defect Rates

At IBM Rochester, lines of code data is based on instruction statements (logical LOC) and includes executable code and data definitions but excludes comments. LOC counts are obtained for the total product and for the new and changed code of the new release. Because the LOC count is based on source instructions, the two size metrics are called *shipped source instructions* (*SSI*) and new and *changed source instructions* (*CSI*), respectively. The relationship between the SSI count and the CSI count can be expressed with the following formula:

$$
\begin{aligned}
\text{SSI (current release)} = &\ \text{SSI (previous release)} \\
&+ \text{CSI (new and changed code instructions for} \\
&\quad \text{current release)} \\
&- \text{deleted code (usually very small)} \\
&- \text{changed code (to avoid double count in both} \\
&\quad \text{SSI and CSI)}
\end{aligned}
$$

Defects after the release of the product are tracked. Defects can be field defects, which are found by customers, or internal defects, which are found internally. The several postrelease defect rate metrics per thousand SSI (KSSI) or per thousand CSI (KCSI) are:

(1) Total defects per KSSI (a measure of code quality of the total product)

(2) Field defects per KSSI (a measure of defect rate in the field)

(3) Release-origin defects (field and internal) per KCSI (a measure of development quality)

(4) Release-origin field defects per KCSI (a measure of development quality per defects found by customers)

Metric (1) measures the total release code quality, and metric (3) measures the quality of the new and changed code. For the initial release where the entire product is new, the two metrics are the same. Thereafter, metric (1) is affected by aging and the improvement (or deterioration) of metric (3). Metrics (1) and (3) are process measures; their field counterparts, metrics (2) and (4) represent the customer's perspective. Given an estimated defect rate (KCSI or KSSI), software developers can minimize the impact to customers by finding and fixing the defects before customers encounter them.

Customer's Perspective

The defect rate metrics measure code quality per unit. It is useful to drive quality improvement from the development team's point of view. Good practice in software quality engineering, however, also needs to consider the customer's perspective. Assume that we are to set the defect rate goal for release-to-release improvement of one product. From the customer's point of view, the defect rate is not as relevant as the total number of defects that might affect their business. Therefore, a good defect rate target should lead to a release-to-release reduction in the total number of defects, regardless of size. If a new release is larger than its predecessors, it means the defect rate goal for the new and changed code has to be significantly better than that of the previous release in order to reduce the total number of defects.

Consider the following hypothetical example:

Initial Release of Product Y

KCSI = KSSI = 50 KLOC
Defects/KCSI = 2.0
Total number of defects = $2.0 \times 50 = 100$

Second Release

KCSI = 20
KSSI = 50 + 20 (new and changed lines of code) − 4 (assuming 20% are changed
     lines of code) = 66
Defect/KCSI = 1.8 (assuming 10% improvement over the first release)
Total number of additional defects = $1.8 \times 20 = 36$

Third Release

KCSI = 30
KSSI = 66 + 30 (new and changed lines of code) − 6 (assuming the same % (20%)
     of changed lines of code) = 90
Targeted number of additional defects (no more than previous release) = 36
Defect rate target for the new and changed lines of code: 36/30 = 1.2 defects/KCSI
or lower

From the initial release to the second release the defect rate improved by 10%. However, customers experienced a 64% reduction [(100 − 36)/100] in the number of defects because the second release is smaller. The size factor works against the third release because it is much larger than the second release. Its defect rate has to be one-third (1.2/1.8) better than that of the second release for the number of new defects not to exceed that of the second release. Of course, sometimes the difference between the two defect rate targets is very large and the new defect rate target is deemed not achievable. In those situations, other actions should be planned to improve the quality of the base code or to reduce the volume of postrelease field defects (i.e., by finding them internally).

Function Points

Counting lines of code is but one way to measure size. Another one is the *function point*. Both are surrogate indicators of the opportunities for error (OFE) in the defect density metrics. In recent years the function point has been gaining acceptance in application development in terms of both productivity (e.g., function points per person-year) and quality (e.g., defects per function point). In this section we provide a concise summary of the subject.

A *function* can be defined as a collection of executable statements that performs a certain task, together with declarations of the formal parameters and local variables manipulated by those statements (Conte et al., 1986). The ultimate measure of software productivity is the number of functions a development team can produce given a certain amount of resource, regardless of the size of the software in lines of code. The defect rate metric, ideally, is indexed to the number of functions a software provides. If defects per unit of functions is low, then the software should have better quality even though the defects per KLOC value could be higher—when the functions were implemented by fewer lines of code. However, measuring functions is theoretically promising but realistically very difficult.

The function point metric, originated by Albrecht and his colleagues at IBM in the mid-1970s, however, is something of a misnomer because the technique does not measure functions explicitly (Albrecht, 1979). It does address some of the problems associated with LOC counts in size and productivity measures, especially the differences in LOC counts that result because different levels of languages are used. It is a weighted total of five major components that comprise an application:

- ☐ Number of external inputs (e.g., transaction types) × 4
- ☐ Number of external outputs (e.g., report types) × 5
- ☐ Number of logical internal files (files as the user might conceive them, not physical files) × 10
- ☐ Number of external interface files (files accessed by the application but not maintained by it) × 7
- ☐ Number of external inquiries (types of online inquiries supported) × 4

These are the average weighting factors. There are also low and high weighting factors, depending on the complexity assessment of the application in terms of the five components (Kemerer and Porter, 1992; Sprouls, 1990):

- ☐ External input: low complexity, 3; high complexity, 6
- ☐ External output: low complexity, 4; high complexity, 7
- ☐ Logical internal file: low complexity, 7; high complexity, 15
- ☐ External interface file: low complexity, 5; high complexity, 10
- ☐ External inquiry: low complexity, 3; high complexity, 6

The complexity classification of each component is based on a set of standards that define complexity in terms of objective guidelines. For instance, for the external output component, if the number of data element types is 20 or more and the number of file types referenced is 2 or more, then complexity is high. If the number of data element types is 5 or fewer and the number of file types referenced is 2 or 3, then complexity is low.

With the weighting factors, the first step is to calculate the function counts (FCs) based on the following formula:

$$FC = \sum_{i=1}^{5} \sum_{j=1}^{3} w_{ij} \times x_{ij}$$

where w_{ij} are the weighting factors of the five components by complexity level (low, average, high) and x_{ij} are the numbers of each component in the application.

The second step involves a scale from 0 to 5 to assess the impact of 14 general system characteristics in terms of their likely effect on the application. The 14 characteristics are:

1. Data communications
2. Distributed functions
3. Performance
4. Heavily used configuration
5. Transaction rate
6. Online data entry
7. End-user efficiency
8. Online update
9. Complex processing
10. Reusability
11. Installation ease
12. Operational ease
13. Multiple sites
14. Facilitation of change

The scores (ranging from 0 to 5) for these characteristics are then summed, based on the following formula, to arrive at the value adjustment factor (VAF)

$$VAF = 0.65 + 0.01 \sum_{i=1}^{14} c_i$$

where c_i is the score for general system characteristic i. Finally, the number of function points is obtained by multiplying function counts and the value adjustment factor:

$$FP = FC \times VAF$$

This equation is a simplified description of the calculation of function points. One should consult the fully documented methods, such as the International Function Point User's Group Standard (IFPUG, 1999), for a complete treatment.

Over the years the function point metric has gained acceptance as a key productivity measure in the application world. In 1986 the IFPUG was established. The IFPUG counting practices committee is the de facto standards organization for function point counting methods (Jones, 1992, 2000). Classes and seminars on function points counting and applications are offered frequently by consulting firms and at software conferences. In application contract work, the function point is often used to measure the amount of work, and quality is expressed as defects per function point. In systems and real-time software, however, the function point has been slow to gain acceptance. This is perhaps due to the incorrect impression that function points work only for information systems (Jones, 2000), the inertia of the LOC-related practices, and the effort required for function points counting. Intriguingly, similar observations can be made about function point use in academic research.

There are also issues related to the function point metric. Fundamentally, the meaning of function point and the derivation algorithm and its rationale may need more research and more theoretical groundwork. There are also many variations in counting function points in the industry and several major methods other than the IFPUG standard. In 1983, Symons presented a function point variant that he termed the Mark II function point (Symons, 1991). According to Jones (2000), the Mark II function point is now widely used in the United Kingdom and to a lesser degree in Hong Kong and Canada. Some of the minor function point variants include feature points, 3D function points, and full function points. In all, based on the comprehensive software benchmark work by Jones (2000), the set of function point variants now include at least 25 functional metrics. Function point counting can be time-consuming and expensive, and accurate counting requires certified function point specialists. Nonetheless, function point metrics are apparently more robust than LOC-based data with regard to comparisons across organizations, especially studies involving multiple languages and those for productivity evaluation.

Example: Function Point Defect Rates

In 2000, based on a large body of empirical studies, Jones published the book *Software Assessments, Benchmarks, and Best Practices.* All metrics used throughout the book are based on function points. According to his study (1997), the average number of software defects in the U.S. is approximately 5 per function point during the entire software life cycle. This number represents the total number of defects found and measured from early software requirements throughout the life cycle of the software, including the defects reported by users in the field. Jones also estimates the defect removal efficiency of software organizations by level of the capability maturity model (CMM) developed by the Software Engineering Institute (SEI). By applying the defect removal efficiency to the overall defect rate per function point, the following defect rates for the delivered software were estimated. The time frames for these defect rates were not specified, but it appears that these defect rates are for the maintenance life of the software. The estimated defect rates per function point are as follows:

- □ SEI CMM Level 1: 0.75
- □ SEI CMM Level 2: 0.44
- □ SEI CMM Level 3: 0.27
- □ SEI CMM Level 4: 0.14
- □ SEI CMM Level 5: 0.05

4.1.2 Customer Problems Metric

Another product quality metric used by major developers in the software industry measures the problems customers encounter when using the product. For the defect rate metric, the numerator is the number of valid defects. However, from the customers' standpoint, all problems they encounter while using the software product, not just the valid defects, are problems with the software. Problems that are not valid defects may be usability problems, unclear documentation or information, duplicates of valid defects (defects that were reported by other customers and fixes were available but the current customers did not know of them), or even user errors. These so-called non-defect-oriented problems, together with the defect problems, constitute the total problem space of the software from the customers' perspective.

The problems metric is usually expressed in terms of problems per user month (PUM):

PUM = Total problems that customers reported (true defects and
non-defect-oriented problems) for a time period
÷ Total number of license-months of the software during the period

where

> Number of license-months = Number of install licenses of the software
> × Number of months in the calculation period

PUM is usually calculated for each month after the software is released to the market, and also for monthly averages by year. Note that the denominator is the number of license-months instead of thousand lines of code or function point, and the numerator is all problems customers encountered. Basically, this metric relates problems to usage. Approaches to achieve a low PUM include:

- ☐ Improve the development process and reduce the product defects.
- ☐ Reduce the non-defect-oriented problems by improving all aspects of the products (such as usability, documentation), customer education, and support.
- ☐ Increase the sale (the number of installed licenses) of the product.

The first two approaches reduce the numerator of the PUM metric, and the third increases the denominator. The result of any of these courses of action will be that the PUM metric has a lower value. All three approaches make good sense for quality improvement and business goals for any organization. The PUM metric, therefore, is a good metric. The only minor drawback is that when the business is in excellent condition and the number of software licenses is rapidly increasing, the PUM metric will look extraordinarily good (low value) and, hence, the need to continue to reduce the number of customers' problems (the numerator of the metric) may be undermined. Therefore, the total number of customer problems should also be monitored and aggressive year-to-year or release-to-release improvement goals set as the number of installed licenses increases. However, unlike valid code defects, customer problems are not totally under the control of the software development organization. Therefore, it may not be feasible to set a PUM goal that the total customer problems cannot increase from release to release, especially when the sales of the software are increasing.

The key points of the defect rate metric and the customer problems metric are briefly summarized in Table 4.1. The two metrics represent two perspectives of product quality. For each metric the numerator and denominator match each other well: Defects relate to source instructions or the number of function points, and problems relate to usage of the product. If the numerator and denominator are mixed up, poor metrics will result. Such metrics could be counterproductive to an organization's quality improvement effort because they will cause confusion and wasted resources.

The customer problems metric can be regarded as an intermediate measurement between defects measurement and customer satisfaction. To reduce customer problems, one has to reduce the functional defects in the products and, in addition, improve other factors (usability, documentation, problem rediscovery, etc.). To improve

TABLE 4.1
Defect Rate and Customer Problems Metrics

	Defect Rate	Problems per User-Month (PUM)
Numerator	Valid and unique product defects	All customer problems (defects and nondefects, first time and repeated)
Denominator	Size of product (KLOC or function point)	Customer usage of the product (user-months)
Measurement perspective	Producer—software development organization	Customer
Scope	Intrinsic product quality	Intrinsic product quality plus other factors

customer satisfaction, one has to reduce defects and overall problems and, in addition, manage factors of broader scope such as timing and availability of the product, company image, services, total customer solutions, and so forth. From the software quality standpoint, the relationship of the scopes of the three metrics can be represented by the Venn diagram in Figure 4.1.

4.1.3 Customer Satisfaction Metrics

Customer satisfaction is often measured by customer survey data via the five-point scale:

- ☐ Very satisfied
- ☐ Satisfied
- ☐ Neutral
- ☐ Dissatisfied
- ☐ Very dissatisfied.

Satisfaction with the overall quality of the product and its specific dimensions is usually obtained through various methods of customer surveys. For example, the specific parameters of customer satisfaction in software monitored by IBM include the CUPRIMDSO categories (capability, functionality, usability, performance, reliability, installability, maintainability, documentation/information, service, and overall); for Hewlett-Packard they are FURPS (functionality, usability, reliability, performance, and service).

Based on the five-point-scale data, several metrics with slight variations can be constructed and used, depending on the purpose of analysis. For example:

(1) Percent of completely satisfied customers
(2) Percent of satisfied customers (satisfied and completely satisfied)

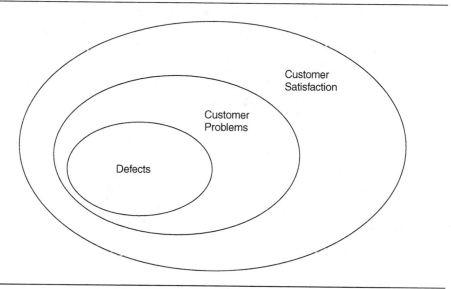

FIGURE 4.1
Scopes of Three Quality Metrics

   (3) Percent of dissatisfied customers (dissatisfied and completely dissatisfied)

   (4) Percent of nonsatisfied (neutral, dissatisfied, and completely dissatisfied)

Usually the second metric, percent satisfaction, is used. In practices that focus on reducing the percentage of nonsatisfaction, much like reducing product defects, metric (4) is used.

   In addition to forming percentages for various satisfaction or dissatisfaction categories, the weighted index approach can be used. For instance, some companies use the *net satisfaction index* (*NSI*) to facilitate comparisons across product. The NSI has the following weighting factors:

   ☐ Completely satisfied = 100%
   ☐ Satisfied = 75%
   ☐ Neutral = 50%
   ☐ Dissatisfied = 25%
   ☐ Completely dissatisfied = 0%

NSI ranges from 0% (all customers are completely dissatisfied) to 100% (all customers are completely satisfied). If all customers are satisfied (but not completely satisfied), NSI will have a value of 75%. This weighting approach, however, may be masking the satisfaction profile of one's customer set. For example, if half of the customers are completely satisfied and half are neutral, NSI's value is also 75%, which is equivalent to the scenario that all customers are satisfied. If satisfaction is a good indicator of product loyalty, then half completely satisfied and half neutral is certainly less positive than all satisfied. Furthermore, we are not sure of the rationale behind giving a 25% weight to those who are dissatisfied. Therefore, this example of NSI is not a good metric; it is inferior to the simple approach of calculating percentage of specific categories. If the entire satisfaction profile is desired, one can simply show the percent distribution of all categories via a histogram. A weighted index is for data summary when multiple indicators are too cumbersome to be shown. For example, if customers' purchase decisions can be expressed as a function of their satisfaction with specific dimensions of a product, then a purchase decision index could be useful. In contrast, if simple indicators can do the job, then the weighted index approach should be avoided.

4.2 In-Process Quality Metrics

Because our goal is to understand the programming process and to learn to engineer quality into the process, in-process quality metrics play an important role. In-process quality metrics are less formally defined than end-product metrics, and their practices vary greatly among software developers. On the one hand, in-process quality metrics simply means tracking defect arrival during formal machine testing for some organizations. On the other hand, some software organizations with well-established software metrics programs cover various parameters in each phase of the development cycle. In this section we briefly discuss several metrics that are basic to sound in-process quality management. In later chapters on modeling we will examine some of them in greater detail and discuss others within the context of models.

4.2.1 Defect Density During Machine Testing

Defect rate during formal machine testing (testing after code is integrated into the system library) is usually positively correlated with the defect rate in the field. Higher defect rates found during testing is an indicator that the software has experienced higher error injection during its development process, unless the higher testing defect rate is due to an extraordinary testing effort—for example, additional testing or a new testing approach that was deemed more effective in detecting defects. The rationale for the positive correlation is simple: Software defect density never follows the uniform distribution. If a piece of code or a product has higher testing defects, it is a result of more effective testing or it is because of higher latent defects in the code. Myers (1979) discusses a counterintuitive principle that the more defects found during testing, the more defects will be found later. That principle is another expression of the positive correlation between defect rates during testing and in the field or between defect rates between phases of testing.

This simple metric of defects per KLOC or function point, therefore, is a good indicator of quality while the software is still being tested. It is especially useful to monitor subsequent releases of a product in the same development organization. Therefore, release-to-release comparisons are not contaminated by extraneous factors. The development team or the project manager can use the following scenarios to judge the release quality:

- ☐ If the defect rate during testing is the same or lower than that of the previous release (or a similar product), then ask: Does the testing for the current release deteriorate?
  - If the answer is no, the quality perspective is positive.
  - If the answer is yes, you need to do extra testing (e.g., add test cases to increase coverage, blitz test, customer testing, stress testing, etc.).

- ☐ If the defect rate during testing is substantially higher than that of the previous release (or a similar product), then ask: Did we plan for and actually improve testing effectiveness?
  - If the answer is no, the quality perspective is negative. Ironically, the only remedial approach that can be taken at this stage of the life cycle is to do more testing, which will yield even higher defect rates.
  - If the answer is yes, then the quality perspective is the same or positive.

4.2.2 Defect Arrival Pattern During Machine Testing

Overall defect density during testing is a summary indicator. The pattern of defect arrivals (or for that matter, times between failures) gives more information. Even with the same overall defect rate during testing, different patterns of defect arrivals indicate different quality levels in the field. Figure 4.2 shows two contrasting patterns for both the defect arrival rate and the cumulative defect rate. Data were plotted from 44 weeks before code-freeze until the week prior to code-freeze. The second pattern, represented by the charts on the right side, obviously indicates that testing started late, the test suite was not sufficient, and that the testing ended prematurely.

The objective is always to look for defect arrivals that stabilize at a very low level, or times between failures that are far apart, before ending the testing effort and releasing the software to the field. Such declining patterns of defect arrival during testing are indeed the basic assumption of many software reliability models. The time unit for observing the arrival pattern is usually weeks and occasionally months. For reliability models that require execution time data, the time interval is in units of CPU time.

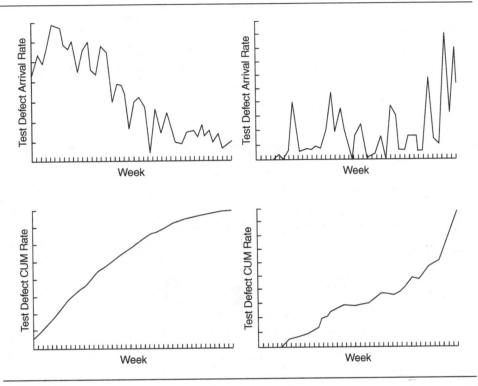

FIGURE 4.2
Two Contrasting Defect Arrival Patterns During Testing

When we talk about the defect arrival pattern during testing, there are actually three slightly different metrics, which should be looked at simultaneously:

☐ The defect arrivals (defects reported) during the testing phase by time interval (e.g., week). These are the raw number of arrivals, not all of which are valid defects.

☐ The pattern of valid defect arrivals—when problem determination is done on the reported problems. This is the true defect pattern.

☐ The pattern of defect backlog overtime. This metric is needed because development organizations cannot investigate and fix all reported problems immediately. This metric is a workload statement as well as a quality statement. If the defect backlog is large at the end of the development cycle and a lot of fixes have yet to be integrated into the system, the stability of the system (hence its quality) will be affected. Retesting (regression test) is needed to ensure that targeted product quality levels are reached.

4.2.3 Phase-Based Defect Removal Pattern

The phase-based defect removal pattern is an extension of the test defect density metric. In addition to testing, it requires the tracking of defects at all phases of the development cycle, including the design reviews, code inspections, and formal verifications before testing. Because a large percentage of programming defects is related to design problems, conducting formal reviews or functional verifications to enhance the defect removal capability of the process at the front end reduces error injection. The pattern of phase-based defect removal reflects the overall defect removal ability of the development process.

With regard to the metrics for the design and coding phases, in addition to defect rates, many development organizations use metrics such as inspection coverage and inspection effort for in-process quality management. Some companies even set up "model values" and "control boundaries" for various in-process quality indicators. For example, Cusumano (1992) reports the specific model values and control boundaries for metrics such as review coverage rate, review manpower rate (review work hours/number of design work hours), defect rate, and so forth, which were used by NEC's Switching Systems Division.

Figure 4.3 shows the patterns of defect removal of two development projects: project A was front-end loaded and project B was heavily testing-dependent for removing defects. In the figure, the various phases of defect removal are high-level design review (I0), low-level design review (I1), code inspection (I2), unit test (UT), component test (CT), and system test (ST). As expected, the field quality of project A outperformed project B significantly.

4.2.4 Defect Removal Effectiveness

Defect removal effectiveness (or efficiency, as used by some writers) can be defined as follows:

$$DRE = \frac{\text{Defects removed during a development phase}}{\text{Defects latent in the product}} \times 100\%$$

Because the total number of latent defects in the product at any given phase is not known, the denominator of the metric can only be approximated. It is usually estimated by:

Defects removed during the phase + defects found later

The metric can be calculated for the entire development process, for the front end (before code integration), and for each phase. It is called *early defect removal*

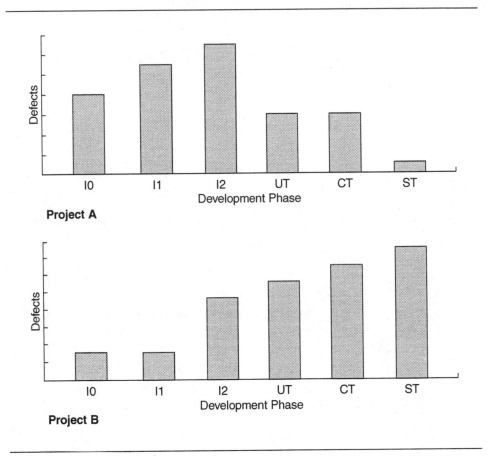

FIGURE 4.3
Defect Removal by Phase for Two Products

and *phase effectiveness* when used for the front end and for specific phases, re-spectively. The higher the value of the metric, the more effective the develop-ment process and the fewer the defects escape to the next phase or to the field. This metric is a key concept of the defect removal model for software development. (In Chapter 6 we give this subject a detailed treatment.) Figure 4.4 shows the DRE by phase for a real software project. The weakest phases were unit test (UT), code inspections (I2), and component test (CT). Based on this metric, action plans to improve the effectiveness of these phases were established and deployed.

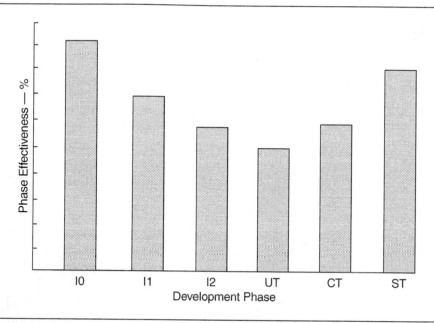

FIGURE 4.4
Phase Effectiveness of a Software Project

4.3 Metrics for Software Maintenance

When development of a software product is complete and it is released to the market, it enters the maintenance phase of its life cycle. During this phase the defect arrivals by time interval and customer problem calls (which may or may not be defects) by time interval are the de facto metrics. However, the number of defect or problem arrivals is largely determined by the development process before the maintenance phase. Not much can be done to alter the quality of the product during this phase. Therefore, these two de facto metrics, although important, do not reflect the quality of software maintenance. What can be done during the maintenance phase is to fix the defects as soon as possible and with excellent fix quality. Such actions, although still not able to improve the defect rate of the product, can improve customer satisfaction to a large extent. The following metrics are therefore very important:

- ☐ Fix backlog and backlog management index
- ☐ Fix response time and fix responsiveness
- ☐ Percent delinquent fixes
- ☐ Fix quality

4.3.1 Fix Backlog and Backlog Management Index

Fix backlog is a workload statement for software maintenance. It is related to both the rate of defect arrivals and the rate at which fixes for reported problems become available. It is a simple count of reported problems that remain at the end of each month or each week. Using it in the format of a trend chart, this metric can provide meaningful information for managing the maintenance process. Another metric to manage the backlog of open, unresolved, problems is the backlog management index (BMI).

$$\text{BMI} = \frac{\text{Number of problems closed during the month}}{\text{Number of problem arrivals during the month}} \times 100\%$$

As a ratio of number of closed, or solved, problems to number of problem arrivals during the month, if BMI is larger than 100, it means the backlog is reduced. If BMI is less than 100, then the backlog increased. With enough data points, the techniques of control charting can be used to calculate the backlog management capability of the maintenance process. More investigation and analysis should be triggered when the value of BMI exceeds the control limits. Of course, the goal is always to strive for a BMI larger than 100. A BMI trend chart or control chart should be examined together with trend charts of defect arrivals, defects fixed (closed), and the number of problems in the backlog.

Figure 4.5 is a trend chart by month of the numbers of opened and closed problems of a software product, and a pseudo-control chart for the BMI. The latest release of the product was available to customers in the month for the first data points on the two charts. This explains the rise and fall of the problem arrivals and closures. The mean BMI was 102.9%, indicating that the capability of the fix process was functioning normally. All BMI values were within the upper (UCL) and lower (LCL) control limits—the backlog management process was in control. (*Note:* We call the BMI chart a pseudo-control chart because the BMI data are autocorrelated and therefore the assumption of independence for control charts is violated. Despite not being "real" control charts in statistical terms, however, we found pseudo-control charts such as the BMI chart quite useful in software quality management. In Chapter 5 we provide more discussions and examples.)

A variation of the problem backlog index is the ratio of number of opened problems (problem backlog) to number of problem arrivals during the month. If the index is 1, that means the team maintains a backlog the same as the problem arrival rate. If the index is below 1, that means the team is fixing problems faster than the problem arrival rate. If the index is higher than 1, that means the team is losing ground in their problem-fixing capability relative to problem arrivals. Therefore, this variant index is also a statement of fix responsiveness.

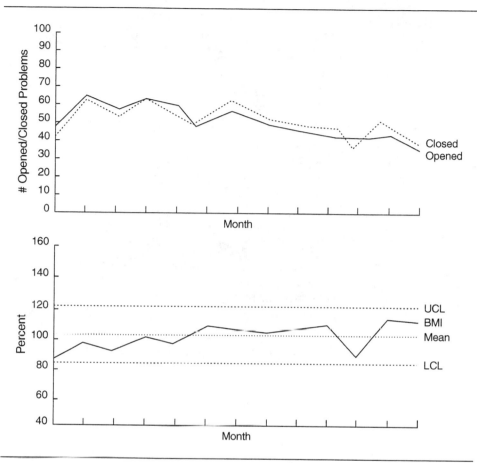

FIGURE 4.5

Opened Problems, Closed Problems, and Backlog Management Index by Month

4.3.2 Fix Response Time and Fix Responsiveness

For many software development organizations, guidelines are established on the time limit within which the fixes should be available for the reported defects. Usually the criteria are set in accordance with the severity of the problems. For the critical situations in which the customers' businesses are at risk due to defects in the software product, software developers or the software change teams work around the clock to fix the problems. For less severe defects for which circumventions are available, the required fix response time is more relaxed. The fix response time metric is usually calculated as follows for all problems as well as by severity level:

Mean time of all problems from open to closed

If there are data points with extreme values, medians should be used instead of mean. Such cases could occur for less severe problems for which customers may be satisfied with the circumvention and didn't demand a fix. Therefore, the problem may remain open for a long time in the tracking report.

In general, short fix response time leads to customer satisfaction. However, there is a subtle difference between fix responsiveness and short fix response time. From the customer's perspective, the use of averages may mask individual differences. The important elements of fix responsiveness are customer expectations, the agreed-to fix time, and the ability to meet one's commitment to the customer. For example, John takes his car to the dealer for servicing in the early morning and needs it back by noon. If the dealer promises noon but does not get the car ready until 2 o'clock, John will not be a satisfied customer. On the other hand, Julia does not need her mini van back until she gets off from work, around 6 P.M. As long as the dealer finishes servicing her van by then, Julia is a satisfied customer. If the dealer leaves a timely phone message on her answering machine at work saying that her van is ready to pick up, Julia will be even more satisfied. This type of fix responsiveness process is indeed being practiced by automobile dealers who focus on customer satisfaction.

In this writer's knowledge, the systems software development of Hewlett-Packard (HP) in California and IBM Rochester's systems software development have fix responsiveness processes similar to the process just illustrated by the automobile examples. In fact, IBM Rochester's practice originated from a benchmarking exchange with HP some years ago. The metric for IBM Rochester's fix responsiveness is operationalized as percentage of delivered fixes meeting committed dates to customers.

4.3.3 Percent Delinquent Fixes

The mean (or median) response time metric is a central tendency measure. A more sensitive metric is the percentage of delinquent fixes. For each fix, if the turnaround time greatly exceeds the required response time, then it is classified as delinquent:

$$\text{Percent delinquent fixes} = \frac{\text{Number of fixes that exceeded the response time criteria by severity level}}{\begin{array}{c}\text{Number of fixes}\\ \text{delivered in a specified time}\end{array}} \times 100\%$$

This metric, however, is not a metric for real-time delinquent management because it is for closed problems only. Problems that are still open must be factored into the calculation for a real-time metric. Assuming the time unit is 1 week, we propose that the percent delinquent of problems in the active backlog be used. *Active backlog* refers to all opened problems for the week, which is the sum of the existing backlog at the beginning of the week and new problem arrivals during the week. In other words, it contains the total number of problems to be processed for the week—the total workload. The number of delinquent problems is checked at the end of the week. Figure 4.6 shows the real-time delivery index diagrammatically.

It is important to note that the metric of percent delinquent fixes is a cohort metric. Its denominator refers to a cohort of problems (problems closed in a given period of time, or problems to be processed in a given week). The cohort concept is important because if it is operationalized as a cross-sectional measure, then invalid metrics will result. For example, we have seen practices in which at the end of each week the number of problems in backlog (problems still to be fixed) and the number of delinquent open problems were counted, and the percent delinquent problems was calculated. This cross-sectional counting approach neglects problems that were processed and closed before the end of the week, and will create a high delinquent index when significant improvement (reduction in problems backlog) is made.

4.3.4 Fix Quality

Fix quality or the number of defective fixes is another important quality metric for the maintenance phase. From the customer's perspective, it is bad enough to encounter functional defects when running a business on the software. It is even worse if the fixes turn out to be defective. A fix is defective if it did not fix the reported problem, or if it fixed the original problem but injected a new defect. For mission-critical software, defective fixes are detrimental to customer satisfaction.

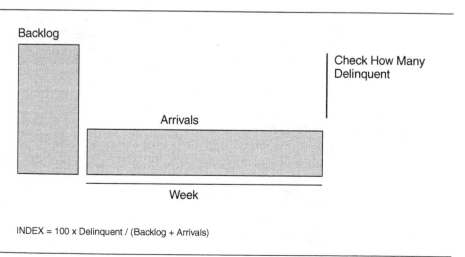

INDEX = 100 x Delinquent / (Backlog + Arrivals)

FIGURE 4.6
Real-Time Delinquency Index

The metric of percent defective fixes is simply the percentage of all fixes in a time interval (e.g., 1 month) that are defective.

A defective fix can be recorded in two ways: Record it in the month it was discovered or record it in the month the fix was delivered. The first is a customer measure, the second is a process measure. The difference between the two dates is the latent period of the defective fix. It is meaningful to keep track of the latency data and other information such as the number of customers who were affected by the defective fix. Usually the longer the latency, the more customers are affected because there is more time for customers to apply that defective fix to their software system.

There is an argument against using percentage for defective fixes. If the number of defects, and therefore the fixes, is large, then the small value of the percentage metric will show an optimistic picture, although the number of defective fixes could be quite large. This metric, therefore, should be a straight count of the number of defective fixes. The quality goal for the maintenance process, of course, is zero defective fixes without delinquency.

4.4 Examples of Metrics Programs

4.4.1 Motorola

Motorola's software metrics program is well articulated by Daskalantonakis (1992). By following the Goal/Question/Metric paradigm of Basili and Weiss (1984), goals were identified, questions were formulated in quantifiable terms, and metrics were established. The goals and measurement areas identified by the Motorola Quality Policy for Software Development (QPSD) are listed in the following.

Goals
- ☐ Goal 1: Improve project planning.
- ☐ Goal 2: Increase defect containment.
- ☐ Goal 3: Increase software reliability.
- ☐ Goal 4: Decrease software defect density.
- ☐ Goal 5: Improve customer service.
- ☐ Goal 6: Reduce the cost of nonconformance.
- ☐ Goal 7: Increase software productivity.

Measurement Areas
- ☐ Delivered defects and delivered defects per size
- ☐ Total effectiveness throughout the process
- ☐ Adherence to schedule
- ☐ Accuracy of estimates
- ☐ Number of open customer problems

☐ Time that problems remain open
☐ Cost of nonconformance
☐ Software reliability

For each goal the questions to be asked and the corresponding metrics were also formulated. In the following, we list the questions and metrics for each goal:[1]

Goal 1: Improve Project Planning

Question 1.1: What was the accuracy of estimating the actual value of project schedule?

Metric 1.1 : Schedule Estimation Accuracy (SEA)

$$SEA = \frac{\text{Actual project duration}}{\text{Estimated project duration}}$$

Question 1.2: What was the accuracy of estimating the actual value of project effort?

Metric 1.2 : Effort Estimation Accuracy (EEA)

$$EEA = \frac{\text{Actual project effort}}{\text{Estimated project effort}}$$

Goal 2: Increase Defect Containment

Question 2.1: What is the currently known effectiveness of the defect detection process prior to release?

Metric 2.1: Total Defect Containment Effectiveness (TDCE)

$$TDCE = \frac{\text{Number of prerelease defects}}{\substack{\text{Number of prerelease defects} \\ + \text{Number of postrelease defects}}}$$

Question 2.2: What is the currently known containment effectiveness of faults introduced during each constructive phase of software development for a particular software product?

Metric 2.2: Phase Containment Effectiveness for phase *i* (PCEi)

1. *Source:* From Daskalantonakis, M. K., "A Practical View of Software Measurement and Implementation Experiences Within Motorola (1001–1004)," *IEEE Transactions on Software Engineering,* Vol. 18, No. 11 (November 1992): 998–1010. Copyright © IEEE, 1992. Used with permission to reprint.

$$PCEi = \frac{\text{Number of phase } i \text{ errors}}{\text{Number of phase } i \text{ errors} + \text{Number of phase } i \text{ defects}}$$

Note: From Daskalantonakis's definition of *error* and *defect*, it appears that Motorola's use of the two terms differs from what was discussed earlier in this chapter. To understand the preceding metric, consider Daskalantonakis's definitions:

- □ *Error:* A problem found during the review of the phase where it was introduced.
- □ *Defect:* A problem found later than the review of the phase where it was introduced.
- □ *Fault:* Both errors and defects are considered faults.

Goal 3: Increase Software Reliability

Question 3.1: What is the rate of software failures, and how does it change over time?

Metric 3.1: Failure Rate (FR)

$$FR = \frac{\text{Number of failures}}{\text{Execution time}}$$

Goal 4: Decrease Software Defect Density

Question 4.1: What is the normalized number of in-process faults, and how does it compare with the number of in-process defects?

Metric 4.1a: In-process Faults (IPF)

$$IPF = \frac{\text{In-process faults caused by incremental software development}}{\text{Assembly-equivalent delta source size}}$$

Metric 4.1b: In-process Defects (IPD)

$$IPF = \frac{\text{In-process defects caused by incremental software development}}{\text{Assembly-equivalent delta source size}}$$

Question 4.2: What is the currently known defect content of software delivered to customers, normalized by Assembly-equivalent size?

Metric 4.2a: Total Released Defects (TRD) total

$$TRD \text{ total} = \frac{\text{Number of released defects}}{\text{Assembly-equivalent total source size}}$$

Metric 4.2b: Total Released Defects (TRD) delta

$$\text{TRD delta} = \frac{\text{Number of released defects caused by incremental software development}}{\text{Assembly-equivalent total source size}}$$

Question 4.3: What is the currently known customer-found defect content of software delivered to customers, normalized by Assembly-equivalent source size?

Metric 4.3a: Customer-Found Defects (CFD) total

$$\text{CFD total} = \frac{\text{Number of customer -found defects}}{\text{Assembly-equivalent total source size}}$$

Metric 4.3b: Customer-Found Defects (CFD) delta

$$\text{CFD delta} = \frac{\text{Number of customer -found defects caused by incremental software development}}{\text{Assembly-equivalent total source size}}$$

Goal 5: Improve Customer Service

Question 5.1 What is the number of new problems opened during the month?
Metric 5.1: New Open Problems (NOP)

NOP = Total new postrelease problems opened during the month

Question 5.2 What is the total number of open problems at the end of the month?
Metric 5.2: Total Open Problems (TOP)

TOP = Total postrelease problems that remain open at the
     end of the month

Question 5.3: What is the mean age of open problems at the end of the month?
Metric 5.3: Mean Age of Open Problems (AOP)

AOP = (Total time postrelease problems remaining open
     at the end of the month have been open)/(Number of open post
     release problems remaining open at the end of the month)

Question 5.4: What is the mean age of the problems that were closed during the month?

Metric 5.4: Mean Age of Closed Problems (ACP)

ACP = (Total time postrelease problems closed within
         the month were open)/(Number of open postrelease
         problems closed within the month)

Goal 6: Reduce the Cost of Nonconformance

Question 6.1: What was the cost to fix postrelease problems during the month?

Metric 6.1: Cost of Fixing Problems (CFP)

CFP = Dollar cost associated with fixing postrelease
         problems within the month

Goal 7: Increase Software Productivity

Question 7.1: What was the productivity of software development projects (based on source size)?

Metric 7.1a: Software Productivity total (SP total)

$$\text{SP total} = \frac{\text{Assembly-equivalent total source size}}{\text{Software development effort}}$$

Metric 7.1b: Software Productivity delta (SP delta)

$$\text{SP delta} = \frac{\text{Assembly-equivalent delta source size}}{\text{Software development effort}}$$

From the preceding goals one can see that metrics 3.1, 4.2a, 4.2b, 4.3a, and 4.3b are metrics for end-product quality, metrics 5.1 through 5.4 are metrics for software maintenance, and metrics 2.1, 2.2, 4.1a, and 4.1b are in-process quality metrics. The others are for scheduling, estimation, and productivity.

In addition to the preceding metrics, which are defined by the Motorola Software Engineering Process Group (SEPG), Daskalantonakis describes in-process metrics that can be used for schedule, project, and quality control. Without getting into too many details, we list these additional in-process metrics in the following. [For details and other information about Motorola's software metrics program, see Daskalantonakis's original article (1992).] Items 1 through 4 are for project status/control and items 5 through 7 are really in-process quality metrics that can provide information about the status of the project and lead to possible actions for further quality improvement.

1. *Life-cycle phase and schedule tracking metric:* Track schedule based on life-cycle phase and compare actual to plan.

2. *Cost/earned value tracking metric:* Track actual cumulative cost of the project versus budgeted cost, and actual cost of the project so far, with continuous update throughout the project.
3. *Requirements tracking metric:* Track the number of requirements change at the project level.
4. *Design tracking metric:* Track the number of requirements implemented in design versus the number of requirements written.
5. *Fault-type tracking metric:* Track causes of faults.
6. *Remaining defect metrics:* Track faults per month for the project and use Rayleigh curve to project the number of faults in the months ahead during development.
7. *Review effectiveness metric:* Track error density by stages of review and use control chart methods to flag the exceptionally high or low data points.

4.4.2 Hewlett-Packard

Grady and Caswell (1986) offer a good description of Hewlett-Packard's software metric program, including both the primitive metrics and computed metrics that are widely used at HP. Primitive metrics are those that are directly measurable and accountable such as control token, data token, defect, total operands, LOC, and so forth. Computed metrics are metrics that are mathematical combinations of two or more primitive metrics. The following is an excerpt of HP's computed metrics:[1]

Average fixed defects/working day: self-explanatory.

Average engineering hours/fixed defect: self-explanatory.

Average reported defects/working day: self-explanatory.

Bang: "A quantitative indicator of net usable function from the user's point of view" (DeMarco, 1982). There are two methods for computing Bang. Computation of Bang for function-strong systems involves counting the tokens entering and leaving the function multiplied by the weight of the function. For data-strong systems it involves counting the objects in the database weighted by the number of relationships of which the object is a member.

Branches covered/total branches: When running a program, this metric indicates what percentage of the decision points were actually executed.

Defects/KNCSS: Self-explanatory (KNCSS—Thousand noncomment source statements).

Defects/LOD: Self-explanatory (LOD—Lines of documentation not included in program source code).

Defects/testing time: Self-explanatory.

1. *Source:* Grady, R. B., and D. L. Caswell, *Software Metrics: Establishing A Company-Wide Program,* pp. 225–226. Englewood Cliffs, N.J.: Prentice-Hall. Copyright © 1986 Prentice-Hall, Inc. Used with permission to reprint.

Design weight: "Design weight is a simple sum of the module weights over the set of all modules in the design" (DeMarco, 1982). Each module weight is a function of the token count associated with the module and the expected number of decision counts which are based on the structure of data.

NCSS/engineering month: Self-explanatory.

Percent overtime: Average overtime/40 hours per week.

Phase: engineering months/total engineering months: Self-explanatory.

Of these metrics, defects/KNCSS and defects/LOD are end-product quality metrics. Defects/testing time is a statement of testing effectiveness, and branches covered/ total branches is testing coverage in terms of decision points. Therefore, both are meaningful in-process quality metrics. Bang is a measurement of functions and NCSS/engineering month is a productivity measure. Design weight is an interesting measurement but its use is not clear. The other metrics are for workload, schedule, project control, and cost of defects.

As Grady and Caswell point out, this list represents the most widely used computed metrics at HP, but it may not be comprehensive. For instance, many others are discussed in other sections of their book. For example, customer satisfaction measurements in relation to software quality attributes are a key area in HP's software metrics. As mentioned earlier in this chapter, the software quality attributes defined by HP are called FURPS (functionality, usability, reliability, performance, and supportability). Goals and objectives for FURPS are set for software projects. Furthermore, to achieve the FURPS goals of the end product, measurable objectives using FURPS for each life-cycle phase are also set (Grady and Caswell, 1986, pp. 159–162).

MacLeod (1993) describes the implementation and sustenance of a software inspection program in an HP division. The metrics used include average hours per inspection, average defects per inspection, average hours per defect, and defect causes. These inspection metrics, used appropriately in the proper context (e.g., comparing the current project with previous projects), can be used to monitor the inspection phase (front end) of the software development process.

4.4.3 IBM Rochester

Because many examples of the metrics used at IBM Rochester have already been discussed or will be elaborated on later, here we give just an overview. Furthermore, we list only selected quality metrics; metrics related to project management, productivity, scheduling, costs, and resources are not included.

☐ Overall customer satisfaction as well as satisfaction with various quality attributes such as CUPRIMDS (capability, usability, performance, reliability, install, maintenance, documentation/information, and service).

☐ Postrelease defect rates such as those discussed in section 4.1.1.

☐ Customer problem calls per month

☐ Fix response time

☐ Number of defective fixes

☐ Backlog management index

☐ Postrelease arrival patterns for defects and problems (both defects and non-defect-oriented problems)

☐ Defect removal model for the software development process

☐ Phase effectiveness (for each phase of inspection and testing)

☐ Inspection coverage and effort

☐ Compile failures and build/integration defects

☐ Weekly defect arrivals and backlog during testing

☐ Defect severity

☐ Defect cause and problem component analysis

☐ Reliability: mean time to initial program loading (IPL) during testing

☐ Stress level of the system during testing as measured in level of CPU use in terms of number of CPU hours per system per day during stress testing

☐ Number of system crashes and hangs during stress testing and system testing

☐ Models for postrelease defect estimation

☐ Various customer feedback metrics at the end of the development cycle before the product is shipped

☐ S curves for project progress comparing actual to plan for each phase of development such as number of inspections conducted by week, LOC integrated by week, number of test cases attempted and succeeded by week, and so forth.

4.5 Collecting Software Engineering Data

The challenge of collecting software engineering data is to make sure that the collected data can provide useful information for project, process, and quality management and, at the same time, that the data collection process will not be a burden on development teams. Therefore, it is important to consider carefully what data to collect. The data must be based on well-defined metrics and models, which are used to drive improvements. Therefore, the goals of the data collection should be established and the questions of interest should be defined before any data is collected. Data classification schemes to be used and the level of precision must be carefully specified. The collection form or template and data fields should be pretested. The amount of data to be collected and the number of metrics to be used need not be overwhelming. It is more important that the information extracted from the data be focused, accurate, and useful than that it be plentiful. Without being metrics driven, overcollection of data could be wasteful. Overcollection of data is quite common when people start to measure software without an a priori specification of purpose, objectives, profound versus trivial issues, and metrics and models.

Gathering software engineering data can be expensive, especially if it is done as part of a research program, For example, the NASA Software Engineering Laboratory spent about 15% of their development costs on gathering and processing data on hundreds of metrics for a number of projects (Shooman, 1983). For large commercial development organizations, the relative cost of data gathering and processing should be much lower because of economy of scale and fewer metrics. However, the cost of data collection will never be insignificant. Nonetheless, data collection and analysis, which yields intelligence about the project and the development process, is vital for business success. Indeed, in many organizations, a tracking and data collection system is often an integral part of the software configuration or the project management system, without which the chance of success of large and complex projects will be reduced.

Basili and Weiss (1984) propose a data collection methodology that could be applicable anywhere. The schema consists of six steps with considerable feedback and iteration occurring at several places:

1. Establish the goal of the data collection.
2. Develop a list of questions of interest.
3. Establish data categories.
4. Design and test data collection forms.
5. Collect and validate data.
6. Analyze data.

The importance of the validation element of a data collection system or a development tracking system cannot be overemphasized.

In their study of NASA's Software Engineering Laboratory projects, Basili and Weiss (1984) found that software data are error-prone and that special validation provisions are generally needed. Validation should be performed concurrently with software development and data collection, based on interviews with those people supplying the data. In cases where data collection is part of the configuration control process and automated tools are available, data validation routines (e.g., consistency check, range limits, conditional entries, etc.) should be an integral part of the tools. Furthermore, training, clear guidelines and instructions, and an understanding of how the data are used by people who enter or collect the data enhance data accuracy significantly.

The actual collection process can take several basic formats such as reporting forms, interviews, and automatic collection using the computer system. For data collection to be efficient and effective, it should be merged with the configuration management or change control system. This is the case in most large development organizations. For example, at IBM Rochester the change control system covers the entire development process, and online tools are used for plan change control, development items and changes, integration, and change control after integration (defect fixes). The tools capture data pertinent to schedule, resource, and project status, as well as quality indicators. In general, change control is more prevalent after the code is integrated. This is one of the reasons that in many organizations defect data are usually available for the testing phases but not for the design and coding phases.

With regard to defect data, testing defects are generally more reliable than inspection defects. During testing, a "bug" exists when a test case cannot execute or when the test results deviate from the expected outcome. During inspections, the determination of a defect is based on the judgment of the inspectors. Therefore, it is important to have a clear definition of an inspection defect. The following is an example of such a definition:

> *Inspection defect:* A problem found during the inspection process which, if not fixed, would cause one or more of the following to occur:

> ☐ A defect condition in a later inspection phase
> ☐ A defect condition during testing
> ☐ A field defect
> ☐ Nonconformance to requirements and specifications
> ☐ Nonconformance to established standards such as performance, national language translation, and usability

For example, misspelled words are not counted as defects, but would be if they were found on a screen that customers use. Using nested IF-THEN-ELSE structures instead of a SELECT statement would not be counted as a defect unless some standard or performance reason dictated otherwise.

Figure 4.7 is an example of an inspection summary form. The form records the total number of inspection defects and the LOC estimate for each part (module), as well as defect data classified by defect origin and defect type. The following guideline pertains to the defect type classification by development phase:

> *Interface defect:* An interface defect is a defect in the way two separate pieces of logic communicate. These are errors in communication between:

> Components
>
> Products
>
> Modules and subroutines of a component
>
> User interface (e.g., messages, panels)

Examples of interface defects per development phase follow.

Product: _____   Component: _____   Release: _____

Inspection Type: _____   (RQ SD I0 I1 I2 U1 U2)

Description: _____

Defect Counts

Tot for Inspection / Part Name	LOC	By Defect Origin					By Defect Type			Total
		RQ	SD	I0	I1	I2	LO	IF	DO	

Total Preparation Hrs: ____ . ____   Total Inspection Hrs: ____ . ____

Total Persons Attended: ____   Inspection Date: ____/____/____

Reinspection Required? ____   (Y/N)

Defect Types:
  DO = Documentation
  IF = Interface
  LO = Logic

Defect Origins and Inspection Types:
  RQ = Requirements
  SD = System Design
  I0 = High-Level Design
  I1 = Low-Level Design
  I2 = Code

FIGURE 4.7
An Inspection Summary Form

High-Level Design (I0)

Use of wrong parameter

Inconsistent use of function keys on user interface (e.g., screen)

Incorrect message used

Presentation of information on screen not usable

Low-Level Design (I1)

Missing required parameters (e.g., missing parameter on module)

Wrong parameters (e.g., specified incorrect parameter on module)

Intermodule interfaces: input not there, input in wrong order

Intramodule interfaces: passing values/data to subroutines

Incorrect use of common data structures

Misusing data passed to code

Code (I2)

Passing wrong values for parameters on macros, application program interfaces (APIs), modules

Setting up a common control block/area used by another piece of code incorrectly

Not issuing correct exception to caller of code

Logic defect: A logic defect is one that would cause incorrect results in the function to be performed by the logic. High-level categories of this type of defect are as follows:

Function: capability not implemented or implemented incorrectly

Assignment: initialization

Checking: validate data/values before use

Timing: management of shared/real-time resources

Data Structures: static and dynamic definition of data

Examples of logic defects per development phase follow.

High-Level Design (I0)

Invalid or incorrect screen flow

High-level flow through component missing or incorrect in the review package

Function missing from macros you are implementing

Using a wrong macro to do a function that will not work (e.g., using XXXMSG to receive a message from a program message queue, instead of YYYMSG).

Missing requirements

Missing parameter/field on command/in database structure/on screen you are implementing

Wrong value on keyword (e.g., macro, command)

Wrong keyword (e.g., macro, command)

Low-Level Design (I1)

Logic does not implement I0 design

Missing or excessive function

Values in common structure not set

Propagation of authority and adoption of authority (lack of or too much)

Lack of code page conversion

Incorrect initialization

Not handling abnormal termination (conditions, cleanup, exit routines)

Lack of normal termination cleanup

Performance: too much processing in loop that could be moved outside of loop

Code (I2)

Code does not implement I1 design

Lack of initialization

Variables initialized incorrectly

Missing exception monitors

Exception monitors in wrong order

Exception monitors not active

Exception monitors active at the wrong time

Exception monitors set up wrong

Truncating of double-byte character set data incorrectly (e.g., truncating before shift in character)

Incorrect code page conversion

Lack of code page conversion

Not handling exceptions/return codes correctly

Documentation defect: A documentation defect is a defect in the description of the function (e.g., prologue of macro) that causes someone to do something wrong based on this information. For example, if a macro prologue contained an incorrect description of a parameter that caused the user of this macro to use the parameter incorrectly, this would be a documentation defect against the macro.

Examples of documentation defects per development phase follow.

High-Level Design (I0)

Incorrect information in prologue (e.g., macro)

Misspelling on user interface (e.g., screen)

Wrong wording (e.g., messages, command prompt text)

Using restricted words on user interface

Wording in messages, definition of command parameters is technically incorrect

Low-Level Design (I1)

Wrong information in prologue (e.g., macros, program, etc.)

Missing definition of inputs and outputs of module, subroutines, etc.

Insufficient documentation of logic (comments tell what but not why)

Code (I2)

Information in prologue not correct or missing

Wrong wording in messages

Second-level text of message technically incorrect

Insufficient documentation of logic (comments tell what but not why)

Incorrect documentation of logic

4.6 Summary

Software quality metrics focus on the quality aspects of the product, process, and project. They can be grouped into three categories in accordance with the software life cycle: end-product quality metrics, in-process quality metrics, and maintenance quality metrics. This chapter gives several examples for each category, summarizes the metrics programs at Motorola, Hewlett-Packard, and IBM Rochester, and discusses data collection.

□ *Product quality metrics*

–Mean time to failure

–Defect density

–Customer-reported problems

–Customer satisfaction

□ *In-process quality metrics*

–Phase-based defect removal pattern

–Defect removal effectiveness

–Defect density during formal machine testing

–Defect arrival pattern during formal machine testing

Recommendations for Small Organizations

To my knowledge, there is no correlation between the existence of a metrics program and the size of the organization, or between the effectiveness of using metrics in software development and team size. For small teams that are starting to implement a metrics program with minimum resources, I recommend the following:

1. Implement the defect arrival metric during the last phase of testing, augmented by a qualitative indicator of the number of critical problems (or show stoppers) and the nature of these problems. The latter is a subset of total defects. These indicators provide important information with regard to the quality of the software and its readiness to ship to customers. For example, if the defect arrival metric is trending down to a sufficiently low level and the number of show stoppers is small and becoming sparser as the test progresses, one can forecast a positive quality posture of the product in the field, and vice versa.

2. After the product is shipped, a natural metric is the number of defects coming in from the field over time. As defects are reported, the organization fixes these defects for their customers, normally in the form of individual fixes, fix packages, or frequent software upgrades, depending on the organization's maintenance strategy. The inevitable question is, how many outstanding defects need to be fixed; in other words, how big is the fix backlog. If the organization intends to compare its fix efficiency to the volume of defect arrivals, the backlog management index metric can be formed easily without additional data.

3. When a product size metric is available, the above metrics can be normalized to form other metrics such as defect density curves over time, during testing or when the product is in the field, and overall defect rate of the product, for a specific duration or for the maintenance life of the product. These normalized metrics can serve as baselines for other projects by

---

☐ *Maintenance quality metrics*

　–Fix backlog

　–Backlog management index

　–Fix response time and fix responsiveness

　–Percent delinquent fixes

　–Defective fixes

With regard to in-process data, generally those at the back end (e.g., testing defects) are more reliable than those at the front end (e.g., design reviews and inspections). To improve data reliability, it is important to establish definitions and examples (e.g., what constitutes a defect during design reviews). Furthermore, validation must be an integral part of the data collection system and should be performed concurrently with software development and data collection.

the team, in terms of both process capacity (in-process metrics) and quality of delivered products. When enough empirical data is accumulated, correlational studies between in-process data and field data of the organization can improve the predictability and consistency of product development. If the operational definitions of the metrics are consistent, cross-organization comparisons can be made.

Of the two product size metrics discussed in this chapter, I recommend function points (FP) over lines of code (LOC) for the many reasons discussed. However, accurate function point counting requires certified function point specialists and it can be time-consuming and expensive. If LOC data is already available, the *backfiring* method, a conversion ratio method between logical source code statements and equivalent volumes of functions points can be used. Such conversion ratios for a set of languages were published by Jones (2000; see p. 78, Table 3.5), and the average ratios (average number of source statements (LOC) per function point) by language are as follows:

Basic Assembly	320
Macro Assembly	213
C	128
FORTRAN	107
COBOL	107
Pascal	91
PL/I	80
Ada83	71
C++	53
Ada95	49
Visual Basic	32
Smalltalk	21
SQL	12

This discussion of a few simple and useful metrics as the beginning of a good metrics practice is from the quality perspective. For overall project management, it is well known that the most basic variables to measure are product size, effort (e.g., person-year), and development cycle time.

References

1. Albrecht, A. J., "Measuring Application Development Productivity," *Proceedings of the Joint IBM/SHARE/GUIDE Application Development Symposium,* October 1979, pp. 83–92.
2. Basili, V. R., and D. M. Weiss, "A Methodology for Collecting Valid Software Engineering Data," *IEEE Transactions on Software Engineering,* Vol. SE-10, 1984, pp. 728–738.
3. Boehm, B. W., *Software Engineering Economics,* Englewood Cliffs, N.J.: Prentice-Hall, 1981.
4. Conte, S. D., H. E. Dunsmore, and V. Y. Shen, *Software Engineering Metrics and Models,* Menlo Park, Calif.: Benjamin/Cummings, 1986.
5. Cusumano, M. A., "Objectives and Context of Software Measurement, Analysis and Control," Massachusetts Institute of Technology Sloan School of Management Working Paper 3471-92, October 1992.
6. Daskalantonakis, M. K., "A Practical View of Software Measurement and Implementation Experiences Within Motorola," *IEEE Transactions on Software Engineering,* Vol. SE-18, 1992, pp. 998–1010.

7. DeMarco, T., *Controlling Software Projects,* New York: Yourdon Press, 1982.
8. Fenton, N. E., and S. L. Pfleeger, *Software Metrics: A Rigorous Approach,* 2nd ed., Boston: International Thomson Computer Press, 1997.
9. Grady, R. B., and D. L. Caswell, *Software Metrics: Establishing a Company-Wide Program,* Englewood Cliffs, N.J.: Prentice-Hall, 1986.
10. IFPUG, IFPUG Counting Practices Manual, Release 4.1, Westerville, Ohio: International Function Point Users Group, 1999.
11. Jones, C., *Programming Productivity,* New York: McGraw-Hill, 1986.
12. Jones, C., "Critical Problems in Software Measurement," Burlington, Mass.: Software Productivity Research, 1992.
13. Jones, C., *Assessment and Control of Software Risks,* Englewood Cliffs, N. J.: Yourdon Press, 1994.
14. Jones, C., *Applied Software Measurement, Assuring Productivity and Quality,* 2nd ed., New York: McGraw-Hill, 1997.
15. Jones, C., *Software Assessments, Benchmarks, and Best Practices,* Boston: Addison-Wesley, 2000.
16. Kemerer, C. F., "Reliability of Function Point Measurement: A Field Experiment," Massachusetts Institute of Technology Sloan School of Management Working Paper 3193-90-MSA, January 1991.
17. Kemerer, C. F., and B. S. Porter, "Improving the Reliability of Function Point Measurement: An Empirical Study," *IEEE Transactions on Software Engineering,* Vol. 18, No. 11, November 1992, pp. 1011–1024.
18. Littlewood, B., and L. Strigini, "The Risks of Software," *Scientific American,* November 1992, pp. 62–75.
19. MacLeod, J. M., "Implementing and Sustaining a Software Inspection Program in an R&D Environment," *Hewlett-Packard Journal,* June 1993, pp. 60–63.
20. Myers, G. J., *The Art of Software Testing,* New York: John Wiley & Sons, 1979.
21. Oman, P., and S. L. Pfleeger (ed.), *Applying Software Metrics,* Los Alamitos: IEEE Computer Society Press, 1997.
22. Shooman, M. L., *Software Engineering: Design, Reliability, and Management,* New York: McGraw-Hill, 1983.
23. Sprouls, J., *IFPUG Function Point Counting Practices Manual, Release 3.0,* Westerville, Ohio: International Function Point Users Group, 1990.
24. Symons, C. R., *Software Sizing and Estimating: Mk II FPA (Function Point Analysis),* Chichester, United Kingdom: John Wiley & Sons, 1991.

5

Applying the Seven Basic Quality Tools in Software Development

The basic statistical tools for quality control promoted by Ishikawa (1989) are widely used in manufacturing productions. They have indeed become an integral part of the quality control literature, and have been known as Ishikawa's seven basic tools. This chapter describes the application of these tools for process and quality control in software development. There are many ways to analyze software metrics; the applications of Ishikawa's seven tools represent a set of basic operations. Keep in mind that these statistical tools are for process and quality control at the project and organization level and, hence, are useful for project leaders and process experts. In contrast, they do not provide specific information to software developers on how to improve the quality of their designs or implementation. Also, because not all these tools are equally useful for small projects where statistical patterns of parameters of the development process are less obvious, the benefits of statistics may not be realized. The box at the end of the chapter offers specific recommendations for small teams. In addition, although the benefits of these tools have long been proved in manufacturing operations, their use and roles in software development has not been widely recognized. For instance, the use of control charts in manufacturing production can ensure a certain end-product quality once the process is defined and the control limits are set. In software development, however, the process is complex and involves a high degree of creativity and mental activity. It is extremely difficult, if not impossible, to define the process capability of software development in statistical terms. Therefore, achieving statistical process control in software development may mean a lot more than control charting. It may require, for example, new development technology, CASE tools, and the use of defect models and reliability estimating techniques. However, good use of the seven basic tools can lead to positive long-term results for process improvement and quality management in software development.

The following sections begin with a brief description of the tools, followed by a discussion of each tool with examples of its applications. Where appropriate, the influences of these tools on process improvement and on decision making are also described. The examples are either from software engineering literature or from software projects developed at IBM in Rochester, Minnesota. In addition to the seven basic tools, we discuss the relations diagram, which is effective for small team brainstorming and particularly useful in displaying cause-and-effect relationships.

5.1 Ishikawa's Seven Basic Tools

Ishikawa's seven basic tools for quality control are checklist (or check sheet), Pareto diagram, histogram, scatter diagram, run chart, control chart, and cause-and-effect diagram. Figure 5.1 shows a simple representation of the tools.

A check sheet is a paper form with printed items to be checked. Its main purposes are to facilitate gathering data and to arrange data while collecting it so the data can be easily used later. Another type of check sheet is the check-up confirmation sheet. It is concerned mainly with the quality characteristics of a process or a product. To distinguish this confirmation check sheet from the ordinary data-gathering check sheet, we use the term *checklist*. In most software development environments, the data-gathering aspect is automated electronically and goes far beyond the data-gathering checksheet approach, which has been used in manufacturing production. Our discussion on this tool, therefore, is confined to checklists.

A Pareto diagram is a frequency chart of bars in descending order; the frequency bars are usually associated with types of problems. It is named after a nineteenth-century Italian economist named Vilfredo Pareto (1848–1923), who expounded his principle in terms of the distribution of wealth—that a large share of the wealth is owned by a small percentage of the population. In 1950 Juran applied the principle to the identification of quality problems—that most of the quality problems are due to a small percentage of the possible causes. In software development, the X-axis for a Pareto diagram is usually the defect cause and the Y-axis the defect count. By arranging the causes based on defect frequency, a Pareto diagram can identify the few causes that account for the majority of defects. It indicates which problems should be solved first in eliminating defects and improving the operation. Pareto analysis is commonly referred to as the 80–20 principle (20% of the causes account for 80% of the defects), although the cause-defect relationship is not always in an 80–20 distribution.

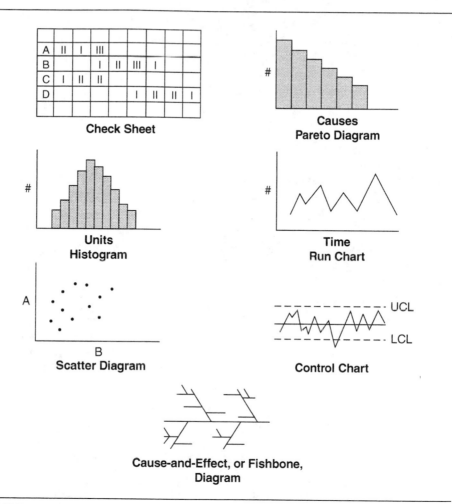

FIGURE 5.1
Ishikawa's Seven Basic Tools for Quality Control

The histogram is a graphic representation of frequency counts of a sample or a population. The X-axis lists the unit intervals of a parameter (e.g., severity level of software defects) ranked in ascending order from left to right, and the Y-axis contains the frequency counts. In a histogram, the frequency bars are shown by the order of the X variable, whereas in a Pareto diagram the frequency bars are shown by order of the frequency counts. The purpose of the histogram is to show the distribution characteristics of a parameter such as overall shape, central tendency, dispersion, and skewness. It enhances understanding of the parameter of interest.

A scatter diagram vividly portrays the relationship of two interval variables. In a cause-effect relationship, the X-axis is for the independent variable and the Y-axis for the dependent variable. Each point in a scatter diagram represents an observation of both the dependent and independent variables. Scatter diagrams aid data-based decision making (e.g., if action is planned on the X variable and some effect is expected on the Y variable). One should always look for a scatter diagram when the correlation coefficient of two variables is presented. As discussed in Chapter 3, this is because the method for calculating the correlation coefficient is highly sensitive to outliers, and a scatter diagram can clearly expose any outliers in the relationship. Second, the most common correlation coefficient is Pearson's product moment correlation coefficient, which assumes a linear relationship. If the relationship is nonlinear, the Pearson correlation coefficient may show no relationship; therefore, it may convey incorrect or false information.

A run chart tracks the performance of the parameter of interest over time. The X-axis is time and the Y-axis is the value of the parameter. A run chart is best used for trend analysis, especially if historical data are available for comparisons with the current trend. Ishikawa (1989) includes various graphs such as the pie chart, bar graph, compound bar graph, and circle graph under the section that discusses run charts. An example of a run chart in software is the weekly number of open problems in the backlog; it shows the development team's workload of software fixes.

A control chart can be regarded as an advanced form of a run chart for situations where the process capability can be defined. It consists of a central line, a pair of control limits (and sometimes a pair of warning limits within the control limits), and values of the parameter of interest plotted on the chart, which represent the state of a process. The X-axis is real time. If all values of the parameter are within the control limits and show no particular tendency, the process is regarded as being in a controlled state. If they fall outside the control limits or indicate a trend, the process is considered out of control. Such cases call for causal analysis and corrective actions are to be taken.

The cause-and-effect diagram, also known as the fishbone diagram, was developed by Ishikawa and associates in the early 1950s in Japan. It was first used to explain factors that affect the production of steel. It is included in the Japanese Industrial Standards terminology for quality control (Kume, 1989). It shows the relationship between a quality characteristic and factors that affect that characteristic. Its layout resembles a fishbone, with the quality characteristic of interest labeled at the fish head, and factors affecting the characteristics placed where the bones are located. While the scatter diagram describes a specific bivariate relationship in detail, the cause-and-effect diagram identifies all causal factors of a quality characteristic in one chart.

5.2 Checklist

The checklist plays a significant role in software development. As a senior software development manager at a major software organization observed, checklists that summarize the key points of the process are much more effective than the lengthy process documents (Bernstein, 1992). At IBM Rochester, the software development process consists of multiple phases, for example, requirements (RQ), system architecture (SD), high-level design (HLD), low-level design (LLD), code development (CODE), unit tests (UT), integration and building (I/B), component tests (CT), system tests (ST), and early customer programs (EP). Each phase has a set of tasks to complete and the phases with formal hand-off have entry and exit criteria. Checklists help developers and programmers ensure that all tasks are complete and that the important factors or quality characteristics of each task are covered. Several examples of checklists are design review checklist, code inspection checklist, moderator (for design review and code inspection) checklist, pre-code-integration (into the system library) checklist, entrance and exit criteria for system tests, and product readiness checklist.

The use of checklists is pervasive. Checklists, used daily by the entire development community, are developed and revised based on accumulated experience. Checklists are often a part of the process documents. Their daily use also keeps the processes alive.

Another type of checklist is the common error list, which is part of the stage kickoffs of the defect prevention process (DPP). As discussed in Chapter 2, DPP involves three key steps: (1) analysis of defects to trace the root causes, (2) action teams to implement suggested actions, and (3) stage kickoff meetings as the major feedback mechanism. Stage kickoff meetings are conducted by the technical teams at the beginning of each development phase. Reviewing lists of common errors and brainstorming on how to avoid them is one of the focus areas (Mays et al., 1990).

Perhaps the most outstanding checklist at IBM Rochester software development is the PTF checklist. PTF is the abbreviation for program temporary fix, which is the fix delivered to customers when they encounter defects in the software system. Defective PTFs are detrimental to customer satisfaction and have always been a strong focus area at IBM Rochester. By implementing an automated PTF checklist and other action items (e.g., formal inspection of software fixes, root cause analysis of defective fixes, and regular refresher classes on the fix process so that developers can be up to date when they need to develop and deliver a fix), IBM Rochester has reduced the percentage of defective fixes to a mimum, below the 1% level. Note that the PTF checklist is just one part of the fix quality improvement approach; however, there is no doubt it played an important role in IBM Rochester's fix quality.

The PTF checklist was developed based on analysis of vast experiences accumulated over the years and is being reexamined and revised on a continuous basis. Starting as an online checklist, it has evolved into an automated expert system that is ingrained with the software fix process. When the fix process is invoked, the expert system automatically provides the advice and step-by-step guidance to software developers. As a result the process discipline is enforced. Figure 5.2 shows several items on the PTF checklist.

____ Qn[1] (Y, N) It is critical that you fix the exact problem described in the APAR/PTR problem description. If the problem description is vague, you can't be sure that you are fixing the problem the customer reported. Is the problem description in the APAR/PTR[2] specific and are you fixing that specific problem?

____ Qn (Y, N) Did this PTF require a change to a macro or include? If yes, WARNING: Don't change the size or offsets of an include. There are probably hard-coded references to the various offsets and you may introduce a defect.

> ____ a. (Y, N) Is the macro/include a CUE, Common Use Element?

> > ☐ Every effort must be made to develop PTFs that do not require changes to a CUE.

> > > • If a change is required, the change must be made such that only the changed modules need to be recompiled and all other modules function correctly with the unchanged CUE.

> > > • If a change is required to the CUE that cannot be isolated to the changed modules, then a temporary restriction should be considered based on APAR severity and availability of a circumvention.

If you must still PTF a CUE,

> > ☐ (Y, N) Has this fix been released and approved by the CUE coordinator? Contact XXX.

> ____ b. (Y, N) Is the macro or include used by more than one module/component?

To help you determine if the macro or include is used by more than one module/component, do the following:

> > ☐ If possible, ask the originator of the code.

> > ☐ Use the YYY command to search for occurrences. Make sure you scan all affected versions for the release you are PTFing.

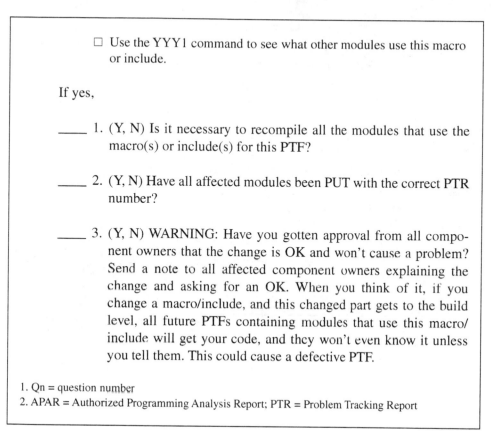

☐ Use the YYY1 command to see what other modules use this macro or include.

If yes,

_____ 1. (Y, N) Is it necessary to recompile all the modules that use the macro(s) or include(s) for this PTF?

_____ 2. (Y, N) Have all affected modules been PUT with the correct PTR number?

_____ 3. (Y, N) WARNING: Have you gotten approval from all component owners that the change is OK and won't cause a problem? Send a note to all affected component owners explaining the change and asking for an OK. When you think of it, if you change a macro/include, and this changed part gets to the build level, all future PTFs containing modules that use this macro/include will get your code, and they won't even know it unless you tell them. This could cause a defective PTF.

1. Qn = question number
2. APAR = Authorized Programming Analysis Report; PTR = Problem Tracking Report

FIGURE 5.2
Sample Items from the PTF Checklist

5.3 Pareto Diagram

Pareto analysis helps by identifying areas that cause most of the problems, which normally means you get the best return on investment when you fix them. It is most applicable in software quality because software defects or defect density never follow a uniform distribution. Rather, almost as a rule of thumb, there are always patterns of clusterings—defects cluster in a minor number of modules or components, a few causes account for the majority of defects, some tricky installation problems account for most of the customer complaints, and so forth. It is, therefore, not surprising to see Pareto charts in software engineering literature. For example, Daskalantonakis (1992) shows an example of Motorola's Pareto analysis for identifying major sources of requirement changes that enabled in-process corrective actions to be taken. Grady and Caswell (1986) show a Pareto analysis of software defects by category for four Hewlett-Packard software projects. The top three types (new function or different processing required, existing data need to be organized/ presented differently, and user needs additional data fields) account for more than one-third of the defects. By focusing on these prevalent defect types, determining probable causes, and instituting process improvements, Hewlett-Packard was able to achieve significant quality improvements.

Figure 5.3 shows an example of a Pareto analysis of the causes of defects for an IBM Rochester product. Interface problems (INTF) and data initialization problems (INIT) were found to be the dominant causes for defects in that product. By focusing on these two areas throughout the design, implementation, and test processes, and by conducting technical education by peer experts, significant improvement was observed. The other defect causes in the figure include complex logical problems (CPLX), translation-related national language problems (NLS), problems related to addresses (ADDR), and data definition problems (DEFN).

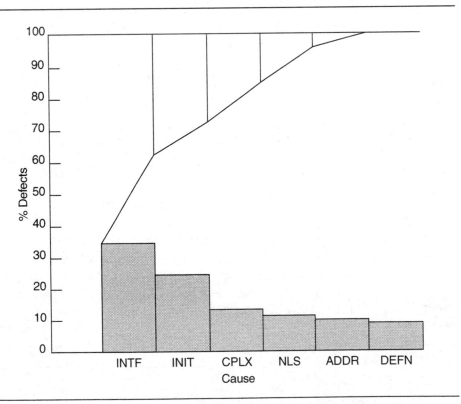

FIGURE 5.3
Pareto Analysis of Software Defects

Another example of Pareto analysis is the problem component analysis conducted at IBM Rochester. The AS/400 software system consists of many products and components. To ensure good return on investment in quality improvement resources, a component problem index based on three indicators was calculated for each release of the software system, and for significant improvements strong focus was placed on the problem components. The problem index is a composite index of three indicators:

☐ Postrelease defects from the new and changed code of the release per thousand new and changed source instructions (defects of current release origin per KCSI). If the components defect rate is
  - the same or less than the system target, then score = 0.
  - higher than system target but less than twice the system target, then score = 1.
  - higher than or equal to twice the system target but less than three times the system target, then score = 2.
  - three or more times the system target, then score = 3.

☐ All postrelease defects are normalized to the total shipped source instructions of the component (all defects per KSSI). This is the defect rate for the entire component including base code from previous releases, ported code, and new and changed code. The scoring criteria are the same as above.

☐ Actual number of defects categorized by quartiles. If the component is in the first quartile, then score = 0, and so forth. This indicator is from the customers' perspective because customers may not care about the lines of code for the functions and the normalized defect rates. They care about the number of defects they encounter. This indicator may not be fair to large components that will have a greater number of defects even if their defect density is the same as others. However, the purpose of the index is not for quality comparison, but to guide the improvement effort. Thus this indicator was included.

The composite component problem index ranges from 0 to 9. Components with an index of 5 and higher are considered problem components. From a Pareto analysis of a product, 27% of the components had an index of 5 and higher; they accounted for about 70% of field defects (Figure 5.4). As a result of this type of Pareto analysis, formal line items for improving problem components (e.g., component restructure, module breakup, complexity measurement and test coverage, and intramodule cleanup) were included in the development plan and have effected significant positive results.

Note: Figure 5.4 is not a Pareto chart in its strict sense because the frequencies are not rank ordered. For a Pareto chart, the frequencies are always in strictly descending order, and the cumulative percentage line is a piecewise convex curve. If we take a two-category view (5* + components versus others), then it is a Pareto chart.

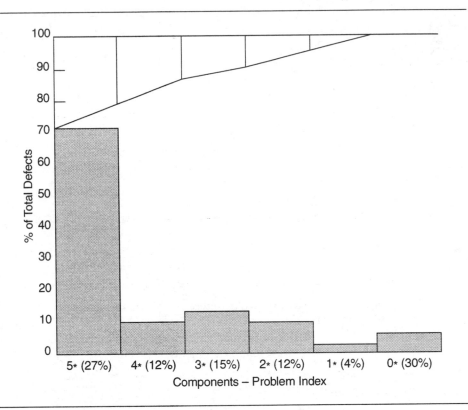

FIGURE 5.4
Pareto Diagram of Defects by Component Problem Index

5.4 Histogram

Figure 5.5 shows two examples of histograms used for software project and quality management. Panel A shows the defect frequency of a product by severity level (from 1 to 4 with 1 being the most severe and 4 the least). Defects with different severity levels differ in their impact on customers. Less severe defects usually have circumventions available and to customers they mean inconvenience. In contrast, high-severity defects may cause system downtime and affect customers' business. Therefore, given the same defect rate (or number of defects), the defect severity histogram tells a lot more about the quality of the software. Panel B shows the frequency of defects during formal machine testing by number of days the defect reports have been opened (1–7 days, 8–14, 15–21, 22–28, 29–35, and 36+). It reflects the response time in fixing defects during the formal testing phases; it is also a workload statement. Figure 5.6 shows the customer satisfaction profile of a software product in terms of very satisfied, satisfied, neutral, dissatisfied, and very dissatisfied. Although

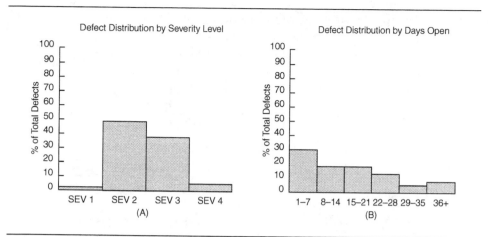

FIGURE 5.5
Two Histograms

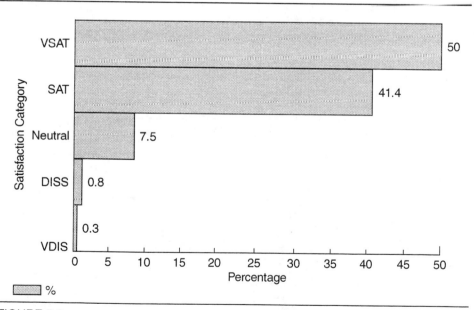

FIGURE 5.6
Profile of Customer Satisfaction with a Software Product

one can construct various metrics with regard to the categories of satisfaction level, a simple histogram conveys the complete information at a glance.

As the examples show, the measurement scale of the data is either interval, ratio, or ordinal (reference the level of measurement discussions in section 3.2 of Chapter 3). If the measurement scale is nominal (e.g., types of software and models of development process), the ordering of the X-axis in a histogram no longer has significance. Such charts are commonly referred to as bar charts. Both histograms and bar charts are frequently used in software development.

5.5 Run Charts

Run charts are also frequently used for software project management; numerous real-life examples can be found in books and journals on software engineering. For example, the weekly arrival of defects and defect backlog during the formal machine testing phases can be monitored via run charts. These charts serve as real-time statements of quality as well as workload. Often these run charts are compared to the historical data or a projection model so that the interpretation can be placed into proper perspective. Another example is tracking the percentage of software fixes that exceed the fix response time criteria. The goal is to ensure timely deliveries of fixes to customers.

Figure 5.7 shows a run chart for the weekly percentage of delinquent open reports of field defects (defect reports that were not yet closed with fixes by the

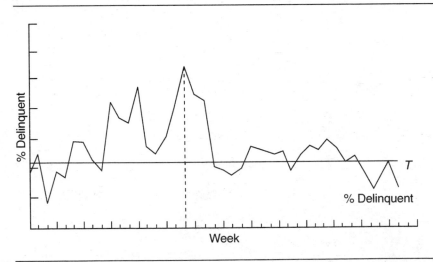

FIGURE 5.7
Run Chart of Percentage of Delinquent Fixes

response time criteria) of an IBM Rochester product. The horizontal line (denoted by the letter T) is the target delinquency rate. The dashed vertical line denotes the time when special remedial actions were rolled out to combat the high delinquency rate. For each delinquent defect report, causal analysis was done and corresponding actions implemented. A sample of the cause categories and the actions implemented are shown in Figure 5.8. As a result, the delinquent-defect report rate was brought down to target in about one month. The rate fluctuated around the target for about four months and eventually was brought under control. (The acronym APAR in

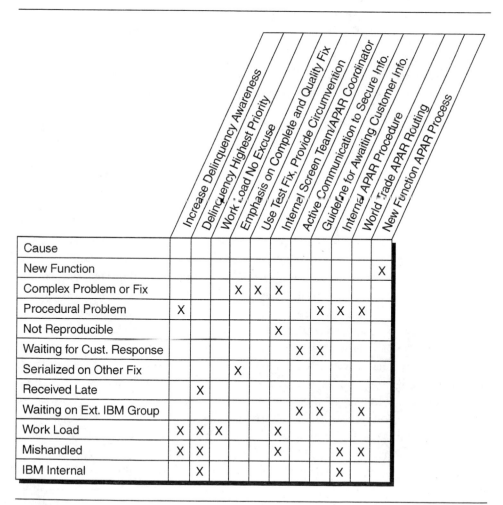

FIGURE 5.8
Causes of and Actions to Reduce Delinquent Fixes

Figure 5.8 stands for Authorized Programming Analysis Report, which refers to reports of postrelease problem.)

Another type of run chart used by many software development organizations for project and schedule management is the S curve, which tracks the cumulative progress of the parameter of interest over time compared to the plan. At IBM Rochester, parameters that are tracked for every project in terms of actual versus planned include:

☐ Completion of design review over time
☐ Completion of code inspection over time
☐ Completion of code integration over time
☐ Completion of component test in terms of number of test cases attempted and successful over time
☐ Completion of system test in terms of number of test cases attempted and successful over time
☐ Other parameters related to project and quality management

5.6 Scatter Diagram

Compared to other tools, the scatter diagram is more difficult to apply. It usually relates to investigative work and requires precise data. It is often used with other techniques such as correlational analysis, regression, and statistical modeling.

Figure 5.9 is a scatter diagram that illustrates the relationship between McCabe's complexity index and defect level. Each data point represents a program module with the X coordinate being its complexity index and the Y coordinate its defect level. Because program complexity can be measured as soon as the program is complete, whereas defects are discovered over a long time, the positive correlation between the two allows us to use program complexity to predict defect level. Furthermore, we can reduce the program complexity when it is developed (as measured by McCabe's index), thereby reducing the chance for defects. Reducing complexity can also make programs easier to maintain. Some component teams of the AS/400 operating system adopt this approach as their strategy for quality and maintainability improvement. Program modules with high-complexity indexes are the targets for analysis and possible module breakup, encapsulation, intramodule cleanup, and other actions. Of course, low-complexity indexes coupled with high defects are clear indications of modules that are poorly designed or implemented and should also be scrutinized.

Other examples of the scatter diagram include the relationships among defects, fan-in and fan-out, quality index of the same components between the current and previous releases, the relationship between testing defect rates and field defect rates, and so forth. We have gained insights in software quality engineering through the investigations of such relationships.

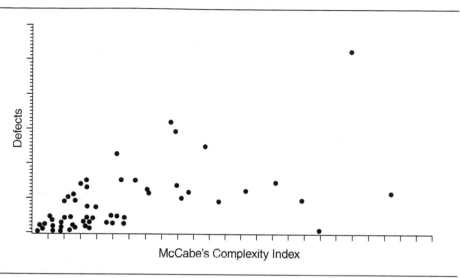

FIGURE 5.9
Scatter Diagram of Program Complexity and Defect Level

In software development, reuse is perhaps the most significant factor in improving productivity. The quality of the new software, however, is often constrained by the latent defects or design limitations in the legacy code. For the AS/400 software system, some products were developed by reusing components of products on the IBM System/38 platform. To examine the relationship of the defect rate of the reused components between the two platforms, we used the scatter diagrams. Figure 5.10 is a scatter diagram for one product. In the figure, each data point represents a component, with the X coordinate indicating its defect rate in the System/38 platform and the Y coordinate indicating its defect rate in the AS/400 platform. Although there are changes and modifications to the AS/400 product and additional reviews and tests were conducted, clearly the correlation (0.69) is quite strong. Also shown are both the linear regression line (the diagonal line) and the 95% confidence interval (area between the two broken lines).

We then proceeded to classify the scattergram into four quadrants according to the medians of the component defect rates on the AS/400 and System/38 platforms (Figure 5.11). Such classification allows different analysis and improvement strategies to be applied to different groups of components.

☐ The components in the upper right quadrant (stars) are the chronic problem components. The fact that these components sustained high defect rates in spite of years of aging on the System/38 platform implies that significant actions (e.g., examination of the design structure, a rewrite of error-prone modules, etc.) need to be considered.

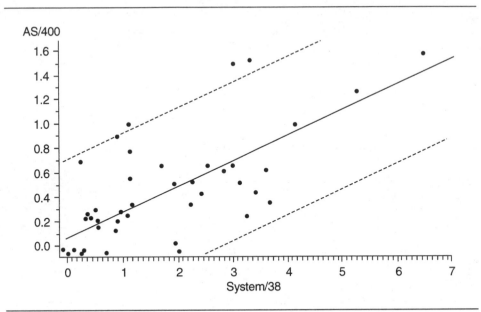

FIGURE 5.10
Correlation of Defect Rates of Reused Components Between Two Platforms

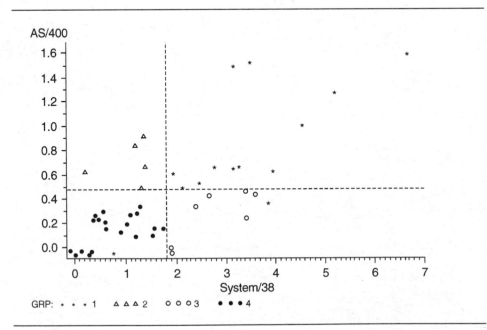

FIGURE 5.11
Grouping of Reused Components Based on Defect Rate Relationship

□ The components in the upper left quadrant (triangles) are components with low defect rates on System/38 but high on AS/400. The improvement strategy should focus on the nature of the enhancements on AS/400 and the process the development teams used.

□ Those in the lower right quadrant (circles) are the components that had high defect rates on System/38 but low on AS/400. The changes to these components for AS/400 and the actions taken during the AS/400 development should be examined to shed light for other components.

□ In the lower left quadrant (darkened circles) are components that have low defect rates in both platforms. The focus of analysis should be on their usage and if the usage is not low, on their design structure.

5.7 Control Chart

The control chart is a powerful tool for achieving statistical process control (SPC). However, in software development it is difficult to use control charts in the formal SPC manner. It is a formidable task, if not impossible, to define the process capability of a software development process. In production environments, process capability is the inherent variation of the process in relation to the specification limits. The smaller the process variation, the better the process's capability. Defective parts are parts that are produced with values of parameters outside the specification limits. Therefore, direct relationships exist among specifications, process control limits, process variations, and product quality. The smaller the process variations, the better the product quality will be. Such direct correlations, however, do not exist or at least have not been established in the software development environment.

In statistical terms, process capability is defined:

$$C_p = \frac{|\text{USL} - \text{LSL}|}{6 \text{ sigma}}$$

where USL and LSL are the upper and lower engineering specification limits, respectively, sigma is the standard deviation of the process, and 6 sigma represents the overall process variation.

If a unilateral specification is affixed to some characteristics, the capability index may be defined:

$$C_p = \frac{|\text{USL} - u|}{3 \text{ sigma}}$$

where u is the process mean, or

$$C_p = \frac{|u - \text{LSL}|}{3 \text{ sigma}}$$

In manufacturing environments where many parts are produced daily, process variation and process capability can be calculated in statistical terms and control charts can be used on a real-time basis. Software differs from manufacturing in several aspects and such differences make it very difficult, if not impossible, to arrive at useful estimates of the process capability of a software development organization. The difficulties include:

☐ Specifications for most defined metrics are nonexistent or poorly related to real customer needs. Well-defined specifications based on customer requirements that can be expressed in terms of metrics are lacking for practically all software projects (more accurately, they are extremely difficult to derive).

☐ Software is design and development, not production, and it takes various phases of activity (architecture, design, code, test, etc.) and considerable time to complete one project. Therefore, the life-cycle concept is more applicable to software than control charts, which are more applicable to sequential data from ongoing operations.

☐ Related to the above, metrics and models specific to software and the life-cycle concept have been and are still being developed (e.g., software reliability models, defect removal models, and various in-process metrics) and they are going through the maturing process. These models and metrics seem to be more effective than control charts for interpreting the software patterns and for product quality management.

☐ Even with the same development process, there are multiple common causes (e.g., tools, methods, types of software, types of components, types of program modules) that lead to variations in quality. The typical use of control charts in software projects regularly mix data from multiple common cause systems.

☐ There are also the behavioral aspects of process implementation (e.g., skills, experience, rigor of process implementation) that cause variations in the quality of the product (Layman et al., 2002).

☐ Many assumptions that underlie control charts are not being met in software data. Perhaps the most critical one is that data variation is from homogeneous sources of variation; this critical assumption is not usually met because of the aforementioned factors. Therefore, even with exact formulas and the most suitable type of control charts, the resultant control limits are not always useful. For instance, the control limits in software applications are often too wide to be useful.

☐ Within a software development organization, multiple processes are often used, and technology and processes change fast.

□ Even when a process parameter is under control in the sense of control charts, without the direct connection between process limits and end-product quality, what does it mean in terms of process capability?

Despite these issues, control charts are useful for software process improvement—when they are used in a relaxed manner. That means that control chart use in software is not in terms of formal statistical process control and process capability. Rather, they are used as tools for improving consistency and stability. On many occasions, they are not used on a real-time basis for ongoing operations. They are more appropriately called pseudo-control charts.

There are many types of control chart. The most common are the X-bar and S charts for sample averages and standard deviations, and the X-bar and R charts for sample averages and sample ranges. There are also median charts, charts for individuals, the p chart for proportion nonconforming, the np chart for number nonconforming, the c chart for number of nonconformities, the u chart for nonconformities per unit, and so forth. For X-bar and S charts or X-bar and R charts, the assumption of the statistical distribution of the quality characteristic is the normal distribution. For the p and the np charts, the assumption of statistical distribution is the binomial distribution. For the c and the u charts, it is assumed that the distribution of the quality characteristic is the Poisson distribution. For details, see a text in statistical quality control (e.g., Montgomery (1985)).

The most approximate charts for software applications are perhaps the p chart, when percentages are involved, and the u chart, when defect rates are used. The control limits are calculated as the value of the parameter of interest (X-bar or p, for example) plus/minus three standard deviations. One can also increase the sensitivity of the chart by adding a pair of warning limits, which are normally calculated as the value of the parameter plus/minus two standard deviations. As the calculation of standard deviations differs among types of parameters, the formulas for control limits (and warning limits) also differ.

For example, control limits for defect rates (u chart) can be calculated as follows:

$$\text{Upper limit} = \bar{\mu} + 3\sqrt{\frac{\bar{\mu}}{n_i}}$$

$$\text{Lower limit} = \bar{\mu} - 3\sqrt{\frac{\bar{\mu}}{n_i}}$$

where $\bar{\mu}$, value for the center line, is the cumulative defect rate (weighted average of defect rates) across the subgroups, and n_i is the size of subgroup i for the calculation of defect rate (e.g., the number of lines of source code or the number of function points). Usually the subgroups used as the unit for calculating and controlling defect rates could be program modules, components, design review sessions of similar length in time, design segments, code segments for inspections, and units of document reviews. Note that in the formula, n_i is the subgroup size and therefore the control limits are calculated for each sample. Therefore the control limits will be different for each data point (subgroup) in the control chart. The second approach is to base the control chart on an average sample size, resulting in an approximate set of control limits. This requires the assumption that future sample size (subgroup size) will not differ greatly from those previously observed. If this approach is used, the control limits will be constant and the resulting control chart will not look as complex as the control chart with variable limits (Montgomery, 1985). However, if the sample sizes vary greatly, the first approach should be used.

Control limits for percentages (e.g., effectiveness metric) can be calculated as follows:

$$\text{Upper limit} = \bar{p} + 3\sqrt{\frac{\bar{p}(1-\bar{p})}{n_i}}$$

$$\text{Lower limit} = \bar{p} - 3\sqrt{\frac{\bar{p}(1-\bar{p})}{n_i}}$$

where $\bar{p}$, the center line, is the weighted average of individual percentages and n_i is the size of subgroup i. Like the μ chart, either the approach for variable control limits or the approach for constant control limits (provided the sample sizes don't vary greatly) can be used. If the true value of p is known, or is specified by management (e.g., a specific target of defect removal effectiveness), then p should be used in the formulas, instead of $\bar{p}$.

Some examples of metrics from the software development process can be control charted, for instance, inspection defects per thousand lines of source code (KLOC) or function point, testing defects per KLOC or function point, phase effectiveness, and defect backlog management index (as discussed in Chapter 4). Figure 5.12 shows a pseudo-control chart on testing defects per KLOC by component for a project at IBM Rochester, from which error-prone components were identified for further in-depth analysis and actions. In this case, the use of the control chart involved more than one iteration. In the first iteration, components with defect rates outside the control limits (particularly high) were identified. (It should be noted that in this example the control chart is one-sided with only the upper control limit.)

In the second iteration, the previously identified error-prone components were removed and the data were plotted again, with a new control limit (Figure 5.13). This process of "peeling the onion" permitted the identification of the next set of potentially defect-prone components, some of which may have been masked on the initial

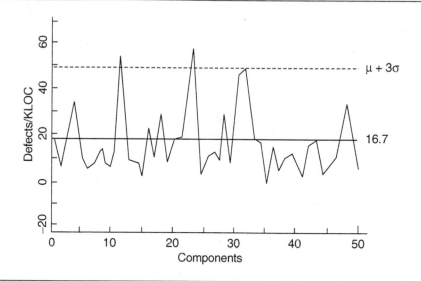

FIGURE 5.12
Pseudo-Control Chart of Test Defect Rate—First Iteration

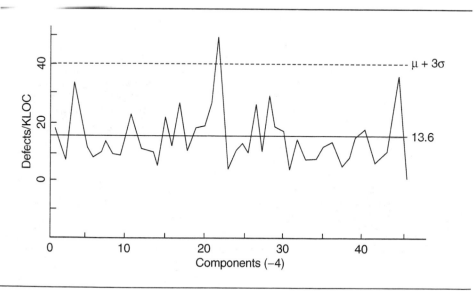

FIGURE 5.13
Pseudo-Control Chart of Test Defect Rate—Second Iteration

charts. This process can continue for a few iterations. Priority of improvement actions as they relate to available resources can also be determined based on the order of iteration in which problem components are identified (Craddock, 1988). At each iteration, the out-of-control points should be removed from the analysis only when their causes have been understood and plans put in place to prevent their recurrence.

Another example, also from IBM Rochester, is charting the inspection effectiveness by area for the several phases of reviews and inspections, as shown in Figure 5.14. Effectiveness is a relative measure in percentage, with the numerator being the number of defects removed in a development phase and the denominator the total number of defects found in that phase, plus defects found later (for detailed discussion on this subject, see Chapter 6). In the figure, each data point represents the inspection effectiveness of a functional development area. The four panels represent

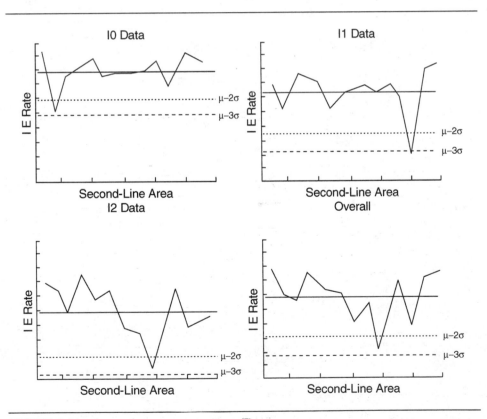

FIGURE 5.14
Pseudo-Control Chart of Inspection Effectiveness

high-level design review (I0), low-level design review (I1), code inspection (I2), and overall effectiveness combining all three phases (lower right). Areas with low effectiveness (below the warning and control limits) as well as those with the highest effectiveness were studied and contributing factors identified. As a result of this control charting and subsequent work, the consistency of the inspection effectiveness across the functional areas was improved.

In recent years, control charts in software applications have attracted attention. The importance of using quantitative metrics in managing software development is certainly more recognized now than previously. A related reason may be the promotion of quantitative management by the capability maturity model (CMM) of the Software Engineering Institute (SEI) at the Carnegie Mellon University. The concept and terminology of control charts are very appealing to software process improvement professionals. A quick survey of the examples of control chart applications in software in the literature, however, supported and confirmed the challenges discussed earlier. For instance, many of the control limits in the examples were too wide to be useful. For such cases, simple run charts with common sense for decision making would be more useful and control charts might not be needed. There were also cases with a one-sided control limit or a lower control limit close to zero. Both types of cases were likely due to problems related to multiple common causes and sample size. The multiple common cause challenge was discussed earlier. With regard to sample size, again, a production environment with ongoing operations is more able to meet the challenge. The subgroup sample size can be chosen according to statistical considerations in a production environment, such as specifying a sample large enough to ensure a positive lower control limit. In software environments, however, other factors often prohibit operations that are based on statistical considerations. At the same time, it is positive that experts have recognized the problems, begun identifying the specific issues, started the discussions, and embarked on the process of mapping possible solutions (e.g., Layman et al., 2002).

To make control charts more applicable and acceptable in the software environment, a high degree of ingenuity is required. Focused effort in the following three areas by experts of control charts and by software process improvement practitioners will yield fruitful results:

1. The control chart applications in software thus far are the Shewhart control charts. Alternative techniques that could be more applicable to software parameters need to be examined, experimented with, and applied. New techniques may even need to be developed. For example, the cusum (cumulative sum) control chart was developed in the 1950s as an alternative to the Shewhart approach when a small but meaningful change needs to be detected as quickly as possible (Burr and Owen, 1996; Montgomery, 1985).

The cusum technique incorporates all of the information in the sequence of sample values by plotting the cumulative sums of the deviations of the sample values from a target value. It is therefore more sensitive to detect differences. The cusum control charts are used in the semiconductor industry. Would they be more applicable than the traditional control charts to the behaviors of some key parameters in software? Is cusum suitable for cases in which the process target is not a constant (e.g., a model curve)? Can control charts be applied to the S-curve type of situations that are rather common in software development (e.g., the testing progress S curves and the defect density curves that are modeled by software reliability models)? Are there better alternatives? Questions like these are important topics that need further methodology research and empirical studies.

2. Even the basic premise of using the 3-sigma control limits deserves a closer look. Our experience is that even for control charts that are free of problems related to multiple common causes, the 3-sigma control limits are too wide to be useful in software. Judging from some examples in the literature and personal experience, experienced practitioners would have taken actions long before the value of the metric reached the control limits. In general practice, we recommend using warning limits (such as those in Figure 5.14) in addition to control limits, and other criteria that are available in the control chart literature. When control limits are set based on larger sigma values, the risk of false alarm decreases but the control chart becomes less sensitive. On the other hand, when control limits are narrower, the control chart has more power to detect differences but the risk of false alarms becomes higher. There is a need to establish a correlation between the width of control limits and practical experiences based on empirical studies. It will be interesting to conduct experiments with a group of software quality management practitioners, who are experienced in using metrics for project management, to gauge the criteria (or thresholds) for their decision making. The subjects can be asked to assess a group of trend charts with varying degrees of deviation from the targets and to indicate at what level of deviation the cases will become alarming to them. Then control chart techniques can be applied to those charts to derive the control limits and warning limits. The control chart limits then can be correlated with the threshold values of the practitioners.

3. For software process improvement practitioners, the challenge is to select and develop *meaningful* process or quality parameters when control charts are to be used. As a hypothetical example, control charting the backlog of opened problems during the final phase of testing of the software (e.g., system test) may not be a meaningful undertaking if some or all of the following conditions are true:

    □   Problem backlog is a function of problem arrivals, which in turn, is a function of test progress. Defect arrival pattern (cumulative form) usually follows an S-curve pattern.

- The backlog and related parameters follow the life-cycle or phase concept (e.g., with start, ramp-up, plateau, and end stages). In such cases, they may not be compatible with the control charting approach. For system testing, a cycle of 3 to 4 months is normally regarded as long. Assuming week is the time unit for the control chart, the number of data points is limited. The criteria for backlog may also vary over the testing cycle. For instance, near the end of testing, the backlog criteria are normally much more stringent than at the peak of testing.

- The problem fixing task is also done by the same team. In such cases, the team may adopt a strategy that optimizes the overall test process instead of imposing a constant control on one parameter such as problem backlog.

- Simple trend charts of several related parameters (e.g., test progress, defect arrivals, defect backlog, and severe problems) are being shown together, with targets specified at several key dates throughout the test cycle if needed. In such cases, the multiple trend chart approach will be simpler and more effective than control charts. If the baseline trends were available for comparison, one could make inferences about the quality of the current project vis-à-vis the compatible baseline. If some form of statistical quality control is desired, a good approach would be to apply one of the software reliability growth models to project the defect arrival pattern and, based on that, to determine the backlog targets over the test cycle.

In general, data from software maintenance is easier for control charting because it meets the basic assumption of time-related sequential data. For the problem backlog example, even for software maintenance data (i.e., field problem backlog), we recommend using a metric in which the effect of a possible second common cause (such as the cyclical pattern of problem arrivals due to the delivery of new products to the customers) is partialled out. (Refer to the backlog management index discussed in section 4.3.1 in Chapter 4.)

As another hypothetical example, we suggest that metrics related to defect removal effectiveness (see discussions in Chapter 6) are candidates for control charting for software development organizations that deliver a number of products or releases of products within a relatively short period of time. In this case, each product or release is a data point in the control chart. The data is still time related and sequential but the data points are farther apart in time so one could call such charts macrolevel pseudo-control charts. It is established in the software engineering literature that the higher the defect removal effectiveness, the better field quality a product will have. With a number of products or releases in the field, one can even establish an empirical correlation between the defect removal effectiveness values and actual field quality levels (use nonparametric statistics if sample size is small). The results can be used to reset the center line of the control chart. The process capability of the organization can then be measured directly and expressed in SPC languages. When the process is under control, it means that the organization is able to keep delivering products that meet certain quality levels in the field. If a software development organization developed five products and provided two releases of each product each year, in one year there would be ten data points. Therefore, it would not take long to form such a control chart. For more data points and more granular control, the unit of observation can be applied to development teams so a given project will have a number of data points. In addition to the overall defect removal effectiveness, this approach can be applied to the specific effectiveness metrics such as inspection effectiveness and test effectiveness.

As a real-life example, Lipke (2002) applied the control chart techniques successfully to two indicators in project management, based on empirical data at the Oklahoma City Air Logistics Center. The two indicators are schedule performance index (SPI) and cost performance index (CPI), which are expressed in earned value terminology in the project management literature. Simply put, the project schedule or cost is on target when the index is 1, ahead of plan when the index is higher than 1, behind plan when the index is below 1. Such control charts are meaningful because when the project is under way, as long as the two indexes are under control, the final outcome will be successful—in this case, schedule-wise and cost-wise. Lipke also made adjustments to the indexes so that the assumptions of control charts were met.

5.8 Cause-and-Effect Diagram

The cause-and-effect diagram is one of the less frequently used tools in software development. Perhaps the best example among fishbone diagrams is the one given by Grady and Caswell (1986). In its quality improvement effort, the development team on a Hewlett-Packard project first used a Pareto diagram and found that defects associated with register allocation were the most prevalent in their project. With the help of a cause-and-effect diagram, they conducted brainstorming sessions on those problems. As Figure 5.15 shows, they found side effects of register usage and incorrect processor register usage to be the two primary causes. Ultimately, both were found to be caused by incomplete knowledge of the operation of the registers. With this finding, that HP division took aggressive steps to provide proper training and documentation regarding registers and processors prior to subsequent projects. Figure 5.16 shows a fishbone diagram relating the key factors to effective inspections. Such a diagram was part of the process education material for a project at IBM Rochester.

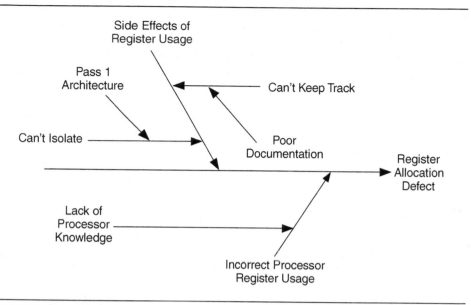

FIGURE 5.15
Cause-and-Effect Diagram

From *Software Metrics: Establishing a Company-Wide Program,* by R. B. Grady and D. L. Caswell, © 1998.
Reprinted by permission of Pearson Education, Inc., Upper Saddle River, N.J.

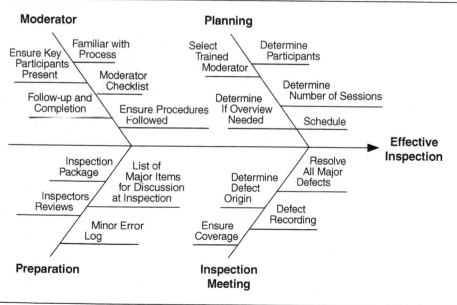

FIGURE 5.16
Cause-and-Effect Diagram of Design Inspection

5.9 Relations Diagram

Ishikawa's seven basic tools are also called the seven old tools or the seven quality control tools. In recent years there emerged the seven new quality planning and management tools, which are the affinity diagram, the relations diagram, the tree diagram, the matrix chart, the matrix data analysis chart, the process decision program chart (PDPC), and the arrow diagram. Although discussion of these seven new tools is not in the scope of this book, it would be remiss not to mention that they may also be useful in software engineering. These seven new tools are mostly qualitative and seem more appropriate for project management and structural brainstorming. Rudisill (1992) reports that a large software development company has automated these seven new tools to facilitate the quality function deployment approach in software development and has gained positive experience, especially in gathering and verifying customers' requirements.

One of the seven new tools that we found very useful over the years is the relations diagram. It displays complex relationships and fosters cause-and-effect thinking. It organizes information from specific to general and surfaces key causes and key effects. It differs from the cause-and-effect diagram in that it displays multiple causes and effects, whereas the cause-and-effect diagram shows one dependent variable (effect) and its cause structure. Figure 5.17 shows a schematic representation of the relations diagram.

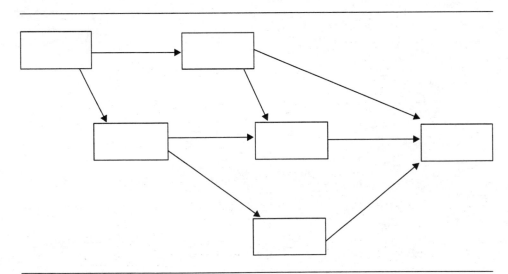

FIGURE 5.17
A Schematic Representation of a Relations Diagram

Figure 5.18 shows a loosely constructed relations diagram (which is somewhat different from the schematic representation in form). It displays the complex cause-and-effect relationships among the factors contributing to the number of customer critical situations for a software product. In this example, a critical situation occurred when a customer's business operations were affected because of issues related to this software product and the customer filed a complaint to the organization that provided the software. The issues could be product quality, the severity and impact of specific defects, technical support issues, ways-of-doing business issues (e.g., e-business issues—business issues related to Internet and this software), and even issues related to business partners.

We found the relations diagram very appealing for complex situations like this example. It is flexible and it fits naturally with the small-team brainstorming process in problem identification and problem solving. In fact, the initial form of the diagram in Figure 5.18 was simply the result of a brainstorming session that was captured on

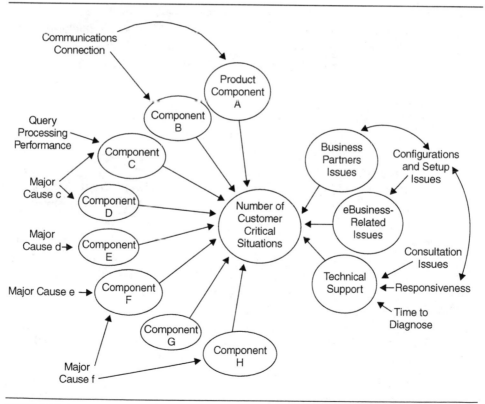

FIGURE 5.18
A Diagram of Complex Relationships Associated with Customer-Critical Situations of a Software Product

a white board. The final form was the cumulative result of subsequent brainstorming sessions, interviews, further analysis, and verifications. The relations diagram can also be supported by quantitative data analysis. For example, the varying sizes of the circles of product components in Figure 5.18 reflect the relative contributions of these components to the number of customer critical situations. For interested experts, multivariate statistical analysis can also be performed to quantify the relationships in a relations diagram because applicable statistical techniques exist. For example, the structural equation models, or path analysis, appear to match well with the relations diagram. Even the two-way relationships among the factors in a relations diagram can be modeled via the recursive structural equation techniques (Duncan, 1975).

5.10 Summary

In recent years, there has been an emerging trend in the software industry to use scientific methods to achieve precision in managing software projects. Many quality engineering and statistical tools that have been used widely in manufacturing are gaining acceptance in software development environments. This chapter discusses the possible applications of the seven basic tools with real-life examples. In many instances, analysis based on these tools has yielded significant effects on software process improvement.

The degree of application of individual tools varies. Some have been used extensively on a daily basis; others are just now being recognized. These tools can be used with each other or with more advanced methods. For instance, the Pareto diagram, cause-and-effect diagram, and scatter diagram can be used together for identifying the dominant problems and their root causes. Control charts can be put in place to monitor process stability, or to determine whether improvements really occur after corrective actions are taken.

The seven basic tools indeed are basic tools. Their real value lies in the consistent and pervasive use by development teams for process improvement. Their impact can be enormous, especially when they are automated and become ingrained in the software development process, as demonstrated by the example of the automated fix checklist at IBM Rochester.

The control chart has been the center of interest of late, perhaps because its concepts and terminology appeal greatly to process improvement professionals. Given the state of art of this tool and, more important, the state of practice in software environments, ingenuity in both methodologies and applications is required for this tool to become a common practice. It is a useful tool for improving process consistency and stability, and therefore for long-term quality improvement.

Although the seven new quality planning and management tools are beyond the intended scope of this chapter, we include the relations diagram in our discussions.

Recommendations for Small Organizations

Most of the basic quality tools can be implemented easily by small teams as well as large organizations. Implementing the scatter diagram and control charts does require that someone on the team has a statistical background.

Run charts, histograms, and bar charts are most often used for status reporting; their implementation comes naturally. Given the pervasive use of presentation software, it would be difficult to find an organization that does not use run charts (or trend charts) and bar charts (or histograms). For small teams starting a metrics program, I recommend a focus on (1) the checklist, (2) the Pareto diagram, and (3) either the relations diagram or the cause-and-effect diagram.

The checklist is an important tool to ensure consistent process implementation and can be applied to many phases and activities throughout the software development process. I have cited many examples in the chapter. Checklists should not be lengthy and, most important, they should be developed based on the team's experience. Starting with one or two checklists for the most important activities, the team can gradually build its experience-based checklists.

These checklists should be reviewed and updated periodically. They then become valuable process artifacts specific to the organization. Experience-based checklists are a good way to make a team a self-learning team and its development process a self-learning process. Like the pilot's checklist before an airplane's takeoff, consistent use of experience-based checklists is a sure way to achieve process control and stability. To derive quantitative indicators from checklists, a team can measure the percentages of the checklist criteria being met for key process activities.

While the checklist is for guiding and reinforcing process implementation, the Pareto diagram is useful for quantitative parameters pertaining to product quality (defects, customer complaints, defective fixes). The relations diagram or the cause-and-effect diagram is a team-oriented tool for problem solving. With effective use of these tools, a team is well equipped for process and quality improvement.

I do not recommend the control chart to small teams starting a metric program. The tool is better suited for the environments in which tracking systems and historical data are well established.

Over the years we found this tool useful for small-team brainstorming and especially for displaying the complex relationships in software environments. We highly recommend it.

Finally, statistical process control (SPC) is not limited to control charting. All the tools discussed in this chapter are important tools recognized in the SPC literature. In software development all these tools, and the many models and metrics discussed in the other chapters, will surely play an ever-increasing role in achieving SPC. We will come back to the discussion on SPC in software development in the final chapter.

References

1. Bernstein, L., "Notes on Software Quality Management," presented at the *International Software Quality Exchange,* San Francisco, March 10–11, 1992, sponsored by the Juran Institute, Wilton, Conn.
2. Burr, A., and M. Owen, *Statistical Methods for Software Quality: Using Metrics to Control Process and Product Quality,* London and New York: International Thomson Computer Press, 1996.
3. Craddock, L. L., "Control Charting in Software Development," *Proceedings Sixth Annual Pacific Northwest Software Quality Conference,* Portland, Oregon, September 1988, pp. 53–70.
4. Daskalantonakis, M. K., "A Practical View of Software Measurement and Implementation Experiences within Motorola," *IEEE Transactions on Software Engineering,* Vol. SE-18, 1992, pp. 998–1010.
5. Duncan, O. D., *Introduction to Structural Equations Models,* New York: Academic Press, 1975.
6. Fenton, N. E., and S. L. Pfleeger, *Software Metrics: A Rigorous Approach,* 2nd ed., London and Boston: International Thomson Computer Press, 1997.
7. Florac, W. A.., and A. D. Carleton, *Measuring the Software Process, Statistical Process Control for Software Process Improvement,* Reading, Mass.: Addison-Wesley, 1999.
8. Grady, R. B., and D. L. Caswell, *Software Metrics: Establishing a Company-Wide Program,* Englewood Cliffs, N.J.: Prentice-Hall, 1986.
9. Ishikawa, K., *Guide to Quality Control,* White Plains, N.Y.: Quality Resource, 1971, 1989.
10. Kume, H., *Statistical Methods for Quality Improvement,* Tokyo: The Association for Overseas Technical Scholarship, 1985, 1989.
11. Layman, B., B. Curtis, J. Puffer, and C. Webet, "Solving the Challenge of Quantitative Management, Section 4: Problems in the Use of Control Charts," SEPG 2002 QM Tutorial, Phoenix, Arizona, February 18–21, 2002.
12. Lipke, W., "Statistical Process Control of Project Performance," *CrossTalk, The Journal of Defense Software Engineering,* Vol. 15, No. 3, March 2002, pp. 15–18.
13. Mays, R. G., C. L. Jones, G. J. Holloway, and D. P. Studinski, "Experiences with Defect Prevention," *IBM Systems Journal,* Vol. 29, No. 1, February 1990, pp. 4–32.
14. Montgomery, D. C., *Introduction to Statistical Quality Control,* New York: John Wiley & Sons, 1985.
15. Rudisill, D., "QCASE: A New Paradigm for Computer-Aided Software Engineering," *International Software Quality Exchange 92 Conference Proceedings,* San Francisco, Calif., March 10–11, 1992, sponsored by the Juran Institute, Wilton, Conn., pp. 4A-19–4A-34.
16. Snedecor, G. W., and W. G. Cochran, *Statistical Methods,* 7th ed., Ames, Iowa: The Iowa State University Press.

6

Defect Removal Effectiveness

The concept of defect removal effectiveness and its measurements are central to software development. Defect removal is one of the top expenses in any software project and it greatly affects schedules. Effective defect removal can lead to reductions in the development cycle time and good product quality. For improvements in quality, productivity, and cost, as well as schedule, it is important to use better defect prevention and removal technologies to maximize the effectiveness of the project. It is important for all projects and development organizations to measure the effectiveness of their defect removal processes.

In Chapter 4 we briefly touched on the metrics of defect removal effectiveness and fault containment. In this chapter we elaborate on the concept, its measurements, and its use in the phase-based defect removal model. After a brief literature review, we take a closer look at the defect injection and removal activities of the phases of a typical development process. Using a matrix approach to cross-tabulate defect data in terms of defect origin and phase of defect discovery (where found), we provide a detailed example of calculating the values of the overall defect removal effectiveness, the inspection effectiveness, the test effectiveness as well as the phase-specific defect removal effectiveness. We then establish the formulas of these indexes based on the defect origin/where found matrix. Next we elaborate the role of defect removal effectiveness in quality planning with more examples. We discuss the cost effectiveness of phase defect removal and also the defect removal effectiveness levels in the context of the capability maturity model (CMM) before summarizing the chapter.

Before we begin, a point on terminology is in order. Some writers use the terms *defect removal efficiency, error detection efficiency, fault containment, defect removal effectiveness*, and the like. In this book we prefer the term *effectiveness* rather than *efficiency*. *Efficiency* implies the element of time, *effectiveness* is related to the extent of impact and we think the latter is more appropriate. In the following sections we may sometimes use the two terms interchangeably, especially when we refer to the definitions and metrics of other writers.

6.1 Literature Review

In the 1960s and earlier, when software development was simply "code and test" and software projects were characterized by cost overruns and schedule delays, the only defect removal step was testing. In the 1970s, formal reviews and inspections were recognized as important to productivity and product quality, and thus were adopted by development projects. As a result, the value of defect removal as an element of he development process strengthened. In his classic article on design and code inspections, Fagan (1976) touches on the concept of defect removal effectiveness. He defined error detection efficiency as:

$$\frac{\text{Errors found by an inspection}}{\text{Total errors in the product before inspection}} \times 100\%$$

In an example of a COBOL application program Fagan cites, the total error detection efficiency for both design and code inspection was 82%. Such a degree of efficiency seemed outstanding. Specifically, the project found 38 defects per KNCSS (thousand noncommentary source statements) via design and code inspections, and 8 defects per KNCSS via unit testing and preparation for acceptance testing. No defects were found during acceptance testing or in actual usage in a six-month period. From this example we know that defects found in the field (actual usage of the software) were included in the denominator of Fagan's calculation of defect removal efficiency.

Intriguingly, the concept of defect removal effectiveness and its measurements were seldom discussed in the literature, as its importance would merit, until the mid-1980s (Jones, 1986). Not surprisingly, Jones's definition, stated here, is very similar to Fagan's:

$$\text{Removal efficiency} = \frac{\text{Defects found by removal operation}}{\text{Defects present at removal operation}} \times 100\%$$

$$= \frac{\text{Defect found}}{\text{Defects found } + \text{Defects not found}} \times 100\%$$
$$\text{(found later)}$$

In Jones's definition, defects found in the field are included in the denominator of the formula.

IBM's Federal Systems Division in Houston, Texas, developed mission-specific space shuttle flight software for the National Aeronautics and Space Administration (NASA) and was well known for its high product quality. The space shuttle is "fly-by-wire"; all the astronaut's commands are sent from flight-deck controls to the computers, which then send out electronic commands to execute a given function. There are five computers onboard the shuttle. The Primary Avionics Software System (on-board software) is responsible for vehicle guidance, navigation, flight control, and numerous systems management and monitoring functions, and also provides the interface from the vehicle to crew and ground communications systems. The onboard software contains about 500,000 lines of source code. In addition, there are about 1.7 million lines of code for the ground software systems used to develop and configure the onboard system for shuttle missions (Kolkhorst and Macina, 1988).

IBM Houston won many quality awards from NASA and from the IBM Corporation for its outstanding quality in the space shuttle flight systems. For example, it received the first NASA Excellence Award for Quality and Productivity in 1987 (Ryan, 1987), and in 1989 it won the first Best Software Laboratory Award from the IBM Corporation. Its shuttle onboard software (PASS) achieved defect-free quality since 1985, and the defect rate for the support systems was reduced to an extraordinarily low level. IBM Houston took several key approaches to improve its quality, one of which is the focus on rigorous and formal inspections. Indeed, in addition to design and code inspections, the IBM Houston software development process contained the phase of formal requirements analysis and inspection. The requirements, which are specified in precise terms and formulas, are much like the low-level design documents in commercial software. The rationale for the heavy focus on the front end of the process, of course, is to remove defects as early as possible in the software life cycle. Indeed, one of the four metrics IBM used to manage quality is the early detection percentage, which is actually inspection defect removal effectiveness. From Ryan (1987) and Kolkhorst and Macina (1988):

$$\text{Early detection percentage} = \frac{\text{Number of major inspection errors}}{\text{Total number of errors}} \times 100\%$$

where total number of errors is the sum of major inspection errors and valid discrepancy reports (discrepancy report is the mechanism for tracking test defects).

According to IBM Houston's definitions, a major inspection error is any error found in a design or code inspection that would have resulted in a valid discrepancy report (DR) if the error had been incorporated into the software. Philosophical differences, errors in comments or documentation, and software maintenance issues are inspection errors that may be classified as minor and do not enter into this count.

Valid DRs document that the code fails to meet the letter, intent, or operational purpose of the requirements. These DRs require a code fix, documented waiver, or user note to the customer. From the preceding formula it appears that the denominator does not include defects from the field, when the software is being used by customers. In this case, however, it is more a conceptual than a practical difference because the number of field defects for the shuttle software systems is so small.

IBM Houston's data also substantiated a strong correlation between inspection defect removal effectiveness and product quality (Kolkhorst and Macina, 1988). For software releases from November 1982 to December 1986, the early detection percentages increased from about 50% to more than 85%. Correspondingly, the product defect rates decreased monotonically from 1984 to 1986 by about 70%. Figures 6.1 and 6.2 show the details.

The effectiveness measure by Dunn (1987) differs little from Fagan's and from Jones's second definition. Dunn's definition is:

$$E = \frac{N}{N + S} \times 100\%$$

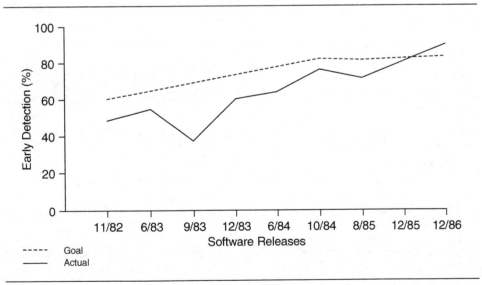

FIGURE 6.1
Early Detection of Software Errors

From "Developing Error-Free Software," by *IEEE AES Magazine:* 25–31. Copyright © 1988 IEEE. Reprinted with permission.

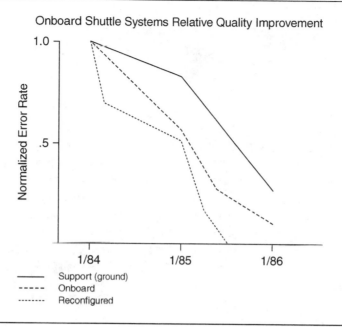

FIGURE 6.2

Relative Improvement of Software Types

From "Developing Error-Free Software," by *IEEE AES Magazine:* 25–31. Copyright © 1988 IEEE. Reprinted with permission.

where

E = Effectiveness of activity (development phase)

N = Number of faults (defects) found by activity (phase)

S = Number of faults (defects) found by subsequent activities (phases)

According to Dunn (1987), this metric can be tuned by selecting only defects present at the time of the activity and susceptible to detection by the activity.

Daskalantonakis (1992) describes the metrics used at Motorola for software development. Chapter 4 gives a brief summary of those metrics. Two of the metrics are in fact for defect removal effectiveness: total defect containment effectiveness (TDCE) and phase containment effectiveness (PCE_i). For immediate reference, we restate the two metrics:

$$TDCE = \frac{\text{Number of prerelease defects}}{\text{Number of prerelease defects} \ + \text{Number of postrelease defects}}$$

$$\text{PCE}_i = \frac{\text{Number of phase } i \text{ errors}}{\text{Number of phase } i \text{ errors} + \text{Number of phase } i \text{ defects}}$$

where phase i errors are problems found during that development phase in which they were introduced, and phase i defects are problems found later than the development phase in which they were introduced.

The definitions and metrics of defect removal effectiveness just discussed differ little from one to another. However, there are subtle differences that may cause confusion. Such differences are negligible if the calculation is for the overall effectiveness of the development process, or there is only one phase of inspection. However, if there are separate phases of activities and inspections before code integration and testing, which is usually the case in large-scale development, the differences could be significant. The reason is that when the inspection of an early phase (e.g., high-level design inspection) took place, the defects from later phases of activities (e.g., coding defects) could not have been injected into the product yet. Therefore, "defects present at removal operation" may be very different from (less than) "defects found plus defect found later" or "$N + S$." In this regard Dunn's (1987) view on the fine tuning of the metric is to the point. Also, Motorola's PCE_i could be quite different from others. In the next section we take a closer look at this metric.

6.2 A Closer Look at Defect Removal Effectiveness

To define defect removal effectiveness clearly, we must first understand the activities in the development process that are related to defect injections and to removals. Defects are injected into the product or intermediate deliverables of the product (e.g., design document) at various phases. It is wrong to assume that all defects of software are injected at the beginning of development. Table 6.1 shows an example of the activities in which defects can be injected or removed for a development process.

For the development phases before testing, the development activities themselves are subject to defect injection, and the reviews or inspections at end-of-phase activities are the key vehicles for defect removal. For the testing phases, the testing itself is for defect removal. When the problems found by testing are fixed incorrectly, there is another chance to inject defects. In fact, even for the inspection steps, there are chances for bad fixes. Figure 6.3 describes the detailed mechanics of defect injection and removal at each step of the development process. From the figure, defect removal effectiveness for each development step, therefore, can be defined as:

$$\frac{\text{Defects removed (at the step)}}{\text{Defects existing on step entry} + \text{Defects injected during development (of the step)}} \times 100\%$$

TABLE 6.1
Activities Associated with Defect Injection and Removal

Development Phase	Defect Injection	Defect Removal
Requirements	Requirements-gathering process and the development of programming functional specifications	Requirement analysis and review
High-level design	Design work	High-level design inspections
Low-level design	Design work	Low-level design inspections
Code implementation	Coding	Code inspections
Integration/build	Integration and build process	Build verification testing
Unit test	Bad fixes	Testing itself
Component test	Bad fixes	Testing itself
System test	Bad fixes	Testing itself

This is the conceptual definition. Note that defects removed is equal to defects detected minus incorrect repairs. If an ideal data tracking system existed, all elements in Figure 6.3 could be tracked and analyzed. In reality, however, it is extremely difficult to reliably track incorrect repairs. Assuming the percentages of incorrect repair or bad fixes are not high (based on my experience), defects removed can be approximated by defects detected. From experience with the AS/400, about 2% are bad fixes during testing, so this assumption seems reasonable. If the bad-fix percentage is high, one may want to adjust the effectiveness metric accordingly, if an estimate is available.

To derive an operational definition, we propose a matrix approach by cross-classifying defect data in terms of the development phase in which the defects are found (and removed) and the phases in which the defects are injected. This requires that for each defect found, its origin (the phase where it was introduced) be decided

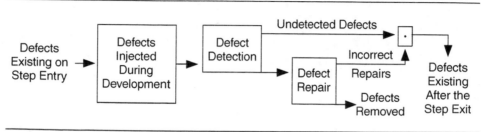

FIGURE 6.3
Defect Injection and Removal During One Process Step

Defect Origin

	Require-ments	High-Level Design	Low-Level Design	Code	Unit Test	Com-ponent Test	System Test	Field	Total
RQ	—								—
I0	49	681							730
I1	6	42	681						729
I2	12	28	114	941					1095
UT	21	43	43	223	2				332
CT	20	41	61	261	—	4			387
ST	6	8	24	72	—	—	1		111
Field	8	16	16	40	—	—	—	1	81
Total	122	859	939	1537	2	4	1	1	3465

(left axis label: Where Found)

FIGURE 6.4
Defect Data Cross-Tabulated by Where Found (Phase During Which Defect Was Found) and Defect Origin

by the inspection group (for inspection defects) or by agreement between the tester and the developer (for testing defects). Let us look at the example in Figure 6.4.

Once the defect matrix is established, calculations of various effectiveness measures are straightforward. The matrix is triangular because the origin of a defect is always at or prior to the current phase. In this example, there were no formal requirements inspections so we are not able to assess the effectiveness of the requirements phase. But in the requirements phase, defects can be injected that can be found later in the development cycle. Therefore, the requirements phase also appears in the matrix as one of the defect origins. The diagonal values for the testing phases represent the number of bad fixes. In this example all bad fixes are detected and fixed, again correctly, within the same phase. In some cases, however, bad fixes may go undetected until subsequent phases.

Based on the conceptual definition given earlier, we calculate the various effectiveness metrics as follows.

High-Level Design Inspection Effectiveness; IE (I0)

Defects removed at I0: 730

Defects existing on step entry (escapes from requirements phase): 122

Defects injected in current phase: 859

$$IE~(I0) = \frac{730}{122 + 859} \times 100\% = 74\%$$

Low-Level Design Inspection Effectiveness; IE (I1)

Defects removed at I1: 729

Defects existing on step entry (escapes from requirements phase and I0):
$122 + 859 - 730 = 251$

Defects injected in current phase: 939

$$IE~(I1) = \frac{729}{251 + 939} \times 100\% = 61\%$$

Code Inspection Effectiveness; IE (I2)

Defects removed at I1: 1095

Defects existing on step entry (escapes from requirements phase, I0 and I1):
$122 + 859 + 939 - 730 - 729 = 461$

Defects injected in current phase: 1537

$$IE~(I2) = \frac{1095}{461 + 1537} \times 100\% = 55\%$$

Unit Test Effectiveness; TE (UT)

Defects removed at I1: 332

Defects existing on step entry (escapes from all previous phases):
$122 + 859 + 939 + 1537 - 730 - 729 - 1095 = 903$

Defects injected in current phase (bad fixes): 2

$$TE~(UT) = \frac{332}{903 + 2} \times 100\% = \frac{332}{905} \times 100\% = 37\%$$

For the testing phases, the defect injection (bad fixes) is usually a small number. In such cases, effectiveness can be calculated by an alternative method (Dunn's formula or Jones's second formula as discussed earlier). In cases with a high bad-fixes rate, the original method should be used.

Effectiveness =

$$\frac{\text{Defects removed at current phase}}{\text{Defects removed at current phase} + \text{Defects removed at subsequent phases}} \times 100\%$$

$$\text{TE (UT)} = \frac{332}{332 + 387 + 111 + 81} \times 100\% = \frac{332}{911} \times 100\% = 36\%$$

Component Test Effectiveness; TE (CT)

$$\text{TE (CT)} = \frac{387}{387 + 111 + 81} \times 100\% = 67\%$$

System Test Effectiveness; TE (ST)

$$\text{TE (ST)} = \frac{111}{111 + 81} \times 100\% = 58\%$$

Overall Inspection Effectiveness; IE

$$\text{IE} = \frac{730 + 729 + 1095}{122 + 859 + 939 + 1537} \times 100\% = \frac{2554}{3457} \times 100\% = 74\%$$

or

$$\text{IE} = \frac{\text{Defects removed by inspections}}{\text{All defects}} \times 100\% = \frac{730 + 729 + 1095}{3465} \times 100\% = 74\%$$

Overall Test Effectiveness; TE

$$\text{TE} = \frac{332 + 387 + 111}{332 + 387 + 111 + 81} \times 100\% = 91\%$$

Overall Defect Removal Effectiveness of the Process; DRE

$$\text{DRE} = \left(1 - \frac{81}{3465}\right) \times 100\% = 97.7\%$$

To summarize, the values of defect removal effectiveness from this example are as follows:

I0: 74%

I1: 61%

I2: 55%

Overall Inspection Defect Removal Effectiveness: 74%

UT: 36%

CT: 67%

ST: 58%

Overall Test Defect Removal Effectiveness: 91%

Overall Defect Removal Effectiveness of the Process: 97.7%

From the matrix of Figure 6.4 it is easy to understand that the PCE_i used by Motorola is somewhat different from phase defect removal effectiveness. PCE_i refers to the ability of the phase inspection to remove defects introduced during a particular phase, whereas phase defect removal effectiveness as discussed here refers to the overall ability of the phase inspection to remove defects that were present at that time. The latter includes the defects introduced at that particular phase as well as defects that escaped from previous phases. Therefore, the phase containment effectiveness (PCE) values will be higher than the defect removal effectiveness values based on the same data. The PCE_i values of our example are as follows.

I0: 681/859 = 79%

I1: 681/939 = 73%

I2: 941/1537 = 61%

UT: 2/2 = 100%

CT: 4/4 = 100%

ST: 1/1 = 100%

Assume further that the data in Figure 6.4 are the defect data for a new project with 100,000 lines of source code (100 KLOC). Then we can calculate a few more interesting metrics such as the product defect rate, the phase defect removal rates, phase defect injection rates, the percent distribution of defect injection by phase, and phase-to-phase defect escapes. For instance, the product defect rate is 81/100 KLOC = 0.81 defects per KLOC in the field (for four years of customer usage). The phase defect removal and injection rates are shown in Table 6.2.

Having gone through the numerical example, we can now formally state the operational definition of defect removal effectiveness. The definition requires information of all defect data (including field defects) in terms both of defect origin and at which stage the defect is found and removed. The definition is based on the defect origin/where found matrix.

Let $j = 1, 2, \ldots, k$ denote the phases of software life cycle.

Let $i = 1, 2, \ldots, k$ denote the inspection or testing types associated with the life-cycle phases including the maintenance phase (phase k).

TABLE 6.2
Phase Defect Removal and Injection Rates from Figure 6.3

Phase	Defects/KLOC (removal)	Defect Injection per KLOC	Total Defect Injection (%)
Requirements	—	1.2	3.5
High-level design	7.3	8.6	24.9
Low-level design	7.3	9.4	27.2
Code	11.0	15.4	44.5
Unit test	3.3	—	
Component test	3.9	—	
System test	1.1	—	
Total	33.9	34.6	100.1

Then matrix M (Figure 6.5) is the defect origin/where found matrix. In the matrix, only cells N_{ij}, where $i \geq j$ (cells at the lower left triangle), contain data. Cells on the diagonal (N_{ij} where $i = j$) contain the numbers of defects that were injected and detected at the same phase; cells below the diagonal (N_{ij} where $i > j$) contain the numbers of defects that originated in earlier development phases and were detected later. Cells above the diagonal are empty because it is not possible for an earlier development phase to detect defects that are originated in a later phase. The row marginals ($N_{i.}$) of the matrix are defects by removal activity, and the column marginals ($N_{.j}$) are defects by origin.

Phase defect removal effectiveness (PDRE$_i$) can be phase inspection effectiveness [IE(i)] or phase test effectiveness [TE(i)]

$$\text{PDE}_i = \frac{N_{i.}}{\sum_{m=1}^{i} N_{.m} - \sum_{m=1}^{i-1} N_{m.}}$$

Phase defect containment effectiveness (PDCE$_i$)

$$\text{PDCE}_i = \frac{N_{ii}}{N_{.i}}$$

Overall inspection effectiveness (IE)

$$\text{IE} = \frac{\sum_{i=1}^{i} N_{i.}}{\sum_{i=1}^{k} N_{i.} = N}$$

Where Found \ Defect Origin	$j=1$	$j=2$	$j=3$	*	*	*	*	$j=k$	
$i=1$	N_{11}								$N_1.$
$i=2$	*	N_{22}							$N_2.$
$i=3$	*	*	N_{33}						$N_3.$
*	*	*	*	*					.
*	N_{ij} $(i>=j)$	*	*	*	*				$Ni.$
*	*	*	*	*	*	N_{ij} $(i=j)$			.
*	*	*	*	*	*	*	*		.
$i=k$	*	*	*	*	*	*	*	N_{kk}	$N_K.$
	$N*1$	$N*2$	$N*3$	*	*	$N*j$	*	$N*k$	N-Grand Total

FIGURE 6.5
Defect Origin/Where Found Matrix—Matrix M

where I is the number of inspection phases.

Overall test effectiveness (TE)

$$\text{TE} = \frac{\sum_{i=I+1}^{k-1} N_{i.}}{\sum_{i=I+1}^{k} N_{i.}}$$

where $I+1, I+2, \ldots, k-1$ are the testing phases.

Overall defect removal effectiveness (DRE) of the development process:

$$\text{DRE} = \frac{\sum_{i=1}^{k-1} N_{i.}}{N}$$

6.3 Defect Removal Effectiveness and Quality Planning

Phase defect removal effectiveness and related metrics associated with effectiveness analyses (such as defect removal and defect injection rates) are useful for quality planning and quality management. These measurements clearly indicate which phase of the development process we should focus on for improvement (e.g., unit testing in our example in Figure 6.4). Effectiveness analyses can be done for the entire project as well as for local areas, such as at the component level and specific departments in an organization, and the control chart technique can be used to enforce consistent improvement across the board (e.g., Figure 5.14 in Chapter 5). Longitudinal release-to-release monitoring of these metrics can give a good feel for the process capability of the development organization. In addition, experiences from previous releases provide the basis for phase-specific target setting and for quality planning.

6.3.1 Phase-Based Defect Removal Model

The phase-based defect removal model (DRM) summarizes the relationships among three metrics—defect injection, defect removal, and effectiveness. The DRM takes a set of error-injection rates and a set of phase-effectiveness rates as input, then models the defect removal pattern step by step. It takes a simplified view of Figure 6.3 and works like this:

Defects at exit of a development step = Defects escaped from previous step
+ Defects injected in current step
− Defects removed in current step

For example, the metrics derived from data in Figure 6.4 can be modeled step by step as shown in Table 6.3.

Now if we are planning for the quality of a new release, we can modify the values of the parameters based on the set of improvement actions that we are going to take. If we plan to improve the effectiveness of I2 and unit tests by 5%, how much can we expect to gain in the final product quality? What are the new targets for defect rates for each phase (before the development team exits the phase)? If we invest in a defect prevention process and in an intensive program of technical education and plan to reduce the error injection rate by 10%, how much could we gain? Approximate answers to questions like these could be obtained through the DRM, given that the DRM is developed from the organization's experience with similar development processes.

Be aware that the DRM is a quality management tool, not a device for software reliability estimation. Unlike the other parametric models that we will discuss in later chapters, the DRM cannot reliably estimate the product quality level. It cannot do so

ample of Phase-Based Defect Removal Model

se	(A) Defect Escaped from Previous Phase (per KLOC)	(B) Defect Injection (per KLOC)	Subtotal (A+B)	Removal Effectiveness	Defect Removal (per KLOC)	Defects at Exit of Phase (per KLOC)
quirements	—	1.2	1.2	—	—	1.2
h-level design	1.2	8.6	9.82	× 74%	= 7.3	2.5
v-level design	2.5	9.4	11.9	× 61%	= 7.3	4.6
le	4.6	15.4	20.0	× 55%	= 11.0	9.0
test	9.0	—	9.0	× 36%	= 3.2	5.8
nponent test	5.8	—	5.8	× 67%	= 3.9	1.9
tem test	1.9	—	1.9	× 58%	= 1.1	0.8
d	0.8					

because the error injection rates may vary from case to case even for the same development team. The rationale behind this model is that if one can ensure that the defect removal pattern by phase is similar to one's experience, one can reasonably expect that the quality of the current project will be similar.

6.3.2 Some Characteristics of a Special Case Two-Phase Model

Remus and Zilles (1979) elaborate the mathematical relationships of defect removal effectiveness, the number of defects found during the front end of the development process (before the code is integrated), the number found during testing, and the number remaining when the product is ready to ship to customers. They derived some interesting characteristics of the defect removal model in a special case:

1. There are only two phases of defect removal.
2. The defect removal effectiveness for the two phases is the same.

The percentage of bad fixes is one of the parameters in the Remus and Zilles model; the derivation involves more than twenty formulas. Here we take a simplified approach without taking bad fixes into account. Interestingly, despite taking a different approach, we arrive at the same conclusion as Remus and Zilles did.

Assume there are two broad phases of defect removal activities:

1. Those activities handled directly by the development team (design reviews, code inspections, unit test) for large software projects take place before the code is integrated into the system library.
2. The formal machine tests after code integration.

Further assume that the defect removal effectiveness of the two broad phases is the same. Define:

MP = Major problems found during reviews/inspections and unit testing (from phase 1); these are the problems that if not fixed, will result in testing defects or defects in the field.

PTR = Problem tracking report after code integration: errors found during formal machine tests.

μ = MP/PTR, $\mu > 1$ (*Note:* The higher the value of μ, the more effective the front end.)

Q = Number of defects in the released software—defects found in the field (customer usage).

TD = Total defects for the life of the software = MP + PTR + Q.

By definition of effectiveness:

$$\text{Phase 1 effectiveness E1} = \frac{MP}{TD}$$

$$\text{therefore}: MP = E1 \times TD \quad (6.1)$$

$$\text{Phase 2 effectiveness E2} = \frac{PTR}{TD - MP}$$

$$\text{therefore}: PTR = E2 \times (TD - MP) \quad (6.2)$$

By the assumption that the two phases have the same effectiveness:

$$E1 = E2$$

$$\frac{MP}{TD} = \frac{PTR}{TD - MP}$$

Thus,

$$PTR = \frac{(TD - MP) \times MP}{TD} \quad (6.3)$$

Then,

$$Q = TD\,(1 - E1)\,(1 - E2)$$

$$= TD\,(1 - E1)^2$$

$$= TD\left(1 - \frac{MP}{TD}\right)^2$$

$$= \frac{TD^2 - 2\,TD\,MP + MP^2}{TD}$$

$$= (TD - MP)\frac{(TD - MP)}{TD}$$

$$= (TD - MP)\frac{(TD - MP) \times MP}{TD} \times \frac{1}{MP}$$

$$= (TD - MP) \times PTR \times \frac{1}{MP} \quad [\text{from Eq. (6.3)}]$$

$$= \frac{1}{\mu} \times (TD - MP)$$

$$= \frac{1}{\mu} \times (Q + MP + PTR - MP)$$

$$= \frac{1}{\mu} \times (Q + PTR)$$

Therefore,

$$Q = \frac{PTR}{\mu - 1} \quad (6.4)$$

By the same token, it can be shown that:

$$Q = \frac{MP}{\mu(\mu - 1)} \quad (6.5)$$

Furthermore, from the definition of μ:

$$\mu = \frac{MP}{PTR}$$

$$= \frac{E1 \times TD}{E2 \times (TD - MP)}$$

$$= \frac{TD}{TD - MP} \quad [E1 = E2]$$

$$= \frac{TD}{PTR + Q} \begin{bmatrix} TD = MP + PTR + Q \\ TD - MP = PTR + Q \end{bmatrix}$$

$$\mu(PTR + Q) = TD$$

$$\mu(Q\mu - Q + Q) = TD \quad [\text{from Eq. (6.4)}, \ PTR = Qu - Q]$$

Therefore,

$$Q = TD/\mu^2 \quad (6.6)$$

Equations (6.4) through (6.6) can be useful for quality planning. The equations can be applied to absolute numbers as well as to normalized rates (e.g., defects per KLOC). Given the number of MP and μ, or PTR and μ, one can estimate the number of defects that remained in the product by Equations (6.4) and (6.5). Also, assuming we use the lifetime defect rate (TD) of a predecessor product to approximate the TD of the product being developed, given a target product quality level to shoot for, Equation (6.6) can determine the value of μ that we need to achieve in order to reach the target. Choosing a specific value of μ determines how much focus a project should have on front-end defect removal. Once the μ target is set, the team can determine the defect removal techniques to use (e.g., formal inspection, function verification by owner, team verifications, rigorous unit testing, etc.). For example, if we use the data from the example of Figure 6.4 (TD = 34.6 defects/KLOC, $Q = 0.81$ defects/KLOC for life of customer use), then the value of μ should be:

$$0.81 = 34.6/\mu^2$$
$$\mu^2 = 34.6/0.81 = 42.7$$
$$\mu = 6.5$$

This means that if the effectiveness is the same for the two phases, then the number of defects to be removed by the first phase must be at least 6.5 times of the number to be removed by testing in order to achieve the quality target. Note that the equations described in this section are valid only under the assumptions stated. They cannot be generalized. Although Equations (6.4) and (6.5) can be used to estimate product quality, this special case DRM is still not a projection model. The equal effectiveness assumption cannot be verified until the product defect rate Q is known or estimated via an independent method. If this assumption is violated, the results will not be valid.

6.4 Cost Effectiveness of Phase Defect Removal

In addition to the defect removal effectiveness by phase per se, the cost of defect removal must be considered for efficient quality planning. Defect removal at earlier development phases is generally less expensive. The closer the defects are found relative to where and when they are injected, the less the removal and rework effort. Fagan (1976) contends that rework done at the I0, I1, and I2 inspection levels can be 10 to 100 times less expensive than if work done in the last half of the process (formal testing phases after code integration). According to Freedman and Weinberg (1982, 1984), in large systems, reviews can reduce the number of errors that reach the testing phases by a factor of 10, and such reductions cut testing costs, including review costs, by 50% to 80%. Remus (1983) studied the cost of defect removal during the three major life-cycle phases of design and code inspection, testing, and customer use (maintenance phase) based on data from IBM's Santa Teresa (California) Laboratory. He found the cost ratio for the three phases to be 1 to 20 to 82.

Based on sample data from IBM Rochester, we found the defect removal ratio for the three phases for the AS/400 similar to Remus's, at 1 to 13 to 92. *Caution:* These numbers may not be interpreted straightforwardly because defects that escaped to the later testing phases and to the field are more difficult to find. When we invest and improve the front end of the development process to prevent these more difficult defects from escaping to the testing phases and to the field, the ratios may decrease. Nonetheless, as long as the marginal costs of additional front-end defect removal remains less than testing and field maintenance, additional investment in the front end is warranted.

Our sample study also revealed interesting but understandable findings. The cost of defect removal is slightly higher for I0 inspection than for I1 and I2 (Figure 6.6). The main reason for this is that external interfaces are being impacted and more personnel are involved in the I0 inspection meetings. The cost for creating and answering a problem trouble report during testing (i.e., problem determination cost) is correlated with the testing phase, defect origin, and defect severity (1 being the most severe and 4 the least) (Figure 6.7).

In his work on software inspection, Gilb (1993, 1999) conducted thorough analysis with ample data. The findings corroborate with those discussed here and

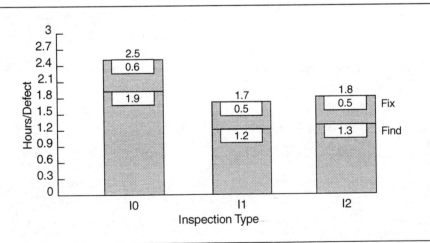

FIGURE 6.6
Cost of Defect Removal by Inspection Phase

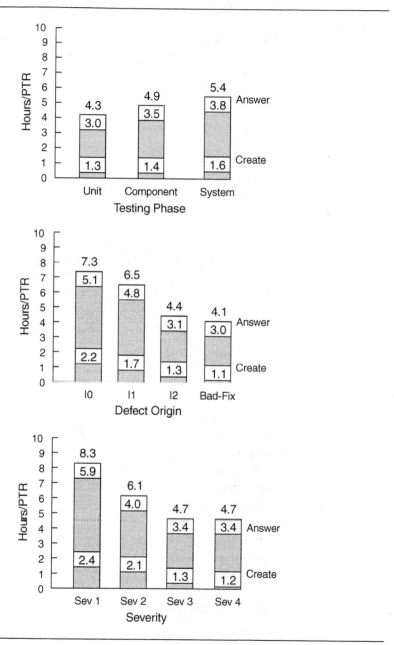

FIGURE 6.7
Cost of Creating and Answering a Problem Trouble Report by Several Variables

support the general argument that software inspection not only improves the quality of the product, but also is beneficial to the economics of the project and the organization.

Although front-end defect removal activities in the form of reviews, walk-throughs, and inspections are less expensive than testing, in general practice, these methods are not rigorous enough. Fagan's inspection method is a combination of a formal review, an inspection, and a walkthrough. It consists of five steps:

1. overview (for communications and education)
2. preparation (for education)
3. inspection (to find errors and to walk through every line of code)
4. rework (to fix errors), and
5. follow-up (to ensure all fixes are applied correctly)

Such a combination has made Fagan's method somewhat more formal and there-fore more effective than earlier methods. The Active Design Reviews method, intro-duced by Parnas and Weiss (1985), represents an important advance. The approach involves conducting several brief reviews rather than one large review, thereby avoid-ing many of the difficulties of conventional reviews. Knight and Myers (1991) pro-posed the phased inspection method to improve the rigor of the process. It consists of a series of coordinated partial inspections called phases (therefore, the term is used differently). Each phase is designed to achieve a desirable property in the product (e.g., portability, reusability, or maintainability), and the responsibilities of each inspector are specified and tracked.

Knight and Myers defined two types of phase. The first type, referred to as a *single-inspector phase,* is a rigidly formatted process driven by a list of unambiguous checks, for examples, internal documentation, source code layout, source code read-ability, programming practices, and local semantics. The second type of phase, designed to check for those properties of the software that cannot be captured in a precise yes or no statement (such as functionality and freedom from defects), is called the *multi-inspector phase.* Multiple personnel conduct independent examina-tions and then compare findings to reach reconciliation. To facilitate and enforce the process, the phased inspection method also involves use of an online computer tool. The tool contains navigation facilities for displaying the work product, documenta-tion display facilities, facilities for the inspector to record comments, and facilities to enforce the inspection process.

Advances such as the preceding offer organizations much promise for improving the front-end defect removal effectiveness. Beyond reviews and inspections, one can even adopt formal methods such as the Cleanroom functional verification (as dis-cussed in Chapter 2).

6.5 Defect Removal Effectiveness and Process Maturity Level

Based on a special study commissioned by the Department of Defense, Jones (Software Productivity Research, 1994; Jones, 2000) estimates the defect removal effectiveness for organizations at different levels of the development process capability maturity model (CMM):

- ☐ Level 1: 85%
- ☐ Level 2: 89%
- ☐ Level 3: 91%
- ☐ Level 4: 93%
- ☐ Level 5: 95%

These values can be used as comparison baselines for organizations to evaluate their relative capability with regard to this important parameter.

In a discussion on quantitative process management (a process area for Capability Maturity Model Integration, CMMI, level 4) and process capability baselines, Curtis (2002) shows the estimated baselines for defect removal effectiveness by phase of defect insertion (or defect origin in our terminology). The cumulative percentages of defects removed up through acceptance test (the last phase before the product is shipped) by phase insertion, for CMMI level 4, are shown in Table 6.4. Based on historical and recent data from three software engineering organizations at General Dynamics Decision Systems, Diaz and King (2002) report the phase containment effectiveness by CMM level as follows:

- ☐ Level 2: 25.5%
- ☐ Level 3: 41.5%
- ☐ Level 4: 62.3%
- ☐ Level 5: 87.3%

TABLE 6.4

Cumulative Percentages of Defects Removed by Phase for CMMI Level 4

Phase Inserted	Cumulative % of Defects Removed Through Acceptance Test
Requirements	94%
Top-level design	95%
Detailed design	96%
Code and unit test	94%
Integration test	75%
System test	70%
Acceptance test	70%

It is not clear how many key phases are there in the development process for these projects and the extent of variations in containment effectiveness across phases. It appears that these statistics represent the average effectiveness for peer reviews and testing for a number of projects at each maturity level. Therefore, these statistics perhaps could be roughly interpreted as overall inspection effectiveness or overall test effectiveness.

According to Jones (2000), in general, most forms of testing are less than 30% efficient. The cumulative efficiency of a sequence of test stages, however, can top 80%.

These findings demonstrate a certain level of consistency among each other and with the example in Figure 6.4. The Figure 6.4 example is based on a real-life project. There was no process maturity assessment conducted for the project but the process was mature and quantitatively managed. Based on the key process practices and the excellent field quality results, the project should be at level 4 or level 5 of a process maturity scale.

More empirical studies and findings on this subject will surely produce useful knowledge. For example, test effectiveness and inspection effectiveness by process

---

Recommendations for Small Organizations

Defect removal effectiveness is a direct indicator of the capability of a software development process in removing defects before the software is shipped. It is one of few, perhaps the only, process indicators that bear a direct correlation with the quality of the software's field performance. In this chapter we examine several aspects of defect removal effectiveness including (1) overall effectiveness, (2) inspection effectiveness, (3) test effectiveness, (4) phase-specific effectiveness, and (5) the role of defect removal effectiveness in quality planning. For small organizations starting a metrics program with constrained resources, I recommend the following approach:

1. Start with the overall defect removal effectiveness indicator and the test effectiveness indicator.

2. Assess the stability or variations of these indicators across projects and implement systematic actions to improve them.

3. Compare with industry baselines (such as those discussed in section 6.5) to determine the organization's process maturity level with regard to this parameter. Because defect removal effectiveness is a relative percentage measure, comparisons across teams and organizations are possible.

4. Also start to examine inspection effectiveness, and loop back to step 2 for continuous improvement.

5. If a tracking system is established, then gather data about defect origins (in addition to where defects were found) and start implementing phase-specific effectiveness metrics to guide specific improvements.

The combination of where-found and defect-origin data is useful for many occasions, not just for phase effectiveness calculation. For example, defect cause analysis including phase origin during the testing phase of the project often provides

maturity, characteristics of distributions at each maturity level, and variations across the type of software are all areas for which reliable benchmark baselines are needed.

6.6 Summary

Effective defect removal during the development process is central to the success of a software project. Despite the variations in terms of terminology and operational definitions (error detection efficiency, removal efficiency, early detection percentage, phase defect removal effectiveness, phase defect containment effectiveness, etc.), the importance of the concept of defect removal effectiveness and its measurements is well recognized. Literature and industry examples substantiate the hypothesis that effective front-end defect removal leads to improved quality of the end product. The relative cost of front-end defect removal is much lower than the cost of formal testing at the back end and the maintenance phase when the product is in the field.

To measure phase defect removal effectiveness, it is best to use the matrix approach in which the defect data are cross-tabulated in terms of defect origin and the phase in which the defects are found. Such an approach permits the estimation of

clues for further actions before shipping the product. However, tracking both where-found and phase-origin data for all defects does require additional resources.

If resources are constrained and data tracking for the front-end of the process (e.g., requirements, design reviews, and code inspections) is not available, then use the test effectiveness metric. But in terms of improvement actions, a focus on the entire development process is important and strongly recommended. Indeed, even for organizations with more mature metrics programs, tracking and data for the front-end of the development process normally are less rigorous than the testing phases. For small organizations starting a metrics program with minimum resources and with the intent to keep the number of metrics to the minimum, using the test effectiveness indicator for measurement while maintaining the overall process focus on requirements, design, coding, and testing is a good strategy. With or without metrics, the importance of a strong focus on requirements, designs, and reviews can never be overstated. Good requirements-gathering and analysis techniques can reduce the volume of requirements changes and secondary requirements significantly.

Good design and programming practices with effective defect prevention and removal are crucial for the stability and predictability of the back end of the development process. Projects that bypass design and code inspections may seem to be ahead of schedule—until testing begins. When testing begins, a deluge of unexpected errors could bring the project to a standstill, and the development team can get locked into a cycle of finding bugs, attempting to fix them, and retesting that can stretch out for months.

phase defect injection and phase defect removal. In general, the shorter the time between defect origin and defect discovery, the more effective and the less expensive the development process will be. The special case of the two-phase defect removal model even provides a link between the relative effectiveness of front-end defect removal and the estimated outcome of the quality of the product.

Based on recent studies, defect removal effectiveness by the level of process maturity has been assessed and comparison baselines have been established. Organizations with established data on their defect removal effectiveness can make comparisons to the baselines and assess their maturity level with regard to this important parameter.

In quality planning it is important that, in addition to the final quality goals, factors such as the defect model, the phase defect removal targets, the process and specific methods used, the possible effectiveness of the methods, and so forth be examined. Inclusion of these factors in early planning facilitates achievement of the software's quality goals.

It should be noted that defect removal effectiveness and defect removal models are useful quality planning and management tools. However, they are not equipped for quality or reliability projections; they are not predictive models. In the next several chapters, we discuss the parametric models that were developed to perform such tasks.

References

1. Daskalanatonakis, M. K., "A Practical View of Software Measurement and Implementation Experiences within Motorola," *IEEE Transactions on Software Engineering,* Vol. SE-18, 1992, pp. 998–1010.
2. Dunn, R. H., "The Quest for Software Reliability," *Handbook of Software Quality Assurance,* G. G. Schulmeyer and J. I. McManus, Eds., New York: Van Nostrand Reinhold, 1987, pp. 342–384.
3. Curtis, B., "Quantitative Process Management and Process Capability Baselines," SEPG 2002 QM Tutorial, Phoenix, Arizona, SEPG 2002, February 18–21.
4. Diaz, M., and J. King, "How CMM Impacts Quality, Productivity, Rework, and the Bottom Line," *CrossTalk, The Journal of Defense Software Engineering,* Vol. 15, No. 3, March 2002, pp. 9–14.
5. Fagan, M. E., "Design and Code Inspections to Reduce Errors in Program Development," *IBM Systems Journal,* Vol. 15, No. 3, 1976, pp. 182–211.
6. Freedman, D. P., and G. M. Weinberg, *Handbook of Walkthroughs, Inspections, and Technical Reviews,* Boston, Mass.: Little, Brown and Company, 1982.
7. Freedman, D. P., and G. M. Weinberg, "Reviews, Walkthroughs, and Inspections," *IEEE Transactions on Software Engineering,* Vol. SE-10, No. 1, January 1984, pp. 68–72.
8. Gilb T., and D. Graham, *Software Inspection,* Reading, Mass.: Addison-Wesley, 1993.
9. Gilb, T., "Optimizing Software Engineering Specification Quality Control Processes (Inspections)" SPIN Team Leader Course, Washington, D.C. SPIN Chapter, June 15–18, 1999.

10. Jones, C., *Programming Productivity,* New York: McGraw-Hill, 1986.
11. Jones, C., *Software Assessments, Benchmarks, and Best Practices,* Boston: Addison-Wesley, 2000.
12. Knight, K. C., and E. A. Myers, "Phased Inspections and Their Implementation," *ACM SIGSOFT Software Engineering Notes,* Vol. 16, No. 3, July 1991, pp. 29–35.
13. Kolkhorst, B. G., and A. J. Macina, "Developing Error-Free Software," *IEEE AES Magazine,* November 1988, pp. 25–31.
14. Parnas, D. W., and D. M. Weiss, "Active Design Reviews: Principles and Practices," *Proceedings of Eighth International Conference on Software Engineering,* London, England, IEEE Computer Society, August 1985.
15. Remus, H., "Integrated Software Validation in the View of Inspections/Review," *Proceedings of the Symposium on Software Validation,* Darmstadt, Germany, Amsterdam: North Holland, 1983, pp. 57–64.
16. Remus, H., and S. Zilles, "Prediction and Management of Program Quality," *Proceedings of the Fourth International Conference on Software Engineering,* Munich, IEEE Computer Society, 1979, pp. 341–350.
17. Ryan, J., "This Company Hates Surprises: The IBM Federal Systems Division Leaves No Stone Unturned in Its Quest to Produce Error-Free Software for NASA's Space Shuttle," *Quality Progress,* September 1987, pp. 12–16.
18. Software Productivity Research, Quality and Productivity of the SEI CMM, Burlington, Mass.: *Software Productivity Research,* 1994.

7

The Rayleigh Model

Having discussed defect removal effectiveness and the phase-based defect removal model, this chapter discusses a formal model of software reliability: the Rayleigh model. The Rayleigh model is a parametric model in the sense that it is based on a specific statistical distribution. When the parameters of the statistical distribution are estimated based on the data from a software project, projections about the defect rate of the project can be made based on the model.

7.1 Reliability Models

Software reliability models are used to assess a software product's reliability or to estimate the number of latent defects when it is available to the customers. Such an estimate is important for two reasons: (1) as an objective statement of the quality of the product and (2) for resource planning for the software maintenance phase. The criterion variable under study is the number of defects (or defect rate normalized to lines of code or function points) in specified time intervals (weeks, months, etc.), or the *time between failures*. Reliability models can be broadly classified into two categories: static models and dynamic models (Conte et al., 1986). A static model uses other attributes of the project or program modules to estimate the number of defects in the software. A dynamic model, usually based on statistical distributions, uses the current development defect patterns to estimate end-product reliability. A static model of software quality estimation has the following general form:

$$y = f(x_1, x_2, \ldots, x_k) + e$$

where the dependent variable y is the defect rate or the number of defects, and the independent variables x_i are the attributes of the product, the project, or the process through which the product is developed. They could be size, complexity, skill level, count of decisions, and other meaningful measurements. The error term is e (because models don't completely explain the behavior of the dependent variable).

Estimated coefficients of the independent variables in the formula are based on data from previous products. For the current product or project, the values of the independent variables are measured, then plugged into the formula to derive estimates of the dependent variable—the product defect rate or number of defects.

Static models are static in the sense that the estimated coefficients of their parameters are based on a number of previous projects. The product or project of interest is treated as an additional observation in the same population of previous projects. In contrast, the parameters of the dynamic models are estimated based on multiple data points gathered to date from the product of interest; therefore, the resulting model is specific to the product for which the projection of reliability is attempted.

Observation and experience shows that static models are generally less superior than dynamic models when the unit of analysis is at the product level and the purpose is to estimate product-level reliability. Such modeling is better for hypothesis testing (to show that certain project attributes are related to better quality or reliability) than for estimation of reliability. When the unit of analysis is much more granular, such as at the program module level, the static models can be powerful—not for product-level reliability estimates, but for providing clues to software engineers on how to improve the quality of their design and implementation. The complexity metrics and models are good examples of this type of modeling, and in Chapter 11 we discuss this topic in more detail.

Dynamic software reliability models, in turn, can be classified into two categories: those that model the entire development process and those that model the back-end testing phase. The former is represented by the Rayleigh model. The latter is represented by the exponential model and other reliability growth models, which are the subject of Chapter 8. A common denominator of dynamic models is that they are expressed as a function of time in development or its logical equivalent (such as development phase).

7.2 The Rayleigh Model

The Rayleigh model is a member of the family of the Weibull distribution. The Weibull distribution has been used for decades in various fields of engineering for reliability analysis, ranging from the fatigue life of deep-groove ball bearings to electron tube failures and the overflow incidence of rivers. It is one of the three known extreme-value distributions (Tobias, 1986). One of its marked characteristics is that the tail of its probability density function approaches zero asymptotically, but never reaches it. Its cumulative distribution function (CDF) and probability density function (PDF) are:

$$\text{CDF}: \; F(t) = 1 - e^{-(t/c)^m}$$

$$\text{PDF}: \; f(t) = \frac{m}{t}\left(\frac{t}{c}\right)^m e^{(t/c)^m}$$

where m is the shape parameter, c is the scale parameter, and t is time. When applied to software, the PDF often means the defect density (rate) over time or the defect arrival pattern and the CDF means the cumulative defect arrival pattern.

Figure 7.1 shows several Weibull probability density curves with varying values for the shape parameter m. For reliability applications in an engineering field, the choice of a specific model is not arbitrary. The underlying assumptions must be considered and the model must be supported by empirical data. Of the Weibull family, the two models that have been applied in software reliability are the models with the shape parameter value $m = 2$ and $m = 1$.

The Rayleigh model is a special case of the Weibull distribution when $m = 2$. Its CDF and PDF are:

$$\text{CDF}: \; F(t) = 1 - e^{-(t/c)^2}$$

$$\text{PDF}: \; f(t) = \frac{2}{t}\left(\frac{t}{c}\right)^2 e^{-(t/c)^2}$$

The Rayleigh PDF first increases to a peak and then decreases at a decelerating rate. The c parameter is a function of t_m, the time at which the curve reaches its peak. By taking the derivative of $f(t)$ with respect to t, setting it to zero and solving the equation, t_m can be obtained.

$$t_m = \frac{c}{\sqrt{2}}$$

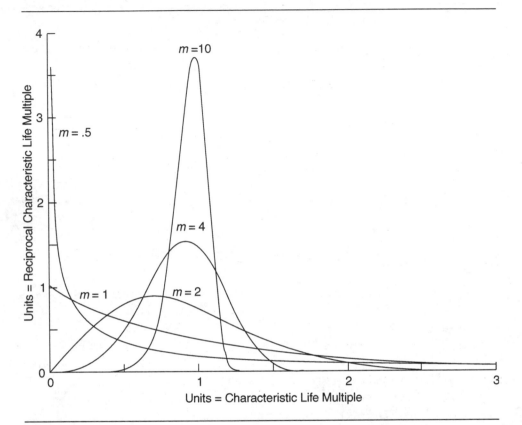

FIGURE 7.1
Weibull Probability Density

After t_m is estimated, the shape of the entire curve can be determined. The area below the curve up to t_m is 39.35% of the total area.

The preceding formulas represent a standard distribution; specifically the total area under the PDF curve is 1. In actual applications, a constant K is multiplied to the formulas (K is the total number of defects or the total cumulative defect rate). If we also substitute

$$c = t_m \sqrt{2}$$

in the formulas, we get the following. To specify a model from a set of data points, K and t_m are the parameters that need to be estimated.

$$F(t) = K\left[1 - e^{-(1/2t^2_m)t^2}\right]$$

$$f(t) = K\left[\left(\frac{1}{t_m}\right)^2 t\, e^{-(1/2t^2_m)t^2}\right]$$

It has been empirically well established that software projects follow a life-cycle pattern described by the Rayleigh density curve (Norden, 1963; Putnam, 1978). Early applications of the model in software were mainly for staffing estimation over time for the life cycle of software projects. More recent work demonstrated that the defect removal pattern of software projects also follows the Rayleigh pattern.

In 1982 Trachtenberg (1982) examined the month-by-month error histories of software projects and found that the composite error pattern of those projects resembled a Rayleigh-like curve. In 1984 Gaffney of the IBM Federal Systems Division reported the development of a model based on defect counts at six phases of the development process commonly used in IBM: high-level design inspections, low-level design inspections, code inspections, unit test, integration test, and system test. Gaffney observed that the defect pattern of his data by the six-phase development process followed a Rayleigh curve. Following the system test phase is the phase of field use (customer use). The number of latent defects in the field is the target for estimation.

By developing a Rayleigh model to fit his data, Gaffney was able to project the expected latent defects in the field. Putnam's work includes the application of the Rayleigh model in estimating the number of software defects, in addition to his well-known work on software size and resource estimation (Putnam and Myers, 1992). By validating the model with systems for which defect data are available (including the space shuttle development and radar development projects), Putnam and Myers (1992) found that the total actual defects were within 5% to 10% of the defects predicted from the model. Data fits of a few other systems, for which the validity of the data is doubtful, however, were not so good. As in Trachtenberg's study, the time unit for the Rayleigh model in Putnam and Myers's application is expressed in terms of months from the project start.

Figure 7.2 shows a Rayleigh curve that models the defect removal pattern of an IBM AS/400 product in relation to a six-step development process, which is very similar to that used by Gaffney. Given the defect removal pattern up through system test (ST), the purpose is to estimate the defect rate when the product is shipped: the post general-availability phase (GA) in the figure. In this example the X-axis is the development phase, which can be regarded as one form of logical equivalent of time. The phases other than ST and GA in the figure are: high-level design review (I0), low-level design review (I1), code inspection (I2), unit test (UT), and component test (CT).

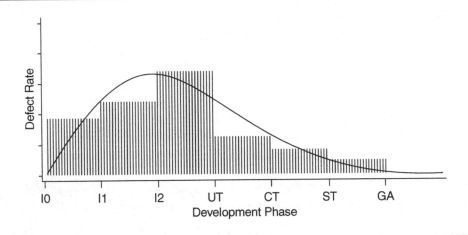

FIGURE 7.2
Rayleigh Model

7.3 Basic Assumptions

Using the Rayleigh curve to model software development quality involves two basic assumptions. The first assumption is that the defect rate observed during the development process is positively correlated with the defect rate in the field, as illustrated in Figure 7.3. In other words, the higher the curve (more area under it), the higher the field defect rate (the GA phase in the figure), and vice versa. This is related to the concept of error injection. Assuming the defect removal effectiveness remains relatively unchanged, the higher defect rates observed during the development process are indicative of higher error injection; therefore, it is likely that the field defect rate will also be higher.

The second assumption is that given the same error injection rate, if more defects are discovered and removed earlier, fewer will remain in later stages. As a result, the field quality will be better. This relationship is illustrated in Figure 7.4, in which the areas under the curves are the same but the curves peak at varying points. Curves that peak earlier have smaller areas at the tail, the GA phase.

Both assumptions are closely related to the "Do it right the first time" principle. This principle means that if each step of the development process is executed properly with minimum errors, the end product's quality will be good. It also implies that if errors are injected, they should be removed as early as possible, preferably before the formal testing phases when the costs of finding and fixing the defects are much higher than that at the front end.

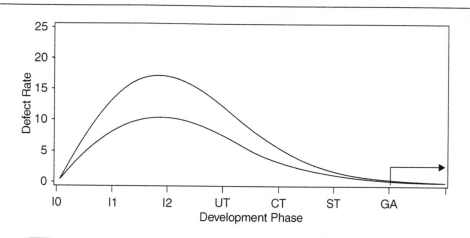

FIGURE 7.3
Rayleigh Model Illustration I

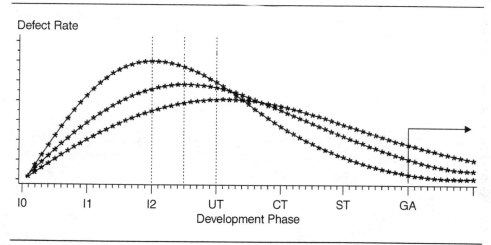

FIGURE 7.4
Rayleigh Model Illustration II

To formally examine the assumptions, we conducted a hypothesis-testing study based on component data for an AS/400 product. A *component* is a group of modules that perform specific functions such as spooling, printing, message handling, file handling, and so forth. The product we used had 65 components, so we had a good-sized sample. Defect data at high-level design inspection (I0), low-level design inspection (I1), code inspection (I2), component test (CT), system test (ST), and operation (customer usage) were available. For the first assumption, we expect significant positive correlations between the in-process defect rates and the field defect rate. Because software data sets are rarely normally distributed, robust statistics need to be used. In our case, because the component defect rates fluctuated widely, we decided to use Spearman's rank-order correlation. We could not use the Pearson correlation because correlation analysis based on interval data, and regression analysis for that matter, is very sensitive to extreme values, which may lead to misleading results.

Table 7.1 shows the Spearman rank-order correlation coefficients between the defect rates of the development phases and the field defect rate. Significant correlations are observed for I2, CT, ST, and all phases combined (I0, I1, I2, CT, and ST). For I0 and I1 the correlations are not significant. This finding is not surprising because (1) I0 and I1 are the earliest development phases and (2) in terms of the defect removal pattern, the Rayleigh curve peaks after I1.

Overall, the findings shown in Table 7.1 strongly substantiate the first assumption of the Rayleigh model. The significance of these findings should be emphasized because they are based on component-level data. For any type of analysis, the more granular the unit of analysis, the less chance it will obtain statistical significance. At the product or system level, our experience with the AS/400 strongly supports this assumption. As another case in point, the space shuttle software system developed by IBM Houston has achieved a minimal defect rate (the onboard software is even defect free). The defect rate observed during the IBM Houston development process (about 12 to 18 defects per KLOC), not coincidentally, is much lower than the industry average (about 40 to 60 defects per KLOC).

To test the hypothesis with regard to the second assumption of the Rayleigh model, we have to control for the effects of variations in error injection. Because error injection varies among components, cross-sectional data are not suitable for the task. Longitudinal data are better, but what is needed is a good controlled experi-

TABLE 7.1
Spearman Rank Order Correlations

Phase	Rank-Order Correlation	n	Significance Level
I0	.11	65	Not significant
I1	.01	65	Not significant
I2	.28	65	.02
CT	.48	65	.0001
ST	.49	65	.0001
All (I0, I1, I2, CT, ST)	.31	65	.01

ment. Our experience indicates that even developing different functions by the same team in different releases may be prone to different degrees of error. This is especially the case if one release is for a major-function development and the other release is for small enhancements.

In a controlled experiment situation, a pool of developers with similar skills and experiences must be selected and then randomly assigned to two groups, the experiment group and the control group. Separately the two groups develop the same functions at time 1 using the same development process and method. At time 2, the two groups develop another set of functions, again separately and again with the same functions for both groups. At time 2, however, the experiment group intentionally does much more front-end defect removal and the control group uses the same method as at time 1. Moreover, the functions at time 1 and time 2 are similar in terms of complexity and difficulty. If the testing defect rate and field defect rate of the project by the experiment group at time 2 are clearly lower than that at time 1 after taking into account the effect of time (which is reflected by the defect rates of the control groups at the two times), then the second assumption of the Rayleigh model is substantiated.

Without data from a controlled experiment, we can look at the second assumption from a somewhat relaxed standard. In this regard, IBM Houston's data again lend strong support for this assumption. As discussed in Chapter 6, for software releases by IBM Houston for the space shuttle software system from November 1982 to December 1986, the early detection percentages increased from about 50% to more than 85%. Correspondingly, the product defect rates decreased monotonically by about 70% (see Figures 6.1 and 6.2 in Chapter 6). Although the error injection rates also decreased moderately, the effect of early defect removal is evident.

7.4 Implementation

Implementation of the Rayleigh model is not difficult. If the defect data (defect counts or defect rates) are reliable, the model parameters can be derived from the data by computer programs (available in many statistical software packages) that use statistical functions. After the model is defined, estimation of end-product reliability can be achieved by substitution of data values into the model.

Figure 7.5 shows a simple example of implementation of the Rayleigh model in SAS, which uses the nonlinear regression procedure. From the several methods in nonlinear regression, we chose the DUD method for its simplicity and efficiency (Ralston and Jennrich, 1978). DUD is a derivative-free algorithm for nonlinear least squares. It competes favorably with even the best derivative-based algorithms when evaluated on a number of standard test problems.

```
/****************************************************************/
/*                                                            */
/*  SAS program for estimating software latent-error rate based */
/*      on the Rayleigh model using defect removal data during  */
/*      development                                           */
/*                                                            */
/* ---------------------------------------------------------- */
/*                                                            */
/*  Assumes: A 6-phase development process: High-level design(I0)*/
/*           Low-level design (I1), coding(I2), Unit test (UT),  */
/*           Component test (CT), and System test (ST).       */
/*                                                            */
/*  Program does:                                             */
/*      1) estimate Rayleigh model parameters                 */
/*      2) plot graph of Rayleigh curve versus actual defect rate */
/*         on a GDDM79 terminal screen (e.g., 3279G)          */
/*      3) perform chi-square goodness-of-fit test, indicate  */
/*         whether the model is adequate or not               */
/*      4) derive latent error estimate                       */
/*                                                            */
/*  User input required:                                      */
/*      A: input defect rates and time equivalents of         */
/*         the six development phases                         */
/*      B: initial values for iteration                       */
/*      C: defect rates                                       */
/*      D: adjustment factor specific to product/development  */
/*          site                                              */
/*                                                            */
/****************************************************************/
TITLE1 'RAYLEIGH MODEL - DEFECT REMOVAL PATTERN';
OPTIONS label center missing=0 number linesize=95;

/****************************************************************/
/*                                                            */
/*  Set label value for graph                                 */
/*                                                            */
/****************************************************************/
proc format;
    value jx 0='I0'
             1='I1'
             2='I2'
             3='UT'
             4='CT'
             5='ST'
             6='GA'
             7=' '
             ;


/****************************************************************/
/*                                                            */
/*  Now we get input data                                     */
/*                                                            */
/****************************************************************/
```

FIGURE 7.5
An SAS Program for the Rayleigh Model

```
data temp;

/*---------------------------------------------------------------*/
/*  INPUT A:                                                     */
/*  In the INPUT statement below, Y is the defect removal rate   */
/*  per KLOC, T is the time equivalent for the development       */
/*  phases:  0.5 for I0, 1.5 for I1, 2.5 for I2, 3.5 for UT,     */
/*  4.5 for CT, and 5.5 for ST.                                  */
/*  Input data follows the CARDS statement.                      */
/*---------------------------------------------------------------*/
     INPUT Y T;
CARDS;
9.2    0.5
11.9   1.5
16.7   2.5
5.1    3.5
4.2    4.5
2.4    5.5
;
/*****************************************************************/
/*                                                               */
/* Now we estimate the parameters of the Rayleigh distribution   */
/*                                                               */
/*****************************************************************/
proc NLIN method=dud outest=out1;
/*---------------------------------------------------------------*/
/* INPUT B:                                                      */
/* The non-linear regression procedure requires initial input    */
/* for the K and R parameters in the PARMS statement.  K is      */
/* the defect rate/KLOC for the entire development process, R is */
/* the peak of the Rayleigh curve.  NLIN takes these initial     */
/* values and the input data above, goes through an iteration    */
/* procedure, and comes up with the final estimates of K and R.  */
/* Once K and R are determined, we can specify the entire        */
/* Rayleigh curve, and subsequently estimate the latent-error    */
/* rate.                                                         */
/*---------------------------------------------------------------*/
     PARMS K=49.50 to 52 by 0.1
           R=1.75 to 2.00 by 0.01;
     *bounds K<=50.50,r>=1.75;
 model y=(1/R**2)*t*K*exp((-1/(2*r**2))*t**2);

data out1; set out1;
     if _TYPE_ = 'FINAL';
proc print data=out1;




/*****************************************************************/
/*                                                               */
/* Now we prepare to plot the graph                              */
/*                                                               */
/*****************************************************************/
/*---------------------------------------------------------------*/
/* Specify the entire Rayleigh curve based on the estimated      */
```

FIGURE 7.5 (*Continued*)

```
/* parameters                                                  */
/*-----------------------------------------------------------*/
data out2; set out1;
     B=1/(2*R**2);
     do I=1 to 140;
         J=I/20;
         RAY=exp(-B*(J-0.05)**2) - exp(-B*J**2);
         DEF=ray*K*20;
         output ;
     end;
label DEF='DEFECT RATE';
/*-----------------------------------------------------------*/
/* INPUT C:                                                    */
/* Prepare for the histograms in the graph, values on the right */
/* hand side of the assignment statements are the actual       */
/* defect removal rates--same as those for the INPUT statement */
/*-----------------------------------------------------------*/
data out2 ; set out2;
if 0<=J<1 then DEF1=9.2 ;
if 1<=J<2 then DEF1=11.9 ;
if 2<=J<3 then DEF1=16.7 ;
if 3<=J<4 then DEF1=5.1 ;
if 4<=J<5 then DEF1=4.2 ;
if 5<=J<=6 then DEF1=2.4 ;
label J='DEVELOPMENT PHASES';
;


/*************************************************************/
/*                                                          */
/* Now we plot the graph on a GDDM79 terminal screen(e.g., 3279G)*/
/* The graph can be saved and plotted out through graphics  */
/* interface such as APGS                                   */
/*                                                          */
/*************************************************************/
     goptions device=GDDM79;
   * GOPTIONS DEVICE=GDDMfam4 GDDMNICK=p3820 GDDMTOKEN=img240x
          HSIZE=8 VSIZE=11;
   * OPTIONS DEVADDR=(.,.,GRAPHPTR);

proc gplot data=out2;
 plot DEF*J  DEF1*J/overlay vaxis=0 to 25 by 5 vminor=0 fr
                       hminor=0;
     symbol1 i=joint v=none c=red;
     symbol2 i=needle v=none    c=green;
     format j jx.;

/*************************************************************/
/*  Now we compute the chi-square goodness-of-fit test      */
/*     Note that the CDF should be used instead of          */
/*     the PDF.  The degree of freedom is                   */
/*     n-1-#parameters, in this case, n-1-2                 */
/*                                                          */
/*************************************************************/
data out1; set out1;
     DO i=1 to 6;
     OUTPUT;
     END;
     keep K R;
```

FIGURE 7.5
An SAS Program for the Rayleigh Model (*Continued*)

```
    data temp2; merge out1 temp;
        T=T + 0.5;
        T_1 = T-1;
        b=1/(R*R*2);
        E_rate = K*(exp(-b*T_1*T_1) - exp(-b*T*T));
        CHI_sq = ( y  - E_rate)**2 / E_rate;
proc sort data=temp2; by T;
data temp2; set temp2; by T;
        if T=1 then T_chisq = 0;
        T_chisq + CHI_sq;


proc sort data=temp2; by K T;
data temp3; set temp2; by K T;
        if LAST.K;
        df = T-1-2;
        p= 1- PROBCHI(T_chisq, df);
        IF p>0.05 then
            RESULT='Chi-square test indicates that model is adequate.    ';
        ELSE
            RESULT='Chi-square test indicates that model is inadequate. ' ;

        keep T_chisq df p RESULT;
proc print data=temp3;


/*********************************************************************/
/*   INPUT D - the value of ADJUST                               */
/*   Now we estimate the latent-error rate.  The Rayleigh model  */
/*   is known to under-estimate.                                 */
/*   To have good predictive validity, it                       */
/*   is important to use an adjustment factor based on the       */
/*   prior experience of your product.                          */
/*********************************************************************/
data temp4; set temp2; by K T;
        if LAST.K;

        ADJUST = 0.15;

        E_rate = K*exp(-b*T*T);
        Latent= E_rate + ADJUST;
        label Latent = 'Latent Error Rate per KCSI';
        keep Latent;
proc print data=temp4 label;



  RUN;
CMS FILEDEF * CLEAR ;
ENDSAS;
```

FIGURE 7.5 (*Continued*)

The SAS program estimates model parameters, produces a graph of fitted model versus actual data points on a GDDM79 graphic terminal screen (as shown in Figure 7.2), performs chi square goodness-of-fit tests, and derives estimates for the latent-error rate. The probability (p value) of the chi square test is also provided. If the test results indicate that the fitted model does not adequately describe the observed data ($p > .05$), a warning statement is issued in the output. If proper graphic support is available, the colored graph on the terminal screen can be saved as a file and plotted via graphic plotting devices.

In the program of Figure 7.5, r represents t_m as discussed earlier. The program implements the model on a six-phase development process. Because the Rayleigh model is a function of time (as are other reliability models), input data have to be in terms of defect data by time. The following time equivalent values for the development phases are used in the program:

I0 — 0.5
I1 — 1.5
I2 — 2.5
UT — 3.5
CT — 4.5
ST — 5.5

Implementations of the Rayleigh model are available in industry. One such example is the Software LIfe-cycle Model tool (SLIM) developed by Quantitative Software Management, Inc., of McLean, Virginia. SLIM is a software product designed to help software managers estimate the time, effort, and cost required to build medium and large software systems. It embodies the software life-cycle model developed by Putnam (Putnam and Myers, 1992), using validated data from many projects in the industry. Although the main purpose of the tool is for life-cycle project management, estimating the number of software defects is one of the important elements. Central to the SLIM tool are two important management indicators. The first is the productivity index (PI), a "big picture" measure of the total development capability of the organization. The second is the manpower buildup index (MBI), a measure of staff buildup rate. It is influenced by scheduling pressure, task concurrency, and resource constraints. The inputs to SLIM include software size (lines of source code, function points, modules, or uncertainty), process productivity (methods, skills, complexity, and tools), and management constraints (maximum people, maximum budget, maximum schedule, and required reliability). The outputs from SLIM include the staffing curve, the cumulative cost curve over time, probability of project success over time, reliability curve and the number of defects in the product, along with other metrics. In SLIM the X-axis for the Rayleigh model is in terms of months from the start of the project.

As a result of Gaffney's work (1984), in 1985 the IBM Federal Systems Division at Gaithersburg, Maryland, developed a PC program called the Software Error Estimation Reporter (STEER). The STEER program implements a discrete version of the Rayleigh model by matching the input data with a set of 11 stored Rayleigh patterns and a number of user patterns. The stored Rayleigh patterns are expressed in terms of percent distribution of defects for the six development phases mentioned earlier. The matching algorithm involves taking logarithmic transformation of the input data and the stored Rayleigh patterns, calculating the separation index between the input data and each stored pattern, and choosing the stored pattern with the lowest separation index as the best-fit pattern.

Several questions arise about the STEER approach. First, the matching algorithm is somewhat different from statistical estimation methodologies, which derive estimates of model parameters directly from the input data points based on proved procedures. Second, it always produces a best-match pattern even when none of the stored patterns is statistically adequate to describe the input data. There is no mention of how little of the separation index indicates a good fit. Third, the stored Rayleigh patterns are far apart; specifically, they range from 1.00 to 3.00 in terms of t_m, with a huge increment of 0.25. Therefore, they are not sensitive enough for estimating the latent-error rate, which is usually a very small number.

There are, however, circumventions to the last two problems. First, use the separation index conservatively; be skeptical of the results if the index exceeds 1.00. Second, use the program iteratively: After selecting the best-match pattern (for instance, the one with $t_m = 1.75$), calculate a series of slightly different Rayleigh patterns that center at the best-match pattern (for instance, patterns ranging from $t_m = 1.50$ to $t_m = 2.00$, with an increment of 0.05 or 0.01), and use them as user patterns to match with the input data again. The outcome will surely be a better "best match."

When used properly, the first two potential weak points of STEER can become its strong points. In other words, STEER plays down the role of formal parameter estimation and relies heavily on matching with existing patterns. If the feature of self-entered user patterns is used well (e.g., use defect patterns of projects from the same development organizations that have characteristics similar to those of the project for which estimation of defects is sought), then empirical validity is established. From our experience in software reliability projection, the most important factor in achieving predictive validity, regardless of the model being used, is to establish empirical validity with historical data.

Table 7.2 shows the defect removal patterns of a number of projects, the defect rates observed during the first year in the field, the life-of-product (four years) projection based on the first-year data, and the projected total latent defect rate (life-of-product) from STEER. The data show that the STEER projections are very close to the LOP projections based on one year of actual data. One can also observe that the

TABLE 7.2
Defect Removal Patterns and STEER Projections

			Defects Per KLOC							
Project	LOC	Language	High-Level Design	Low-Level Design	Code	Unit Test	Integration Test	System Test	First-Year Field Defect	LOP Field Defect
A	680K	Jovial	4	—	13	5	4	2	0.3	0.6
B	30K	PL/1	2	7	14	9	7	—	3.0	6.0
C	70K	BAL	6	25	6	3	2	0.5	0.2	0.4
D	1700K	Jovial	4	10	15	4	3	3	0.4	0.8
E	290K	ADA	4	8	13	—	8	0.1	0.3	0.6
F	70K	—	1	2	4	6	5	0.9	1.1	2.2
G	540K	ADA	2	5	12	12	4	1.8	0.6	1.2
H	700K	ADA	6	7	14	3	1	0.4	0.2	0.4

defect removal patterns and the resulting field defects lend support to the basic assumptions of the Rayleigh model as discussed earlier. Specifically, more front-loaded defect patterns lead to lower field defect rates and vice versa.

7.5 Reliability and Predictive Validity

In Chapter 3 we examined issues associated with reliability and validity. In the context of modeling, reliability refers to the degree of change in the model output due to chance fluctuations in the input data. In specific statistical terms, reliability relates closely to the confidence interval of the estimate: The narrower the confidence interval, the more reliable the estimate, and vice versa. Confidence interval, in turn, is related to the sample size: Larger samples yield narrower confidence intervals. Therefore, for the Rayleigh model, which is implemented on a six-phase development process, the chance of having a satisfactory confidence interval is very slim. My recommendation is to use as many models as appropriate and rely on intermodel reliability to establish the reliability of the final estimates. For example, in addition to the Rayleigh model, one can attempt the exponential model or other reliability growth models (see Chapter 8). Although the confidence interval for each model estimate may not be satisfactory, if the estimates by different models are close to each other, confidence in the estimates is strengthened. In contrast, if the estimates from different models are not consistent, we will not have much confidence in our estimates even if the confidence interval for each single estimate is small. In such cases, more investigation is needed to understand and to reconcile the differences across models before a final estimate is decided.

Predictive validity refers simply to the accuracy of model estimates. The foremost thing to achieve predictive validity is to make sure that the input data are accurate and reliable. As discussed in an earlier chapter, there is much room for improvement in data quality in the software industry in general, including defect tracking in software development. Within the development process, usually the tracking system and the data quality are better at the back end (testing) than at the front end (requirements analysis, design reviews, and code inspections). Without accurate data, it is impossible to obtain accurate estimates.

Second, and not less important, to establish predictive validity, model estimates and actual outcomes must be compared and empirical validity must be established. Such empirical validity is of utmost importance because the validity of software reliability models, according to the state of the art, is context specific. A model may work well in a certain development organization for a group of products using certain development processes, but not in dissimilar environments. No universally good software reliability model exists. By establishing empirical validity, we ensure that the model works in the intended context. For instance, when applying the Rayleigh to the AS/400 data, we verified the model based on many releases of the System/38 and System/36 data. We found that the Rayleigh model consistently underestimated the software field defect rate. To improve its predictive validity, we calibrated the model output with an adjustment factor, which is the mean difference between the Rayleigh estimates and the actual defect rates reported. The calibration is logical, given the similar structural parameters in the development process among the three computer systems, including organization, management, and work force.

Interestingly, Wiener-Ehrlich and associates also found that the Rayleigh model underestimated the manloading scores of a software project at the tail (Wiener-Ehrlich et al., 1984). It may be that the model is really too optimistic for software applications. A Weibull distribution with an m of less than 2 (for example, 1.8) might work better for software. This is a worthwhile research topic if reliable and complete data (including process as well as field defect data) for a large number of projects are available. It should be cautioned that when one models the data with the Weibull distribution to determine the value of the m parameter, one should be sure to use the complete data set. If incomplete data are used (e.g., in-process data for the current project), the m value thus obtained will be artificially high, which will lead to underestimates of the software defects. This is because m is the shape parameter of the Weibull distribution; it will fit the shape of the data points available during the estimation process. Therefore, for in-process data, a fixed m value should be used when modeling with the Weibull distribution. We have seen examples of misuse of the Weibull distribution with in-process data, resulting in invalid estimates of software defects.

To further test our observation that the Rayleigh model underestimates the tail end of the distribution of software data, we started to look for a meaningful set of data from another organization. We obtained the field defect arrival data for a systems software that was developed at IBM in Austin, Texas. The data set contains more than sixty monthly data points, representing the entire life cycle of field defects of the software. We fitted a number of software reliability models including the Rayleigh and the Weibull with several m values. As shown in Figure 7.6, we found that the Weibull model with $m = 1.8$ gave a better fit of the distribution than the Rayleigh model, although both passed the goodness-of-fit test.

The three cases of Rayleigh underestimation discussed are from different software development organizations, and the time frame spans sixteen years from 1984 to 2000. Although more research is needed, based on the reasons discussed here, we recommend the use of Weibull with $m = 1.8$ in Rayleigh applications when estimation accuracy at the tail end is critical.

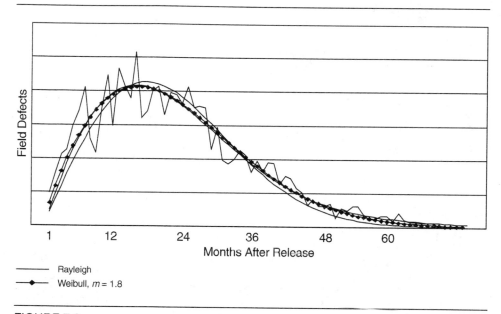

FIGURE 7.6
Rayleigh Model Versus Weibull Distribution with $m = 1.8$

7.6 Summary

The Rayleigh model is a special case of the Weibull distribution family, which has been widely used for reliability studies in various fields. Supported by a large body of empirical data, software projects were found to follow a life-cycle pattern described by the Rayleigh curve, for both resource and staffing demand and defect discovery/removal patterns. The Rayleigh model is implemented in several software products for quality assessment. It can also be implemented easily via statistical software packages, such as the example provided in this chapter.

Compared to the phase-based defect removal model, the Rayleigh model is a formal parametric model that can be used for projecting the latent software defects when the development work is complete and the product is ready to ship to customers. The rationale behind the model fits well with the rationale for effective software development. Specifically, while the defect removal effectiveness approach focuses on defect removal, the Rayleigh encompasses both defect prevention (reduction in defect rates) and early defect removal.

In addition to quality projection, another strength of the Rayleigh model is that it provides an excellent framework for quality management. After we discuss the reliability growth models in the next chapter, in Chapter 9 we will revisit the Rayleigh model in its capacity as a quality management model.

References

1. Conte, S. D., H. E. Dunsmore, and V. Y. Shen, *Software Engineering Metrics and Models,* Menlo Park, Calif.: Benjamin/Cummings, 1986.
2. Gaffney, Jr., J. E., "On Predicting Software Related Performance of Large-Scale Systems," *CMG XV,* San Francisco, December 1984.
3. Norden, P. V., "Useful Tools for Project Management," *Operations Research in Research and Development,* B. V. Dean, Ed., New York: John Wiley & Sons, 1963.
4. Putnam, L. H., "A General Empirical Solution to the Macro Software Sizing and Estimating Problem," *IEEE Transactions on Software Engineering,* Vol. SE-4, 1978, pp. 345–361.
5. Putnam, L. H., and W. Myers, *Measures for Excellence: Reliable Software on Time, Within Budget,* Englewood Cliffs, N.J.: Yourdon Press, 1992.
6. Ralston, M. L., and R. I. Jennrich, "DUD, a Derivative-Free Algorithm for Nonlinear Least Squares," *Technometrics,* Vol. 20, 1978, pp. 7–14.
7. Tobias, P. A., and D. C. Trindade, *Applied Reliability,* New York: Van Nostrand Reinhold, 1986.
8. Trachtenberg, M., "Discovering How to Ensure Software Reliability," *RCA Engineer,* Jan./Feb. 1982, pp. 53–57.
9. Wiener-Ehrlich, W. K., J. R. Hamrick, and V. F. Rupolo, "Modeling Software Behavior in Terms of a Formal Life Cycle Curve: Implications for Software Maintenance," *IEEE Transactions on Software Engineering,* Vol. SE-10, 1984, pp. 376–383.

8

Exponential Distribution and Reliability Growth Models

Continuing our discussion of software reliability models, in this chapter we cover the class of models called the *reliability growth models*. We first discuss the exponential model; then we concisely describe several notable reliability growth models in the literature; and in later sections we discuss several issues such as model assumptions, criteria for model evaluation, the modeling process, the test compression factor, and estimating the distribution of estimated field defects over time.

In contrast to Rayleigh, which models the defect pattern of the entire development process, reliability growth models are usually based on data from the formal testing phases. Indeed it makes more sense to apply these models during the final testing phase when development is virtually complete, especially when the testing is customer oriented. The rationale is that defect arrival or failure patterns during such testing are good indicators of the product's reliability when it is used by customers. During such postdevelopment testing, when failures occur and defects are identified and fixed, the software becomes more stable, and reliability grows over time. Therefore models that address such a process are called reliability growth models.

8.1 The Exponential Model

The exponential model is another special case of the Weibull family, with the shape parameter m equal to 1. It is best used for statistical processes that decline monotonically to an asymptote. Its cumulative distribution function (CDF) and probability density function (PDF) are

$$\text{CDF}: F(t) = 1 - e^{-(t/c)}$$
$$= 1 - e^{-\lambda t}$$

$$\text{PDF}: f(t) = \frac{1}{c} e^{-(t/c)}$$
$$= \lambda e^{-\lambda t}$$

where c is the scale parameter, t is time, and $\lambda = 1/c$. Applied to software reliability, λ is referred to as the *error detection rate* or *instantaneous failure rate*. In statistical terms it is also called the *hazard rate*.

Again the preceding formulas represent a standard distribution—the total area under the PDF curve is 1. In actual application, the total number of defects or the total cumulative defect rate K needs to be multiplied to the formulas. K and lambda (λ) are the two parameters for estimation when deriving a specific model from a data set.

The exponential distribution is the simplest and most important distribution in reliability and survival studies. The failure data of much equipment and many processes are well described by the exponential distribution: bank statement and ledger errors, payroll check errors, light bulb failure, automatic calculating machine failure, radar set component failure, and so forth. The exponential distribution plays a role in reliability studies analogous to that of normal distribution in other areas of statistics.

In software reliability the exponential distribution is one of the better known models and is often the basis of many other software reliability growth models. For instance, Misra (1983) used the exponential model to estimate the defect-arrival rates for the shuttle's ground system software of the National Aeronautics and Space Administration (NASA). The software provided the flight controllers at the Johnson Space Center with processing support to exercise command and control over flight operations. Data from an actual 200-hour flight mission indicate that the model worked very well. Furthermore, the mean value function (CDF) of the Goel-Okumoto (1979) nonhomogeneous Poisson process model (NPPM) is in fact the exponential model.

Figures 8.1 and 8.2 show the exponential model applied to the data of one of the AS/400 software products. We have modeled the weekly defect arrival data since the start of system test, when the development work was virtually complete. The system-testing stage uses customer interfaces, tests external requirements, and simulates end-user application environments. The pattern of defect arrivals during this stage, therefore, should be indicative of the latent defect rate when the system is shipped.

Like the Rayleigh model, the exponential model is simple and quick to implement when powerful statistical software is available. For example, it can be implemented via SAS programs similar to the one shown in Figure 7.5 of the previous chapter. Of course, if a high degree of usability and various scenarios are desired, more elaborate software is needed.

Besides programming, the following should be taken into consideration when applying the exponential distribution for reliability projection or estimating the number of software defects. First, as with all types of modeling and estimation, the more accurate and precise the input data, the better the outcome. Data tracking for software reliability estimation is done either in terms of precise CPU execution time or on a calendar-time basis. Normally execution-time tracking is for small projects or special reliability studies; calendar-time tracking is common for commercial

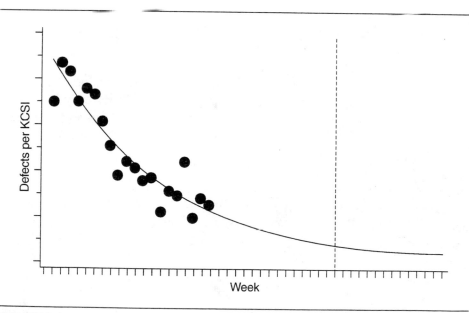

FIGURE 8.1
Exponential Model—Density Distribution

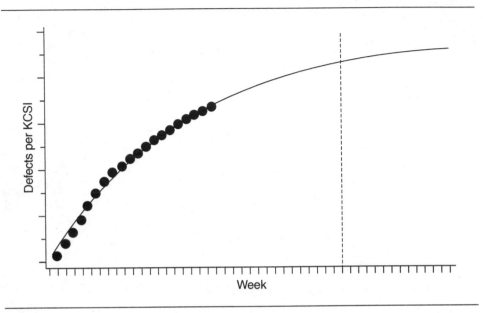

FIGURE 8.2
Exponential Model—Cumulative Distribution

development. When calendar-time data are used, a basic assumption for the exponential model is that the testing effort is homogeneous throughout the testing phase. Ohba (1984) notes that the model does not work well for calendar-time data with a nonhomogeneous time distribution of testing effort. Therefore, this assumption must be examined when using the model. For instance, in the example shown in Figures 8.1 and 8.2 the testing effort remained consistently high and homogeneous throughout the system test phase; a separate team of testers worked intensively based on a predetermined test plan. The product was also large (>100 KLOC) and therefore the trend of the defect arrival rates tended to be stable even though no execution-time data were available.

To verify the assumption, indicators of the testing effort, such as the person-hours in testing for each time unit (e.g., day or week), test cases run, or the number of variations executed, are needed. If the testing effort is clearly not homogeneous, some sort of normalization has to be made. Otherwise, models other than the exponential distribution should be considered.

As an example of normalization, let us assume the unit of calendar time is a week and it is clear that the weekly testing effort is not homogeneous. Further assume that weekly data on the number of person-hours in testing are known. Simple adjustments such as the following can reduce artificial fluctuations in the data and can make the model work better:

1. Accumulate the total person-hours in testing for the entire testing phase and calculate the average number of person-hours in testing per week, n.
2. Starting from the beginning of testing, calculate the defect rates (or defect count) for each n person-hour units. Allocate the defect rates to the calendar week in sequence. Specifically, allocate the defect rate observed for the first n person-hours of testing to the first week; allocate the defect rate observed for the second n person-hours of testing to the second week, and so forth.
3. Use the allocated data as weekly input data for the model.

Second, the more data points available, the better the model will perform—assuming there is an adequate fit between the model and the data. The question is: When the test is in progress, how much data is needed for the model to yield reasonably adequate output? Ehrlich and associates (1990) investigated this question using data from AT&T software that was a transmission measurement system for remote testing of special service circuits. They assessed the predictive validity of the exponential model with data at 25%, 50%, 60%, 70%, and 80% into test, and at test completion. They found that at 25% into test the model results were way off. At 50% the results improved considerably but were still not satisfactory. At 60% into test, the exponential model had satisfactory predictive validity. Although it is not clear whether these findings can be generalized, they provide a good reference point for real-time modeling.

8.2 Reliability Growth Models

The exponential model can be regarded as the basic form of the software reliability growth models. For the past two decades, software reliability modeling has been one of the most active areas in software engineering. More than a hundred models have been proposed in professional journals and at software conferences, each with its own assumptions, applicability, and limitations. Unfortunately, not many models have been tested in practical environments with real data, and even fewer models are in use. From the practical software development point of view, for some models the cost of gathering data is too expensive; some models are not understandable; and some simply do not work when examined. For instance, Elbert and associates (1992) examined seven reliability models with data from a large and complex software system that contained millions of lines of source code. They found that some models gave reasonable results, and others provided unrealistic estimates. Despite a good fit between the model and the data, some models predicted the probability of error detection as a negative value. The range of the estimates of the defects of the system from these models is incredibly wide—from 5 to 6 defects up to 50,000.

Software reliability growth models can be classified into two major classes, depending on the dependent variable of the model. For the *time between failures models,* the variable under study is the time between failures. This is the earliest class of models proposed for software reliability assessment. It is expected that the failure times will get longer as defects are removed from the software product. A common approach of this class of model is to assume that the time between, say, the $(i − 1)$st and the ith failures follows a distribution whose parameters are related to the number of latent defects remaining in the product after the $(i − 1)$st failure. The distribution used is supposed to reflect the improvement in reliability as defects are detected and removed from the product. The parameters of the distribution are to be estimated from the observed values of times between failures. Mean time to next failure is usually the parameter to be estimated for the model.

For the *fault count models* the variable criterion is the number of faults or failures (or normalized rate) in a specified time interval. The time can be CPU execution time or calendar time such as hour, week, or month. The time interval is fixed a priori and the number of defects or failures observed during the interval is treated as a random variable. As defects are detected and removed from the software, it is expected that the observed number of failures per unit time will decrease. The number of remaining defects or failures is the key parameter to be estimated from this class of models.

The following sections concisely describe several models in each of the two classes. The models were selected based on experience and may or may not be a good representation of the many models available in the literature. We first summarize three time between failures models, followed by three fault count models.

8.2.1 Jelinski-Moranda Model

The Jelinski-Moranda (J-M) model is one of the earliest models in software reliability research (Jelinski and Moranda, 1972). It is a time between failures model. It assumes N software faults at the start of testing, failures occur purely at random, and all faults contribute equally to cause a failure during testing. It also assumes the fix time is negligible and that the fix for each failure is perfect. Therefore, the software product's failure rate improves by the same amount at each fix. The hazard function (the instantaneous failure rate function) at time t_i, the time between the $(i − 1)$st and ith failures, is given

$$Z(t_i) = \phi[N − (i − 1)]$$

where N is the number of software defects at the beginning of testing and ϕ is a proportionality constant. Note that the hazard function is constant between failures but decreases in steps of ϕ following the removal of each fault. Therefore, as each fault is removed, the time between failures is expected to be longer.

8.2.2 Littlewood Models

The Littlewood (LW) model is similar to the J-M model, except it assumes that different faults have different sizes, thereby contributing unequally to failures (Littlewood, 1981). Larger-sized faults tend to be detected and fixed earlier. As the number of errors is driven down with the progress in test, so is the average error size, causing a law of diminishing return in debugging. The introduction of the error size concept makes the model assumption more realistic. In real-life software operation, the assumption of equal failure rate by all faults can hardly be met, if at all. Latent defects that reside in code paths that rarely get executed by customers' operational profiles may not be manifested for years.

Littlewood also developed several other models such as the Littlewood nonhomogeneous Poisson process (LNHPP) model (Miller, 1986). The LNHPP model is similar to the LW model except that it assumes a continuous change in instantaneous failure rate rather than discrete drops when fixes take place.

8.2.3 Goel-Okumoto Imperfect Debugging Model

The J-M model assumes that the fix time is negligible and that the fix for each failure is perfect. In other words, it assumes perfect debugging. In practice, this is not always the case. In the process of fixing a defect, new defects may be injected. Indeed, defect fix activities are known to be error-prone. During the testing stages, the percentage of defective fixes in large commercial software development organizations may range from 1% or 2% to more than 10%. Goel and Okumoto (1978) proposed an imperfect debugging model to overcome the limitation of the assumption. In this model the hazard function during the interval between the $(i-1)$st and the ith failures is given

$$Z(t_i) = [N - p(i-1)]\lambda$$

where N is the number of faults at the start of testing, p is the probability of imperfect debugging, and λ is the failure rate per fault.

8.2.4 Goel-Okumoto Nonhomogeneous Poisson Process Model

The NHPP model (Goel and Okumoto, 1979) is concerned with modeling the number of failures observed in given testing intervals. Goel and Okumoto propose that the cumulative number of failures observed at time t, $N(t)$, can be modeled as a non-homogeneous Poisson process (NHPP)—as a Poisson process with a time-dependent failure rate. They propose that the time-dependent failure rate follows an exponential distribution. The model is

$$P\{N(t) = y\} = \frac{[m(t)]^y}{y!} e^{-m(t)}, \quad y = 0, 1, 2, \ldots$$

where

$$m(t) = a(1 - e^{-bt})$$

$$\lambda(t) \equiv m'(t) = abc^{-bt}$$

In the model, $m(t)$ is the expected number of failures observed by time t; $\lambda(t)$ is the failure density; a is the expected number of failures to be observed eventually; and b is the fault detection rate per fault. As seen, $m(t)$ and $\lambda(t)$ are the cumulative distribution function $[F(t)]$ and the probability density function $[f(t)]$, respectively, of the exponential function discussed in the preceding section. The parameters a and b correspond to K and λ. Therefore, the NHPP model is a straight application of the exponential model. The reason it is called NHPP is perhaps because of the emphasis on the probability distribution of the estimate of the cumulative number of failures at a specific time t, as represented by the first equation. Fitting the model curve from actual data and for projecting the number of faults remaining in the system, is done mainly by means of the mean value, or cumulative distribution function (CDF).

Note that in this model the number of faults to be detected, a, is treated as a random variable whose observed value depends on the test and other environmental factors. This is fundamentally different from models that treat the number of faults to be a fixed unknown constant.

The exponential distribution assumes a pattern of decreasing defect rates or failures. Cases have been observed in which the failure rate first increases and then decreases. Goel (1982) proposed a generalization of the Goel-Okumoto NHPP model by allowing one more parameter in the mean value function and the failure density function. Such a model is called the Goel generalized nonhomogeneous Poisson process model;

$$m(t) = a(1 - e^{-bt^c})$$
$$\lambda(t) \equiv m'(t) = abc\, e^{-bt^c} t^{c-1}$$

where a is the expected number of faults to be eventually detected, and b and c are constants that reflect the quality of testing. This mean value function and failure density function is actually the Weibull distribution, which we discussed in Chapter 7. When the shape parameter m (in the Goel model, it is c) equals 1, the Weibull distribution becomes the exponential distribution; when m is 2, it then becomes the Rayleigh model.

8.2.5 Musa-Okumoto Logarithmic Poisson Execution Time Model

Similar to the NHPP model, in the Musa-Okumoto (M-O) model the observed number of failures by a certain time, τ, is also assumed to be a nonhomogeneous Poisson process (Musa and Okumoto, 1983). However, its mean value function is different. It attempts to consider that later fixes have a smaller effect on the software's reliability than earlier ones. The logarithmic Poisson process is claimed to be superior for highly nonuniform operational user profiles, where some functions are executed much more frequently than others. Also the process modeled is the number of failures in specified execution-time intervals (instead of calendar time). A systematic approach to convert the results to calendar-time data (Musa et al., 1987) is also provided. The model, therefore, consists of two components—the execution-time component and the calendar-time component.

The mean value function of this model is

$$u(\tau) = \frac{1}{\theta} \ln(\lambda_0 \theta_\tau + 1)$$

where λ is the initial failure intensity, and θ is the rate of reduction in the normalized failure intensity per failure.

8.2.6 The Delayed S and Inflection S Models

With regard to the software defect removal process, Yamada et al. (1983) argue that a testing process consists of not only a defect detection process, but also a defect isolation process. Because of the time needed for failure analysis, significant delay can occur between the time of the first failure observation and the time of reporting. They offer the delayed S-shaped reliability growth model for such a process, in which the observed growth curve of the cumulative number of detected defects is S-shaped. The model is based on the nonhomogeneous Poisson process but with a different mean value function to reflect the delay in failure reporting,

$$m(t) = k\left[1 - (1 + \lambda t)\, e^{-\lambda t}\right]$$

where t is time, λ is the error detection rate, and K is the total number of defects or total cumulative defect rate.

In 1984, Ohba proposed another S-shaped reliability growth model—the inflection S model (Ohba, 1984). The model describes a software failure detection phenomenon with a mutual dependence of detected defects. Specifically, the more failures we detect, the more undetected failures become detectable. This assumption brings a certain realism into software reliability modeling and is a significant improvement over the assumption used by earlier models—the independence of faults in a program. Also based on the nonhomogeneous Poisson process, the model's mean value function is

$$I(t) = K \frac{1 - e^{-\lambda t}}{1 + i\, e^{-\lambda t}}$$

where t is time, λ is the error detection rate, i is the inflection factor, and K is the total number of defects or total cumulative defect rate.

The delayed S and inflection S models can be regarded as accounting for the learning period during which testers become familiar with the software at the beginning of a testing period. The learning period is associated with the delayed or inflection patterns as described by the mean value functions. The mean value function (CDF) and the failure density function (PDF) curves of the two models, in comparison with the exponential model, are shown in Figure 8.3. The exponential model assumes that the peak of defect arrival is at the beginning of the system test phase, and continues to decline thereafter; the delayed S model assumes a slightly delayed peak; and the inflection S model assumes a later and sharper peak.

8.3 Model Assumptions

Reliability modeling is an attempt to summarize the complex reality in precise statistical terms. Because the physical process being modeled (the software failure phenomenon) can hardly be expected to be so precise, unambiguous statements of the assumptions are necessary in the development of a model. In applications, the models perform better when the underlying assumptions are met, and vice versa. In other words, the more reasonable the assumptions, the better a model will be. From the preceding summary of several reliability growth models, we can see that earlier models tend to have more restrictive assumptions. More recent models tend to be able to deal with more realistic assumptions. For instance, the J-M model's five assumptions are:

1. There are N unknown software faults at the start of testing.
2. Failures occur randomly—times between failures are independent.
3. All faults contribute equally to cause a failure.

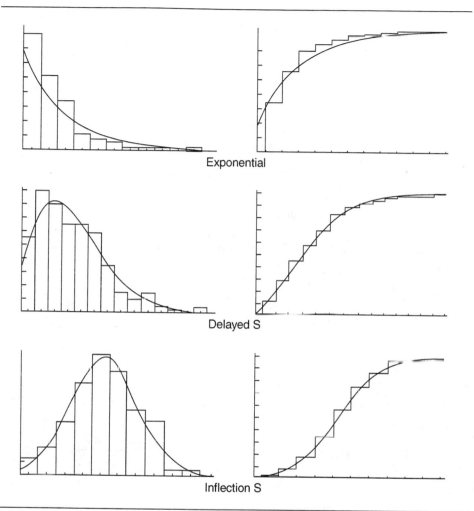

Exponential

Delayed S

Inflection S

FIGURE 8.3
Exponential, Delayed S, and Inflection S Models—PDF (*left*) and CDF (*right*)

4. Fix time is negligible.
5. Fix is perfect for each failure; there are no new faults introduced during correction.

Together these assumptions are difficult to meet in practical development environments. Although assumption 1 does not seem to pose problems, all the others pose limitations to the model. The Littlewood models, with the concept of error size, overcame the restriction imposed by assumption 3. The Goel-Okumoto imperfect debugging model is an attempt to improve assumptions 4 and 5.

Assumption 2 is used in all time between failures models. It requires that successive failure times be independent of each other. This assumption could be met if successive test cases were chosen randomly. However, the test process is not likely to be random; testing, especially functional testing, is not based on independent test cases. If a critical fault is discovered in a code segment, the tester may intensify the testing of associated code paths and look for other faults. Such activities may mean a shorter time to next failure. Strict adherence to this assumption therefore is not likely. Care should be taken, however, to ensure some degree of independence in data points when using the time between failures models.

The previous assumptions pertain to the time between failures models. In general, assumptions of the time between failures models tend to be more restrictive. Furthermore, time between failures data are more costly to gather and require a higher degree of precision.

The basic assumptions of the fault count model are as follows (Goel, 1985):

1. Testing intervals are independent of each other.
2. Testing during intervals is reasonably homogeneous.
3. Numbers of defects detected during nonoverlapping intervals are independent of each other.

As discussed earlier, the assumption of a homogeneous testing effort is the key to the fault count models. If this assumption is not met, some normalization effort or statistical adjustment should be applied. The other two assumptions are quite reasonable, especially if the model is calendar-time based with wide enough intervals (e.g., weeks).

For both classes of models, the most important underlying assumption is that of effective testing. If the test process is not well planned and test cases are poorly designed, the input data and the model projections will be overly optimistic. If the models are used for comparisons across products, then additional indicators of the effectiveness or coverage of testing should be included for the interpretation of results.

8.4 Criteria for Model Evaluation

For reliability models, in 1984 a group of experts (Iannino et al., 1984) devised a set of criteria for model assessment and comparison. The criteria are listed as follows, by order of importance as determined by the group:

☐ *Predictive validity:* The capability of the model to predict failure behavior or the number of defects for a specified time period based on the current data in the model.

☐ *Capability:* The ability of the model to estimate with satisfactory accuracy quantities needed by software managers, engineers, and users in planning and managing software development projects or controlling change in operational software systems.

☐ *Quality of assumptions:* The likelihood that the model assumptions can be met, and the assumptions' plausibility from the viewpoint of logical consistency and software engineering experience.

☐ *Applicability:* The model's degree of applicability across different software products (size, structure, functions, etc.).

☐ *Simplicity:* A model should be simple in three aspects: (1) simple and inexpensive to collect data, (2) simple in concept and does not require extensive mathematical background for software development practitioners to comprehend, and (3) readily implemented by computer programs.

From the practitioner's point of view and with recent observations of software reliability models, we contend that the most important criteria are predictive validity, simplicity, and quality of assumptions, in that order of importance. Capability and applicability are less significant. As the state of the art is still maturing and striving to improve its most important objective (predictive accuracy), the extra criteria of demanding more functions (capability) for multiple environments (applicability) seems burdensome. Perhaps the accuracy of software reliability models can best be summarized as follows: Some models sometimes give good results, some are almost universally awful, and none can be trusted to be accurate at all times (Brocklehurst and Littlewood, 1992). A model with good predictive validity but poor capability and narrow applicability is certainly superior to one with good capability and wide applicability but with very poor ability to predict.

In contrast to the order of importance determined by the 1984 group, we think that simplicity is much more important, second only to predictive validity. Experts in software reliability models are usually academicians who are well versed in mathematics and statistics. Many modeling concepts and terminologies are outside the discipline of computer science, let alone easy to comprehend and implement by software developers in the industry. As mentioned earlier, some reliability models have not been tested and used in real-life development projects simply because they are not understandable. Simplicity, therefore, is a key element in bridging the gap between the state of the art and the state of practice in software reliability modeling.

The quality of the assumptions is also very important. Early models tend to have restrictive and unrealistic assumptions. More recent models tend to have more realistic assumptions. Better assumptions make the model more convincing and more acceptable by software practitioners; they also lead to better predictive validity.

8.5 Modeling Process

To model software reliability, the following process or similar procedures should be used.

1. Examine the data. Study the nature of the data (fault counts versus times between failures), the unit of analysis (CPU hour, calendar day, week, month, etc.), the data tracking system, data reliability, and any relevant aspects of the data. Plot the data points against time in the form of a scatter diagram, analyze the data informally, and gain an insight into the nature of the process being modeled. For example, observe the trend, fluctuations, and any peculiar patterns and try to associate the data patterns with what was happening in the testing process. As another example, sometimes if the unit of time is too granular (e.g., calendar-time in hours of testing), the noise of the data may become too large relative to the underlying system pattern that we try to model. In that case, a larger time unit such as day or week may yield a better model.
2. Select a model or several models to fit the data based on an understanding of the test process, the data, and the assumptions of the models. The plot in step 1 can provide helpful information for model selection.
3. Estimate the parameters of the model. Different methods may be required depending on the nature of the data. The statistical techniques (e.g., the maximum likelihood method, the least-squares method, or some other method) and the software tools available for use should be considered.
4. Obtain the fitted model by substituting the estimates of the parameters into the chosen model. At this stage, you have a specified model for the data set.
5. Perform a goodness-of-fit test and assess the reasonableness of the model. If the model does not fit, a more reasonable model should be selected with regard to model assumptions and the nature of the data. For example, is the lack of fit due to a few data points that were affected by extraneous factors? Is the time unit too granular so that the noise of the data obscures the underlying trend?
6. Make reliability predictions based on the fitted model. Assess the reasonableness of the predictions based on other available information—actual performance of a similar product or of a previous release of the same product, subjective assessment by the development team, and so forth.

To illustrate the modeling process with actual data, the following sections give step-by-step details on the example shown in Figures 8.1 and 8.2. Table 8.1 shows the weekly defect rate data.

Step 1

The data were weekly defect data from the system test, the final phase of the development process. During the test process the software was under formal change con-

TABLE 8.1
Weekly Defect Arrival Rates and Cumulative Rates

Week	Defects/KLOC Arrival	Defects/KLOC Cumulative
1	.353	.353
2	.436	.789
3	.415	1.204
4	.351	1.555
5	.380	1.935
6	.366	2.301
7	.308	2.609
8	.254	2.863
9	.192	3.055
10	.219	3.274
11	.202	3.476
12	.180	3.656
13	.182	3.838
14	.110	3.948
15	.155	4.103
16	.145	4.248
17	.221	4.469
18	.095	4.564
19	.140	4.704
20	.126	4.830

trol—any defects found are tracked by the electronic problem tracking reports (PTR) and any change to the code must be done through the PTR process, which is enforced by the development support system. Therefore, the data were reliable. The density plot and cumulative plot of the data are shown in Figures 8.1 and 8.2 (ignore temporarily the fitted curves).

Step 2

The data indicated an overall decreasing trend (of course, with some noises), therefore the exponential model was chosen. For other products, we had used the delayed S and inflection S models. Also, the assumption of the S models, specifically the delayed reporting of failures due to problem determination and the mutual dependence of defects, seems to describe the development process correctly. However, from the trend of the data we did not observe an increase-then-decrease pattern, so we chose the exponential model. We did try the S models for goodness of fit, but they were not as good as the exponential model in this case.

Step 3

We used two methods for model estimation. In the first method, we used an SAS program similar to the one shown in Figure 7.5 in Chapter 7, which used a nonlinear regression approach based on the DUD algorithm (Ralston and Jennrich, 1978). The second method relies on the Software Error Tracking Tool (SETT) software developed by Falcetano and Caruso at IBM Kingston (Falcetano and Caruso, 1988). SETT implemented the exponential model and the two S models via the Marquardt nonlinear least-squares algorithm. Results of the two methods are very close. From the DUD nonlinear regression methods, we obtained the following values for the two parameters K and λ.

$$K = 6.597$$
$$\lambda = 0.0712$$

The asymptotic 95% confidence intervals for the two parameters are:

	Lower	Upper
K	5.643	7.552
λ	0.0553	0.0871

Step 4

By fitting the estimated parameters from step 3 into the exponential distribution, we obtained the following specified model

$$f(t) = 6.597 \times 0.0712 \times e^{-0.0712t}$$

$$F(t) = 6.597(1 - e^{-0.0712t})$$

where t is the week number since the start of system test.

Step 5

We conducted the Kolmogorov-Smirnov goodness-of-fit test (Rohatgi, 1976) between the observed number of defects and the expected number of defects from the model in step 4. The Kolmogorov-Smirnov test is recommended for goodness-of-fit testing for software reliability models (Goel, 1985). The test statistic is as follows:

$$D(n) = x \mid F^*(x) - F(x) \mid$$

where n is sample size, $F^*(x)$ is the normalized observed cumulative distribution at each time point (normalized means the total is 1), and $F(x)$ is the expected cumulative distribution at each time point, based on the model. In other words, the statistic compares the normalized cumulative distributions of the observed rates and the expected rates from the model at each point, then takes the absolute difference. If the maximum difference, $D(n)$, is less than the established criteria, then the model fits the data adequately.

Table 8.2 shows the calculation of the test. Column (A) is the third column in Table 8.1. Column (B) is the cumulative defect rate from the model. The $F^*(x)$ and $F(x)$ columns are the normalization of columns (A) and (B), respectively. The maximum of the last column, $|F^*(x) - F(x)|$, is .02329. The Kolmogorov-Smirnov test statistic for $n = 20$, and p value = .05 is .294 (Rohatgi, 1976, p. 661, Table 7).

TABLE 8.2
Weekly Defect Arrival Rates and Cumulative Rates

Week	Observed Defects/KLOC Cumulative (A)	Model Defects/KLOC Cumulative (B)	$F^*(x)$	$F(x)$	$\|F^*(x) - F(x)\|$
1	.353	.437	.07314	.09050	.01736
2	.789	.845	.16339	.17479	.01140
3	1.204	1.224	.24936	.25338	.00392
4	1.555	1.577	.32207	.32638	.00438
5	1.935	1.906	.40076	.39446	.00630
6	2.301	2.213	.47647	.45786	.01861
7	2.609	2.498	.54020	.51691	.02329
8	2.863	2.764	.59281	.57190	.02091
9	3.055	3.011	.63259	.62311	.00948
10	3.274	3.242	.67793	.67080	.00713
11	3.476	3.456	.71984	.71522	.00462
12	3.656	3.656	.75706	.75658	.00048
13	3.838	3.842	.79470	.79510	.00040
14	3.948	4.016	.81737	.83098	.01361
15	4.103	4.177	.84944	.86438	.01494
16	4.248	4.327	.87938	.89550	.01612
17	4.469	4.467	.92515	.92448	.00067
18	4.564	4.598	.94482	.95146	.00664
19	4.704	4.719	.97391	.97659	.00268
20	4.830	4.832	1.00000	1.00000	.00000

$D(n) = .02329$

Because the $D(n)$ value for our model is .02329, which is less than .294, the test indicates that the model is adequate.

Step 6

We calculated the projected number of defects for the four years following completion of system test. The projection from this model was very close to the estimate from the Rayleigh model and to the actual field defect data.

At IBM Rochester we have been using the reliability modeling techniques for estimating the defect level of software products for some years. We found the Rayleigh, the exponential, and the two S-type models to have good applicability to AS/400's process and data. We also rely on cross-model reliability to assess the reasonableness of the estimates. Furthermore, historical data are used for model calibration and for adjustment of the estimates. Actual field defect data confirmed the predictive validity of this approach; the differences between actual numbers and estimates are small.

8.6 Test Compression Factor

As the example and other cases in the literature illustrate (for example, Misra, 1983; Putnam and Myers, 1992), a fair degree of accuracy to project the remaining number of defects can be achieved by software reliability models, based on testing data. This approach works especially well if the project is large, where defect arrivals tend not to fluctuate much; if the system is not for safety-critical missions; and if environment-specific factors are taken into account when choosing a model. For safety-critical systems, the requirements for reliability and, therefore, for reliability models, are much more stringent.

Even though the projection of the total number of defects (or defect rates) may be reasonably accurate, it does not mean that one can extend the model density curve from the testing phase to the maintenance phase (customer usage) directly. The defect arrival patterns of the two phases may be quite different, especially for commercial projects. During testing the sole purpose is to find and remove defects; test cases are maximized for defect detection, therefore, the number of defect arrivals during testing is usually higher. In contrast, in customers' applications it takes time to encounter defects—when the applications hit usual scenarios. Therefore, defect arrivals may tend to spread. Such a difference between testing-defect density and field-defect density is called the *compression factor*. The value of the compression factor varies, depending on the testing environments and the customer usage profiles. It is expected to be larger when the test strategy is based on partition and limit testing and smaller for random testing or customer-environment testing. In the assessment by Elbert and associates (1992) on three large-scale commercial projects, the compression factor was 5 for two projects and 30 for a third. For projects that have extensive customer beta tests, models based on the beta test data may be able to extrapolate to the field use phase.

Figure 8.4 shows a real-life example of compression of defect density between testing and initial data from the field. For the upper panel, the upper curve represents the extrapolated cumulative defect rate based on testing data. The lower curve is the actual cumulative field defect rate. Although the points of the two curves at four years in the life of product are close, the upper curve has a much faster buildup rate. The difference is even more drastic in the lower panel, in which the two defect density curves are contrasted. The extrapolated curve based on testing data is front loaded and declines much faster. In vivid contrast, the actual field defect arrival is

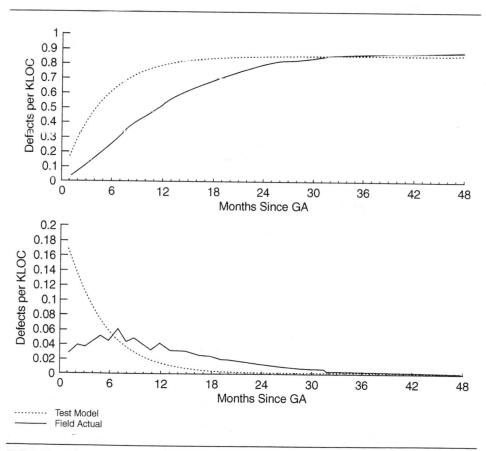

FIGURE 8.4

Compression Illustration—Cumulative and Density Curves

much more spread out. It even follows a different density pattern (a delayed S or a Rayleigh-like pattern).

8.7 Estimating the Distribution of Total Defects over Time

Based on the discussions in the previous section, it is apparent that for software maintenance planning, we should (1) use the reliability models to estimate the total number of defects or defect rate only and (2) spread the total number of defects into arrival pattern over time based on historical patterns of field defect arrivals.

The field defect arrival patterns, in turn, can be modeled by the same process. Our experience with several operating systems indicates that the arrival curves follow the Rayleigh, the exponential, or the S models. Figure 8.5 shows the field

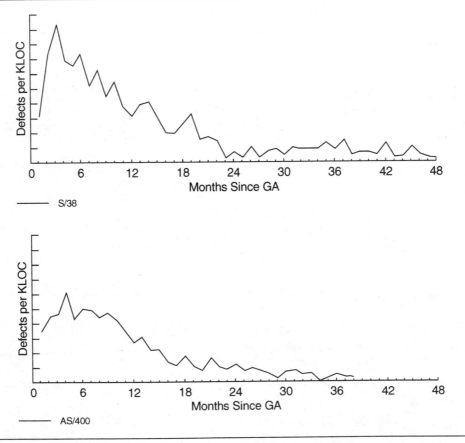

FIGURE 8.5
Field Defect Arrival Pattern—System/38 and AS/400 Operating Systems

defect arrival patterns of a major release of both the System/38 and the AS/400 operating systems. As discussed in Chapter 7, Figure 7.6 shows the field defect arrivals pattern of another IBM system software, which can be modeled by the Rayleigh curve or the Weibull distribution with the shape parameter, m, equal to 1.8.

The field defect arrival pattern may differ for different types of software. For example, in software for large systems it takes longer for latent defects to be detected and reported. The life of field defect arrivals can be longer than three years. For applications software, the arrival distribution is more concentrated and usually lasts about two years. We call the former the slow ramp-up pattern and the latter the fast ramp-up pattern. Based on a number of products for each category, we derived the distribution curves for both patterns, as shown in Figure 8.6. The areas under the two curves are the same, 100%. Tables 8.3 and 8.4 show the percent distribution by month for the two patterns. Because the defect arrival distribution pattern may depend on the type of software and industry segment, one should establish one's own pattern based on historical data. If the defect arrival patterns cannot be modeled by a known reliability model, we recommend using a nonparametric method (e.g., 3-point moving average) to smooth the historical data to reveal a pattern and then calculate the percent distribution over time.

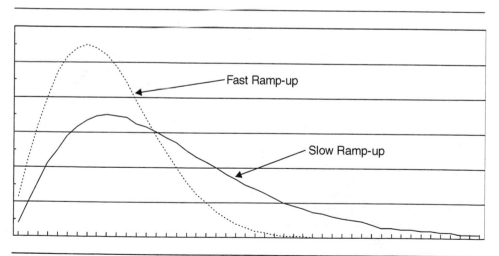

FIGURE 8.6
Two Patterns of Field Defect Arrivals—Areas Under the Curves Are the Same

TABLE 8.3
Monthly Percent Distribution of Field Defect Arrivals—Slow Ramp-up Pattern

Month	%	Month	%	Month	%	Month	%
1	0.554	13	4.505	25	1.940	37	0.55
2	1.317	14	4.366	26	1.802	38	0.41
3	2.148	15	4.158	27	1.594	39	0.41
4	2.911	16	3.950	28	1.386	40	0.34
5	3.465	17	3.742	29	1.247	41	0.34
6	4.019	18	3.465	30	1.178	42	0.27
7	4.366	19	3.188	31	1.040	43	0.27
8	4.643	20	2.980	32	0.970	44	0.20
9	4.782	21	2.772	33	0.832	45	0.20
10	4.851	22	2.495	34	0.762	46	0.13
11	4.782	23	2.287	35	0.693	47	0.13
12	4.712	24	2.079	36	0.624	48	0.06
Year 1 Cumulative	42.550	Year 2 Cumulative	82.537	Year 3 Cumulative	96.605	Year 4 Cumulative	100

TABLE 8.4
Monthly Percent Distribution of Field Defect Arrivals—Fast Ramp-up Pattern

Month	%	Month	%	Month	%
1	1.592	13	5.398	25	0.277
2	3.045	14	4.706	26	0.208
3	4.429	15	4.014	27	0.128
4	5.536	16	3.391	28	0.069
5	6.505	17	2.768	29	0.069
6	7.128	18	2.215	30	0.069
7	7.474	19	1.730		
8	7.612	20	1.384		
9	7.474	21	1.038		
10	7.197	22	0.761		
11	6.713	23	0.554		
12	6.090	24	0.415		
Year 1 Cumulative	70.795	Year 2 Cumulative	99.169	Year 2.5 Cumulative	99.999

8.8 Summary

The exponential distribution, another special case of the Weibull distribution family, is the simplest and perhaps most widely used distribution in reliability and survival studies. In software, it is best used for modeling the defect arrival pattern at the back end of the development process—for example, the final test phase. When calendar-time (versus execution-time) data are used, a key assumption for the exponential model is that the testing effort is homogeneous throughout the testing phase. If this assumption is not met, normalization of the data with respect to test effort is needed for the model to work well.

In addition to the exponential model, numerous software reliability growth models have been proposed, each with its own assumptions, applicability, and limitations. However, relatively few have been verified in practical environments with industry data, and even fewer are in use. Based on the criteria variable they use, software reliability growth models can be classified into two major classes: *time between failures models* and *fault count models*. In this chapter we summarize several well-known models in each class and illustrate the modeling process with a real-life example. From the practitioner's vantage point, the most important criteria for evaluating and choosing software reliability growth models are predictive validity, simplicity, and quality of assumptions.

Recommendations for Small Projects

The Rayleigh model discussed in Chapter 7 and the models discussed in this chapter are used to project a software's quality performance in the field (e.g., failure rate or number of defects) based on data gathered during the development of the project. Data requirements for these models are no different from those for other metrics discussed in previous chapters. The size of the teams or the development organizations does not affect implementation of these models. They do require modeling tools and personnel with sufficient statistical modeling training. For organizations that do not meet one or both of these requirements, I recommend a nonparametric method, which requires only pencils, paper, and a calculator, and which is based on the principles of simplicity and empirical validity.

The recommended method simply makes use of the test effectiveness metric discussed in Chapter 6. Assuming the level of test effectiveness is established via previous similar projects, with the volume of testing defects for the current project available, the volume of field defects can be estimated via the test effectiveness formula. Specifically, use the following three-step approach:

1. Select one or more previous projects that are comparable to the current project. Examine and establish the test effectiveness level and its variants (e.g., average, standard deviation, interval estimates) of these projects.

2. Gather the testing defect data from the current project, estimate the number of field defects based on the test effectiveness formula and the established test effectiveness value. If possible, con-

duct interval estimates (using data on standard deviations) as well as point estimates.

3. Based on the pattern of defect arrivals over time from history (discussed in section 8.6), spread out the total number of estimated field defects into years, quarters, or even months for more precise maintenance planning.

As an example, the ratios of the number of defects found during the system test to the number of field defects in a year for four software projects are as follows:

- Project A: 1.54
- Project B: 1.55
- Project C: 1.50
- Project D: 1.34

In other words, the system test effectiveness for Project A is $1.54 / (1.54+1) = 60.6\%$, and so forth. The average ratio for the four projects is 1.48 and average test effectiveness is 59.7%. Suppose the system test for the current project found 74 defects, using the average ratio of average test effectiveness, the number of field defects of the current project within a year in the field is estimated to be 50 (74/1.48).

Interval estimate is usually a better approach than point estimate. To derive an interval estimate (with a lower bound and an upper bound), the size of the sample (in this case $n = 4$), its standard deviation, and the t-distribution will be involved. For details, refer to a text on statistical methods such as Snedecor and Cochran (1980, pp. 54–59).

To cross-validate our estimate for this example, we also looked into a similar ratio for the four previous projects, by including the testing defects from two other tests (in addition to system test). The ratios are as follows:

- Project A: 2.93
- Project B: 3.03
- Project C: 3.26
- Project D: 2.84

In other words, the cumulative test effectiveness of two other tests and the system test for Project A is 2.93 / (2.93 + 1) = 74.6%. Using this new set of ratios, we came up with another estimate that is close to the first estimate. Therefore, our confidence on the robustness of the estimates increased. If the two estimates differ significantly, then apparently some judgment has to be made.

Caution: An implicit assumption of this simple method for defect estimation is that the defect arrival patterns during testing are similar. If they are not, the validity of this method will be compromised. If the pattern for the current project is in vivid contrast to comparable projects, such as the case shown in Figure 4.2, then the empirical validity of this method may not be established. In that case, we don't recommend using this method.

When the total number of field defects is estimated, estimating the pattern of arrivals over time can be based on history, which is organization- and product-type specific. If there are considerable fluctuations in the history data, the three-point moving average can be used to come up with a smooth pattern. If no history data is available, assess the type of software and, if applicable, use the distribution pattern in Table 8.3 or Table 8.4.

It is worth noting that for systems software, our observation is that the yearly distribution pattern is roughly similar to the half-life decay pattern of carbon dating. In other words, defect volume in the first year is about half of the total defects over the life of defect arrivals of the product, and in the second year, it is about half of the remaining defects, and so forth. If nothing is available and only a high-level yearly spread is needed, this half-life decay pattern could be used for systems software.

Software reliability models are most often used for reliability projection when development work is complete and before the software is shipped to customers. They can also be used to model the failure pattern or the defect arrival pattern in the field and thereby provide valuable input to maintenance planning.

References

1. Brocklehurst, S., and B. Littlewood, "New Ways to Get Accurate Reliability Measurements," *IEEE Software*, July 1992, pp. 34–42.
2. Ehrlich, W. K., S. K. Lee, and R. H. Molisani, "Applying Reliability Measurement: A Case Study," *IEEE Software*, March 1990, pp. 46–54.
3. Elbert, M. A., R. C. Howe, and T. F. Weyant, "Software Reliability Modeling," *ASQC Quality Congress Transactions*, Nashville, Tenn., 1992, pp. 933–940.

4. Falcetano, M. J., and J. M. Caruso, IBM Kingston, New York, Private Communication, 1988.

5. Goel, A. L., "Software Reliability Modeling and Estimation Techniques," Report RADC-TR-82-263, Rome Air Development Center, October 1982.

6. Goel, A. L., "Software Reliability Models: Assumptions, Limitations, and Applicability," *IEEE Transactions on Software Engineering,* Vol. SE-11, 1985, pp. 1411–1423.

7. Goel, A. L., and K. Okumoto, "An Analysis of Recurrent Software Failures in a Real-Time Control System," *Proceedings ACM Annual Technology Conference,* Washington, D.C., 1978, pp. 496–500.

8. Goel, A. L., and K. Okumoto, "A Time-Dependent Error-Detection Rate Model for Software Reliability and Other Performance Measures," *IEEE Transactions on Reliability,* Vol. R-28, 1979, pp. 206–211.

9. Hong, G. Y., "Present and Future of Software Reliability Engineering," *QC Focus,* No. 35, January/February, 1998 pp. 5–10.

10. Iannino, A., J. D. Musa, K. Okumoto, and B. Littlewood, "Criteria for Software Reliability Model Comparisons," *IEEE Transactions on Software Engineering,* Vol. SE-10, 1984, pp. 687–691.

11. Jelinski, Z., and P. Moranda, "Software Reliability Research," *Statistical Computer Performance Evaluation,* W. Freiberger, Ed., New York: Academic Press, 1972, pp. 465–484.

12. Littlewood, B., "Stochastic Reliability Growth: A Model for Fault Removal in Computer Programs and Hardware Designs," *IEEE Transactions on Reliability,* Vol. R-30, 1981, pp. 313–320.

13. Lyu, M. R., and A. Nikora, "Applying Reliability Models More Effectively," *IEEE Software,* July 1992, pp. 43–52.

14. Miller, D. R., "Exponential Order Statistic Models of Software Reliability Growth," *IEEE Transactions on Software Engineering,* Vol. SE-12, 1986, pp. 12–24.

15. Misra, P. N., "Software Reliability Analysis," *IBM Systems Journal,* Vol. 22, 1983, pp. 262–270.

16. Musa, J. D., A. Iannino, and K. Okumoto, *Software Reliability: Measurement, Prediction, Application,* New York: McGraw-Hill, 1987.

17. Musa, J. D., and K. Okumoto, "A Logarithmic Poisson Execution Time Model for Software Reliability Measurement," *Proceedings Seventh International Conference on Software Engineering,* Los Alamitos, Calif.: IEEE Computer Society Press, 1983, pp. 230–238.

18. Ohba, M., "Software Reliability Analysis Models," *IBM Journal of Research and Development,* Vol. 28, 1984, pp. 428–443.

19. Putnam, L.H., and W. Myers, *Measures for Excellence: Reliable Software on Time, Within Budget,* Englewood Cliffs, N.J.: Yourdon Press, 1992.

20. Ralston, M. L., and R. I. Jennrich, "DUD, a Derivative-Free Algorithm for Nonlinear Least Squares," *Technometrics,* Vol. 20, 1978, pp. 7–14.

21. Rohatgi, V. K., *An Introduction to Probability Theory and Mathematical Statistics,* New York: John Wiley & Sons, 1976.

22. Snedecor, G. W. and W. G. Cochran, *Statistical Methods,* 7th ed., Ames, Iowa: The Iowa State University Press, 1980.

23 Wiener-Ehrlich, W. K., J. R. Hamrick, and V. F. Rupolo, "Modeling Software Behavior in Terms of a Formal Life Cycle Curve: Implications for Software Maintenance," *IEEE Transactions on Software Engineering,* Vol. SE-10, 1984, pp. 376–383.

24. Xie, M., and G. Y. Hong, "A Study of the Sensitivity of Software Release Time," *Journal of Systems and Software* 44, 1998, pp. 163–168.

25. Xie, M., G. Y. Hong, and C. Wohlin "Software Reliability Prediction Incorporating Information from a Similar Project," *Journal of Systems and Software* 49, 1999, pp. 43–48.
26. Xie, M., and G. Y. Hong, "Software Reliability Modeling and Analysis," Book chapter in *Handbook of Statistics 20: Advances in Reliability,* edited by N. Balakrishnan and C. R. Rao, Elsevier Science, 2002.
27. Yamada, S., M. Ohba, and S. Osaki, "S-Shaped Reliability Growth Modeling for Software Error Detection," *IEEE Transactions on Reliability,* Vol. R-32, 1983, pp. 475–478.

9

Quality Management Models

Chapters 7 and 8 discuss models for reliability estimations. In this chapter we discuss models that can be used for quality management. We also give examples of in-process quality reports that support the models and discuss a method of in-process defect type analysis—the orthogonal defect classification.

It is important to assess the quality of a software product, project the number of defects, or estimate the mean time to next failure when development work is complete. It is more important to monitor and manage the quality of the software when it is under development. Such a task is the purpose of the software quality management models and in-process metrics. Although some models can be used for both reliability estimations and quality management, as we will see in later sections, how the models are used for quality management is different from that for reliability estimations. On the one hand, quality management models must provide early signs of warning or of improvement so that timely actions can be planned and implemented. On the other hand, they can be less precise and less mathematical than predictive models.

For a development organization, to be helpful the quality management model(s) must cover the early development phases. Models based on data collected at the end of the development process allow little time for action, if needed. The reliability growth models, which are based on system-test data when development work is virtually complete, therefore, may not be as useful for in-process quality management as for reliability assessment. Nonetheless, the reliability growth models are useful for quality management in terms of tracking status and determining when to end system testing for a specific predetermined quality goal.

Unlike the reliability models, which are numerous and include constantly emerging new ones, there are few models for in-process quality management in the literature. The following sections describe models that we have developed or have used.

9.1 The Rayleigh Model Framework

Perhaps the most important principle in software engineering is "do it right the first time." This principle speaks to the importance of managing quality throughout the development process. Our interpretation of the principle, in the context of software quality management, is threefold:

- ☐ The best scenario is to prevent errors from being injected into the development process.
- ☐ When errors are introduced, improve the front end of the development process to remove as many of them as early as possible. Specifically, in the context of the waterfall development process, rigorous design reviews and code inspections are needed. In the Cleanroom methodology, function verification by the team is used.
- ☐ If the project is beyond the design and code phases, unit tests and any additional tests by the developers serve as gatekeepers for defects to escape the front-end process before the code is integrated into the configuration management system (the system library). In other words, the phase of unit test or pre-integration test (the development phase prior to system integration) is the last chance to do it right the "first time."

The Rayleigh model is a good overall model for quality management. It articulates the points on defect prevention and early defect removal related to the preceding items. Based on the model, if the error injection rate is reduced, the entire area under the Rayleigh curve becomes smaller, leading to a smaller projected field defect rate. Also, more defect removal at the front end of the development process will lead to a lower defect rate at later testing phases and during maintenance. Both scenarios aim to lower the defects in the latter testing phases, which in turn lead to fewer defects in the field. The relationship between formal machine-testing defects and field defects, as described by the model, is congruent with the famous counterintuitive principle in software testing by Myers (1979), which basically states that the more defects found during formal testing, the more that remained to be found later. The reason is that at the late stage of formal testing, error injection of the development process (mainly during design and code implementation) is basically determined (except for bad fixes during testing). High testing defect rates indicate that the error injection is high; if no extra effort is exerted, more defects will escape to the field.

If we use the iceberg analogy to describe the relationship between testing and field defect rates, the tip of the iceberg is the testing defect rate and the submerged part is the field defect rate. The size of the iceberg is equivalent to the amount of error injection. By the time formal testing starts, the iceberg is already formed and its size determined. The larger its tip, the larger the entire iceberg. To reduce the submerged part, extra effort must be applied to expose more of the iceberg above the water. Figure 9.1 shows a schematic representation of the iceberg analogy.

A Rayleigh model derived from a previous release or from historical data can be used to track the pattern of defect removal of the project under development. If the current pattern is more front loaded than the model would predict, it is a positive sign, and vice versa. If the tracking is via calendar time such as month or week (versus by development phase), when enough data points are available, early estimation of model parameters can be performed. Quality projections based on early data would not be reliable compared to the final estimate at the end of the development cycle. Nonetheless, for in-process quality management, the data points can indicate the direction of the quality in the current release so that timely actions can be taken.

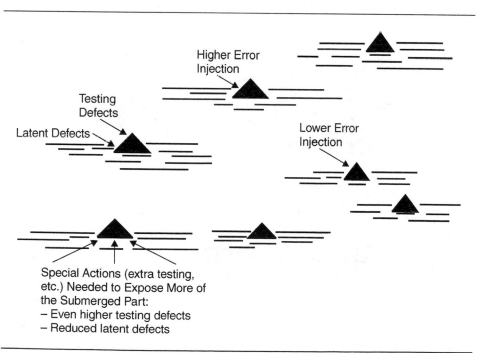

FIGURE 9.1

Iceberg Analogy—Error Injection, Testing Defects, and Latent Defects

Perhaps more important than for quality projections, the Rayleigh framework can serve as the basis for quality improvement strategy—especially the two principles associated with defect prevention and early defect removal. At IBM Rochester the two principles are in fact the major directions for our improvement strategy in development quality. For each direction, actions are formulated and implemented. For instance, to facilitate early defect removal, actions implemented include focus on the design review/code inspection (DR/CI) process; deployment of moderator training (for review and inspection meeting); use of an inspection checklist; use of in-process escape measurements to track the effectiveness of reviews and inspections; use of mini builds to flush out defects by developers before the system library build takes place; and many others. Plans and actions to reduce error injection include the laboratory-wide implementation of the defect prevention process; the use of CASE tools for development; focus on communications among teams to prevent interface defects; and others. The bidirectional quality improvement strategy is illustrated in Figure 9.2 by the Rayleigh model.

In summary, the goal is to shift the peak of the Rayleigh curve to the left while lowering it as much as possible. The ultimate target of IBM Rochester's strategy is to achieve the defect injection/removal pattern represented by the lowest curve, one with an error injection rate similar to that of IBM Houston's space shuttle software projects. In the figure, the Y-axis represents the defect rate. The development phases represented by the X-axis are high-level design review (I0), low-level design review (I1), code inspection (I2), unit test (UT), component test (CT), system test (ST), and product general availability (GA, or field quality, Fd).

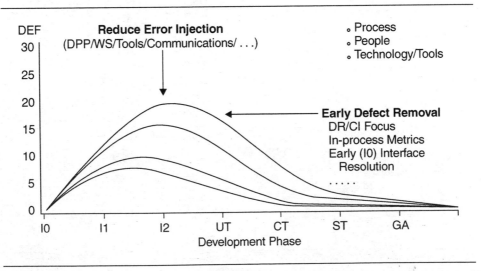

FIGURE 9.2
Rayleigh Model—Directions for Development Quality Improvement

This type of strategy can be implemented whether the defect removal pattern of an organization follows a Rayleigh curve or not. If not, the discrete phase-based defect model can be used. The key is that the phase-based defect removal targets are set to reflect an earlier defect removal pattern compared to the baseline. Then action plans should be implemented to achieve the targets. Figure 9.3 shows the defect removal patterns of several releases of a systems software developed at IBM Rochester. As can be seen from the curves, the shifting of the defect removal patterns does reflect improvement in the two directions of (1) earlier peaking of the defect curves, and (2) lower overall defect rates. In the figure, the *Y*-axis is the number of defects normalized per thousand new and changed source instructions (KCSI). The development phases on the *X*-axis are the same as those in Figure 9.2.

One major problem with the defect removal model is related to the assumption of the error injection rate. When setting defect removal targets for a project, error injection rates can be estimated based on previous experience. However, there is no way to determine how accurate such estimates are when applied to the current release. When tracking the defect removal rates against the model, lower actual defect removal could be the result of lower error injection or poor reviews and inspections. In contrast, higher actual defect removal could be the result of higher

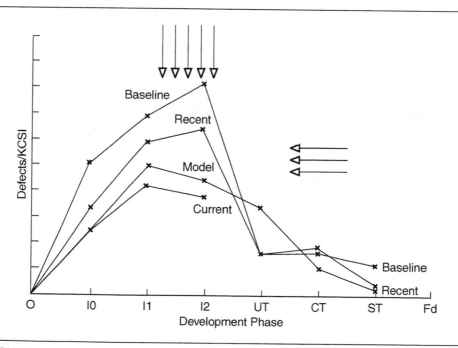

FIGURE 9.3

An Example of Improvement of the Defect Removal Pattern

error injection or better reviews and inspections. From the in-process defect removal data of the project under development, how do we know which scenario (better defect removal, higher error injection, lower error injection, or poorer defect removal) fits the project? To solve this problem, additional indicators must be incorporated into the context of the model for better interpretation of the data.

One such additional indicator is the quality of the process execution. For instance, at IBM Rochester the metric of inspection effort (operationalized as the number of hours the team spent on design and code inspections normalized per thousand lines of source code inspected) is used as a proxy indicator for how rigorous the inspection process is executed. This metric, combined with the inspection defect rate, can provide useful interpretation of the defect model. Specifically, a 2×2 matrix such as that shown in Figure 9.4 can be used. The high–low comparisons are between actual data and the model, or between the current and previous releases of a product. Each of the four scenarios imparts valuable information.

- ☐ *Best case scenario—high effort/low defect rate:* The design/code was cleaner before inspections, and yet the team spent enough effort in DR/CI (design review/code inspection) that good quality was ensured.
- ☐ *Good/not bad scenario—high effort/high defect rate:* Error injection may be high, but higher effort spent is a positive sign and that may be why more defects were removed. If effort is significantly higher than the model target, this may be a good scenario.

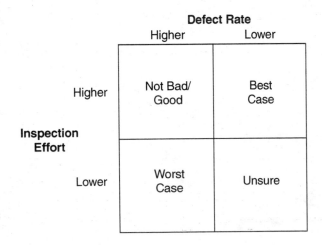

FIGURE 9.4

Inspection Effort/Defect Rate Scenarios Comparing Actuals to Model

□ *Unsure scenario—low effort/low defect rate:* Not sure whether the design and code were better, therefore less time was needed for inspection or inspections were hastily done, so fewer defects were found. In this scenario, we need to rely on the team's subjective assessment and other information for a better determination.

□ *Worst case scenario—low effort/high defect rate:* High error injection but inspections were not rigorous enough. Chances are more defects remained in the design or code at the exit of the inspection process.

The matrix is formed by combining the scenarios of an effort indicator and an outcome indicator. We call this approach to evaluating the quality of the project under development the effort/outcome model. The model can be applied to any phase of the development process with any pairs of meaningful indicators. In Chapter 10, we discuss the application of the model to testing data in details. We contend that the effort/ outcome model is a very important framework for in-process quality management.

Figures 9.5 and 9.6 show a real-life example of the high effort/high defect rate scenario from two software products. Compared to a predecessor product, the

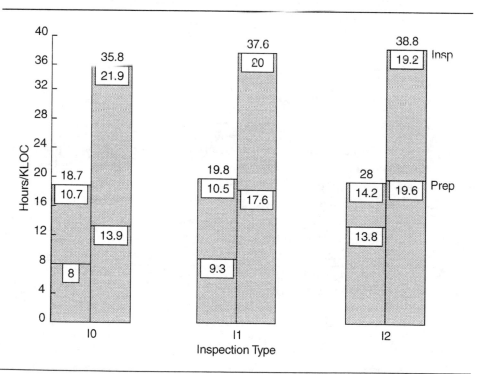

FIGURE 9.5
Inspection Effort Comparison by Phase of Two Products

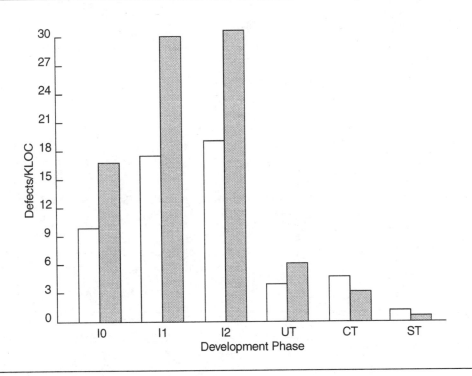

FIGURE 9.6
Defect Removal Patterns of Two Products

inspection effort of this product increased by more than 60%, and as a result the defect removal during the design and code inspection process was much higher than that of the predecessor product. As a result of the front-end effort, the test defect rate was significantly lower, and better field quality was observed. When development work was almost complete and lower test defect rates were observed, it was quite clear that the product would have better quality. However, during the front-end development it would have been difficult to interpret the defect removal pattern without the effort/defect matrix as part of the defect model. This example falls into the good/not bad scenario in Figure 9.4.

9.2 Code Integration Pattern

Among the major phases of any development process (i.e., requirements/analysis, design, code, test, and customer validation), code development is perhaps the most fundamental activity. Completion of coding and unit testing, and therefore the integration of code into the system library (to be ready for formal testing) is perhaps the most concrete intermediate deliverable of a project. Code completion by no means implies that the project is near completion. The earlier the code is complete and integrated into the system library relative to the project completion date, the better chance it will be adequately tested. In most software development projects, code completion does not occur only once for the entire project. Different pieces of function are completed at different times, within a certain calendar-time range on the project schedule. There is a common practice of continual code integration into the system library and the starting of component tests (functional tests), usually until the start of system testing. The pattern of code integration over time, relative to the product delivery date, therefore, is a crucial variable for schedule and quality management.

Figure 9.7 shows the code integration pattern of a systems software relative to the product's ship date. The vertical bars are the amount of code completed and integrated into the system library over time. Their values are expressed via the first Y-axis. The S curve is the cumulative percentage of code integrated over time, and is represented by the second Y-axis.

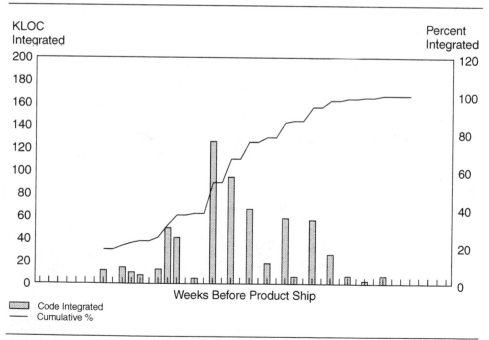

FIGURE 9.7
Code Integration Pattern of a Systems Software

We call the code integration pattern a pattern, not a model. However, meaningful use of this pattern can make it function like a heuristic model. There are at least three meaningful ways to use it:

☐ Establish a plan code integration curve as early in the development cycle as possible. Normally at the beginning of the project, team leaders are able to put down target dates for key activities of the line items they are responsible for, such as design complete, design review complete, code complete and integration, and testing start and completion. Use the plan curve to track the progress of code completion and integration.

☐ As early as a plan curve is available, study its pattern and take early actions to improve the pattern. For example, the S curve with a concave pattern at the top, such as the example in Figure 9.7, is a normal and healthy pattern. If the S curve shows some steep step increases at the right hand side, then it is a back-end loaded integration pattern, which may pose risks to testing schedules, defect arrival pattern during testing, and even schedules and quality outcome of the project.

☐ Perform project-to-project or release-to-release comparisons when baselines are available. Assess the feasibility of the current project based on the comparison results and take early actions.

Figure 9.8 shows a project-to-project comparison of code integration patterns. Products X, Y, and A are completed projects with positive quality in the field. Product B is a new project in the beginning stage, with the code integration plan just established. Product B's pattern is clearly back-end loaded with steep increases in the S curve up through the end of the code integration cycle. More important, it is significantly different from the other three projects, via the Kolmogorov-Smirnov test (Rohatgi, 1984). If the difference is not statistically significant, the plan can be recovered via effective quality improvement actions and sound project management practices. For examples, break big chunks of functions into smaller pieces and allow the pieces that get done earlier to integrate into the system library earlier, analyze the amount of new function and workload distribution across teams and balance the workload, or take actions on the front-end analysis and design work and attempt to move up the starting date of code integration. When the difference is statistically significant, it means that the feasibility of the project—on-time delivery with a field quality level similar to that of previous projects—is in question. In other words, the process capability of the development organization is being challenged. In such cases, the structural parameters of the project may need to be reevaluated. By "structural parameters," we mean the delivery date, the schedule, the amount of functions to be developed and delivered, the quality goals, and so forth. The project team can use this metric to articulate the team's evaluation to the executive project sponsor.

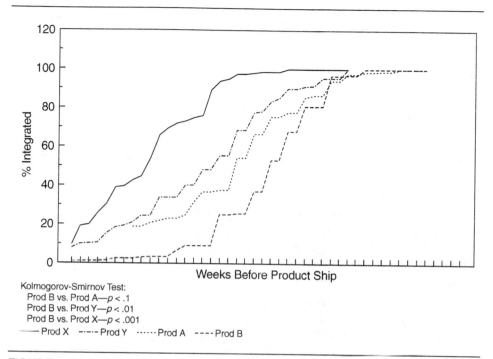

FIGURE 9.8
Code Integration Patterns of Four Projects

The code integration pattern metric is a simple and useful project management and quality management tool. Its objective fits perfectly with the overall framework of the Rayleigh model that the earlier defect removal, the better. We also recommend that the development team capture its experiences over time and derive its own "heuristic model." The model may include heuristic values of parameters such as a lower limit (the best pattern), an upper limit (the most challenged pattern and yet the project was completed successfully), the largest step function in the code integration process that was handled successfully, the strategies that can transform a negative pattern to an acceptable one, and other meaningful parameters and criteria pertinent to the model's objectives. This metric should be implemented by software projects of all kinds and sizes, and can be implemented easily with well-established tracking system, a simple Lotus 1-2-3 spreadsheet, or pencil and paper.

9.3 The PTR Submodel

Although the Rayleigh model, which covers all phases of the development process, can be used as the overall defect model, we need more specific models for better tracking of development quality. For example, the testing phases may span several months. For the waterfall process we used in previous examples, formal testing phases include component test, component regression test, and system test. For in-process quality management, one must also ensure that the chronological pattern of testing defect removal is on track. To derive a testing defect model, once again the Rayleigh model or other parametric models can be used if such models adequately describe the testing defect arrival patterns.

If the existing parametric models do not fit the defect patterns, special models for assessing in-process quality have to be developed. Furthermore, in many software projects, there is a common practice that the existing reliability models may not be able to address: the practice of continual code integration. As discussed in the previous section, sequential chunks of code are integrated when ready and this integration occurs throughout the development cycle until the system testing starts. To address this situation, we developed a simple nonparametric PTR submodel for testing defect tracking. It is called a PTR model because in many development organizations testing defects are tracked via some kind of problem tracking report (PTR), which is a part of the change control process during testing. Valid PTRs are, therefore, valid code defects. It is a submodel because it is part of the overall defect removal model. Simply put, the PTR submodel spreads over time the number of defects that are expected to be removed during the machine-testing phases so that more precise tracking is possible. It is a function of three variables:

1. Planned or actual lines of code integrated over time
2. Expected overall PTR rate (per thousand lines of code or per function point)
3. PTR-surfacing pattern after the code is integrated

The expected overall PTR rate can be estimated from historical data. Lines-of-code (LOC) integration over time is usually available in the current implementation plan. The PTR-surfacing pattern after code integration depends on both testing activities and the driver-build schedule. For instance, if a new driver is built every week, the PTR discovery/fix/integration cycle will be faster than that for drivers built biweekly or monthly. Assuming similar testing efforts, if the driver-build schedule differs from that of the previous release, adjustment to the previous release pattern is needed. If the current release is the first release, it is more difficult to establish a base pattern. Once a base pattern is established, subsequent refinements are relatively easy. For example, the following defect discovery pattern was observed for the first release of an operating system:

Month 1: 17%
Month 2: 22%
Month 3: 20%

Month 4: 16%

Month 5: 12%

Month 6: 9%

Month 7: 4%

To derive the PTR model curve, the following steps can be used:

1. Determine the code integration plan; plot the lines of code (or amount of function points) to be integrated over time (see Figure 9.9).
2. For each code integration, multiply the expected PTR rate by the KLOC for each planned integration to get the expected number of PTRs for each integration.
3. Spread over time the number of PTRs for each integration based on the PTR spread pattern and sum the number of PTRs for each time point to get the model curve.
4. Update the model when the integration plan (e.g., KLOC to be integrated over time) changes or actual integration data become available.

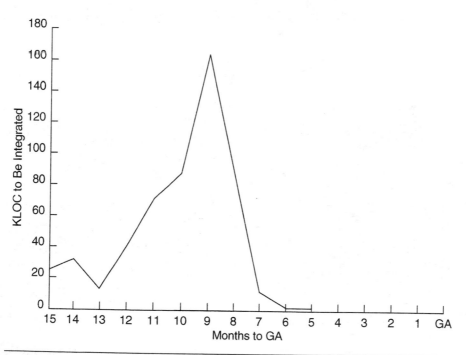

FIGURE 9.9

Planned KLOC Integration over Time of a Software Project

5. Plot the curve and track the current project in terms of months from the
    product's general availability (GA) date.

A calculator or a simple spreadsheet program is sufficient for the calculations
involved in this model.

Figure 9.10 shows an example of the PTR submodel with actual data. The code
integration changes over time during development, so the model is updated periodically. In addition to quality tracking, the model serves as a powerful quality impact
statement for any slip in code integration or testing schedule. Specifically, any delay
in development and testing will skew the model to the right, and the intersection of
the model line and the imaginary vertical line of the product's ship date (GA date)
will become higher.

Note that the PTR model is a nonparametric model and is not meant for projection. Its purpose is to enable the comparison of the actual testing defect arrival versus
an expected curve for in-process quality management. Compared to the model curve,
if the actual defect arrivals increase and peak earlier and decline faster relative to the
product's ship date, that is positive, and vice versa. When data from the previous

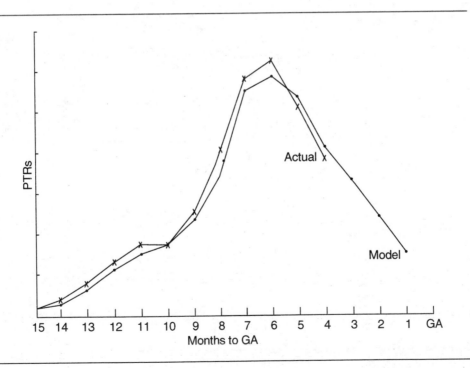

FIGURE 9.10
PTR Submodel

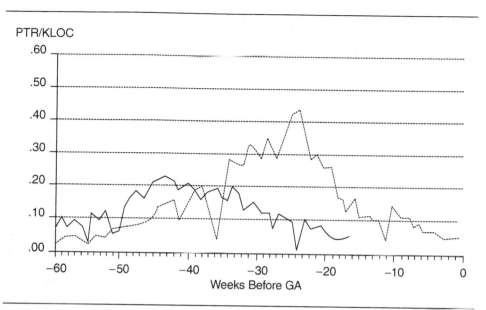

FIGURE 9.11
Testing Defect Arrival Patterns of Two Releases of a Product

release of the same product are available, and the code integration over time is similar for the two releases, the simplest way to gauge the testing defect arrival pattern is to use the curve of the previous release as the model. One can also fit a software reliability model to the data to obtain a smooth model curve. Our experience indicates that the Rayleigh model, the Weibull distribution, the delayed S model and the inflection S model (see discussions in Chapter 8) are all candidate models for the PTR data. Whether the model fits the data, however, depends on the statistical goodness-of-fit test.

Figure 9.11 shows such a comparison. Given that the test coverage and effectiveness of the releases are comparable, the PTR arrival patterns suggest that the current release will have a substantially lower defect rate. The data points are plotted in terms of number of weeks before product shipment. The data points associated with an abrupt decline in the early and later segments of the curves represent Christmas week and July 4th week, respectively. In Chapter 10, we will discuss the PTR-related metrics with details in the context of software testing.

9.4 The PTR Arrival and Backlog Projection Model

Near the end of the development cycle, a key question to ask is whether the scheduled code-freeze date can be met without sacrificing quality. Will the PTR arrival and backlog decrease to the predetermined desirable levels by the code-freeze date? The PTR submodel discussed earlier is clearly not able to accomplish this task because it is a tracking tool, not a projection tool. In contrast, the exponential model and other reliability growth models based on system test data, while being sufficient for the task, require data points well into the system test phase. Moreover, the analytic models may or may not be adequate depending on the goodness of fit. For cases like this, other types of modeling approaches may be needed. Here we present an example that we call the PTR arrival and backlog projection models. Its purpose is to project the PTR arrivals and backlog at the end of the development process. Analytical models aside, our approach was to derive empirical models based on data from the current project. If we were able to capture key explanatory variables in the models, we should be able to tap the correct message of the data with a certain degree of confidence. In this regard, the general linear model approach is readily available. From experience, we know that polynomial time terms combined with relevant variables usually form good projection models.

This model is different from the exponential model in several aspects. First, the time frame covers all machine testing (all PTRs) after the code is integrated (part of unit test, component test, component regression test, and system test). The exponential model applies only to defect arrivals during system test. Second, the data for this model are PTR arrivals and backlog, while the exponential model includes only valid PTRs (defects).

In our model building, the following sets of predictor variables were tested and their relationships with PTR arrival and backlog were specified:

☐ *Chronological time:* The rationale is to capture the chronological pattern of the development process. It is well known that software development has a life cycle of systematic processes. The specific time trend, however, varies among systems. It may be linear or polynomial patterns of second degree or higher, a Fourier series, or some other forms.

☐ *Time lag variables:* This set of variables is relevant because the data are of a time series nature and we need to assess the length of memory of these time series processes. Is this week's PTR number affected by the PTR occurrence of the preceding five weeks? four weeks? or the preceding fourth and third weeks but not the immediate two weeks? Does this process have memory at all? Testing this set of variables can give answers to questions like these.

☐ *Cumulative thousand lines of code (KLOC) integrated:* This variable is important because code was not integrated at only one point in time. Throughout the development cycle, pieces of code were integrated into the system library for testing. The number of PTRs is strongly related to the size of the code being tested.

☐ *Significant activities such as the onset of component test, system test, and other events:* This set of variables is dichotomous, with 1 denoting the presence of the event and 0 denoting its absence.

Prior to statistical testing of significance, scatterplots were used to examine the patterns of bivariate relationships and to detect outliers (Figures 9.12 and 9.13). For PTR arrival, a few obvious outliers were found, namely, the weeks of Thanksgiving, Christmas, and New Year's Day. The conspicuously low PTR arrivals for these weeks were apparently attributed to fewer working days as well as fewer programmers,

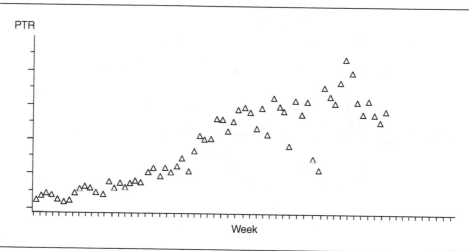

FIGURE 9.12
PTR Arrival by Week

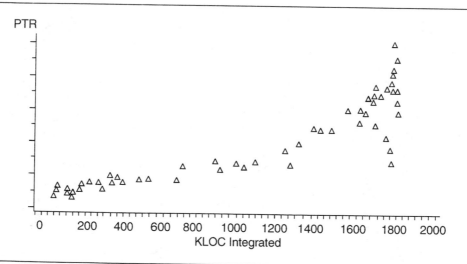

FIGURE 9.13
PTR Arrival by KLOC Integrated

which were artifacts of our calendar-time data. The values for these weeks, therefore, were replaced by the medians of the five consecutive data points centering at the weeks of interest. Likewise, values for the weeks of Memorial Day, Independence Day, and Labor Day were replaced, although they were not particularly low. For the backlog data, no adjustment is necessary because the data are cumulative.

When the patterns of bivariate relationships were specified and separate significance tests performed, the independent variables were put together in a model and their net effects were estimated simultaneously by the method of least squares. For both the arrival and backlog data, several models were attempted and the final model was chosen based on the highest R^2 value.

The number of PTR weekly arrivals was found to be a linear combination of a cubic pattern of time, a quadratic pattern of KLOC, the number of arrivals in the preceding week, and the presence or absence of the system test:

$$\text{PTR arrival} = \text{Constant} + f\,(\text{Week, Week}^2, \text{Week}^3, \text{KLOC, KLOC}^2,$$
$$\text{\# Arrivals in preceding week, System test}) + e$$

The equation of the model is as follows:

$$\begin{aligned}
\text{PTR arrival} = \ & 107.28764 \\
& - 3.22800 \times \text{Week} + 0.78017 \times \text{Week}^2 \\
& - 0.01048 \times \text{Week}^3 \\
& - 0.29980 \times \text{KLOC} + 0.00015 \times \text{KLOC}^2 \\
& + 0.18030 \times \text{\# Arrivals in preceding week} \\
& + 140.50424 \times \text{System test}
\end{aligned}$$

The model was highly significant ($F = 169.6$, $df_1 = 7$, $df_2 = 55$, p = 0.0001), as were its component terms. All independent variables together accounted for 95.6% of the variation of the arrival data. This R^2 translates to a multiple correlation of 0.978 between the model and the actual data.

Figure 9.14 compares the PTR arrival projection model with actual data points for the projection period. The model produces a projection that is accurate within one week in terms of when the PTR arrivals would decrease to the predetermined desirable level prior to code-freeze. A PTR backlog model was likewise established and the projection was borne out very well.

This analysis shows that the PTR arrival and backlog processes at the end of the development cycle are predictable with fairly good accuracy. Both our models are sufficiently strong, explaining about 95% of the total variation of the dependent variables. Both series of projections were borne out amazingly well, and were within one week in estimating the time of meeting the criteria levels.

This approach can be used in similar situations where projections for future dates are needed. It is especially useful when analytical models are not applicable.

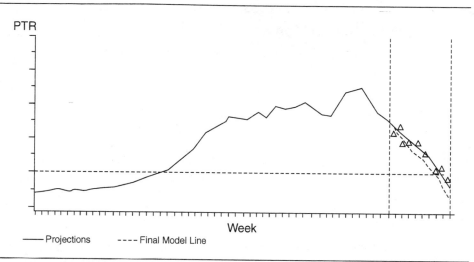

FIGURE 9.14
PTR Arrival Projection Model

Source: Kan, S. H., "Modeling and Software Development Quality," *IBM Systems Journal,* Vol. 30, No. 3, 1991, pp. 351–362. Copyright © 1991 International Business Machines Corporation. Reprinted with permission from *IBM Systems Journal.*

For the projections to be accurate, however, it requires a fairly large number of data points and the data collected must pass the last inflection point of the process. Another key is to capture significant variables in the model in order to obtain the highest R^2 possible. After the initial model is derived, updates should be done when new data points become available. It is advisable to attempt different projection scenarios based on differing assumptions, thereby giving a broader perspective for the assessment.

At the beginning of a process when few data points are available, analytical models or models based on experience can be derived for management purposes. When sufficient data are available, the best model can be determined based on goodness-of-fit tests. Combined with graphic techniques, the modeling approach is a very useful tool for software project management.

Unlike other models discussed, the PTR arrival and backlog projection models are really a modeling approach rather than a specific model. Statistical expertise, modeling experience, and a thorough understanding of the data are necessary in order to deal with issues pertaining to model assumptions, variables specification, and final model selection. A desirable outcome often depends on the model's R^2 and on the validity of the assumptions.

9.5 Reliability Growth Models

Although reliability growth models are meant for reliability assessment, they are also useful for quality management at the back end of the development process. Models developed from a previous product or a previous release of the same product can be used to track the testing defects of the current product. To have significant improvement, the defect arrival rate (or failure density) of the current project must fall below the model curve. Figure 9.15 shows an example from a systems software product developed at IBM Rochester. Each data point represents a weekly defect arrival rate during the system test phase. The defect arrival patterns represented by the triangles and circles indicate two later releases of the same product. Compared to the baseline model curve, both new releases witnessed a significant reduction in defect rate during the system test phase.

As a second example, when another product was just about at the start of system testing, the PTR arrival rates were unusually high compared to the model. It was clear that proceeding in a business-as-usual manner would not result in meeting the product's quality goal. A special quality improvement program (QIP) was then pro-

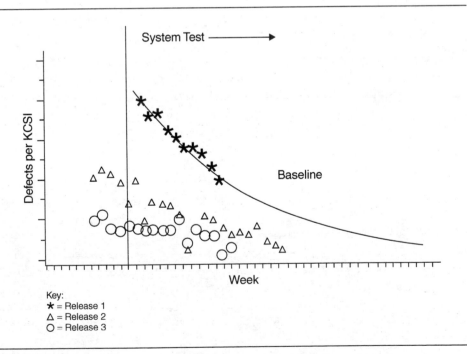

FIGURE 9.15
Reliability Growth Model for Quality Management

posed, evaluated, approved, and swiftly implemented. The QIP involved five extra activities:

1. *Blitz testing*—"artistic" testing in stressful environments
2. *Customer evaluation*—customers conducting testing in the development laboratory
3. *Code inspections*—additional inspections of error-prone modules, especially routines that are difficult to test such as the error recovery/exception handling routines
4. *Design reviews*—rereview of designs of suspect components and modules
5. *Extension of system test*—improvement of test suites and extension of testing schedules to allow thorough final test execution

Because of the special QIP activities, the product ship date was delayed one month. As a result, more than 250 would-be field defects were found and removed. The field quality of the product, evidenced by field defect arrivals reported in later years, improved significantly.

Figure 9.16 shows the defect arrival pattern of the product during system test. The data points represent the weekly defect rate (per thousand new and changed code—KCSI). The asterisks represent the defect arrival from the originally planned

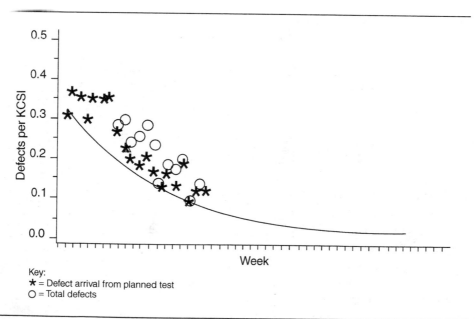

FIGURE 9.16
High Defect Arrival During System Test Compared to Model

system test. The circles represent the total defect rates including the additional defects discovered and removed via the QIP activities. Since the QIP activities and defects were specially marked in the defect tracking system, we were able to assess the additional defect removal by the program.

One of the advantages of using the reliability growth models as a quality management tool is that comparisons can be made when the first data points become available. If unfavorable signs are detected (e.g., defect arrivals are much too high), timely actions can be taken. In contrast, for reliability assessment and projection, a substantial amount of data has to be available for the models to be reliable. For models with an inflection point (such as the delayed S and inflection S models), data must be available beyond the inflection point if the models are to work. As discussed in the preceding chapter, studies show that the exponential process model needs to have data from about 60% of the system test in order to provide reasonably adequate fit and projection. Therefore, the reliability models can be used more liberally for quality management than for reliability projection.

The typical use of reliability models for quality management, as described in the software reliability literature, is to determine the end date of testing given a reliability goal or a specific defect level to be achieved. If the model derived from the current data indicates less-than-desirable quality, then more testing will be done until the reliability reaches the goal. This strategy assumes an abundance of extra test cases is available or the generation of extra test cases is relatively easy. For many commercial development projects, such an assumption may be difficult to meet. Test plans and test cases are developed over time along with design and code development; adding effective test cases is not a task that can be accomplished in a short time. Therefore, actions other than simply prolonging the testing (such as customer beta test, special stress testing, etc.) should also be considered.

Managing development quality based on reliability models at the back end should be used as the last step in the broader context of a series of quality management models. It should not be the sole approach. A software development quality management system should put as much focus as possible at the front end, and actions should be triggered as early as possible if negative indicators are observed. Actions taken at design, code, unit test, code integration time, and even at early formal machine testing time, are apt to be more cost effective and have a smaller chance of affecting the delivery date than later actions. Unfortunately, in the software reliability literature, one often gets the impression that the main way to achieve quality is to keep on testing until the defect arrival rate or the mean time to failure rate reaches the desirable level. Such a testing strategy to achieve quality improvement is not a good one. It is more applicable to research projects than to commercial developments, which often do not have the luxury to react at the back end and to delay delivery. The QIP example given earlier was the last major improvement action of that product, not the only one.

Finally, when interpreting the defect arrival data against a predetermined model, the variable of testing effort or coverage must be taken into consideration. For instance, if the defect arrivals are substantially below the model curve (as is the case in Figure 9.15), questions arise such as, "are the lower defects due to less effective testing or really due to better quality?" In this regard, the effort/outcome model in Figure 9.4 also applies to the testing phases. In Chapter 10, we discuss the effort/outcome model with respect to in-process metrics for testing.

9.6 Criteria for Model Evaluation

As discussed in the previous chapter, we contend that the most important criteria for evaluating reliability models are predictive validity, simplicity, and quality of assumptions, in that order of importance. With regard to quality management models, we propose that timeliness of quality indications, scope of coverage of the development process, and capability be the major criteria for evaluation.

The earlier a model can detect signs of quality problems or improvements, the more time is available for proactive planning. Furthermore, corrections in the early phases of the development process are much less expensive than those made at the back end. See Chapter 6 for discussion of the cost effectiveness of defect removal by development phase.

Model coverage of all phases of the development process is important. To have a good quality end product, quality in the intermediate deliverables at each phase, as defined by the phase entry and exit criteria, is a prerequisite. Each development phase must be managed and appropriate quality actions implemented. In case a single model cannot perform the tasks adequately, the use of multiple models is recommended.

While we contend that capability (other than predictability) is not an important criterion for software reliability models at the current state of the art, it is very important for management models. If "capability" refers to the model's ability to provide information for planning and managing software development projects, that is the purpose of quality management models. For instance, given the current in-process defect injection and removal pattern, will the project be likely to achieve its quality goal? If the effectiveness of the design review process improves by certain points, what is the possible impact on end-product quality? While quality management models may never reach the degree of accuracy and precision that reliability models have (or aim for), it is their capability to provide hints and findings for various in-process management questions that distinguish them as a separate category of software quality engineering model.

9.7 In-Process Metrics and Reports

We have thus far discussed an overall framework and the models associated with the framework for quality management during the development process. To facilitate the implementation of these models, we need a defect tracking and reporting system and a set of related in-process metrics. This is especially true for large development projects that involves many teams. In-process measurements and feedback, therefore, need to be available at various levels, ranging from the component team (several members) level to the entire product and system, which may involve more than one organization. In this section we present some examples of in-process metrics and reports.

Figures 9.17 and 9.18 are examples of reports that can support the implementation of the front end of the Rayleigh model—the design and code inspection phases. Figure 9.17 is the implementation version of the effort/outcome model in Figure 9.3. It is the first part of the inspection report and provides guidelines for interpretation and for actions with regard to the data in Figure 9.18.

Figure 9.18 shows the number of inspections completed by stage (I0, high-level design review; I1, low-level design review; and I2, code inspection). The first part of the upper panel gives information about actual lines of code inspected (Insp Locs), total lines of code in the current plan for the department (DCR Locs), number of defects found, inspection effort in terms of preparation hours and inspection hours, rework hours, and the number of participants at the inspections (#Ats). The second part of the first panel (defined by double dashed lines) shows the normalized metrics such as percent inspection coverage (%Insp CVG), defects per thousand lines of code (Defs/Kloc), preparation hours per KLOC (PrepHr/Kloc), actual inspection hours per KLOC (InspHr/Kloc), total hours on inspection (the sum of preparation time and inspection time) per KLOC (TotHrs/Kloc), rework hours per KLOC (RwrkHr/Kloc) to complete the design or coding phase, and the average number of participants per inspection. The system model in terms of inspection defect rates (Sys Model) and inspection effort (Sys Stddr) are also presented for comparison.

In the second panel the same information for the previous release by the same team or department is shown. The bottom panel shows comparisons according to the scenarios of the effort/outcome model. For each phase of inspection, two comparisons are made: current release compared to the previous release, and current release compared to the system model. Specifically, the first comparison involves comparing "Defs/Kloc" and "TotHrs/Kloc" in the first panel with the corresponding numbers in the second panel. The second comparison involves comparing "Defs/Kloc" with "Sys Model" and "TotHrs/Kloc" with "Sys Stddr" in the first panel (current release). The report also automatically flags the total inspection effort (TotHrs/Kloc) if its

```
                               DEFECT RATE
                Significant HIGHER <-----------------> Significant LOWER
           +----------------------------+----------------------------+
           |          *** H H ***       |        *** H L ***         |
    I      |                            |                            |
    N Sign |    SCENARIO 2: GOOD/NOT BAD |   SCENARIO 1: BEST CASE    |
    S HIGHER                            |                            |
    P      |                            |                            |
    E      | * MAY NEED EMPHASIS ON DEFECT| * ASK IF INSPECTION       |
    C      |     PREVENTION             |     EFFECTIVE?              |
    T      |                            |                            |
    I      | * KEEP UP THE GOOD INSPECTION| * IF YES, INDICATION OF GOOD|
    O      |     EFFORT                 |     QUALITY                |
    N      |                            |                            |
           |----------------------------|----------------------------|
           |          *** L H ***       |        *** L L ***         |
    E Sign |                            |                            |
    F LOWER|    SCENARIO 4: WORST CASE  |   SCENARIO 3: UNSURE        |
    F      |                            |                            |
    O      | * INDICATION OF LOW QUALITY| * LOOK FOR OTHER INDICATORS |
    R      |                            |     SUCH AS REWORK TIME     |
    I      | * CONSIDER REINSPECTION    | * INCREASE INSPECTION EFFORT|
           | * MAY NEED EMPHASIS ON      |                            |
           |     PREVENTION             |                            |
           | * NEED TO INCREASE EFFORT AND|                          |
           |     IMPROVE INSPECTION RIGOR|                            |
           |                            |                            |
           +----------------------------+----------------------------+
```

In addition to the matrix above, also ask these
questions:
- Have all mandatory reviewers attended?
- Were the inspectors well prepared?
- Were all materials covered?
- Was the meeting time adequate for the amount and
  complexity of materials?

FIGURE 9.17
An Inspection Report—Effort/Defect Matrix

value is lower than the system standard (Sys Stddr). As discussed in Chapter 6, inspection defect removal is much more cost effective than testing. Therefore, if a team's inspection effort is below the system standard, the minimum the team should do is to examine if there is enough rigor in their inspections, and if not, take appropriate action.

```
                    Summary Inspection Report            Date:
                  Defect Rate and Inspection Effort       Time:
==================================================================
*** Dept/Comp    A                                  Release  N
---- ------ -------- -------- ------ ------ ------- ------- ------ ------

Insp   #      Insp    DCR            Prep  Insp   Total  Rwrk    #
Type  Insps   Locs    Locs   Defs  Hours Hours   Hours  Hours  Ats
---- ------ -------- -------- ------ ------ ------- ------- ------ ------
I0      64   23604    38077    298  502.1 464.1   966.2  164.2  556
I1      19    9620    38077    203  151.6 158.6   310.2  122.7   86
I2     136   30886    38077   1059  760.6 671.8  1432.4  574.4  529

*** Dept/Comp    A                                  Release  N
---- ------ -------- -------- ------ ------ ------- ------- ------ ------

Insp  %Insp  Defs     Sys    PrepHr InspHr TotHrs  Sys   RwrkHr  #At
Type  CVG   /Kloc    Model   /Kloc  /Kloc  /Kloc  Stddr  /Kloc  /Insp
---- ------ -------- -------- ------ ------ ------- ------- ------ ------
I0    62.0   12.6      7.0    21.3   19.7   40.9   19.6    7.0    8.7
I1    25.3   21.1     15.0    15.8   16.5   32.2   22.8   12.8    4.5
I2    81.1   34.3     13.0    24.6   21.8   46.4   26.0   18.6    3.9

==================================================================
*** Dept/Comp    A                                  Release  N-1
---- ------ -------- -------- ------ ------ ------- ------- ------ ------

Insp   #      Insp    DCR            Prep  Insp   Total  Rwrk    #
Type  Insps   Locs    Locs   Defs  Hours Hours   Hours  Hours  Ats
---- ------ -------- -------- ------ ------ ------- ------- ------ ------
I0      58   42917    51652    679  540.0 413.4   953.4  371.5  627
I1      43   28924    51652    499  264.7 262.2   526.9  210.5  330
I2     107   44904    51652   1168  869.1 734.0  1603.1  620.8  488

*** Dept/Comp    A                                  Release  N-1
---- ------ -------- -------- ------ ------ ------- ------- ------ ------

Insp  %Insp  Defs     Sys    PrepHr InspHr TotHrs  Sys   RwrkHr  #At
Type  CVG   /Kloc    Model   /Kloc  /Kloc  /Kloc  Stddr  /Kloc  /Insp
---- ------ -------- -------- ------ ------ ------- ------- ------ ------
I0    83.1   15.8      7.0    12.6    9.6   22.2   19.6    8.7   10.8
I1    56.0   17.3     15.0     9.2    9.1   18.2   22.8    7.3    7.7
I2    86.9   26.0     13.0    19.4   16.3   35.7   26.0   13.8    4.6
==================================================================
I0 : Compared to previous release        you are at  HL   +------+------+
   : Compared to system standard & model you are at  HH   |  HH  |  HL  |
I1 : Compared to previous release        you are at  HH   |      |      |
   : Compared to system standard & model you are at  HH   |------|------|
I2 : Compared to previous release        you are at  HH   |      |      |
   : Compared to system standard & model you are at  HH   |  LH  |  LL  |
                                                          +------+------+

==================================================================
```

FIGURE 9.18
An Inspection Report—Inspection Effort and Defect Rate

Note that for the effort/defect matrix, the inspection effort indicator is a proxy variable to measure how well the inspection process was executed. It is one, but not the only, operational definition to measure process quality. An alternative could be the inspection team's assessment and the inspection scoring approach. Specifically, instead of (or in addition to) the tracking of inspection effort, the inspection team assesses the effectiveness of the inspection and the quality of the design (or code) at the end of an inspection. Simple checklists such as the one in Table 9.1 can be used.

It is preferable to conduct two assessments for each inspection, one before and one after. Such pre- and postinspection evaluations provide information on the effect of the inspection process. For the preinspection assessment, the questions on inspection effectiveness and whether another inspection is needed may not apply.

The inspection scores can then be used as indicators of the process quality as well as the interim product (design and code) quality. When data on multiple inspections are available, the technique of control charting can be used for in-process quality control. For instance, the team may establish a requirement for mandatory rework or reinspection if the score of a design or an implementation is below the lower control limit.

TABLE 9.1
An Inspection Scoring Checklist

	Response									
	Poor			Acceptable				Excellent		
Design	1	2	3	4	5	6	7	8	9	10
Work meets requirements	1	2	3	4	5	6	7	8	9	10
Understandability of design	1	2	3	4	5	6	7	8	9	10
Extensibility of design	1	2	3	4	5	6	7	8	9	10
Documentation of design	1	2	3	4	5	6	7	8	9	10
Effectiveness of this inspection	1	2	3	4	5	6	7	8	9	10
Does another inspection need to be held?	____Yes			____No						
Code Implementation	1	2	3	4	5	6	7	8	9	10
Work meets design	1	2	3	4	5	6	7	8	9	10
Performance considerations	1	2	3	4	5	6	7	8	9	10
Understandability of implementation	1	2	3	4	5	6	7	8	9	10
Maintainability of implementation	1	2	3	4	5	6	7	8	9	10
Documentation	1	2	3	4	5	6	7	8	9	10
Effectiveness of this inspection	1	2	3	4	5	6	7	8	9	10
Does another inspection need to be held?	____Yes			____No						

When using the inspection scoring approach, factors related to small team dynamics should be considered. Data from this approach may not be unobtrusive and therefore should be interpreted carefully, and in the context of the development organization and the process used. For instance, there may be a tendency among the inspection team members to avoid giving low scores even though the design or implementation is poor. A score of 5 (acceptable) may actually be a 2 or a 3. Therefore, it is important to use a wider response scale (such as the 10-point scale) instead of a narrow one (such as a 3-point scale). A wider response scale provides room to express (and observe) variations and, once enough data are available, develop valid interpretations.

Figure 9.19 is another example of inspection defect reports. The defects are classified in terms of defect origin (RQ = requirements, SD = system design, I0 = high-level design, I1 = low-level design, I2 = code development) and defect type (LO = logic, IF = interface, DO = documentation). The major purpose of the report is to show two metrics—in-process escape rate and percent of interface defects. The concept of in-process escape rate is related to the concept of defect removal effectiveness, which is examined in Chapter 6. The effectiveness metric is a powerful but not an in-process metric. It cannot be calculated until all defect data for the entire development process become available. The in-process escape metric asks the question in a different way. The effectiveness metric asks "what is the percentage of total defects found and removed by this phase of inspection?" The in-process escape metric asks "among the defects found by this phase of inspection, what is the percentage that should have been found by previous phases?" The lower the in-process escape rate, the more likely that the effectiveness of the previous phases was better. The in-process escape metric also supports the early defect removal approach. For example, if among the defects found by I2 (code inspection) there is a high percentage that should have been found by I1 (low-level design review), that means I1 (low-level design) was not done well enough and remedial actions should be implemented.

The rationale for the metric of percentage of interface defects is that a large percentage of defects throughout the development life cycle (from design defects to field defects) is due to interface issues. Furthermore, interface problems are to a large extent related to human communications and, therefore, preventable. Reducing interface defects should be an objective of in-process quality management. One of the objectives of high-level design is to finalize interface issues at the exit of I0 (high-level design review). Therefore, it is logical to see high percentages of interface defects at I0. However, at subsequent phases, if the percentage of interface defects remains high, it implies that the goal of resolving interface issues at I0 has not been achieved. In this example, the predetermined targets for in-process escape rates and for interface defect reduction were also shown in the report, and exceptions were flagged.

9.7 In-Process Metrics and Reports

263

```
                        Summary Inspection Report        Date:
                     By Defect Origin and Defect Type    Time:
========================================================================
*** Dept/Comp         A                             Release  N
---- ----       --------------------    ------------------------------
Insp            <-- Defect Origin -->   <------ % DISTRIBUTIION ------->
Type Defs       RQ  CAI I0   I1   I2     RQ   SD   I0    I1   I2 TOT
---- ----       --------------------    ------------------------------
I0    298       26  15  257   0    0    8.7  5.0  86.2  ---   --- 100%
I1    203        0   0   10  193   0    0.0  0.0   4.9  95.1  --- 100%
I2   1059       11   0   41   97  910   1.0  0.0   3.9   9.2 85.9 100%

---- ---- ------- ----   ------------------    ------------------------
Insp    #   Insp         <- Defect Type ->    <--  Defect   Type  -->
Type Insp Locs Defs        LO   IF   DO       %LO   %IF   %DO  Tot
---- ---- ------- ----   ------------------    ------------------------
I0    64  23604  298       56   79  163      18.8  26.5  54.7  100%
I1    19   9620  203      138    9   56      68.0   4.4  27.6  100%
I2   136  30886 1059      684   65  310      64.6   6.1  29.3  100%
========================================================================
*** Dept/Comp         A                             Release  N-1
---- ----       --------------------    ------------------------------
Insp            <-- Defect Origin -->   <------ % DISTRIBUTIION ------->
Type Defs       RQ  CAI I0   I1   I2     RQ   SD   I0    I1   I2 TOT
---- ----       --------------------    ------------------------------
I0    679       22   2  655   0    0    3.2  0.3  96.5  ---   --- 100%
I1    499        5   0   50  444   0    1.0  0.0  10.0* 89.0  --- 100%
I2   1168        4   1   19  125 1019   0.3  0.1   1.6  10.7 87.2 100%
---- ---- ------- ----   ------------------    ------------------------
Insp    #   Insp         <- Defect Type ->    <--  Defect   Type  -->
Type Insp Locs Defs        LO   IF   DO       %LO   %IF   %DO  Tot
---- ---- ------- ----   ------------------    ------------------------
I0    58  42917  679       95  143  441      14.0  21.1  64.9  100%
I1    43  28924  499      254   35  210      50.9   7.0  42.1  100%
I2   107  44904 1168      668   78  422      57.2   6.7  36.1  100%
========================================================================
*** IN-PROCESS ESCAPE RATE SYSTEM TARGET
I1 defects : <= 5% are escapes from HLD
I2 -"-     : <= 2% are escapes from HLD
I2 -"-     : <= 6% are escapes from LLD

*** INTERFACE DEFECT REDUCTION
I0       : Interface issues finalized at I0 exit
I1 & I2  : Goal is to reduce interface defects to
           <= 5% of total defects

(*)      : EXCEEDS system target significantly (2x+)
           Consider RE-INSPECTION AND OTHER ACTIONS.
(@)      : EXCEEDS system target significantly (2x+).
           Consider RE-INSPECTION AND OTHER ACTIONS. MAKE
           SURE INTERFACE ISSUES ARE FINALIZED AT I0 EXIT.
========================================================================
NOTE: When interpreting * and @, be careful with small numbers.
```

FIGURE 9.19

An Inspection Report—Defect Origin and Defect Type

Figure 9.20 shows a report on unit test coverage and defects. Ideally, unit tests are conducted before the code is integrated into the system library. For various reasons (dependencies, schedule pressures, etc.), it is not uncommon that some unit tests are done after code integration. The in-process metrics and reports, therefore, should reflect the state of practice and encourage defect removal before integration. In Figure 9.20 the columns include the product ID (PROD), the ID of the components (CPID) that the organization owns, the lines of code by components for the current release (DCRLOC), the lines of code that have been unit tested (UTLOC), the unit test coverage so far ($\%CVG = UTLOC \times 100/DCRLOC$), the number of unit test defects found before integration [DEFS (DCR)], the number of unit test defects found after integration and expressed in the form of problem tracking reports (UT PTRs), and the normalized rates. The key interests of the report are the ratio of pre-

```
                   Unit Test Coverage and Defect Report           Date:
                                                                  Time:

               Status = Approved, Integrated, Completed, Closed
               PRODUCT = XX  COMPONENT=ALL  DEPT= B  RELEASE= N

===================================================================
                                                            TOTAL
                               DEFS   UT   TOTAL DEFS/  PTR/ DEFS/
                                                       DCR  DCR
  PROD  CPID DCRLOC  UTLOC  %CVG  (DCR) PTRS  DEFS  UT-
                                                       KLOC KLOC
                                                       KLOC

  ----  ----- ------ ------ ----- ----- ---- ------ ------ ---- -----

  XX    CP1      20     30 100.0    4    1     5   133.3  50.0 250.0
  XX    CP2    4084   4315 100.0   67    9    76    15.5   2.2  18.6
  XX    CP3     175    175 100.0    1    0     1     5.7   0.0   5.7
  XX    CP4    3983   3959  99.4   16    1    17     4.0   0.3   4.3
  XX    CP5    7406   7389  99.8  134   39   173    18.1   5.3  23.4
  XX    CP6    2589   1289  49.8    6    0     6     4.7   0.0   2.3
  XX    CP7    2947   2845  96.5   50    2    52    17.6   0.7  17.6
  XX    CP8     735    700  95.2    8    3    11    11.4   4.1  15.0
  XX    CP9    2570   1292  50.3   16   20    36    12.4   7.8  14.0
  XX    CP10   6888   1300  18.9   19    4    23    14.6   0.6   3.3
  XX    CP11    441    304  68.9    8    4    12    26.3   9.1  27.2
  XX    CP12     2      2 100.0    0    1     1     0.0 500.0 500.0

  ----  ----- ------ ------ ----- ----- ---- ------ ------ ---- -----

  XX    TOTAL 31840  23600  74.1  329   84   413    13.9   2.9  13.3

===================================================================
```

FIGURE 9.20
A Unit Test Coverage and Defect Report

integration defect removal [DEFS (DCR)] to postintegration defects (UT PTRS) and the overall unit test defect rate (TOTAL DEFS/DCR KLOC). The interpretation is that the higher the ratio (the higher defect removal before integration), the better. Components with high unit test defects found after code integration should be examined closely. Comparisons can also be made for the same components between two consecutive releases to reveal if an earlier defect removal pattern is being achieved.

Figure 9.21 shows the test defect rate by phase. In addition to postintegration unit test defects (UT), it shows defects found during the build and integration process (BI), component test (CT), component regression test (CRT), system test (ST), and early customer programs (customer field test, customer early burn-in program, etc.).

```
                    PTR BY TEST ACTIVITY
            DEPT: C     PROD: YY   CPID: ALL     Date:
                    Release:    N                Time:
```

PROD	CPID	UT	BI	CT	CRT	ST	ECP	TOTAL	DCR LOC	DEFS/ KLOC
YY	COMP1	2	0	3	0	0	0	5	1150	1.3
YY	COMP2	2	0	16	6	5	0	29	940	30.9
YY	COMP3	0	0	2	0	1	0	3	0	--
YY	COMP4	1	0	3	2	1	0	7	50	140.0
YY	COMP5	0	0	1	0	2	0	3	1050	2.9
YY	COMP6	1	0	2	3	4	1	11	0	--
YY	COMP7	0	2	4	0	1	0	7	605	11.6
YY	COMP8	1	0	7	0	0	0	8	51	156.9
YY	COMP9	1	1	3	1	1	0	7	172	40.7
YY	COMP10	0	0	1	0	0	0	1	0	--
YY	COMP11	3	0	13	3	8	0	27	1775	15.2
YY	COMP12	0	1	1	0	0	0	2	293	6.8
YY	COMP13	0	0	8	4	5	0	17	800	21.3
YY	COMP14	0	0	1	0	0	0	1	200	5.0
YY	COMP15	1	0	0	0	0	0	1	25	40.0
YY	TOTAL	12	4	65	19	28	1	129	7111	18.1

-- Not applicable

FIGURE 9.21
A Defects by Test Phase Report

The column DCR LOC again shows the lines of new and changed code for the current release. The DEFS/KLOC column shows the defect rate per KLOC. The three components that have 0 in the DCR LOC column did not have new and changed code for that release but took part in the testing effort to remove defects in the existing code.

Data from Figure 9.21, together with data for unit test and the front-end inspections, provide sufficient information for the overall defect removal patterns for the entire development process. These in-process metrics and reports cannot be used in a piecemeal fashion. They should be used together in the context of the quality management models.

In addition to the basic metrics and reports, many other reports are useful for in-process quality management. The first is perhaps the test defect origin report. Similar to the inspection defect origin report, this reports classifies defects for each test phase by where they should have been found. For instance, when a defect is reported during a system test, its test origin (UT, CT, or ST) will be determined by involved parties. Usually it is easier to determine if a certain defect is a system test type defect, than to distinguish the difference between a unit test defect and a component test defect.

Other reports such as severity distribution of test defects, defect cause by test phase, and changes during the test phases due to performance reasons also provide important indicators of the product's quality. Testing defect rates have a strong correlation with field defect rates; the severity of test defects is also a good indicator of the severity distribution of field defects. Severe problems, usually difficult to circumvent, tend to have a more pervasive impact on customer business. Performance changes, especially the late ones, are error-prone activities. If negative signals are detected from these metrics, proactive actions (e.g., special customer evaluation or extended customer burn-in) should be planned before the release of the product.

There are more in-process metrics for testing that are not covered in this chapter. The next chapter provides a more detailed discussion of the subject.

9.8 Orthogonal Defect Classification

Orthogonal defect classification (ODC) is a method for in-process quality management based on defect cause analysis (Chillarege et al., 1992). Defect cause or defect type analysis by phase of development is not new. In many development organizations, metrics associated with defect cause are part of the in-process measurement system. The ODC method asserts that a set of mutually independent cause categories (orthogonal) can be developed, which can be used across phases of development and across products, and that the distribution of these defect types is associated with process phases. The authors contend that a more or less stable "signature profile" of defect type distribution can be established by each phase of the development process. By examining the distribution of defect types, therefore, one can tell which development phase the current project is at, logically. The authors propose eight defect types:

- ☐ Function
- ☐ Interface
- ☐ Checking
- ☐ Assignment
- ☐ Timing/serialization
- ☐ Build/package/merge
- ☐ Documentation
- ☐ Algorithm

The authors contend that functional defects (missing or incorrect functions) are associated with the design phase; interface defects are associated with low-level design; checking with low-level design or code implementation; assignment with code; timing/serialization with low-level design; build/package/merge with library tools; documentation defects with publications; and algorithms with low-level design.

The authors offer several examples of ODC. One example illustrates the high percentage of the defect type "function" found at a late stage in the development cycle. Specifically, the defect discovery time was classified into four periods; the last period corresponded approximately to the system test phase. In the last period the number of defects found almost doubled, and the percentage of defect type "function" increased to almost 50%. Since the defect type "function" is supposed to be found earlier (during the design phase), the observed distribution indicated a clear departure from the expected process behavior. Given that function defects were the cause of the departure, the analysis also suggested an appropriate design reinspection rather than more intensive testing.

In addition to defect type analysis, the ODC method includes defect triggers to improve testing effectiveness. A defect trigger is a condition that allows a defect to surface. By capturing information on defect triggers during testing and for field defects reported by customers, the test team can improve its test planning and test cases to maximize defect discovery.

The trigger part of ODC and its application to testing appear to be more solid than the assertion with regard to the "signature profiles" of defect type. Whether the process associations with defect type can be applied across products or organization uniformly is an open question. Even assuming similar development processes, differences in process details and focus areas may lead to differences in the distribution of defect types and defect causes. For instance, in the example shown in Figure 9.19, final resolution of interface issues is one of the exit criteria of high-level design inspection (I0). Therefore, higher percentages of interface defects are observed at I0, instead of at low-level design (I1). Another variable is the maturity level of the development process, especially in terms of the error injection rate. A defect type distribution for a development organization with an error injection rate of 60 defects per KLOC is likely to be different from that with an error injection rate of 20 defects per KLOC. The actions for reducing error injection or defect prevention are likely to have stronger effects on some defect causes than on others.

With regard to use of a defect type distribution for assessing the progress of the project, the ODC method seems to be too indirect. The several quality management models and the many in-process metrics discussed in this book would be more effective for project and quality management. At the defect analysis level, a more direct approach is to use the defect found (at which phase of development) versus defect origin (or test origin) analysis—see the examples in Figures 6.4 and 9.19.

The ODC method has evolved over the years. More defect attributes have been developed. The attributes classified by ODC when a defect is opened include the following:

- *Activity*—The specific activity that exposed the defect. For example, during system test, a defect occurs when one clicks a button to select a printer. The phase is system test but the activity is function test because the defect surfaced by performing a function test-type activity.
- *Trigger*—The environment or condition that had to exist for the defect to surface.
- *Impact*—This refers to the effect the defect had on the customer if it had escaped to the field, or the effect it would have had if not found during development.

The attributes classified by ODC when a defect fix is known include the following:

- *Target*—What is being fixed: design, code, documentation, and so forth?
- *Defect type*—The nature of the correction made
- *Defect qualifier* (applies to defect type)—Captures the element of nonexistent, wrong, or irrelevant implementation
- *Source*—The origin of the design/code that had the defect
- *Age*—The history of the design/code that had the defect

The ODC defect analysis method has been applied to many projects and successful results have been reported (Bassin et al., 2002; Butcher et al., 2002). The most significant contribution of ODC seems to be in the area of providing data-based assessments leading to improvement of test effectiveness.

Data and resources permitting, we recommend in-depth defect-cause and defect-type analysis be done (whether or not it is according to the ODC classifications) as an integrated part of the in-process metrics in the context of quality management models.

Recommendations for Small Organizations

The Rayleigh model for quality management is a useful framework. I recommend it to development organizations of all sizes. For organizations that don't have data and metrics tracking for all phases of development, simply focus on the strategies and actions along the two directions of improvement: (1) those that will lead to early defect removal and (2) those that will reduce the error injection by the development team. For data tracking and metrics for small organizations that plan to start a metrics practice, I recommend the following:

■ For the front end of the development process, use the inspection scoring checklist (Table 9.1).
■ For the middle of the development process, use the code integration pattern metric and over time establish a heuristic model.
■ For the back end of the development process, use a testing defect related metric or model (Figures 4.2, 9.10, 9.11, 9.15, or 10.5).

Implementation of the three metrics provides support to the Rayleigh model of quality management.

We have discussed the testing defect arrival metric and its variants and recommended it in several chapters. The only point to add is that for small projects, the time unit for this metric doesn't have to be "week." It can be in terms of days or hours of testing and it should be scaled according to the duration of testing and the volume of defect arrivals.

As discussed in section 9.2, the code integration pattern metric is a powerful project management and quality management tool. If can be implemented easily by small and large teams, with or without an established metrics tracking system.

The inspection scoring checklist is perfect for small teams. It is a simple and flexible tool that can be implemented with just paper (the form) and pencil by small organizations starting a metrics program that may not be ready to invest the resources to track and analyze the defects found by design reviews and code inspection. Even in organizations with established metrics practices, metrics tracking for requirements, design, and code is usually accorded less effort than tracking for testing and field quality. The inspection scoring checklist is a good tool for the team's self-improvement. At the same time, it provides two important pieces of information for project and quality management on the front-end implementation of the development process: the quality of the design or code and the effectiveness of the design reviews or code inspections. The checklist can be used with any forms of review or inspection ranging from formal inspection meetings to informal buddy reviews.

Accumulated data gathered via the checklist can be used to establish baselines and to indicate the process capability of the organization. Data from the current project can be compared to the baseline and used as an early predictive indicator. For example, if the average scores of the designs and the effectiveness of design reviews are substantially higher than the norm established by history, one can expect a lower testing defect rate and a lower field defect rate (because of better intrinsic design and/or code quality) even though test effectiveness remains unchanged.

9.9 Summary

Quality management models are valuable for monitoring and managing the quality of software when it is under development. These models emerged from the practical needs of large-scale software development. Unlike reliability models, which are numerous, there are few models for in-process quality management in the literature. Whereas reliability models need to provide precise and predictively valid results, the demand for precision for management models is far less. In contrast, the major criteria for management models are timeliness for quality indications, scope of coverage (of various phases of the development process), and capability (various indicators and attributes of quality). Therefore, when reliability models are used for quality management (instead of being used as prediction tools), a different focus should be applied.

The Rayleigh model (or for that matter the phase-based defect model) provides a nice framework for quality management, covering the entire development process. Within the overall Rayleigh framework, submodels such as the effort/outcome model, the PTR submodel, the PTR arrival and backlog projection models, the reliability growth models, and related in-process metrics provide further specifics.

To implement these models, a good tracking and reporting system and a set of related in-process metrics are important. Defect cause and defect type analysis, such as the ODC method, can lead to more insights and, therefore, effective improvement actions.

References

1. Bassin, K., S. Biyani, and P. Santhanam, "Metrics to Evaluate Vendor Developed Software Based on Test Case Execution Results," *IBM Systems Journal,* Vol. 41, No.1, 2002, pp. 13–30.
2. Butcher, M., H. Munro, and T. Kratschmer, "Improving Software Testing via ODC: Three Case Studies," *IBM Systems Journal,* Vol. 41, No. 1, 2002, pp. 31–44.
3. Chillarege, R., I. S. Bhandari, J. K. Chaar, M. J. Halliday, D. S. Moebus, B. K. Ray, and M-Y. Wong, "Orthogonal Defect Classification—A Concept for In-Process Measurements," *IEEE Transactions on Software Engineering,* Vol. 18, No. 11, November 1992, pp. 943–956.
4. Kan, S. H., "Modeling and Software Development Quality," *IBM Systems Journal,* Vol. 30, No. 3, 1991, pp. 351–362.
5. Myers, G. J., *The Art of Software Testing,* New York: John Wiley & Sons, 1979.
6.   Rohatgi, V. K., *Statistical Inference,* New York: John Wiley & Sons, 1984.

10

In-Process Metrics for Software Testing

In Chapter 9 we discussed quality management models with examples of in-process metrics and reports. The models cover both the front-end design and coding activities and the back-end testing phases of development. The focus of the in-process data and reports, however, are geared toward the design review and code inspection data, although testing data is included. This chapter provides a more detailed discussion of the in-process metrics from the testing perspective.[1] These metrics have been used in the IBM Rochester software development laboratory for some years with continual evolution and improvement, so there is ample implementation experience with them. This is important because although there are numerous metrics for software testing, and new ones being proposed frequently, relatively few are supported by sufficient experiences of industry implementation to demonstrate their usefulness. For each metric, we discuss its purpose, data, interpretation, and use, and provide a graphic example based on real-life data. Then we discuss in-process quality management vis-à-vis these metrics and revisit the metrics

1. This chapter is a modified version of a white paper written for the IBM corporate-wide Software Test Community Leaders (STCL) group, which was published as "In-process Metrics for Software Testing," in *IBM Systems Journal*, Vol. 40, No.1, February 2001, by S. H. Kan, J. Parrish, and D. Manlove. Copyright © 2001 International Business Machines Corporation. Permission to reprint obtained from *IBM Systems Journal*.

framework, the *effort/outcome model*, again with sufficient details on testing-related metrics. Then we discuss some possible metrics for a special test scenario, acceptance test with regard to vendor-developed code, based on the experiences from the IBM 2000 Sydney Olympics project by Bassin and associates (2002). Before we conclude the chapter, we discuss the pertinent question: *How do you know your product is good enough to ship?*

Because the examples are based on IBM Rochester's experiences, it would be useful to outline IBM Rochester's software test process as the context, for those who are interested. The accompanying box provides a brief description.

10.1 In-Process Metrics for Software Testing

In this section, we discuss the key in-process metrics that are effective for managing software testing and the in-process quality status of the project.

10.1.1 Test Progress S Curve (Planned, Attempted, Actual)

Tracking the progress of testing is perhaps the most important tracking task for managing software testing. The metric we recommend is a test progress S curve over time. The X-axis of the S curve represents time units and the Y-axis represents the number of test cases or test points. By "S curve" we mean that the data are cumulative over time and resemble an "S" shape as a result of the period of intense test activity, causing a steep planned test ramp-up. For the metric to be useful, it should contain the following information on one graph:

☐ Planned progress over time in terms of number of test cases or number of test points to be completed successfully by week (or other time unit such as day or hour)
☐ Number of test cases attempted by week (or other time unit)
☐ Number of test cases completed successfully by week (or other time unit)

The purpose of this metric is to track test progress and compare it to the plan, and therefore be able to take action upon early indications that testing activity is falling behind. It is well known that when the schedule is under pressure, testing, especially development testing, is affected most significantly. Schedule slippage occurs day by day and week by week. With a formal test progress metric in place, it is much more difficult for the team to ignore the problem. From the project planning perspective, an S curve forces better planning (see further discussion in the following paragraphs).

Figure 10.2 is an example of the component test metric at the end of the test of a major release of an integrated operating system. As can be seen from the figure, the testing plan is expressed in terms of a line curve, which is put in place before the test

IBM Rochester's Software Test Process

IBM Rochester's systems software development process has a strong focus on the front-end phases such as requirements, architecture, design and design verification, code integration quality, and driver builds. For example, the completion of high-level design review (I0) is always a key event in the system schedule and managed as an intermediate deliverable. At the same time, testing (development tests and independent tests) and customer validation are the key process phases with equally strong focus. As Figure 10.1 shows, the common industry model of testing includes functional test, system test, and customer beta test before the product is shipped. Integration and solution testing can occur before or after the product ships. It is often conducted by customers because the customer's integrated solution may consist of products from different vendors. For IBM Rochester, the first test phase after unit testing and code integration into the system library consists of component test (CT) and component regression test (CRT), which is equivalent to functional test. The next test phase is system test (ST), which is conducted by an independent test group. To ensure entry criteria is met, an acceptance test (STAT) is conducted before system test start. The main path of the test process is from CT → CTR → STAT → ST. Parallel to the main path are several development and independent tests:

■ Along with component test, a stress test is conducted in a large network environment with performance workload running in the background to stress the system.
■ When significant progress is made in component test, a product-level test (PLT),

which focuses on the subsystems of an overall integrated software system (e.g., database, client access, clustering), starts.
■ The network test is a specific product-level test focusing on communications subsystems and related error recovery processes.
■ The independent test group also conducts a software installation test, which runs from the middle of the component test until the end of the system test.

The component test and the component regression test are done by the development teams. The stress test, the product-level test, and the network test are done by development teams in special test environments maintained by the independent test group. The install and system tests are conducted by the independent test team. Each of these different tests plays an important role in contributing to the high quality of an integrated software system for the IBM eServer iSeries and AS/400 computer system. Later in this chapter, another shaded box provides an overview of the system test and its workload characteristics.

As Figure 10.1 shows, several early customer programs occur at the back end of the development process:

■ *Customer invitational program:* Selected customer invited to the development laboratory to test the new functions and latest technologies. This is done when component and component regression tests are near completion.
■ *Internal beta:* The development site uses the latest release for its IT production operations (i.e., eating one's own cooking)
■ *Beta program with business partners*
■ *Customer beta program*

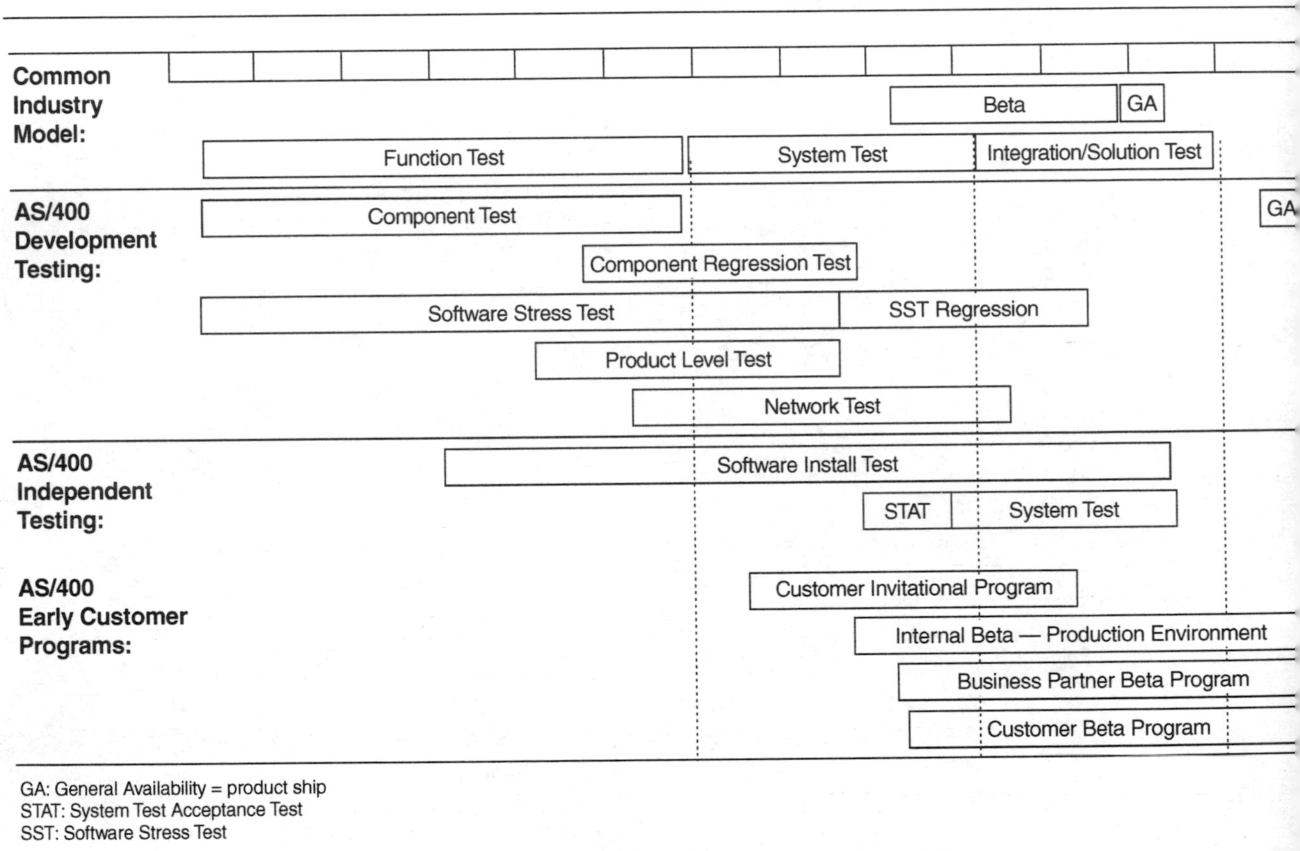

Common Industry Model:											

Common Industry Model:

Beta | GA

Function Test | System Test | Integration/Solution Test

AS/400 Development Testing:

Component Test   GA

Component Regression Test

Software Stress Test | SST Regression

Product Level Test

Network Test

AS/400 Independent Testing:

Software Install Test

STAT | System Test

AS/400 Early Customer Programs:

Customer Invitational Program

Internal Beta — Production Environment

Business Partner Beta Program

Customer Beta Program

GA: General Availability = product ship
STAT: System Test Acceptance Test
SST: Software Stress Test

FIGURE 10.1
IBM Rochester's Software Testing Phases

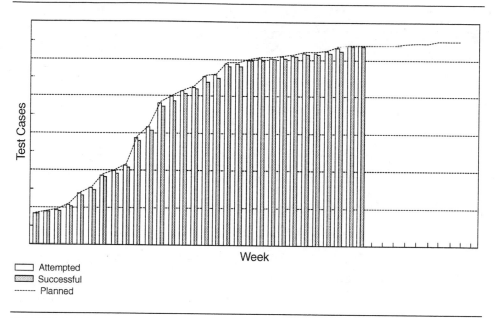

FIGURE 10.2
Sample Test Progress S Curve

begins. The empty bars indicate the cumulative number of test cases attempted and the solid bars represent the number of successful test cases. With the plan curve in place, each week when the test is in progress, two bars (one for attempted and one for successful) are added to the graph. This example shows that during the rapid test ramp-up period (the steep slope of the curve), for some weeks the test cases attempted were slightly ahead of plan (which is possible), and the successes were slightly behind plan.

Because some test cases are more important than others, it is not unusual in software testing to assign scores to the test cases. Using test scores is a normalization approach that provides more accurate tracking of test progress. The assignment of scores or points is normally based on experience, and at IBM Rochester, teams usually use a 10-point scale (10 for the most important test cases and 1 for the least). To track test points, the teams need to express the test plan (amount of testing done every week) and track the week-by-week progress in terms of test points. The example in Figure 10.3 shows test point tracking for a product level test, which was underway, for a systems software. It is noted that there is always an element of subjectivity in the assignment of weights. The weights and the resulting test points should be determined in the test planning stage and remain unchanged during the testing process. Otherwise, the purpose of this metric will be compromised in the reality of schedule pressures. In software engineering, weighting and test score assignment

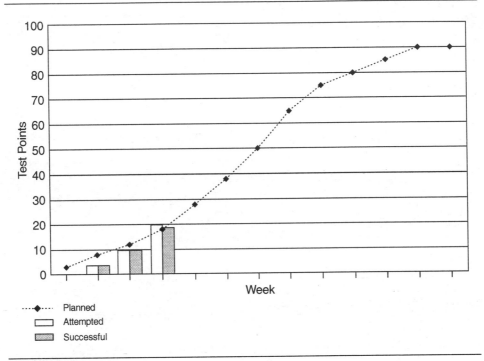

FIGURE 10.3
Test Progress S Curve—Test Points Tracking

remains an interesting area where more research is needed. Possible guidelines from such research will surely benefit the planning and management of software testing.

For tracking purposes, test progress can also be weighted by some measurement of coverage. Coverage weighting and test score assignment consistency become increasingly important in proportion to the number of development groups involved in a project. Lack of attention to tracking consistency across functional areas can result in a misleading view of the overall project's progress.

When a plan curve is in place, the team can set up an in-process target to reduce the risk of schedule slippage. For instance, a disparity target of 15% between attempted (or successful) and planned can be used to trigger additional actions. Although the test progress S curves, as shown in Figures 10.2 and 10.3, give a quick visual status of the progress against the total plan and plan-to-date (the eye can quickly determine if testing is ahead or behind on planned attempts and successes), it may be difficult to discern the exact amount of slippage. This is particularly true for large testing efforts, where the number of test cases is in the hundreds of thousands. For that reason, it is useful to also display the test status in tabular form, as in Table 10.1. The table also shows underlying data broken out by department and

st Progress Tracking—Planned, Attempted, Successful

	No. of Test Cases Planned to Date	Percent of Plan Attempted	Percent of Plan Successful	No. of Planned Test Cases Not Yet Attempted	Percent of Total Attempted	Percent of Total Success
tem	60577	90.19	87.72	5940	68.27	66.10
t A	1043	66.83	28.19	346	38.83	15.60
t B	708	87.29	84.46	90	33.68	32.59
t C	33521	87.72	85.59	4118	70.60	68.88
t D	11275	96.25	95.25	423	80.32	78.53
t E	1780	98.03	94.49	35	52.48	50.04
t F	4902	100.00	99.41	0	96.95	95.93
duct A	13000	70.45	65.10	3841	53.88	49.70
duct B	3976	89.51	89.19	417	66.82	66.50
duct C	1175	66.98	65.62	388	32.12	31.40
duct D	277	0	0	277	0	0
duct E	232	6.47	6.470	214	3.78	3.70

product or component, which helps to identify problem areas. In some cases, the overall test curve may appear to be on schedule, but when progress is viewed only at the system level, because some areas are ahead of schedule, they may mask areas that are behind schedule. Of course, test progress S curves are also used for functional areas and for specific products.

An initial plan curve should be subject to brainstorming and challenges. For example, if the curve shows a very steep ramp-up in a short period of time, the project manager may challenge the team with respect to how doable the plan is or the team's specific planned actions to execute the plan successfully. As a result, better planning will be achieved. *Caution:* Before the team settles on a plan curve and uses it to track progress, a critical evaluation of what the plan curve represents must be made. Is the total test suite considered effective? Does the plan curve represent high test coverage (functional coverage)? What are the rationales for the sequences of test cases in the plan? This type of evaluation is important because once the plan curve is in place, the visibility of this metric tends to draw the whole team's attention to the disparity between attempted, successful, and the planned testing.

Once the plan line is set, any proposed or actual changes to the plan should be reviewed. Plan slips should be evaluated against the project schedule. In general, the baseline plan curve should be maintained as a reference. Ongoing changes to the planned testing schedule can mask schedule slips by indicating that attempts are on track, while the plan curve is actually moving to the right.

In addition, this metric can be used for release-to-release or project-to-project comparisons, as the example in Figure 10.4 shows. For release-to-release comparisons, it is important to use time units (weeks or days) before product ship (or general availability, GA) as the unit for the X-axis. By referencing the ship dates, the comparison provides a true status of the project in process. In Figure 10.4, it can be observed that Release B, represented by the dotted line, is more back-end loaded than Release A, which is represented by the solid line. In this context, the metric is both a quality and a schedule statement for the testing of the project. This is because late testing causes late cycle defect arrivals and therefore negatively affects the quality of the final product. With this type of comparison, the project team can plan ahead (even before the testing starts) to mitigate the risks.

To implement this metric, the test execution plan needs to be laid out in terms of the weekly target, and actual data needs to be tracked on a weekly basis. For small to medium projects, such planning and tracking activities can use common tools such as Lotus 1-2-3 or other project management tools. For large and complex projects, a stronger tools support facility normally associated with the development environment may be needed. Many software tools are available for project management and quality control, including tools for defect tracking and defect projections. Testing tools usually include test library tools for keeping track of test cases and for test automation, test coverage analysis tools, test progress tracking, and defect tracking tools.

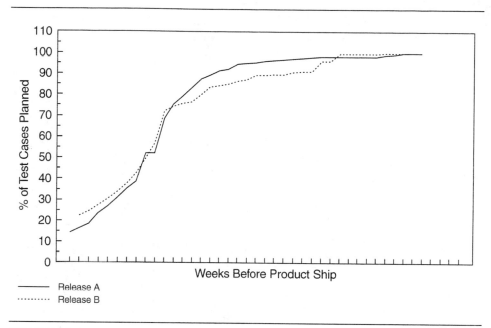

FIGURE 10.4

Test Plan Curve—Release-to-Release Comparison

10.1.2 Testing Defect Arrivals over Time

Defect tracking and management during the testing phase is highly recommended as a standard practice for all software testing. Tracking testing progress and defects are common features of many testing tools. At IBM Rochester, defect tracking is done via the problem tracking report (PTR) tool. We have discussed PTR-related models and reports previously. In this chapter we revisit two testing defect metrics (arrivals and backlog) with more details. We recommend tracking the defect arrival pattern over time, in addition to tracking by test phase. Overall defect density during testing, or for a particular test, is a summary indicator, but not really an in-process indicator. The pattern of defect arrivals over time gives more information. As discussed in Chapter 4 (section 4.2.2), even with the same overall defect rate during testing, different patterns of defect arrivals may imply different scenarios of field quality. We recommend the following for this metric:

☐   Always include data for a comparable baseline (a prior release, a similar project, or a model curve) in the chart if such data is available. If a baseline is not available, at the minimum, when tracking starts, set some expected level of defect arrivals at key points of the project schedule (e.g., midpoint of functional test, system test entry, etc.).

- ☐ The unit for the *X*-axis is weeks (or other time units) before product ship
- ☐ The unit for the *Y*-axis is the number of defect arrivals for the week, or its variants.

Figure 10.5 is an example of this metric for releases of an integrated operating system. For this example, the main goal is release-to-release comparison at the system level. The metric can be used for the defect arrival patterns based on the total number of defects from all test phases, and for defect arrivals for specific tests. It can be used to compare actual data with a PTR arrival model, as discussed in Chapter 9.

Figure 10.5 has been simplified for presentation. The real graph has much more information on it including vertical lines to depict the key dates of the development cycle and system schedules such as last new function integration, development test completion, start of system test, and so forth. There are also variations of the metric: total defect arrivals, severe defects (e.g., severity 1 and 2 defects in a 4-point severity scale), defects normalized to size of the release (new and changed code plus a partial weight for ported code), and total defect arrivals versus valid defects. The main, and the most useful, chart is the total number of defect arrivals. In our projects, we also include a high severity (severity 1 and 2) defect chart and a normalized view as main-stays of tracking. The normalized defect arrival chart can eliminate some of the

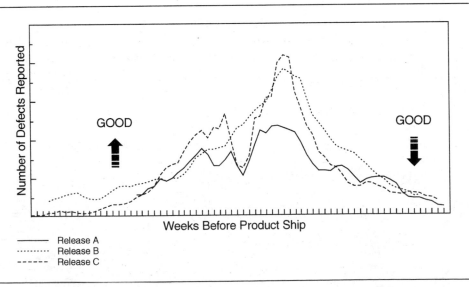

FIGURE 10.5
Testing Defect Arrival Metric

visual guesswork of comparing current progress to historical data. In conjunction with the severity chart, a chart that displays the percentage of severity 1 and 2 PTRs per week can be useful. As Figure 10.6 shows, the percentage of high severity problems increases as the release progresses toward the product ship date. Generally, this is because the urgency for problem resolution increases when approaching product delivery, therefore, the severity of the defects was elevated. Unusual swings in the percentage of high severity problems, however, could signal serious problems and should be investigated.

When do the defect arrivals peak relative to time to product delivery? How does this pattern compare to previous releases? How high do they peak? Do they decline to a low and stable level before delivery? Questions such as these are key to the defect arrival metric, which has significant quality implications for the product in the field. A positive pattern of defect arrivals is one with higher arrivals earlier, an earlier peak (relative to the baseline), and a decline to a lower level earlier before the product ship date, or one that is consistently lower than the baseline when it is certain that the effectiveness of testing is at least as good as previous testing. The tail end of

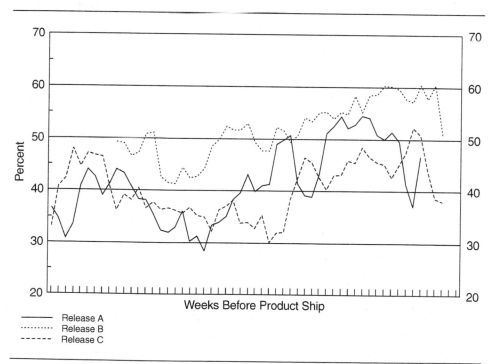

FIGURE 10.6

Testing Defect Arrivals—Percentage of Severity 1 and 2 Defects the curve is especially important because it is indicative of the quality of the product in the field. High defect activity before product delivery is more often than not a sign of quality problems. To interpret the defect arrivals metrics properly, refer to the scenarios and questions discussed in Chapter 4 section 4.2.1.

In addition to being an important in-process metric, the defect arrival pattern is the data source for projection of defects in the field. If we change from the weekly defect arrival curve (a density form of the metric) to a cumulative defect curve (a cumulative distribution form of the metric), the curve becomes a well-known form of the software reliability growth pattern. Specific reliability models, such as those discussed in Chapters 8 and 9, can be applied to the data to project the number of residual defects in the product. Figure 10.7 shows such an example. The actual testing defect data represents the total cumulative defects removed when all testing is complete. The fitted model curve is a Weibull distribution with the shape parameter (m) being 1.8. The projected latent defects in the field is the difference in the Y-axis of the model curve between the product ship date and when the curve is approaching its limit. If there is a time difference between the end date of testing and the product ship date, such as this case, the number of latent defects represented by the section of the model curve for this time segment has to be included in the projected number of defects in the field.

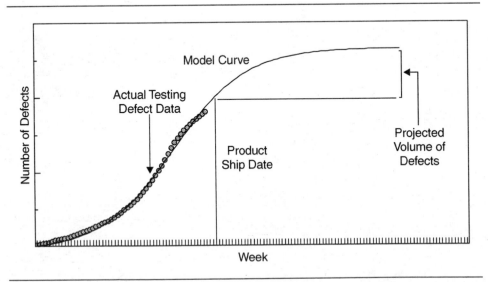

FIGURE 10.7
Testing Defect Arrival Curve, Software Reliability Growth Model,
and Defect Projection

10.1.3 Testing Defect Backlog over Time

We define the number of testing defects (or problem tracking reports, PTRs) remaining at any given time as the defect backlog (PTR backlog). Simply put, defect backlog is the accumulated difference between defect arrivals and defects that were closed. Defect backlog tracking and management is important from the perspective of both test progress and customer rediscoveries. A large number of outstanding defects during the development cycle will impede test progress. When a product is about to ship to customers, a high defect backlog means more customer rediscoveries of the defects already found during the development cycle. For software organizations that have separate teams to conduct development testing and to fix defects, defects in the backlog should be kept at the lowest possible level at all times. For organizations that have the same teams responsible for development testing and fixing defects, however, there are appropriate timing windows in the development cycle for which the priority of focuses may vary. While the defect backlog should be managed at a reasonable level at all times, it should not be the highest priority during a period when making headway in functional testing is the critical-path development activity. During the prime time for development testing, the focus should be on test effectiveness and test execution, and defect discovery should be encouraged to the maximum possible extent. Focusing too early on overall defect backlog reduction may conflict with these objectives. For example, the development team may be inclined not to open defect records. The focus during this time should be on the fix turnaround of the critical defects that impede test progress instead of the entire backlog. Of course, when testing is approaching completion, strong focus for drastic reduction in the defect backlog should take place.

For software development projects that build on existing systems, a large backlog of "aged" problems can develop over time. These aged defects often represent fixes or enhancements that developers believe would legitimately improve the product, but which get passed over during development due to resource or design constraints. They may also represent problems that have been fixed or are obsolete as a result of other changes. Without a concerted effort, this aged backlog can build over time. This is one area of the defect backlog that warrants attention early in the development cycle, even prior to the start of development testing.

Figure 10.8 is an example of the defect backlog metric for several releases of a systems software product. Again, release-to-release comparisons and actual data versus targets are the main objectives. Target X was a point target for a specific event in the project schedule. Target Y was for the period when the product was being readied to ship.

Note that for this metric, a sole focus on the numbers is not sufficient. In addition to the overall reduction, deciding which specific defects should be fixed first is very

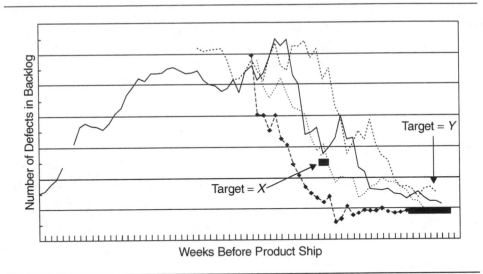

FIGURE 10.8
Testing Defect Backlog Tracking

important in terms of achieving early system stability. In this regard, the expertise and ownership of the development and test teams are crucial.

Unlike defect arrivals, which should not be controlled artificially, the defect backlog is completely under the control of the development organization. For the three metrics we have discussed so far, we recommend the following overall project management approach:

- ☐ When a test plan is in place and its effectiveness evaluated and accepted, manage test progress to achieve an early ramp-up in the S curve.
- ☐ Monitor defect arrivals and analyze the problems (e.g., defect cause analysis and Pareto analysis of problem areas of the product) to gain knowledge for improvement actions. *Do not* artificially control defect arrivals, which is a function of test effectiveness, test progress, and the intrinsic quality of the code (the amount of latent defects in the code). *Do* encourage opening defect records when defects are found.
- ☐ Strongly manage defect backlog reduction and achieve predetermined targets associated with the fix integration dates in the project schedule. Known defects that impede testing progress should be accorded the highest priority.

The three metrics discussed so far are obviously related, and they should be viewed together. We'll come back to this point in the section on the effort/outcome model.

10.1.4 Product Size over Time

Lines of code or another indicator of the project size that is meaningful to the development team can also be tracked as a gauge of the "effort" side of the development equation. During product development, there is a tendency toward growth as requirements and designs are fleshed out. Functions may continue to be added to meet late requirements or the development team wants more enhancements. A project size indicator, tracked over time, can serve as an explanatory factor for test progress, defect arrivals, and defect backlog. It can also relate the measurement of total defect volume to per unit improvement or deterioration. Figure 10.9 shows a project's release size pattern with rapid growth during release definition, stabilization, and then possibly a slight reduction in size toward release completion, as functions that fail to meet schedule or quality objectives are deferred. In the figure, the different segments in the bars represent the different layers in the software system. This metric is also known as an indicator of scope creep. Note that lines of code is only one of the size indicators. The number of function points is another common indicator, especially in application software. We have also seen the number of bytes of memory that the software will use as the size indicator for projects with embedded software.

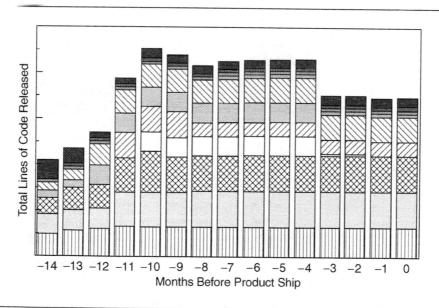

FIGURE 10.9
Lines of Code Tracking over Time

10.1.5 CPU Utilization During Test

For computer systems or software products for which a high level of stability is required to meet customers' needs, it is important that the product perform well under stress. In software testing during the development process, the level of CPU utilization is an indicator of the system's stress.

To ensure that its software testing is effective, the IBM Rochester software development laboratory sets CPU utilization targets for the software stress test and the system test. Stress testing starts at the middle of the component test phase and may run into the system test time frame with the purpose of stressing the system in order to uncover latent defects that cause system crashes and hangs that are not easily discovered in normal testing environments. It is conducted with a network of systems. System test is the final test phase with a customerlike environment. Test environment, workload characteristics, and CPU stress level are major factors contributing to the effectiveness of the test. The accompanying box provides an overview of the IBM Rochester system test and its workload characteristics.

System Test Overview and Workload Characteristics

IBM Rochester's system test serves as a means to provide a predelivery readiness assessment of the product's ability to be installed and operated in customerlike environments. These test environments focus on the total solution, including current release of the operating system, new and existing hardware, and customerlike applications. The resulting test scenarios are written to exercise the operating system and related products in a manner similar to customers' businesses. These simulated environments do not attempt to replicate a particular customer, but represent a composite of customer types in the target market.

The model used for simulating customerlike environments is referred to as the RAISE (Reliability, Availability, Installability, Serviceability, and Ease of use) environment. It is designed to represent an interrelated set of companies that use the IBM products to support and drive their day-to-day business activities. Test scenarios are defined to simulate the different types of end-user activities, workflow, and business applications. They include CPU-intensive applications and interaction-intensive computing. During test execution, the environment is run as a 24-hour-a-day, 7-day-a-week (24x7) operation.

Initially, work items are defined to address complete solutions in the RAISE environment. From these work items come more detailed scenario definitions. These scenarios are written to run in the respective test environment, performing a sequence of tasks and executing a set of test applications to depict some customerlike event. Scenario variations are used to cater test effort to different workloads, operating environments, and run-time duration. The resulting interaction of multiple scenarios executing across a network of systems provides a representation of real end-user environments. This provides an assessment of the overall functionality in the release, especially in terms of customer solutions.

Some areas that scenario testing concentrates on include:

- Compatibility of multiple products running together
- Integration and interoperability of products across a complex network
- Coexistence of multiple products on one hardware platform
- Areas of potential customer dissatisfaction:
  - Unacceptable performance
  - Unsatisfactory installation
  - Migration/upgrade difficulties
  - Incorrect and/or difficult-to-use documentation
  - Overall system usability

As is the case for many customers, most system test activities require more than one system to execute. This fact is essential to understand, from both product integration and usage standpoints, and also because this represents a more realistic, customerlike setup. In driving multiple, interrelated, and concurrent activities across our network, we tend to "shake out" those hard-to-get-at latent problems. In such a complex environment, these types of problems tend to be difficult to analyze, debug, and fix, because of the layers of activities and products used. Additional effort to fix these problems is time well spent, because many of them could easily become critical situations to customers.

Workloads for the RAISE test environments are defined to place an emphasis on stressful, concurrent product interaction. Workload characteristics include:

- Stressing some of the more complex new features of the system
- Running automated tests to provide background workload for additional concurrence and stress testing and to test previous release function for regression
- Verifying that the software installation instructions are accurate and understandable and that the installation function works properly
- Testing release-to-release compatibility, including n to $n-1$ communications connectivity and system interoperability
- Detecting data conversion problems by simulating customers performing installations from a prior release
- Testing availability and recovery functions
- Artistic testing involving disaster and error recovery
- Performing policy-driven system maintenance (e.g., backup, recovery, and applying fixes)
- Defining and managing different security levels for systems, applications, documents, files, and user/group profiles
- Using the tools and publications that are available to the customer or IBM service personnel when diagnosing and resolving problems

Another objective during the RAISE system test is to maintain customer environment systems at stable hardware and software levels for an extended time (one month or more). A guideline for this would be minimum number of unplanned initial program loads (IPL, or reboot) except for maintenance requiring an IPL. The intent is to simulate an active business and detect problems that occur only after the systems and network have been operating for an extended, uninterrupted period of time.

The data in Figure 10.10 indicate the recent CPU utilization targets for the IBM Rochester's system test. Of the five systems in the system test environment, there is one system with a 2-way processor (VA), two systems with 4-way processors (TX and WY), and one system each with 8-way and 12-way processors. The upper CPU utilization limits for TX and WY are much lower because these two systems are used for interactive processing. For the overall testing network, the baseline targets for system test and the acceptance test of system test are also shown.

The next example, shown in Figure 10.11, demonstrates the tracking of CPU utilization over time for the software stress test. There is a two-phase target as represented by the step-line in the chart. The original target was set at 16 CPU hours per system per day on the average, with the following rationale:

- ☐ The stress test runs 20 hours per day, with 4 hours of system maintenance.
- ☐ The CPU utilization target is 80% or higher.

The second phase of the target, set at 18 CPU hours per system per day, is for the back end of the stress test. As the figure shows, a key element of this metric, in addition to comparison of actual and target data, is release-to-release comparison. One can observe that the curve for release C had more data points in the early development cycle, which were at higher CPU utilization levels. This is because pretest runs were conducted prior to availability of the new release content. For all three releases, the CPU utilization metric shows an increasing trend with the stress test progress.

Test System

MN (8W)	TX* (4W)	VA (2W)	WY* (4W)	ND (12W)	Acceptance Test <u>45%**</u> overall
90%	70%	90%	70%	90%	System Test <u>65%**</u> overall
Upper Limits					Baselines

* Priorities set for interactive user response time; 70 percent seems to be the upper limit based on prior release testing.
** Average minimum needed to meet test case and system aging requirements.

FIGURE 10.10
CPU Utilization Targets for Testing Systems

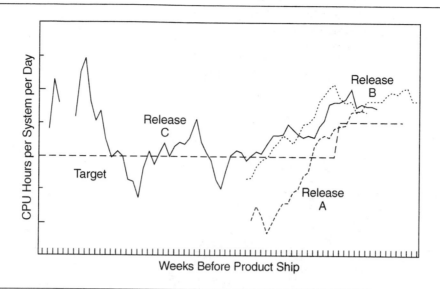

FIGURE 10.11
CPU Utilization Metrics

The CPU utilization metric is used together with the system crashes and hangs metric. This relationship is discussed in the next section.

To collect CPU utilization data, a performance monitor tool runs continuously (24x7) on each test system. Through the communication network, the data from the test systems are sent to a nontest system on a real-time basis. By means of a Lotus Notes database application, the final data can be easily tallied, displayed, and monitored.

10.1.6 System Crashes and Hangs

Hand in hand with the CPU utilization metric is the system crashes and hangs metric. This metric is operationalized as the number of unplanned initial program loads (IPLs, or reboots) because for each crash or hang, the system has to be re-IPLed (rebooted). For software tests whose purpose is to improve the stability of the system, we need to ensure that the system is stressed and testing is conducted effectively to uncover latent defects that would lead to system crashes and hangs, or in general any unplanned IPLs. When such defects are discovered and fixed, stability of the system improves over time. Therefore, the metrics of CPU utilization (stress level) and unplanned IPLs describe the effort aspect and the outcome aspect respectively, of the effectiveness of the test.

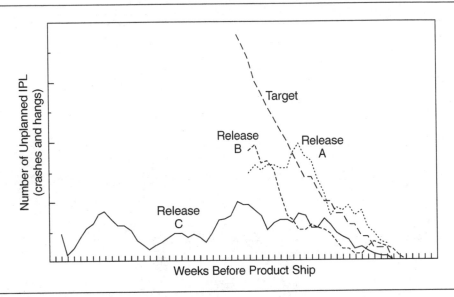

FIGURE 10.12
System Crashes and Hangs Metric

Figure 10.12 shows the system crashes and hangs metric for the same three releases shown in Figure 10.11. The target curve was derived based on data from prior releases by fitting an exponential model.

In terms of data collection, when a system crash or hang occurs and the tester reboots (re-IPLs) the system, the performance monitor and IPL tracking tool produces a screen prompt and requests information about the last system crash or hang. The tester can ignore the prompt temporarily, but it will reappear regularly after a certain time until the questions are answered. Information elicited via this tool includes test system, network ID, tester name, IPL code and reason (and additional comments), system reference code (SRC) if available, data and time system went down, release, driver, PTR number (the defect that caused the system crash or hang), and the name of the product. The IPL reason code consists of the following categories:

- ☐ 001 Hardware problem (unplanned)
- ☐ 002 Software problem (unplanned)
- ☐ 003 Other problem (unplanned)
- ☐ 004 Load fix (planned)

Because the volume and trend of system crashes and hangs are germane to the stability of the product in the field, we highly recommend this in-process metric for software for which stability is an important attribute. These data should also be used to make release-to-release comparisons and as leading indicators to product delivery readiness. While CPU utilization tracking definitely requires a tool, tracking of system crashes and hangs can start with pencil and paper if a disciplined process is in place.

10.1.7 Mean Time to Unplanned IPL

Mean time to failure (MTTF), or mean time between failures (MTBF), are the standard measurements of reliability. In software reliability literature, this metric and various models associated with it have been discussed extensively. Predominantly, the discussions and use of this metric are related to academic research or specific-purpose software systems. To the author's awareness, implementation of this metric is rare in organizations that develop commercial systems. This may be due to several reasons including issues related to single-system versus multiple-systems testing, the definition of a failure, the feasibility and cost in tracking all failures and detailed time-related data (Note: Failures are different from defects or faults; a single defect can cause multiple failures and in different machines) in commercial projects, and the value and return on investment of such tracking.

System crashes and hangs (unplanned IPLs) are the more severe forms of failure. Such failures are clear-cut and easier to track, and metrics based on such data are more meaningful. Therefore, at IBM Rochester, we use mean time to unplanned IPL (MTI) as the software reliability metric. This metric is used only during the system testing period, which, as previously described, is a customerlike system integration test prior to product delivery. Using this metric for other tests earlier in the development cycle is possible but will not be as meaningful because all the components of the system cannot be addressed collectively until the final system test. The formula to calculate the MTI metric is:

$$\text{Weekly MTI} = \sum_{i=1}^{n} W_i \bullet \left(\frac{H_i}{I_i + 1} \right)$$

where
n = Number of weeks that testing has been performed (i.e., the current week of test)
H = Total of weekly CPU run hours
W = Weighting factor
I = Number of weekly (unique) unplanned IPLs (due to software failures)

Basically the formula takes the total number of CPU run hours for each week (H_i), divides it by the number of unplanned IPLs plus 1 ($I_i + 1$), then applies a set of weighting factors to get the weighted MTI number, if weighting is desired. For example, if the total CPU run hours from all test systems for a specific week was 320 CPU hours and there was one unplanned IPL due to a system crash, then the unweighted MTI for that week would be 320/(1+1) = 160 CPU hours. In the IBM Rochester implementation, we apply a set of weighting factors based on results from prior baseline releases. The purpose of weighting factors is to take the outcome from the prior weeks into account so that at the end of the system test (with a duration of 10 weeks), the MTI represents an entire system test statement. It is the practitioner's decision whether to use a weighting factor or how to distribute the weights heuristically. Deciding factors may include type of products and systems under test, test cycle duration, and how the test period is planned and managed.

Figure 10.13 is an example of the MTI metric for the system test of a recent release of an integrated operating system. The X-axis represents the number of weeks before product ship. The Y-axis on the right side is MTI and on the left side is the number of unplanned IPLs. Inside the chart, the shaded areas represent the number of

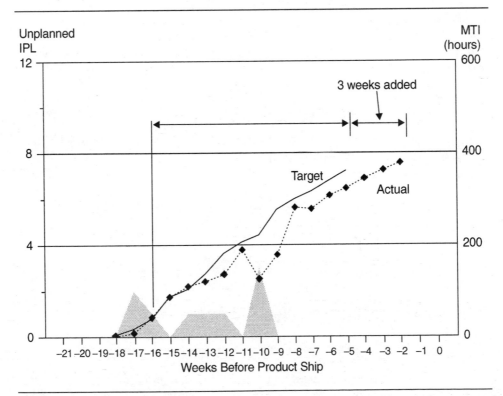

FIGURE 10.13
Mean Time to Unplanned IPL Metric

unique unplanned IPLs (crashes and hangs) encountered. From the start of the acceptance test of the system test, the MTI metric is shown tracking to plan until week 10 before product ship, when three system crashes occurred during one week. From the significant drop of the MTI, it was evident that with the original test plan, there would not be enough burn-in time for the system to reach the MTI target. Because this lack of burn-in time might result in undetected critical problems, additional testing was done and the system test was lengthened by three weeks. The product ship date remained unchanged.

Clearly, discrepancies between actual and targeted MTI should trigger early, proactive decisions to adjust testing plans and schedules to make sure that product ship criteria for burn-in can be achieved. At a minimum, the risks should be well understood and a risk mitigation plan should be developed. Action plans might include:

- ☐ Extending test duration and/or adding resources
- ☐ Providing for a more exhaustive regression test period if one were planned
- ☐ Adding a regression test if one were not planned
- ☐ Taking additional actions to intensify problem resolution and fix turnaround time (assuming that there is enough time available until the test cycle is planned to end)

10.1.8 Critical Problems: Showstoppers

This showstopper parameter is very important because the severity and impact of software defects varies. Regardless of the volume of total defect arrivals, it takes only a few showstoppers to render a product dysfunctional. This metric is more qualitative than the metrics discussed earlier. There are two aspects of this metric. The first is the number of critical problems over time, with release-to-release comparison. This dimension is quantitative. The second, more important, dimension is concerned with the types of the critical problems and the analysis and resolution of each problem.

The IBM Rochester's implementation of this tracking and focus is based on the general criteria that any problem that will impede the overall progress of the project or that will have significant impact on customer's business (if not fixed) belongs to such a list. The tracking normally starts at the middle of the component test phase when a critical problem meeting by the project management team (with representatives from all functional areas) takes place once a week. When it gets closer to system test and product delivery time, the focus intensifies and daily meetings take place. The objective is to facilitate cross-functional teamwork to resolve the problems swiftly. Although there is no formal set of criteria, problems on the critical problem list tend to be problems related to installation, system stability, security, data corruption, and so forth. All problems on the list must be resolved before product delivery.

10.2 In-Process Metrics and Quality Management

On the basis of the previous discussions of specific metrics, we have the following recommendations for implementing in-process metrics for software testing in general:

☐ Whenever possible, use calendar time, instead of phases of the development process, as the measurement unit for in-process metrics. There are some phase-based metrics or defect cause analysis methods available, which we also use. However, in-process metrics based on calendar time provide a direct statement on the status of the project with regard to whether it can be developed on time with desirable quality. As appropriate, a combination of time-based metrics and phase-based metrics may be desirable.

☐ For time-based metrics, use ship date as the reference point for the X-axis and use week as the unit of measurement. By referencing the ship date, the metric portrays the true in-process status and conveys a "marching toward completion" message. In terms of time units, we found that data at the daily level proved to have too much fluctuation and data at the monthly level lost its timeliness, and neither can provide a trend that can be spotted easily. Weekly data proved optimal in terms of both measurement trends and cycles for actions. Of course, when the project is approaching the back end of the development cycle, some metrics may need to be monitored and actions taken daily. For very small projects, the time units should be scaled according to the length of the test cycle and the pattern of defect arrivals. For instance, the example in Chapter 12 (Figure 12.5) shows the relationship between defect arrivals and hours of testing. The testing cycle was about 80 hours so the time unit was hour. One can observe that the defect arrival pattern by hour of testing shows a start, ramp-up, and then stabilizing pattern, which is a positive pattern.

☐ Metrics should indicate "good" or "bad" in terms of quality or schedule. To achieve these objectives, a comparison baseline (a model or some history) should always be established. Metrics should also have a substantial visual component so that "good" and "bad" are observable by the users without significant analysis. In this regard, we recommend frequent use of graphs and trend charts.

☐ Some metrics are subject to strong management actions, whereas a few specific ones should not be intervened with. For example, defect arrival pattern is an important quality indicator of the project. It is driven by test effectiveness and test progress. It should not be artificially controlled. When defects are discovered by testing, defect reports should be opened and tracked. On the other hand, testing progress can be managed. Therefore, defect arrival pattern can be influenced only indirectly via managing the testing. In contrast, defect backlog is completely subject to management and control.

□   Finally, the metrics should be able to drive improvements. The ultimate questions for the value of metrics is, as a result of metrics, what kind and how much improvement will be made and to what extent will the final product quality be influenced?

With regard to the last item in the list, to drive specific improvement actions, sometimes the metrics have to be analyzed at a granular level. As a real-life example, for the test progress and defect backlog (PTR backlog) metrics, the following analysis was conducted and guidelines for action were provided for the component teams for an IBM Rochester project near the end of the component test (CT) phase.

□   Components that were behind in the CT were identified using the following methods:

- Sorting all components by "% of total test cases attempted" and selecting those that are less than 65%. In other words, with less than 3 weeks to component test complete, these components have more than one-third of testing left.
- Sorting all components by "number of planned cases not attempted" and selecting those that have 100 or larger, and adding these components to those identified in step 1. In other words, these several additional components may be on track or not seriously behind percentage-wise, but because of the large number of test cases they have, a large amount of work remains.

  (Because the unit (test case, or test variation) is not of the same weight across components, step 1 was used as the major criterion, supplemented by step 2.)

□   Components with double-digit PTR backlogs were identified.

□   Guidelines for actions were devised:

- If CT is way behind and PTR backlog is not high, the first priority is to focus on finishing CT.
- If CT is on track and PTR backlog is high, the key focus is on reducing PTR backlog.
- If CT is way behind and PTR backlog is high, then these components are really in trouble. GET HELP (e.g., extra resources, temporary help from other component teams who have experience with this component).
- For the rest of the components, continue to keep a strong focus both on finishing CT and reducing PTR backlog.

Furthermore, analysis on defect cause, symptoms, defect origin (in terms of development phase), and where found can provide more information for possible improvement actions. Such analyses are discussed in previous chapters. Tables 10.2 and 10.3 show two examples on defect cause distribution and the distribution of defects found by test phase across development teams for a systems software project. The defect causes are categorized into initialization-related problems (INIT), data

TABLE 10.2
Percent Distribution of Defect Cause by Development Team

Defect Cause	Team A	Team B	Team C	Team D	Team E	Team F	Team G	Team H	Project
Initialization (INIT)	11.5%	9.8%	12.3%	9.6%	10.6%	10.4%	**13.9%**	6.4%	10.6%
Definition (DEFN)	5.5	**34.9**	8.5	6.6	2.8	10.9	9.5	8.3	10.7
Interface (INTF)	10.6	16.3	15.8	**31.3**	8.3	19.3	12.0	11.3	15.6
Logic, algorithm (LGC)	**59.9**	**26.1**	54.2	41.4	54.4	49.7	48.6	**64.9**	50.4
Machine readable information (MRI)	**3.7**	1.4	**3.1**	0.5	0.9	1.8	0.7	1.1	1.7
Complex problems (CPLX)	8.8	11.6	6.1	10.6	**23.0**	7.9	**15.3**	7.9	11.0
TOTAL (n)	100.0% (217)	100.1% (215)	100.0% (260)	100.0% (198)	100.0% (217)	100.0% (394)	100.0% (274)	99.9% (265)	100.0% (2040)

TABLE 10.3
Percent Distribution of Defect Found by Testing Phase by Development Team

Team	UT	CT	CRT	Artistic	PLT	ST	Total (*n*)
A	26.7%	35.9%	9.2%	8.4%	6.9%	**12.9%**	100.0% (217)
B	25.6	24.7	7.4	**38.1**	2.8	**1.4**	100.0 (215)
C	31.9	33.5	9.2	12.3	5.4	7.7	100.0 (260)
D	**41.9**	29.8	11.1	12.1	**1.5**	3.6	100.0 (198)
E	38.2	23.5	11.1	5.0	11.1	**11.1**	100.0 (217)
F	**18.0**	39.1	7.4	3.3	**25.3**	6.9	100.0 (394)
G	**19.0**	29.9	18.3	**21.5**	4.4	6.9	100.0 (274)
H	26.0	36.2	17.7	12.8	4.2	3.1	100.0 (265)
Proejct Overall	27.1%	32.3%	11.4%	13.4%	9.1%	6.7%	100.0% (2040)

definition–related problems (DEFN), interface problems (INTF), logical and algo-rithmic problems (LGC), problems related to messages, translation, and machine-readable information (MRI), and complex configuration and timing problems (CPLX). The test phases include unit test (UT), component test (CT), component regression test (CRT), artistic test, product level test (PLT), and system test (ST). Artistic test is the informal testing done by developers during the formal CT, CRT, and PLT test cycles. It usually results from a "blitz test" focus on specific functions, additional testing triggered by in-process quality indicators, or new test cases in response to newly discovered problems in the field. In both tables, the percentages that are highlighted in bold numbers differ substantially from the pattern for the over-all project.

Metrics are a tool for project and quality management. For many types of projects, including software development, commitment by the teams is very impor-tant. Experienced project managers know, however, that subjective commitment is not enough. Do you commit to the system schedules and quality goals? Will you deliver on time with desirable quality? Even with strong commitment by the devel-opment teams to the project manager, these objectives are often not met for a host of reasons, right or wrong. In-process metrics provide the added value of objective indi-cation. It is the combination of subjective commitments and objective measurements that will make the project successful.

To successfully manage in-process quality and therefore the quality of the final deliverables, in-process metrics must be used effectively. We recommend an inte-grated approach to project and quality management vis-à-vis these metrics in which quality is managed as vigorously as factors such as schedule, cost, and content. Quality should always be an integral part of the project status report and checkpoint reviews. Indeed, many examples described here are metrics for both quality and schedules (those weeks to delivery date measurements) because the two parameters are often intertwined.

One common observation with regard to metrics in software development is that project teams often explain away the negative signs indicated by the metrics. There are two key reasons for this phenomenon. First, in practice many metrics are inadequate to measure the quality of the project. Second, project managers might not be action-oriented or not willing to take ownership of quality management. Therefore, the effectiveness, reliability, and validity of metrics are far more important than the quantity of metrics. We recommend using only a few important and manageable metrics during the project. When a negative trend is observed, an early urgent response can prevent schedule slips and quality deterioration. Such an approach can be supported by setting in-process metric targets. Corrective actions should be triggered when the measurements fall below a predetermined target.

10.2.1 Effort/Outcome Model

It is clear that some metrics are often used together to provide adequate interpretation of the in-process quality status. For example, test progress and defect arrivals (PTR arrivals), and CPU utilization and the number of system crashes and hangs are two obvious pairs. If we take a closer look at the metrics, we can classify them into two groups: those that measure the testing effectiveness or testing effort, and those that indicate the outcome of the test in terms of quality, or the lack thereof. We call the two groups the effort indicators (e.g., test effectiveness assessment, test progress S curve, CPU utilization during test) and the outcome indicators (PTR arrivals—total number and arrivals pattern, number of system crashes and hangs, mean time to unplanned initial program load (IPL)), respectively.

To achieve good test management, useful metrics, and effective in-process quality management, the effort/outcome model should be used. The 2x2 matrix in Figure 10.14 for testing-related metrics is equivalent to that in Figures 9.4 and 9.17 for inspection-related metrics. For the matrix on test effectiveness and the number of defects:

- ☐ Cell 2 is the best-case scenario. It is an indication of good intrinsic quality of the design and code of the software—low error injection during the development process—and verified by effective testing.
- ☐ Cell 1 is a good/not bad scenario. It represents the situation that latent defects were found via effective testing.
- ☐ Cell 3 is the worst-case scenario. It indicates buggy code and probably problematic designs—high error injection during the development process.
- ☐ Cell 4 is the unsure scenario. One cannot ascertain whether the lower defect rate is a result of good code quality or ineffective testing. In general, if the test effectiveness does not deteriorate substantially, lower defects is a good sign.

Outcome (Defects Found)

		Higher	Lower
Effort (Testing Effectiveness)	Better	Cell1 Good/Not Bad	Cell2 Best-Case
	Worse	Cell3 Worst-Case	Cell4 Unsure

FIGURE 10.14
An Effort/Outcome Matrix

It should be noted that in an effort/outcome matrix, the better/worse and higher/lower designations should be carefully determined based on project-to-project, release-to-release, or actual-to-model comparisons. This effort/outcome approach also provides an explanation of Myers (1979) counterintuitive principle of software testing as discussed in previous chapters. This framework can be applied to pairs of specific metrics. For testing and defect volumes (or defect rate), the model can be applied to the overall project level and in-process metrics level. At the overall project level, the effort indicator is the assessment of test effectiveness compared to the baseline, and the outcome indicator is the volume of all testing defects (or overall defect rate) compared to the baseline, when all testing is complete. As discussed earlier, it is difficult to derive a quantitative indicator of test effectiveness. But an ordinal assessment (better, worse, about equal) can be made via test coverage (functional or some coverage measurements), extra testing activities (e.g., adding a separate phase), and so forth.

At the in-process status level, the test progress S curve is the effort indicator and the defect arrival pattern (PTR arrivals) is the outcome indicator. The four scenarios will be as follows:

☐ Positive Scenarios
  • The test progress S curve is the same as or ahead of baseline (e.g., a previous release) and the defect arrival curve is lower (than that of a previous release). This is the cell 2 scenario.
  • The test progress S curve is the same as or ahead of the baseline and the defect arrival is higher in the early part of the curve—chances are the defect arrivals will peak earlier and decline to a lower level near the end of testing. This is the cell 1 scenario.

☐ Negative Scenarios
- The test progress S curve is significantly behind and the defect arrival curve is higher (compared with baseline)—chances are the PTR arrivals will peak later and higher and the problem of late cycle defect arrivals will emerge. This is the cell 3 scenario.
- The test S curve is behind and the defect arrival is lower in the early part of the curve —this is an unsure scenario. This is the cell 4 scenario.

Both cell 3 (worst case) and cell 4 (unsure) scenarios are unacceptable from quality management's point of view. To improve the situation at the overall project level, if the project is still in early development the test plans have to be more effective. If testing is almost complete, additional testing for extra defect removal needs to be done. The improvement scenarios take three possible paths:

1. If the original scenario is cell 3 (worst case), the only possible improvement scenario is cell 1 (good/not bad). This means achieving quality via extra testing.
2. If the original scenario is cell 4 (unsure), the improvement scenario can be one of the following two:
   ☐ Cell 1 (good/not bad) means more testing leads to more defect removal, and the original low defect rate was truly due to insufficient effort.
   ☐ Cell 2 (best case) means more testing confirmed that the intrinsic code quality was good, that the original low defect rate was due to lower latent defects in the code.

For in-process status, the way to improve the situation is to accelerate the test progress. The desirable improvement scenarios take two possible paths:

1. If the starting scenario is cell 3 (worst case), then the improvement path is cell 3 to cell 1 to cell 2.
2. If the starting scenario is cell 4 (unsure), improvement path could be:
   ☐ Cell 4 to cell 2
   ☐ Cell 4 to cell 1 to cell 2

The difference between the overall project level and the in-process status level is that for the latter situation, cell 2 is the only desirable outcome. In other words, to ensure good quality, the defect arrival curve has to decrease to a low level when active testing is still going on. If the defect arrival curve stays high, it implies that there are substantial latent defects in the software. One must keep testing until the defect arrivals show a genuine pattern of decline. At the project level, because the volume of defects (or defect rate) is cumulative, both cell 1 and cell 2 are desirable outcomes from a testing perspective.

Generally speaking, outcome indicators are fairly common; effort indicators are more difficult to establish. Moreover, different types of software and tests may need different effort indicators. Nonetheless, the effort/outcome model forces one to establish appropriate effort measurements, which in turn, drives the improvements in testing. For example, the metric of CPU utilization is a good effort indicator for systems software. In order to achieve a certain level of CPU utilization, a stress environment needs to be established. Such effort increases the effectiveness of the test. The level of CPU utilization (stress level) and the trend of the number of system crashes and hangs are a good pair of effort/outcome metrics.

For integration type software where a set of vendor software are integrated together with new products to form an offering, effort indicators other than CPU stress level may be more meaningful. One could look into a test coverage-based metric including the major dimensions of testing such as:

- Setup
- Install
- Min/max configuration
- Concurrence
- Error-recovery
- Cross-product interoperability
- Cross-release compatibility
- Usability
- Double-byte character set (DBCS)

A five-point score (1 being the least effective and 5 being the most rigorous testing) can be assigned for each dimension and their sum can represent an overall coverage score. Alternatively, the scoring approach can include the "should be" level of testing for each dimension and the "actual" level of testing per the current test plan based on independent assessment by experts. Then a "gap score" can be used to drive release-to-release or project-to-project improvement in testing. For example, assume the test strategy for a software offering calls for the following dimensions to be tested, each with a certain sufficiency level: setup, 5; install, 5; cross-product interoperability, 4; cross-release compatibility, 5; usability, 4; and DBCS, 3. Based on expert assessment of the current test plan, the sufficiency levels of testing are setup, 4; install, 3; and cross-product interoperability, 2; cross-release compatibility, 5; usability, 3; DBCS, 3. Therefore the "should be" level of testing would be 26 and the "actual" level of testing would be 20, with a gap score of 6. This approach may be somewhat subjective but it also involves in the assessment process the experts who can make the difference. Although it would not be easy in real-life implementation, the point here is that the effort/outcome paradigm and the focus on effort metrics have direct linkage to test improvements. Further research in this area or implementation experience will be useful.

For application software in the external user test environment, usage of key features of the software and hours of testing would be good effort indicators, and the number of defects found can be the outcome indicator. Again to characterize the quality of the product, the defect curve must be interpreted with data about feature usage and effort of testing. *Caution:* To define and develop effort indicators, the focus should be on the effectiveness of testing rather than on the person-hour (or person-month) effort in testing per se. A good testing strategy should strive for efficiency (via tools and automation) as well as effectiveness.

10.3 Possible Metrics for Acceptance Testing to Evaluate Vendor-Developed Software

Due to business considerations, a growing number of organizations rely on external vendors to develop the software for their needs. These organizations typically conduct an acceptance test to validate the software. In-process metrics and detailed information to assess the quality of the vendors' software are generally not available to the contracting organizations. Therefore, useful indicators and metrics related to acceptance testing are important for the assessment of the software. Such metrics would be different from the calendar-time–based metrics discussed in previous sections because acceptance testing is normally short and there may be multiple code drops and, therefore, multiple mini acceptance tests in the validation process.

The IBM 2000 Sydney Olympics project was one such project, in which IBM evaluated vendor-delivered code to ensure that all elements of a highly complex system could be integrated successfully (Bassin, Biyani, and Santhanam, 2002). The summer 2000 Olympic Games was considered the largest sporting event in the world. For example, there were 300 medal events, 28 different sports, 39 competition venues, 30 accreditation venues, 260,000 INFO users, 2,000 INFO terminals, 10,000 news records, 35,000 biographical records, and 1.5 million historical records. There were 6.4 million INFO requests per day on the average and the peak Internet hits per day was 874.5 million. For the Venue Results components of the project, Bassin, Biyani, and Santhanam developed and successfully applied a set of metrics for IBM's testing of the vendor software. The metrics were defined based on test case data and test case execution data; that is, when a test case was attempted for a given increment code delivery, an execution record was created. Entries for a test case execution record included the date and time of the attempt, and the execution status, test phase, pointers to any defects found during execution, and other ancillary information. There were five categories of test execution status: pass, completed with errors, fail, not implemented, and blocked. A status of "failed" or "completed with errors" would result in the generation of a defect record. A status of "not implemented" indicated that the test case did not succeed because the targeted function had not yet been implemented, because this was in an incremental code delivery environment. The "blocked" status was used when the test case did not succeed because access to the targeted area was blocked by code that was not functioning correctly. Defect records would not be recorded for these latter two statuses. The key metrics derived and used include the following:

Metrics related to test cases

- ☐ *Percentage of test cases attempted*—used as an indicator of progress relative to the completeness of the planned test effort
- ☐ *Number of defects per executed test case*—used as an indicator of code quality as the code progressed through the series of test activities
- ☐ *Number of failing test cases without defect records*—used as an indicator of the completeness of the defect recording process

Metrics related to test execution records

- ☐ *Success rate*—The percentage of test cases that passed at the last execution was an important indicator of code quality and stability.
- ☐ *Persistent failure rate*—The percentage of test cases that consistently failed or completed with errors was an indicator of code quality. It also enabled the identification of areas that represented obstacles to progress through test activities.
- ☐ *Defect injection rate*—The authors used the percentage of test cases whose status went from pass to fail or error, fail to error, or error to fail, as an indicator of the degree to which inadequate or incorrect code changes were being made. Again, the project involves multiple code drops from the vendor. When the status of a test case changes from one code drop to another, it is an indication that a code change was made.
- ☐ *Code completeness*—The percentage of test executions that remained "not implemented" or "blocked" throughout the execution history was used as an indicator of the completeness of the coding of component design elements.

With these metrics and a set of in-depth defect analysis referenced as orthogonal defect classification, Bassin and associates were able to provide value-added reports, evaluations, and assessments to the project team.

These metrics merit serious considerations for software projects in similar environments. The authors contend that the underlying concepts are useful, in addition to vendor-delivered software, for projects that have the following characteristics:

- ☐ Testers and developers are managed by different organizations.
- ☐ The tester population changes significantly, for skill or business reasons.
- ☐ The development of code is iterative.
- ☐ The same test cases are executed in multiple test activities.

It should be noted these test case execution metrics require tracking at a very granular level. By definition, the unit of analysis is at the execution level of each test case. They also require the data to be thorough and complete. Inaccurate or incomplete data will have much larger impact on the reliability of these metrics than on metrics based on higher-level units of analysis. Planning the implementation of these metrics therefore must address the issues related to the test and defect tracking system as part of the development process and project management system. Among the most important issues are cost and behavioral compliance with regard to the recording of accurate data. Finally, these metrics measure the outcome of test executions. When using these metrics to assess the quality of the product to be shipped, the effectiveness of the test plan should be known or assessed a priori, and the framework of effort/outcome model should be applied.

10.4 How Do You Know Your Product Is Good Enough to Ship?

Determining when a product is good enough to ship is a complex issue. It involves the types of products (e.g., a shrink-wrap application software versus an operating system), the business strategy related to the product, market opportunities and timing, customers requirements, and many more factors. The discussion here pertains to the scenario in which quality is an important consideration and that on-time delivery with desirable quality is the major project goal.

A simplistic view is that one establishes a target for one or several in-process metrics, and if the targets are not met, then the product should not be shipped per schedule. We all know that this rarely happens in real life, and for legitimate reasons. Quality measurements, regardless of their maturity levels, are never as black and white as meeting or not meeting a delivery date. Furthermore, there are situations where some metrics are meeting targets and others are not. There is also the question of how bad is the situation. Nonetheless, these challenges do not diminish the value of in-process measurements; they are also the reason for improving the maturity level of software quality metrics.

In our experience, indicators from at least the following dimensions should be considered together to get an adequate picture of the quality of the product.

- ☐ System stability, reliability, and availability
- ☐ Defect volume
- ☐ Outstanding critical problems
- ☐ Feedback from early customer programs
- ☐ Other quality attributes that are of specific importance to a particular product and its customer requirements and market acceptance (e.g., ease of use, performance, security, and portability.)

When various metrics are indicating a consistent negative message, the product will not be good enough to ship. When all metrics are positive, there is a good chance that the product quality will be positive in the field. Questions arise when some of the metrics are positive and some are not. For example, what does it mean to the field quality of the product when defect volumes are low and stability indicators are positive but customer feedback is less favorable than that of a comparable release? How about when the number of critical problems is significantly higher and all other metrics are positive? In those situations, at least the following points have to be addressed:

☐ Why is this and what is the explanation?
☐ What is the influence of the negative in-process metrics on field quality?
☐ What can be done to control and mitigate the risks?
☐ For the metrics that are not meeting targets, how bad is the situation?

Answers to these questions are always difficult, and seldom expressed in quantitative terms. There may not even be right or wrong answers. On the question of how bad is the situation for metrics that are not meeting targets, the key issue is not one of statistical significance testing (which helps), but one of predictive validity and possible negative impact on field quality after the product is shipped. How adequate the assessment is and how good the decision is depend to a large extent on the nature of the product, experience accumulated by the development organization, prior empirical correlation between in-process metrics and field performance, and experience and observations of the project team and those who make the GO or NO GO decision. The point is that after going through all metrics and models, measurements and data, and qualitative indicators, the team needs to step back and take a big-picture view, and subject all information to its experience base in order to come to a final analysis. The final assessment and decision making should be analysis driven, not data driven. Metric aids decision making, but do not replace it.

Figure 10.15 is an example of an assessment of in-process quality of a release of a systems software product when it was near the ship date. The summary table outlines the indicators used (column 1), key observations of the status of the indicators (column 2), release-to-release comparisons (columns 3 and 4), and an assessment (column 5). Some of the indicators and assessments are based on subjective information. Many parameters are based on in-process metrics and data. The assessment was done about two months before the product ship date, and actions were taken to address the areas of concern from this assessment. The release has been in the field for more than two years and has demonstrated excellent field quality.

Indicator	Observation	Versus Release A	Versus Release B	As
Component Test	Base complete. Product X to complete 7/31.	⇔	⇔	
PTR Arrivals	Peak earlier than Release A and Release B, and lower at back end — for both absolute numbers and normalized (to size) rates.	⇑	⇑	
PTR Severity Distribution	Lower than Release A and Release B at back end.	⇑	⇑	
PTR Backlog	Excellent backlog management, lower than Release A and Release B, and achieved targets at Checkpoint Z. Needs focus for final take-down before product ship.	⇔	⇔	
Number of Pending Fixes	Higher than Release B at same time before product ship. Need focus to minimize customer rediscovery.	⇔	⇓	
Critical Problems	Strong problem management. Number of problems on the critical list similar to Release B.	⇑	⇑	
System Stability – Unplanned IPLs – CPU Run Time	Stability similar to, maybe slightly better than, Release B.	⇑	⇑	
Plan Change	Plan changes not as pervasive as Release B	N/A	⇑	
Timeliness of Translation and National Language Testing	Early and proactive build daily meetings. National language testing behind, but schedules achievable.	⇔	⇔	
Hardware System Test	Target complete: 7/31/xx. Focusing on backlog reduction. XX is a known problem area but receiving focus.	⇑	⇔	

ardware Reliability	Projected to meet target (better than prior releases) for all models.	⇑	⇑	Green
roduct Level Test	Testing continues for components DD and WWDatabase, but no major problems.	⇑	⇔	Green
stall Test	Phase II testing ahead of plan. One of the cleanest releases in install test.	⇑	⇑	Green
erviceability and ograde Testing	Concern with configurator readiness, software order structure in manufacturing.	⇔	⇓	Red: Concer
oftware System Test	Release looks good overall.	⇔	⇔	Green
ervice Readiness	Worldwide service community is on track to be ready to support the release.	⇑	⇑	Green
arly Customer ograms	Good early customer feedback on the release.	⇔	⇔	Green
anufacturing Build d Test	Still early, but no major problems.	⇔	⇔	Green

⇑ : Better than comparison release
⇒ : Same as comparison release
⇓ : Worse than comparison release

10.5 Summary

In this chapter we discuss a set of in-process metrics for the testing phases of the software development process. We provide real-life examples based on implementation experiences at the IBM Rochester software development laboratory. We also revisit the effort/outcome model as a framework for establishing and using in-process metrics for quality management.

There are certainly many more in-process metrics for software test that are not covered here; it is not our intent to provide a comprehensive coverage. Furthermore, not every metric we discuss here is applicable universally. We recommend that the several metrics that are basic to software testing (e.g., the test progress curve, defect arrivals density, critical problems before product ship) be integral parts of all software testing.

It can never be overstated that it is the effectiveness of the metrics that matters, not the number of metrics used. There is a strong temptation for quality practitioners to establish more and more metrics. However, ill-founded metrics are not only useless, they are actually counterproductive and add costs to the project. Therefore, we must take a serious approach to metrics. Each metric should be subjected to the examination of basic principles of measurement theory and be able to demonstrate empirical value. For example, the concept, the operational definition, the measurement scale, and validity and reliability issues should be well thought out. At a macro level, an overall framework should be used to avoid an ad hoc approach. We discuss the effort/outcome framework in this chapter, which is particularly relevant for in-process metrics. We also recommend the Goal/Question/Metric (GQM) approach in general for any metrics (Basili, 1989, 1995).

Recommendations for Small Organizations

For small organizations that don't have a metrics program in place and that intend to practice a minimum number of metrics, we recommend these metrics as basic to software testing: test progress S curve, defect arrival density, and critical problems or showstoppers.

For any projects and organizations we strongly recommend the effort/outcome model for interpreting the metrics for software testing and in managing their in-process quality. Metrics related to the effort side of the equation are especially important in driving improvement of software tests.

Finally, the practice of conducting an evaluation on whether the product is good enough to ship is highly recommended. The metrics and data available to support the evaluation may vary, and so may the quality criteria and the business strategy related to the product. Nonetheless, having such an evaluation based on both quantitative metrics and qualitative assessments is what good quality management is about.

At the same time, to enhance success, one should take a dynamic and flexible approach, that is, tailor the metrics to the needs of a specific team, product, and organization. There must be buy-in by the team (development and test) in order for the metrics to be effective. Metrics are a means to an end—the success of the project—not an end itself. The project team that has intellectual control and thorough understanding of the metrics and data they use will be able to make the right decisions. As such, the use of specific metrics is difficult to be mandated from the top down.

While good metrics can serve as a useful tool for software development and project management, they do not automatically lead to improvement in testing and in quality. They do foster data-based and analysis-driven decision making and provide objective criteria for actions. Proper use and continued refinement by those involved (e.g., the project team, the test community, the development teams) are therefore crucial.

References

1. Basili, V. R., "Software Development: A Paradigm for the Future," *Proceedings 13th International Computer Software and Applications Conference (COMPSAC),* Keynote Address, Orlando, Fla., September 1989.
2. Basili, V. R., "Software Measurement Workshop," University of Maryland, 1995.
3. Bassin, K., S. Biyani, and P. Santhanam, "Metrics to Evaluate Vendor Developed Software Based on Test Case Execution Results," *IBM Systems Journal,* Vol. 41, No. 1, 2002, pp. 13–30.
4. Hailpern, B., and P. Santhanam, "Software Debugging, Testing, and Verification," *IBM Systems Journal,* Vol. 41, No. 1, 2002, pp. 4–12.
5. McGregor, J. D., and D. A. Sykes, *A Practical Guide to Testing Object-Oriented Software,* Boston: Addison-Wesley, 2001.
6. Myers, G. J., *The Art of Software Testing,* New York: John Wiley & Sons, 1979.
7. Ryan, L., "Software Usage Metrics for Real-World Software Testing," *IEEE Spectrum,* April 1998, pp. 64–68.

11

Complexity Metrics and Models

Thus far the reliability and quality management models we have discussed are either at the project or the product level. Both types of model tend to treat the software more or less as a black box. In other words, they are based on either the external behavior (e.g., failure data) of the product or the intermediate process data (e.g., type and magnitude of inspection defects), without looking into the internal dynamics of design and code of the software. In this chapter we describe the relationships between metrics about design and code implementation and software quality. The unit of analysis is more granular, usually at the program-module level. Such metrics and models tend to take an internal view and can provide clues for software engineers to improve the quality of their work.

Reliability models are developed and studied by researchers and software reliability practitioners with sophisticated skills in mathematics and statistics; quality management models are developed by software quality professionals and product managers for practical project and quality management. Software complexity research, on the other hand, is usually conducted by computer scientists or experienced software engineers. Like the reliability models, many complexity metrics and models have emerged in the recent past. In this chapter we discuss several key metrics and models, and describe a real-life example of metric analysis and quality improvement.

11.1 Lines of Code

The lines of code (LOC) count is usually for executable statements. It is actually a count of instruction statements. The interchangeable use of the two terms apparently originated from Assembler program in which a line of code and an instruction statement are the same thing. Because the LOC count represents the program size and complexity, it is not a surprise that the more lines of code there are in a program, the more defects are expected. More intriguingly, researchers found that defect density (defects per KLOC) is also significantly related to LOC count. Early studies pointed to a negative relationship: the larger the module size, the smaller the defect rate. For instance, Basili and Perricone (1984) examined FORTRAN modules with fewer than 200 lines of code for the most part and found higher defect density in the smaller modules. Shen and colleagues (1985) studied software written in Pascal, PL/S, and Assembly language and found an inverse relationship existed up to about 500 lines. Since larger modules are generally more complex, a lower defect rate is somewhat counterintuitive. Interpretation of this finding rests on the explanation of interface errors: Interface errors are more or less constant regardless of module size, and smaller modules are subject to higher error density because of smaller denominators.

More recent studies point to a curvilinear relationship between lines of code and defect rate: Defect density decreases with size and then curves up again at the tail when the modules become very large. For instance, Withrow (1990) studied modules written in Ada for a large project at Unisys and confirmed the concave relationship between defect density (during formal test and integration phases) and module size (Table 11.1). Specifically, of 362 modules with a wide range in size (from fewer than 63 lines to more than 1,000), Withrow found the lowest defect density in the category of about 250 lines. Explanation of the rising tail is readily available. When module size becomes very large, the complexity increases to a level beyond a programmer's immediate span of control and total comprehension. This new finding is also consistent with previous studies that did not address the defect density of very large modules.

Experience from the AS/400 development also lends support to the curvilinear model. In the example in Figure 11.1, although the concave pattern is not as significant as that in Withrow's study, the rising tail is still evident.

The curvilinear model between size and defect density sheds new light on software quality engineering. It implies that there may be an optimal program size that can lead to the lowest defect rate. Such an optimum may depend on language, project, product, and environment; apparently many more empirical investigations are needed. Nonetheless, when an empirical optimum is derived by reasonable methods (e.g., based on the previous release of the same product, or based on a similar product by the same development group), it can be used as a guideline for new module development.

TABLE 11.1
Curvilinear Relationship Between Defect Rate and Module Size—Withrow (1990)

Maximum Source Lines of Modules	Average Defect per 1,000 Source Lines
63	1.5
100	1.4
158	0.9
251	0.5
398	1.1
630	1.9
1000	1.3
>1000	1.4

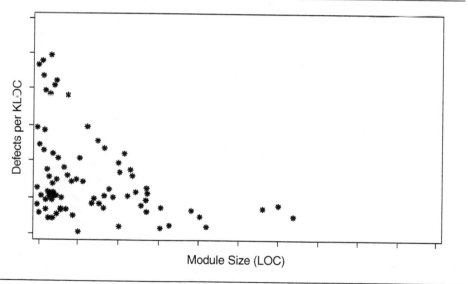

FIGURE 11.1
Curvilinear Relationship Between Defect Rate and Module Size—AS/400 data

11.2 Halstead's Software Science

Halstead (1977) distinguishes software science from computer science. The premise of software science is that any programming task consists of selecting and arranging a finite number of program "tokens," which are basic syntactic units distinguishable by a compiler. A computer program, according to software science, is a collection of tokens that can be classified as either operators or operands. The primitive measures of Halstead's software science are:

n_1 = Number of distinct operators in a program
n_2 = Number of distinct operands in a program
N_1 = Number of operator occurrences
N_2 = Number of operand occurrences

Based on these primitive measures, Halstead developed a system of equations expressing the total vocabulary, the overall program length, the potential minimum volume for an algorithm, the actual volume (number of bits required to specify a program), the program level (a measure of software complexity), program difficulty, and other features such as development effort and the projected number of faults in the software. Halstead's major equations include the following:

Vocabulary (n) $n = n_1 + n_2$

Length (N) $N = N_1 + N_2$
  $= n_1 \log_2 (n_1) + n_2 \log_2 (n_2)$

Volume (V) $V = N \log_2 (n)$
  $= N \log_2 (n_1 + n_2)$

Level (L) $L = V^* / V$
  $= (2/n_1) \times (n_2/N_2)$

Difficulty (D) $D = V / V^*$
 (inverse of level) $= (n_1 / 2) \times (N_2 / n_2)$

Effort (E) $E = V / L$

Faults (B) $B = V / S^*$

where V^* is the minimum volume represented by a built-in function performing the task of the entire program, and S^* is the mean number of mental discriminations (decisions) between errors (S^* is 3,000 according to Halstead).

Halstead's work has had a great impact on software measurement. His work was instrumental in making metrics studies an issue among computer scientists. However, software science has been controversial since its introduction and has been criticized from many fronts. Areas under criticism include methodology, derivations of equations, human memory models, and others. Empirical studies provide little support to the equations except for the estimation of program length. Even for the estimation of program length, the usefulness of the equation may be subject to dispute. To predict program length, data on N_1 and N_2 must be available, and by the time N_1 and N_2 can be determined, the program should be completed or near completion. Therefore, the predictiveness of the equation is limited. As discussed in Chapter 3, both the formula and actual LOC count are functions of N_1 and N_2; thus they appear to be just two operational definitions of the concept of program length. Therefore, correlation exists between them by definition.

In terms of quality, the equation for B appears to be oversimplified for project management, lacks empirical support, and provides no help to software engineers. As $S*$ is taken as a constant, the equation for faults (B) simply states that the number of faults in a program is a function of its volume. This metric is therefore a static metric, ignoring the huge variations in fault rates observed in software products and among modules.

11.3 Cyclomatic Complexity

The measurement of cyclomatic complexity by McCabe (1976) was designed to indicate a program's testability and understandability (maintainability). It is the classical graph theory cyclomatic number, indicating the number of regions in a graph. As applied to software, it is the number of linearly independent paths that comprise the program. As such it can be used to indicate the effort required to test a program. To determine the paths, the program procedure is represented as a strongly connected graph with unique entry and exit points. The general formula to compute cyclomatic complexity is:

$$M = V(G) = e - n + 2p$$

where
$V(G)$ = Cyclomatic number of G
e = Number of edges
n = Number of nodes
p = Number of unconnected parts of the graph

As an example, Figure 11.2 is a control graph of a simple program that might contain two IF statements. If we count the edges, nodes, and disconnected parts of the graph, we see that $e = 8$, $n = 7$, and $p = 1$, and that $M = 8 - 7 + 2 * 1 = 3$.

Note that M is also equal to the number of binary decisions in a program plus 1. If all decisions are not binary, a three-way decision is counted as two binary decisions and an n-way case (select) statement is counted as $n - 1$ binary decisions. The

FIGURE 11.2
Simple Control Graph Example

iteration test in a looping statement is counted as one binary decision. In the preceding simple example, since there are two binary decisions, $M = 2 + 1 = 3$.

The cyclomatic complexity metric is additive. The complexity of several graphs considered as a group is equal to the sum of the individual graphs' complexities. However, it ignores the complexity of sequential statements. Neither does the metric distinguish different kinds of control flow complexity such as loops versus IF-THEN-ELSE statements or cases versus nested IF-THEN-ELSE statements.

To have good testability and maintainability, McCabe recommends that no program module should exceed a cyclomatic complexity of 10. Because the complexity metric is based on decisions and branches, which is consistent with the logic pattern of design and programming, it appeals to software professionals. Since its inception, cyclomatic complexity has become an active area of research and practical applications. Many experts in software testing recommend use of the cyclomatic representation to ensure adequate test coverage; the use of McCabe's complexity measure has been gaining acceptance by practitioners.

Because of its appeal to programmers and researchers, many studies have been conducted to relate McCabe's complexity measure to defect rate, and moderate to strong correlations were observed. For instance, in a study of software metrics of a large SQL product that consisted of about 1300 modules, Troster (1992) found a relatively strong correlation between McCabe's cyclomatic complexity index and the number of test defects ($r = .48$, $n = 1303$, $p = .0001$). Studies found that the complexity index also correlates strongly with program size—lines of code. Will the correlation between complexity and defect remain significant after program size is controlled? In other words, is the correlation between complexity and defects a spurious one, because program size affects both complexity and defect level? Many studies have been done with regard to this question and the findings are not always consistent. There are cases where the correlation disappears after the effect of program size is controlled; in other cases the correlation weakens somewhat but remains significant, suggesting a genuine association between complexity and defect level. Our experience belongs to the latter kind.

Sometimes the disappearance of the correlation between complexity and defect level after accounting for program size may be due to a lack of investigational rigor. It is important that appropriate statistical techniques be used with regard to the nature of the data. For example, Troster observed that the LOC count also correlated with the number of test defects quite strongly ($r = 0.49$, $n = 1296$, $p = 0.001$). To partial out the effect of program size, therefore, he calculated the correlation between McCabe's complexity index and testing defect rate (per KLOC). He found that the correlation totally disappeared with $r = 0.002$ ($n = 1296$, $p = 0.9415$). Had Troster stopped there, he would have concluded that there is no genuine association between complexity and defect level. Troster realized, however, that he also needed to look at the rank-order correlation. Therefore, he also computed the Spearman's rank-order correlation coefficient and found a very respectable association between complexity and defect rate:

Spearman's correlation − 0.27

$n = 1296$ (number of modules)

$p = 0.0001$ (highly statistically significant)

These seemingly inconsistent findings, based on our experience and observation of the Troster study, is due to the nature of software data. As discussed previously, Pearson's correlation coefficient is very sensitive to extreme data points; it can also be distorted if there is a lot of noise in the data. Defect rate data (normalized to KLOC) tend to fluctuate widely and therefore it is difficult to have significant Pearson correlation coefficients. The rank-order correlation coefficient, which is less precise but more robust than the Pearson correlation coefficient, is more appropriate for such data.

As another example, Craddock (1987) reports the use of McCabe's complexity index at low-level design inspections and code inspection (I2). He correlated the number of inspection defects with both complexity and LOC. As shown in Table 11.2, Craddock found that complexity is a better indicator of defects than LOC at the two inspection phases.

Assuming that an organization can establish a significant correlation between complexity and defect level, then the McCabe index can be useful in several ways, including the following:

TABLE 11.2
Correlation Coefficients Between Inspection Defects and Complexity

Inspection Type	Number of Inspections	KLOC	r Lines of Code	r McCabe's Index
I0	46	129.9	0.10	—
I1	41	67.9	0.46	0.69
I2	30	35.3	0.56	0.68

- ☐ To help identify overly complex parts needing detailed inspections
- ☐ To help identify noncomplex parts likely to have a low defect rate and therefore candidates for development without detailed inspections
- ☐ To estimate programming and service effort, identify troublesome code, and estimate testing effort

Later in this chapter we describe an example of complexity study in more detail and illustrate how quality improvement can be made via the focus on complexity reduction.

11.4 Syntactic Constructs

McCabe's cyclomatic complexity index is a summary index of binary decisions. It does not distinguish different kinds of control flow complexity such as loops versus IF-THEN-ELSES or cases versus IF-THEN-ELSES. Researchers of software metrics also studied the association of individual syntactic constructs with defect level. For instance, Shen and associates (1985) discovered that the number of unique operands (n_2) was useful in identifying the modules most likely to contain errors for the three software products they studied. Binder and Poore (1990) empirically supported the concept of local software quality metrics whose formulation is based on software syntactic attributes. Such local metrics may be specific to the products under study or the development teams or environments. However, as long as an empirical association with software quality is established, those metrics could provide useful clues for improvement actions. In selecting such metrics for study, consideration must be given to the question of whether the metric could be acted on.

In studying the quality and syntactic indicators among a sample of twenty modules of a COBOL compiler product, Lo (1992) found that field defects at the module level can be estimated through the following equations:

$$\text{Field defects} = -2.5 + 0.003\text{LOC} + 0.001 \text{ Unique operands}$$
$$(R^2 = 0.66)$$
$$\text{Field defects} = 0.11 \text{ IF-THEN} + 0.03 \text{ Number of calls}$$
$$(R^2 = 0.88)$$

While both equations provide satisfactory results, the findings mean nothing in terms of planning actions for improvement. In a second attempt, which included all 66 modules of the product, Lo examined other syntactic constructs and found the following relationship:

$$\text{Field defects} = 0.15 + 0.23 \text{ DO WHILE} + 0.22 \text{ SELECT}$$
$$+ 0.07 \text{ IF THEN}$$
$$(R^2 = 0.55)$$

In the model, all three metrics are statistically significant, with DO WHILE having the most effect. The DO WHILE metric included both DO WHILE . . . END and DO WHILE TO . . . . ? Although the R^2 of the model decreased, the findings provide useful clues for improvement. Although it is difficult to avoid the use of IF THEN or to change the number of unique operands, it is feasible to reduce the use of a complex construct such as the DO WHILE or SELECT statement. Upon brainstorming with the development team, Lo found that most developers were having difficulty mastering the DO WHILE construct. As a result, minimizing the use of DO WHILE was one of the actions the team took to reduce defects in the compiler product.

11.5 Structure Metrics

Lines of code, Halstead's software science, McCabe's cyclomatic complexity, and other metrics that measure module complexity assume that each program module is a separate entity. Structure metrics try to take into account the interactions between modules in a product or system and quantify such interactions. Many approaches in structure metrics have been proposed. Some good examples include invocation complexity by McClure (1978), system partitioning measures by Belady and Evangelisti (1981), information flow metrics by Henry and Kafura (1981), and stability measures by Yau and Collofello (1980). Many of these metrics and models, however, are yet to be verified by empirical data from software development projects.

Perhaps the most common design structure metrics are the fan-in and fan-out metrics, which are based on the ideas of coupling proposed by Yourdon and Constantine (1979) and Myers (1978):

- □ *Fan-in:* A count of the modules that call a given module
- □ *Fan-out:* A count of modules that are called by a given module

In general, modules with a large fan-in are relatively small and simple, and are usually located at the lower layers of the design structure. In contrast, modules that are large and complex are likely to have a small fan-in. Therefore, modules or components that have a large fan-in and large fan-out may indicate a poor design. Such modules have probably not been decomposed correctly and are candidates for redesign. From the complexity and defect point of view, modules with a large fan-in are expected to have negative or insignificant correlation with defect levels, and modules with a large fan-out are expected to have a positive correlation. In the AS/400 experience, we found a positive correlation between fan-out and defect level, and no correlation between fan-in and defects. However, the standard deviations of fan-in and fan-out were quite large in our data. Therefore, our experience was inconclusive.

Henry and Kafura's structure complexity is defined as:

$$C_p = (\text{fan-in} \times \text{fan-out})^2$$

In an attempt to incorporate the module complexity and structure complexity, Henry and Selig's work (1990) defines a hybrid form of their information-flow metric as

$$HC_p = C_{ip} \times (\text{fan-in} \times \text{fan-out})^2$$

where C_{ip} is the internal complexity of procedure p, which can be measured by any module complexity metrics such as McCabe's cyclomatic complexity.

Based on various approaches to structure complexity and module complexity measures, Card and Glass (1990) developed a system complexity model

$$C_t = S_t + D_t$$

where
C_t = System complexity
S_t = Structural (intermodule) complexity
D_t = Data (intramodule) complexity

They defined relative system complexity as

$$C = C_t / n$$

where n is the number of modules in the system.

Structure complexity is further defined as

$$S = \frac{\sum f^2(i)}{n}$$

where
S   = Structural complexity
$f(i)$ = Fan-out of module i
n = Number of modules in system

and data complexity is further defined as

$$D_i = \frac{V(i)}{f(i)+1}$$

where
D_i = Data complexity of module i
$V(i)$ = I/O variables in module i
$f(i)$ = Fan-out of module i.

$$D = \frac{\sum D(i)}{n}$$

where
D = Data (intramodule) complexity
$D(i)$ = Data complexity of module i
n = Number of new modules in system

Simply put, according to Card and Glass (1990), system complexity is a sum of structural (intermodule) complexity and overall data (intramodule) complexity. Structural complexity is defined as the mean (per module) of squared values of fan-out. This definition is based on the findings in the literature that fan-in is not an important complexity indicator and that complexity increases as the square of connections between programs (fan-out). With regard to data (intramodule) complexity of a module, it is defined as a function that is directly dependent on the number of I/O variables and inversely dependent on the number of fan-outs in the module. The rationale is that the more I/O variables in a module, the more functionality needs to be accomplished by the module and, therefore, the higher internal complexity. On the contrary, more fan-out means that functionality is deferred to modules at lower levels, therefore, the internal complexity of a module is reduced. Finally, the overall data complexity is defined as the average of data complexity of all new modules. In Card and Glass's model, only new modules enter the formula because oftentimes the entire system consists of reused modules, which have been designed, used, aged, and stabilized in terms of reliability and quality.

In a study of eight software projects, Card and Glass found that the system complexity measure was significantly correlated with subjective quality assessment by a senior development manager and with development error rate. Specifically, the correlation between system complexity and development defect rate was 0.83, with complexity accounting for fully 69% of the variation in error rate. The regression formula thus derived was

$$\text{Error rate} = -5.2 + 0.4 \times \text{Complexity}$$

In other words, each unit increase in system complexity increases the error rate by 0.4 (errors per thousand lines of code).

The Card and Glass model appears quite promising and has an appeal to software development practitioners. They also provide guidelines on achieving a low complexity design. When more validation studies become available, the Card and Glass model and related methods may gain greater acceptance in the software development industry.

While Card and Glass's model is for the system level, the system values of the metrics in the model are aggregates (averages) of module-level data. Therefore, it is feasible to correlate these metrics to defect level at the module level. The meanings of the metrics at the module level are as follows:

- D_i = data complexity of module i, as defined earlier
- S_i = structural complexity of module i, that is, a measure of the module's interaction with other modules
- $C_i = S_i + D_i$ = the module's contribution to overall system complexity

In Troster's study (1992) discussed earlier, data at the module level for Card and Glass's metrics are also available. It would be interesting to compare these metrics with McCabe's cyclomatic complexity with regard to their correlation with defect rate. Not unexpectedly, the rank-order correlation coefficients for these metrics are very similar to that for McCabe's (0.27). Specifically, the coefficients are 0.28 for D_i, 0.19 for S_i, and 0.27 for C_i. More research in this area will certainly yield more insights into the relationships of various design and module metrics and their predictive power in terms of software quality.

11.6 An Example of Module Design Metrics in Practice

In this section, we describe an analysis of several module design metrics as they relate to defect level, and how such metrics can be used to develop a software quality improvement plan. Special attention is given to the significance of cyclomatic complexity. Data from all program modules of a key component in the AS/400 software system served as the basis of the analysis. The component provides facilities for message control among users, programs, and the operating system. It was written in PL/MI (a PL/1–like language) and has about 70 KLOC. Because the component functions are complex and involve numerous interfaces, the component has consistently experienced high reported error rates from the field. The purpose of the analysis was to produce objective evidences so that data-based plans can be formulated for quality and maintainability improvement.

The metrics in the analysis include:

- [ ] McCabe's cyclomatic complexity index (CPX).
- [ ] Fan-in: The number of modules that call a given module (FAN-IN).
- [ ] Fan-out: The number of modules that are called by a given module. In AS/400 this metric refers to the number of MACRO calls in the module (MAC).
- [ ] Number of INCLUDES in the module. In AS/400 INCLUDES are used for calls such as subroutines and declarations. The difference between MACRO and INCLUDE is that for INCLUDE there are no parameters passing. For this reason, INCLUDES are not counted as fan-out. However, INCLUDES do involve interface, especially for the common INCLUDES.
- [ ] Number of design changes and enhancements since the initial release of AS/400 (DCR).
- [ ] Previous defect history. This metric refers to the number of formal test defects and field defects in the same modules in System/38, the predecessor midrange computer system of AS/400. This component reused most of the modules in System/38. This metric is denoted PTR38 in the analysis.
- [ ] Defect level in the current system (AS/400). This is the total number of formal test defects and field defects for the latest release when the analysis was done. This metric is denoted DEFS in the analysis.

Our purpose was to explain the variations in defect level among program modules by means of the differences observed in the metrics described earlier. Therefore, DEFS is the dependent variable and the other metrics are the independent variables. The means and standard deviations of all variables in the analysis are shown in Table 11.3. The large mean values of MACRO calls (MAC) and FAN-IN illustrate the complexity of the component. Indeed, as the component provides facilities for message control in the entire operating system, numerous modules in the system have MACRO-call links with many modules of the component. The large standard deviation for FAN-IN also indicates that the chance for significant relationships between fan-in and other variables is slim.

Table 11.4 shows the Pearson correlation coefficients between defect level and other metrics. The high correlations for many factors were beyond expectation. The

TABLE 11.3
Means, Standard Deviations, and Number of Modules

Standard Variable	Mean	Deviation	n
CPX	23.5	23.2	72
FAN-IN	143.5	491.6	74
MAC	61.8	27.4	74
INCLUDES	15.4	9.5	74
DCR	2.7	3.1	75
PTR38	8.7	9.8	63
DEFS	6.5	8.9	75

TABLE 11.4
Correlation Coefficients Between Defect Level and Other Metrics

Variable	Pearson Correlation	n	Significance (p Value)
CPX	.65	72	.0001
FAN-IN	.02	74	Not significant
MAC	.68	74	.0001
INCLUDES	.65	74	.0001
DCR	.78	75	.0001
PTR38	.87	75	.0001

significant correlations for complexity indexes and MACRO calls support the theory that associates complexity with defect level. McCabe's complexity index measures the complexity within the module. FAN-OUT, or MACRO calls in this case, is an indicator of the complexity between modules.

As expected, the correlation between FAN-IN and DEFS was not significant. Because the standard deviation of FAN-IN is large, this finding is tentative. More focused analysis is needed. Theoretically, modules with a large fan-in are relatively simple and are usually located at lower layers of the system structure. Therefore, fan-in should not positively correlate with defect level. The correlation should either be negative or insignificant, as the present case showed.

The high correlation for module changes and enhancement simply illustrates the fact that the more changes, the more chances for injecting defects. Moreover, small changes are especially error-prone. Because most of the modules in this component were designed and developed for the System/38, changes for AS/400 were generally small.

The correlation between previous defect history and current defect level was the strongest (0.87). This finding confirms the view of the developers that many modules in the component are chronic problem components, and systematic plans and actions are needed for any significant quality improvement.

The calculation of Pearson's correlation coefficient is based on the least-squares method. Because the least-squares method is extremely sensitive to outliers, examination of scatterplots to confirm the correlation is mandatory. Relying on the correlation coefficients alone sometimes may be erroneous. The scatter diagram of defect level with McCabe's complexity index is shown in Figure 5.9 in Chapter 5 where we discuss the seven basic quality tools. The diagram appears radiant in shape: low-complexity modules at the low defect level; however, for high-complexity modules, while more are at the high defect level, there are others with low defect levels. Perhaps the most impressive finding from the diagram is the blank area in the upper left part, confirming the correlation between low complexity and low defect level. As can be seen, there are many modules with a complexity index far beyond McCabe's recommended level of 10—probably due to the high complexity of system programs in general, and the component functions specifically.

Figure 11.3 shows the scatter diagrams for defect level with MAC, INCLUDE, DCR, and PTR38. The diagrams confirm the correlations. Because the relationships appear linear, the linear regression lines and confidence intervals are also plotted.

The extreme data point at the upper right corner of the diagrams represents the best known module in the component, which formats a display of messages in a queue and sends it to either the screen or printer. With more than 5,000 lines of source code, it is a highly complex module with a history of many problems.

The next step in our analysis was to look at the combined effect of these metrics on defect level simultaneously. To achieve this task, we used the multiple regression approach. In a multiple regression model, the effect of each independent variable is adjusted for the effects of other variables. In other words, the regression coefficient and the significance level of an independent variable represent the net effect of that variable on the dependent variable—in this case, the defect level. We found that in the combined model, MAC and INCLUDE become insignificant. When we excluded them from the model, we obtained the following:

$$DEFS = -1.796 + 0.597 \times PTR38 + 0.628 \times DCR + 0.051 \times CPX$$

With an R^2 of 0.83, the model is highly significant. Each of the three independent variables is also significant at the 0.05 level. In other words, the model explains 83% of the variations in defect level observed among the program modules.

To verify the findings, we must control for the effect of program size—lines of code. Since LOC is correlated with DEFS and other variables, its effect must be partialled out in order to conclude that there are genuine influences of PTR38, DCR,

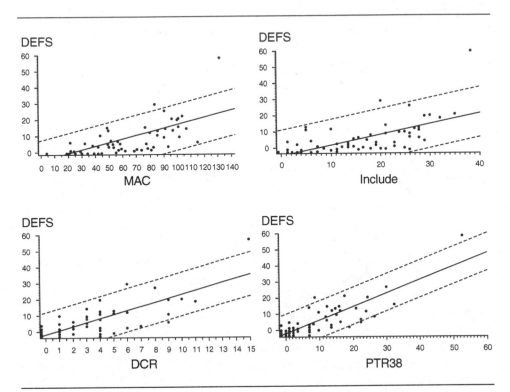

FIGURE 11.3
Scatter Diagram—DEFS with MAC, INCLUDE, DCR, and PTR38

and CPX on DEFS. To accomplish the task, we did two things: (1) normalized the defect level by LOC and used defects per KLOC (DEFR) as the dependent variable and (2) included LOC as one of the independent variables (control variable) in the multiple regression model. We found that with this control, PTR38, DCR, and CPX were still significant at the 0.1 level. In other words, these factors truly represent something for which the length of the modules cannot account. However, the R^2 of the model was only 0.20. We contend that this again is due to the wide fluctuation of the dependent variable, the defect rate. The regression coefficients, their standard errors, t values, and the significance levels are shown in Table 11.5.

This analysis indicates that other than module length, the three most important factors affecting the defect rates of the modules are the number of changes and enhancements, defect history, and complexity level. From the intervention stand-point, since developers have no control over release enhancements, the latter two factors become the best clues for quality improvement actions. The relationships among defect history, complexity, and current defect level are illustrated in Figure 11.4. The

TABLE 11.5
Results of Multiple Regression Model of Defect Rate

Variable	Regression Coefficients	Standard Error	t Value	Significance (p Value)
Intercept	4.631	2.813	1.65	.10
CPX	.115	.066	1.73	.09
DCR	1.108	.561	1.98	.05
PTR38	.359	.220	1.63	.10
LOC	−.014	.005	2.99	.004
R^2	.20			

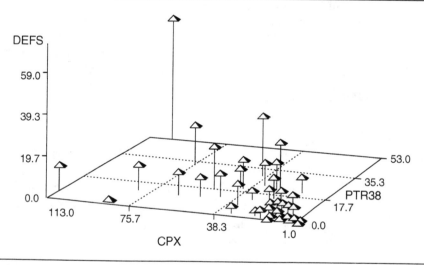

FIGURE 11.4
Scatter Diagrams of DEF, PTR38, and CPX

best return on investment, then, is to concentrate efforts on modules with high defect history (chronic problem modules) and high complexity.

Based on the findings from this analysis and other observations, the component team established a quality improvement plan with staged implementation. The following list includes some of the actions related to this analysis:

☐ Scrutinize the several modules with moderate complexity and yet high defect level. Examine module design and code implementation and take proper actions.

☐ Identify high-complexity and chronic problem modules, do intramodule restructuring and cleanup (e.g., better separation of mainline and subroutines, better comments, better documentation in the prologue, removal of dead code, better structure of source statements). The first-stage target is to reduce the complexity of these modules to 35 or lower.

☐ Closely related to the preceding actions, to reduce the number of compilation warning messages to zero for all modules.

☐ Include complexity as a key factor in new module design, with the maximum not to exceed 35.

☐ Improve test effectiveness, especially for complex modules. Use test coverage measurement tools to ensure that such modules are adequately covered.

☐ Improve component documentation and education.

Since the preceding analysis was conducted, the component team has been making consistent improvements according to its quality plan. Field data from new releases indicate significant improvement in the component's quality.

11.7 Summary

This chapter describes several major metrics and models with regard to software module and design from the viewpoint of the metrics' correlation with defect level. Regardless of whether the metrics are lines of code, the software science metrics, cyclomatic complexity, other syntactic constructs, or structure metrics, these metrics seem to be operational definitions of the complexity of the software design and module implementation. In retrospect, the key to achieving good quality is to reduce the complexity of software design and implementation, given a problem domain for which the software is to provide a solution.

The criteria for evaluation of complexity metrics and models, therefore, rest on their explanatory power and applicability. *Explanatory power* refers to the model's ability to explain the relationships among complexity, quality, and other programming and design parameters. *Applicability* refers to the degree to which the models and metrics can be applied by software engineers to improve their work in design, coding, and testing. This is related to whether the model or metric can provide clues that can lead to specific actions for improvement. As a secondary criterion to explanatory power, congruence between the underlying logic of the model and the reasoning patterns of software engineers also plays a significant role. As a case in point, McCabe's complexity metrics may appeal more to programming development professionals than Halstead's token-based software science. During the design, code, and test phases, software engineers' line of reasoning is determined more in terms of decision points, branches, and paths than in terms of the number of operators and operands.

Recommendations for Small Teams

Complexity metrics and models are by nature small-team metrics. They measure the internal dynamics of design and code of the software, and the unit of analysis is usually at the program-module level. The examples discussed in the chapter are all small-team projects. Even for large organizations, use of these metrics for quality improvement is probably more effective with selected small teams than an across-the-board implementation.

Whether measured by lines of code, cyclomatic complexity, the number of fan-in and fan-out, or specific syntactic constructs, it is important to have empirical validity established before the team decides on an action plan. By *empirical validity* we mean a good correlation exists between the selected metrics and defect rate for the modules owned by the team

and a causality can be inferred (see discussions in Chapter 3). To establish a correlation, data gathering and analysis are needed. In the case that statistical expertise is not readily available to perform complex analysis, simple techniques (e.g., the Pareto diagram, the scatter diagram, and simple tabulations) coupled with good brainstorming by team members will be just as effective. Causality can also be established by individual defect causal analysis. For example, if causal analysis of a number of defects by the team points to modules with high fan-outs, then a causality can be asserted. To aid causal analysis and to organize the causes and effects in a structured manner, the team can use the cause-and-effect diagram and the relations diagram, which are discussed in Chapter 5.

Like software reliability models, perhaps even more so, the validity of complexity metrics and models often depends on the product, the development team, and the development environment. Therefore, one should always be very careful when generalizing findings from specific studies. In this regard, the concept and approach of local software quality metrics seem quite appealing. Specific improvement actions, therefore should be based on pertinent empirical relationships.

References

1. Basili, V. R., and B. T. Perricone, "Software Errors and Complexity: An Empirical Investigation," *Communications of the ACM*, January 1984, pp. 42–52.
2. Belady, L. A., and C. J. Evangelisti, "System Partitioning and Its Measure," *Journal of Systems and Software*, 2, 1981, pp. 23–39.
3. Binder, L., and J. Poore, "Field Experiments with Local Software Quality Metrics," *Software—Practice and Experience*, Vol. 20, No. 7, July 1990, pp. 631–647.
4. Card, D. N., and Robert L. Glass, *Measuring Software Design Quality*, Englewood Cliffs, N.J.: Prentice-Hall, 1990.
5. Craddock, L. L., "Analyzing Cost-of-Quality, Complexity, and Defect Metrics for Software Inspections," Technical Report TR07.844, IBM Rochester, Minn., April 1987.
6. Halstead, M. H., *Elements of Software Science*, New York: Elsevier North Holland, 1977.

7. Henry, S. M., and D. Kafura, "Software Structure Metrics Based on Information Flow," *IEEE Transactions on Software Engineering,* Vol. SE-7, 1981, pp. 510–518.

8. Henry, S. M., and C. Selig, "Predicting Source-Code Complexity at the Design Stage," *IEEE Software,* March 1990, pp. 36–44.

9. Lo, B., "Syntactical Construct Based APAR Projection," IBM Santa Teresa Laboratory Technical Report, California, 1992.

10. McCabe, T. J., "A Complexity Measure," *IEEE Transactions on Software Engineering,* Vol. 2, No. 4, December 1976, pp. 308–320.

11. McClure, C. L., "A Model for Program Complexity Analysis," *Proceedings IEEE Third International Conference on Software Engineering,* May 1978, pp. 149–157.

12. Myers, G. J., *Composite Structured Design,* Wokingham, U.K.: Van Nostrand Reinhold, 1978.

13. Shen, V., T. Yu, S. Thebaut, and L. Paulsen, "Identifying Error-Prone Software—An Empirical Study," *IEEE Transactions on Software Engineering,* Vol. SE-11, No. 4, April 1985, pp. 317–324.

14. Troster, J., "Assessing Design-Quality Metrics on Legacy Software," Software Engineering Process Group, IBM Canada Ltd. Laboratory, North York, Ontario, September 1992.

15. Withrow, C., "Error Density and Size in Ada Software," *IEEE Software,* January 1990, pp. 26–30.

16. Yau, S. S., and J. S. Collofello, "Some Stability Measures for Software Maintenance," *IEEE Transactions on Software Engineering,* Vol. SE-6, 1980, pp. 545–552.

17. Yourdon, E., and L. L. Constantine, *Structured Design,* Englewood Cliffs, N.J.: Prentice-Hall, 1979.

12

Metrics and Lessons Learned for Object-Oriented Projects

In the past decade, many companies have started to deploy objected-oriented (OO) technology in their software development efforts. Object-oriented analysis (OOA), object-oriented design (OOD), and object-oriented languages and programming (OOP) have gained wide acceptance in many software organizations. OO metrics have been proposed in the literature and there have been increased discussions in recent years. In this chapter we discuss the major OO metrics in the literature, and give examples of metrics and data from commercial software projects. We attempt to discuss the metrics from several perspectives including design and complexity, productivity, and quality management. In the last part of the chapter, we discuss the lessons learned from the assessments of a good number of the OO projects over the past decade.

12.1 Object-Oriented Concepts and Constructs

Class, object, method, message, instance variable, and inheritance are the basic concepts of the OO technology. OO metrics are mainly measures of how these constructs are used in the design and development process. Therefore, a short review of definitions is in order.

- A *class* is a template from which objects can be created. It defines the structure and capabilities of an object instance. The class definition includes the state data and the behaviors (methods) for the instances of that class. The class can be thought of as a factory that creates instances as needed. For example, an Account class may have methods to allow deposits and withdrawals, using a balance instance variable to hold the current balance. This definition defines how an Account works, but it is not an actual account.
- An *abstract class* is a class that has no instances, created to facilitate sharing of state data and services among similar, more specialized subclasses.
- A *concrete class* is a class that has instances. For example, there might be a Savings Account class with a number of instances in a bank application.
- An *object* is an instantiation of a class. It is anything that models things in the real world. These things can be physical entities such as cars, or events such as a concert, or abstractions such as a general-purpose account. An object has state (data) and behavior (methods or services), as defined for the class of objects it belongs to.
- A *method* is a class service behavior. It operates on data in response to a message and is defined as part of the declaration of a class. Methods reflect how a problem is broken into segments and the capabilities other classes expect of a given class.
- *Message:* Objects communicate via messages. To request a service from another object, an object sends it a message. This is the only means to get information from an object, because its data is not directly accessible (this is called encapsulation).
- *Instance variable* is a place to store and refer to an object's state data. In traditional programming, this would be a data variable. In OO paradigm, data is made up of instance variables of an object.
- *Inheritance:* Similar classes of objects can be organized into categories called *class hierarchies*. The lower-level classes (called subclasses) can use the services of all the higher classes in their hierarchy. This is called inheritance. *Inheritance* is simply a way of reusing services and data. As an example, Savings accounts are types of general Account, and IRA accounts are types of Savings accounts. The Savings account inherits the capability to handle deposits from the Account class. The number of subclasses in the class hierarchy is called *hierarchy nesting* or *depth of inheritance tree (DIT)*.

Figure 12.1 provides a pictorial description of the OO structures and key concepts. For example, "Account", "SavingsCheckingAccount", "HomeEquity", and "CertificateAccount" are all classes. "Account" is also an abstract class; the other classes are its subclasses, which are concrete classes. "Ken Brown'sSavingsAccount" and "Ken Brown's HomeEquity Account" are objects. The "Account" class has three subclasses or children. "AccountNumber" is an instance variable, also called an attribute, and getBalance() is a method of the "Account" class. All instance variables and methods for the "Account" class are also the instance variables and methods of its subclasses through inheritance. The object "Ken Brown'sSavingsAccount" sends a message to the object "Ken Brown's HomeEquity Account", via the "transfer()"

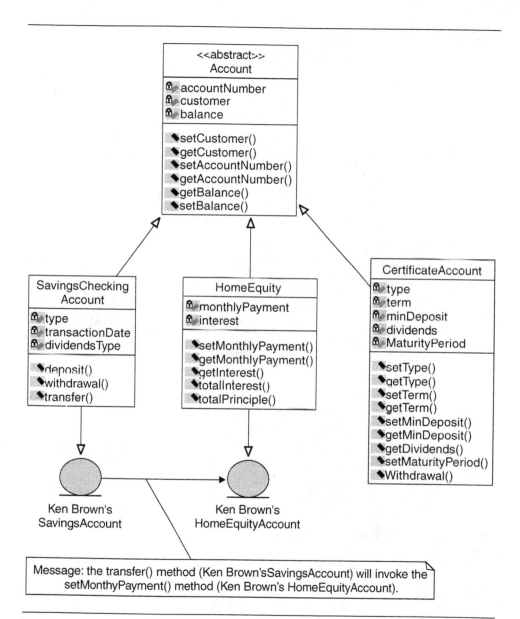

FIGURE 12.1
An Object-Oriented Class Hierarchy

method and thereby invokes the "setMonthlyPayment()" method. Therefore, the class "SavingsCheckingAccount" is coupled to the class "HomeEquity" through the message.

12.2 Design and Complexity Metrics

Classes and methods are the basic constructs for OO technology. The amount of function provided by an OO software can be estimated based on the number of identified classes and methods or its variants. Therefore, it is natural that the basic OO metrics are related to classes and methods, and the size (logical lines of code, or LOC) or function points of the classes and methods. For design and complexity measures, the metrics would have to deal with specific OO characteristics such as inheritance, instance variable, and coupling.

12.2.1 Lorenz Metrics and Rules of Thumb

Based on his experience in OO software development, Lorenz (1993) proposed eleven metrics as OO design metrics. He also provided the rules of thumb for some of the metrics, which we summarized in Table 12.1.

As the table shows, some of these metrics are guidelines for OO design and development rather than metrics in the sense of quantitative measurements. Although most of these eleven metrics are related to OO design and implementation, metric 8 is a statement of good programming practices, metric 9 is a quality indicator, and metric 11 is a metric for validating the OO development process.

With regard to average method size, a large number may indicate poor OO designs and therefore function-oriented coding. For average number of methods per class, a large number is desirable from the standpoint of code reuse because subclasses tend to inherit a larger number of methods from superclasses. However, if the number of methods per object class gets too large, extensibility will suffer. A larger number of methods per object class is also likely to complicate testing as a result of increased complexity. Too many methods in a single class, not counting inherited methods, is also a warning that too much responsibility is being placed in one type of object. There are probably other undiscovered classes. On this point, similar reasoning can be applied to instance variables—a large number of instance variables indicates that one class is doing more than it should. In other words, the design may need refinement.

Inheritance tree depth is likely to be more favorable than breadth in terms of reusability via inheritance. Deeper inheritance trees would seem to promote greater method sharing than would broad trees. On the other hand, a deep inheritance tree may be more difficult to test than a broad one and comprehensibility may be diminished. Deep class hierarchy may be the result of overzealous object creation, almost the opposite concern of having too many methods or instance variables in one class.

The pertinent question therefore is, what should the optimum value be for OO metrics such as the several just discussed? There may not be one correct answer, but the rules of thumb by Lorenz as shown in Table 12.1 are very useful. They were derived based on experiences from industry OO projects. They provide a threshold for comparison and interpretation.

TABLE 12.1.
OO Metrics and Rules of Thumb Recommended by Lorenz (1993)

Metric	Rules of Thumb and Comments
1. Average Method Size (LOC)	Should be less than 8 LOC for Smalltalk and 24 LOC for C++
2. Average Number of Methods per Class	Should be less than 20. Bigger averages indicate too much responsibility in too few classes.
3. Average Number of Instance Variables per Class	Should be less than 6. More instance variables indicate that one class is doing more than it should.
4. Class Hierarchy Nesting Level (Depth of Inheritance Tree, DIT)	Should be less than 6, starting from the framework classes or the root class.
5. Number of Subsystem/Subsystem Relationships	Should be less than the number in metric 6.
6. Number of Class/Class Relationships in Each Subsystem	Should be relatively high. This item relates to high cohesion of classes in the same subsystem. If one or more classes in a subsystem don't interact with many of the other classes, they might be better placed in another subsystem.
7. Instance Variable Usage	If groups of methods in a class use different sets of instance variables, look closely to see if the class should be split into multiple classes along those "service" lines.
8. Average Number of Comment Lines (per Method)	Should be greater than 1.
9. Number of Problem Reports per Class	Should be low (no specifics provided).
10. Number of Times Class Is Reused	If a class is not being reused in different applications (especially an abstract class), it might need to be redesigned.
11. Number of Classes and Methods Thrown Away	Should occur at a steady rate throughout most of the development process. If this is not occurring, one is probably doing an incremental development instead of performing true iterative OO design and development.

Source: Lorenz, 1993.

In 1994 Lorenz and Kidd (1994) expanded their metrics work by publishing a suite of recommended OO metrics with multiple metrics for each of the following categories: method size, method internals, class size, class inheritance, method inheritance, class internals, and class externals. They also showed the frequency distribution of the number of classes for five projects, in the histogram form, along the values of some of the metrics. No numeric parameters of these metrics (e.g., mean or median) were provided, however.

12.2.2 Some Metrics Examples

In early 1993, IBM Object Oriented Technology Council (OOTC) (1993) published a white paper on OO metrics with recommendations to the product divisions. The list included more that thirty metrics, each with a relative importance rating of high, medium, or low. All proposed metrics by Lorenz in 1993 (Table 12.1), with the exception of metrics 5 and 6, were in the IBM OOTC list with a high importance rating. Almost all of the OOTC metrics were included in Lorenz and Kidd's (1994) comprehensive suite. This commonality was not a coincidence because both Lorenz and Kidd were formerly affiliated with IBM and Lorenz was formerly the technical lead of IBM's OOTC. As one would expect, Lorenz's OO metrics rules of thumb were the same as IBM OOTC's. The OOTC also recommended that the average depth of hierarchy be less than 4 for C++ projects. In terms of project size, the OOTC classified projects with fewer than 200 classes as small, projects with 200 to 500 classes as medium, and projects with more than 500 classes as large.

Table 12.2 shows selected metrics for six OO projects developed at the IBM Rochester software development laboratory. Project A was for the lower layer of a large operating system that interacts with hardware microcode; Project B was the development of an operating system itself; Project C was for the software that drives the input and output (IO) devices of a computer system; Project D was for a Visualage application; Project E was for a software for a development environment, which was a joint project with an external alliance; and Project F was for a software that provides graphical operations for a subsystem of an operating system. Based on OOTC's project size categorization, Projects A, B, and C were very large projects, Projects E and F were medium-sized projects, and Project D was a small project.

Compared with the rules of thumb per Lorenz (1993) and IBM OOTC (1993), Project E had a much higher average number of methods per class, a larger class in terms of LOC, and a larger maximum depth of inheritance tree. Project E was a joint project with an external alliance and when code drops were delivered, acceptance testing was conducted by IBM. Our defect tracking during acceptance testing did show a high defect volume and a significantly higher defect rate, even when compared to other projects that were developed in procedural programming. This supports the observation that a deep inheritance tree may be more difficult to test than a

TABLE 12.2
Some OO Metrics for Six Projects

Metric	Project A (C++)	Project B (C++)	Project C (C++)	Project D (IBM Smalltalk)	Project E (OTI Smalltalk)	Project F (Digitalk Smalltalk)	Rules of Thumb
Number of Classes	5,741	2,513	3,000	100	566	492	na
Methods per Class	8	3	7	17	36	21	<20
LOC per Method	21	19	15	5.3	5.2	5.7	<8(S)* <24(C)*
LOC per Class	207	60	100	97	188	117	<160(S)* <480(C)*
Max Depth of Inheritance Tree (DIT)	6	na	5	6	8	na	<6
Avg DIT	na	na	3	4.8	2.8	na	<4 (C)*

(S)* = Smalltalk; (C)* = C++

broad one and comprehensibility may be diminished, thereby allowing more opportunities for error injection.

The metric values for the other projects all fell below the rule-of-thumb thresholds. The average methods per class for projects A, B, and C were far below the threshold of 20, with project B's value especially low. A smaller number of methods per class may mean larger overheads in class interfaces and a negative impact on the software's performance. Not coincidentally, all three projects were not initially meeting their performance targets, and had to undergo significant performance tuning before the products were ready to ship. The performance challenges of these three projects apparently could not be entirely attributed to this aspect of the class design because there were other known factors, but the data demonstrated a good correlation. Indeed, our experience is that performance is a major concern that needs early action for most OO projects. The positive lesson learned from the performance tuning work of these projects is that performance tuning and improvement are easier in OO development than in procedural programming.

12.2.3 The CK OO Metrics Suite

In 1994 Chidamber and Kemerer proposed six OO design and complexity metrics, which later became the commonly referred to CK metrics suite:

☐ *Weighted Methods per Class (WMC):* WMC is the sum of the complexities of the methods, whereas complexity is measured by cyclomatic complexity. If one considers all methods of a class to be of equal complexity, then WMC is simply the number of methods defined in each class. Measuring the cyclomatic complexity is difficult to implement because not all methods are assessable in the class hierarchy due to inheritance. Therefore, in empirical studies, WMC is often just the number of methods in a class, and the average of WMC is the average number of methods per class.

☐ *Depth of Inheritance Tree (DIT):* This is the length of the maximum path of a class hierarchy from the node to the root of the inheritance tree.

☐ *Number of Children of a Class (NOC):* This is the number of immediate successors (subclasses) of a class in the hierarchy.

☐ *Coupling Between Object Classes (CBO):* An object class is coupled to another one if it invokes another one's member functions or instance variables (see the example in Figure 12.1). CBO is the number of classes to which a given class is coupled.

☐ *Response for a Class (RFC):* This is the number of methods that can be executed in response to a message received by an object of that class. The larger the number of methods that can be invoked from a class through messages, the greater the complexity of the class. It captures the size of the response set of a class. The response set of a class is all the methods called by local methods. RFC is the number of local methods plus the number of methods called by local methods.

☐ *Lack of Cohesion on Methods (LCOM):* The cohesion of a class is indicated by how closely the local methods are related to the local instance variables in the class. High cohesion indicates good class subdivision. The LCOM metric measures the dissimilarity of methods in a class by the usage of instance variables. LCOM is measured as the number of disjoint sets of local methods. Lack of cohesion increases complexity and opportunities for error during the development process.

Chidamber and Kemerer (1994) applied these six metrics in an empirical study of two companies, one using C++ and one using Smalltalk. Site A, a software vendor, provided data on 634 classes from two C++ libraries. Site B, a semiconductor manufacturer, provided data on 1,459 Smalltalk classes. The summary statistics are shown in Table 12.3.

The median weighted methods per class (WMC) for both sites were well below the threshold value for the average number of methods (20) as discussed earlier. The DIT maximums exceeded the threshold of 6, but the medians seemed low, especially for the C++ site. The classes for both sites had low NOCs—with medians equal to zero, and 73% of site A and 68% of site B had zero children. Indeed the low values of DIT and NOC led the authors to the observation that the designers might not be taking advantage of reuse of methods through inheritance. Striking differences in CBOs and RFCs were shown between the C++ and Smalltalk sites, with the median values for the Smalltalk site much higher. The contrast reflects the differences in the lan-

TABLE 12.3
Median Values of CK Metrics for Two Companies

	Site A (C++)	Site B (Smalltalk)
WMC (Weighted Methods per Class)	5	10
DIT (Depth of Inheritance Tree)	1(Max. = 8)	3 (Max = 10)
NOC (Number of Children)	0	0
RFC (Response for a Class)	6	29
CBO (Coupling Between Object Classes)	0	9
LCOM (Lack of Cohesion on Methods)	0 (Range: 0–200)	2 (Range: 0–17)

Source: Chidamber and Kemerer, 1993, 1994; Henderson-Sellers, 1995.

guages with regard to OO implementation. Smalltalk has a higher emphasis on pure OO message passing and a stronger adherence to object-oriented principles (Henderson-Sellers, 1995). Last, the distribution of lack of cohesion on methods was very different for the two sites. Overall, this empirical study shows the feasibility of collecting metrics in realistic environments and it highlights the lack of use of inheritance. The authors also suggested that the distribution of the metric values be used for the identification of design outliers (i.e., classes with extreme values).

12.2.4 Validation Studies and Further Examples

To evaluate whether the CK metrics are useful for predicting the probability of detecting faulty classes, Basili and colleagues (1996) designed and conducted an empirical study over four months at the University of Maryland. The study participants were the students of a C++ OO software analysis and design class. The study involved 8 student teams and 180 OO classes. The independent variables were the six CK metrics and the independent variables were the faulty classes and number of faults detected during testing. The LCOM metric was operationalized as the number of pairs of member functions without shared instance variables, minus the number of pairs of member functions with shared instance variables. When the above subtraction is negative, the metric was set to zero. The hypotheses linked high values of the CK metrics to higher probability of faulty classes. Key findings of the study are as follows:

- ☐ The six CK metrics were relatively independent.
- ☐ The lack of use of inheritance was confirmed because of the low values in the DITs and NOCs.
- ☐ The LCOM lacked discrimination power in predicting faulty classes.
- ☐ DITs, RFCs, NOCs, and CBOs were significantly correlated with faulty classes in multivariate statistical analysis.

☐   These OO metrics were superior to code metrics (e.g., maximum level of state-
     ment nesting in a class, number of function declaration, and number of function
     calls) in predicting faulty classes.

This validation study provides positive confirmation of the value of the CK metrics. The authors, however, caution that several factors may limit the generalizability
of results. These factors include: small project sizes, limited conceptual complexity,
and student participants.

In 1997 Chidamber, Darcy, and Kemerer (1997) applied the CK metrics suite to
three financial application software programs and assessed the usefulness of the metrics from a managerial perspective. The three software systems were all developed
by one company. They are used by financial traders to assist them in buying, selling,
recording, and analysis of various financial instruments such as stocks, bonds,
options, derivatives, and foreign exchange positions. The summary statistics of the
CK metrics of these application software are in Table 12.4.

One of the first observed results was the generally small values for the depth of
inheritance tree (DIT) and number of children (NOC) metrics in all three systems, indicating that developers were not taking advantage of the inheritance reuse feature of the
OO design. This result is consistent with the earlier findings of an empirical study by
two of the authors on two separate software systems (Chidamber and Kemerer, 1994).
Second, the authors found that three of the metrics, weighted methods per class (WMC),
response for a class (RFC), and coupling between classes (CBO) were highly correlated, with correlation coefficients above the .85 level. In statistical interpretation, this
implies that for the three software systems in the study, all three metrics were measuring something similar. This finding was in stark contrast to the findings by the validation study by Basilli and colleagues (1995), in which all six CK metrics were found to
be relatively independent. This multi-collinearity versus independence among several
of the CK metrics apparently needs more empirical studies to clarify.

We noted that the metrics values from these three systems are more dissimilar
than similar, especially with regard to the maximum values. This is also true when
including the two empirical data sets in Table 12.3. Therefore, it seems that many
more empirical studies need to be accumulated before preferable threshold values of
the CK metrics can be determined. The authors also made the observation that the
threshold values of these metrics cannot be determined a priori and should be derived
and used locally from each of the data sets. They decided to use the "80-20" principle in the sense of using the 80th percentile and 20th percentile of the distributions to
determine the cutoff points for a "high" or "low" value for a metric. The authors also
recommended that the values reported in their study not be accepted as rules, but
rather practitioners should analyze local data and set thresholds appropriately.

The authors' major objective was to explore the effects of the CK metrics on managerial variables such as productivity, effort to make classes reusable, and design

TABLE 12.4

Summary Statistics of the CK Metrics for Three Financial Software Systems

Software A (45 Classes)	Median	Mean	Maximum
WMC (Weighted Methods per Class)	6	9.27	63
DIT (Depth of Inheritance Tree)	0	0.04	2
NOC (Number of Children)	0	0.07	2
RFC (Response for a Class)	7	13.82	102
CBO (Coupling Between Object Classes)	2	4.51	39
LCOM (Lack of Cohesion on Methods)	0	6.96	90
Software B (27 classes)	**Median**	**Mean**	**Maximum**
WMC (Weighted Methods per Class)	22	20.22	31
DIT (Depth of Inheritance Tree)	1	1.11	2
NOC (Number of Children)	0	0.07	2
RFC (Response for a Class)	33	38.44	93
CBO (Coupling Between Object Classes)	7	8.63	22
LCOM (Lack of Cohesion on Methods)	0	29.37	387
Software C (25 Classes)	**Median**	**Mean**	**Maximum**
WMC (Weighted Methods per Class)	5	6.48	22
DIT (Depth of Inheritance Tree)	2	1.96	3
NOC (Number of Children)	0	0.92	11
RFC (Response for a Class)	7	9.8	42
CBO (Coupling Between Object classes)	0	1.28	8
LCOM (Lack of Cohesion on Methods)	0	4.08	83

Source: Chidamber et al., 1997.

effort. Each managerial variable was evaluated using data from a different project. Productivity was defined as size divided by the number of hours required (lines of code per person hour), and was assessed using data from software A. Assessment of the effort to make classes reusable was based on data from software B. Some classes in software B were reused on another project and the rework effort was recorded and measured in the number of hours spent by the next project staff to modify each class for use in the next project. Assessment on design effort was based on data from software C. Design effort was defined as the amount of time spent in hours to specify the high-level design of each class. Multivariate statistical techniques were employed with class as the unit of analysis and with each managerial variable as the independent variable. The CK metrics were the independent variables; other relevant variables, such as size and specific developers who had superior performance, were included in the models to serve as control variables so that the net effect of the

CK metrics could be estimated. The findings indicated that of the six CK metrics, high levels of CBOs (coupling between object classes) and LCOMs (lack of cohesion on methods) were associated with lower productivity, higher effort to make classes reusable, and greater design effort. In other words, high values of CBO and LCOM were not good with regard to the managerial variables. Specifically, the final regression equation for the productivity evaluation was as follows:

$$Productivity = -6.41 + 0.10 * Size + 48.11*Staff\_4 - 76.57 * HICBO - 33.96*HILCOM$$

The equation indicates that controlling for the size of the classes and the effect of a star performer (STAFF_4), the productivity for classes with high CBO (coupling between object classes) and LCOM (lack of cohesion on methods) values was much lower (again, the authors used the 80th percentile as the cutoff point to define high values). Because productivity was defined as lines of code per person hour, the regression equation indicates that the productivity was 76.57 lines of code per hour lower (than other classes) for classes with high CBO values, and 33.96 lines of code per hour lower for classes with high LCOM values. The effects were very significant! As a side note, it is interesting to note that the productivity of the classes developed by the star performer (STAFF_4) was 48.11 lines of code per hour higher!

This finding is significant because it reflects the strength of the underlying concepts of coupling and cohesion. In practical use, the metrics can be used to flag outlying classes for special attention.

Rosenberg, Stapko, and Gallo (1999) discuss the metrics used for OO projects at the NASA Software Assurance Technology Center (SATC). They recommend the six CK metrics plus three traditional metrics, namely, cyclomatic complexity, lines of code, and comment percentage based on SATC experience. The authors also used these metrics to flag classes with potential problems. Any class that met at least two of the following criteria was flagged for further investigation:

- Response for Class (RFC) > 100
- Response for Class > 5 times the number of methods in the class
- Coupling between Objects (CBO) > 5
- Weighted Methods per Class (WMC) > 100
- Number of Methods > 40

Considerable research and discussions on OO metrics have taken place in recent years, for example, Li and Henry (1993), Henderson-Sellers (1996), De Champeaux (1997), Briand (1999), Kemerer (1999), Card and Scalzo (1999), and Babsiya and Davis (2002). With regard to the direction of OO metrics research, there seems to be agreement that it is far more important to focus on empirical validation (or refutation) of the proposed metrics than to propose new ones, and on their relationships with managerial variables such as productivity, quality, and project management.

12.3 Productivity Metrics

As stated in the preface, productivity metrics are outside the scope of this book. Software productivity is a complex subject that deserves a much more complete treatment than a brief discussion in a book that focuses on quality and quality metrics. For non-OO projects, much research has been done in assessing and measuring productivity and there are a number of well-known books in the literature. For example, see Jones's work (1986, 1991, 1993, 2000). For productivity metrics for OO projects, relatively few research has been conducted and published. Because this chapter is on OO metrics in general, we include a brief discussion on productivity metrics.

Metrics like lines of code per hour, function points per person-month (PM), number of classes per person-year (PY) or person-month, number of methods per PM, average person-days per class, or even hours per class and average number of classes per developer have been proposed or reported in the literature for OO productivity (Card and Scalzo, 1999; Chidamer et al., 1997; IBM OOTC, 1993; Lorenz and Kidd, 1994). Despite the differences in units of measurement, these metrics all measure the same concept of productivity, which is the number of units of output per unit of effort. In OO development, the unit of output is class or method and the common units of effort are PY and PM. Among the many variants of productivity metric, number of classes per PY and number of classes per PM are perhaps the most frequently used.

Let us look at some actual data. For the five IBM projects discussed earlier, data on project size in terms of number of classes were available (Table 12.2). We also tracked the total PYs for each project, from design, through development, to the completion of testing. We did not have effort data for Project E because it was a joint project with an external alliance. The number of classes per PY thus calculated for these projects are shown in Table 12.5. The numbers ranged from 2.8 classes per PM to 6 classes per PM. The average of the projects was 4.4 classes per PM, with a standard deviation of 1.1. The dispersion of the distribution was small in view of the fact that these were separate projects with different development teams, albeit all developed in the same organization. The high number of classes per PM for Project B may be related to the small number of methods per class (3 methods per class) for the project, as discussed earlier. It is also significant to note that the differences between the C++ projects and the Smalltalk projects were small.

Lorenz and Kidd (1994) show data on average number of person-days per class for four Smalltalk projects and two C++ projects, in a histogram format. From the histograms, we estimate the person-days per class for the four Smalltalk projects

TABLE 12.5
Productivity in Terms of Number of Classes per PY for Five OO Projects

	Project A C++	Project B C++	Project C C++	Project D IBM Smalltalk	Project E OTI Smalltalk	Project F Digitalk Smalltalk
Number of Classes	5,741	2,513	3,000	100	566	492
PY	100	35	90	2	na	10
Classes per PY	57.4	71.8	33.3	50	na	49.2
Classes per PM	4.8	6	2.8	4.2	na	4.1
Methods per PM	8	18	20	71	na	86

were 7, 6, 2, and 8, and for the two C++ projects, they were about 23 and 35. The Smalltalk data seem to be close to that of the IBM projects, amounting to about 4 classes per PM. The C++ projects amounted to about one PM or more per class.

Lorenz and Kidd (1994) list the pertinent factors affecting the differences, including user interface versus model class, abstract versus concrete class, key versus support class, framework versus framework-client class, and immature versus mature classes. For example, they observe that key classes, classes that embody the "essence" of the business domain, normally take more time to develop and require more interactions with domain experts. Framework classes are powerful but are not easy to develop, and require more effort. Mature classes typically have more methods but required less development time. Therefore, without a good understanding of the projects and a consistent operational definition, it is difficult to make valid comparisons across projects or organizations.

It should be noted that all the IBM projects discussed here were systems software, either part of an operating system, or related to an operating system or a development environment. The architecture and subsystem design were firmly in place. Therefore, the classes of these projects may belong more to the mature class category. Data on classes shown in the tables include all classes, regardless of whether they were abstract or concrete, and key or support classes.

In a recent assessment of OO productivity, we looked at data from two OO projects developed at two IBM sites, which were developing middleware software related to business frameworks and Web servers. Their productivity numbers are shown in Table 12.6. The productivity numbers for these two projects were much lower than those discussed earlier. These numbers certainly reflected the difficulty in designing and implementing framework-related classes, versus the more mature

TABLE 12.6
Productivity Metrics for Two OO Projects

	Classes (C++)	Methods (C++)	Total PMs	Classes per PM	Methods per PM
Web Server	598	1,029	318	1.9	3.2
Framework	3,215	24,670	2,608	1.2	9.5

classes related to operating systems. The effort data in the table include the end-to-end effort from architecture to design, development, and test. If we confined the measurement to development and test and excluded the effort related to design and architecture, then the metrics value would increase to the following:

Web server: 2.6 classes per PM, 4.5 methods per PM

Framework: 1.9 classes per PM, 14.8 methods per PM

The IBM OOTC's rule of thumb for effort estimate (at the early design stage of a project) is one to three PM per business class (or key class) (West, 1999). In Lorenz and Kidd's (1994) definition, a key class is a class that is central to the business domain being automated. A key class is one that would cause great difficulties in developing and maintaining a system if it did not exist. Since the ratio between key classes and support classes, or total classes in the entire project is not known, it is difficult to correlate this 1 to 3 PM per key class guideline to the numbers discussed above.

In summary, we attempt to evaluate some empirical OO productivity data, in terms of number of classes per PM. With the preceding discussion, we have the following tentative values as a stake in the ground for OO project effort estimation:

- ☐ For project estimate at the early design phase, 1 to 3 PM per business class (or one-third of a class to one class per PM)
- ☐ For framework-related projects, about 1.5 classes per PM
- ☐ For mature class projects for systems software, about 4 classes per PM

Further studies and accumulation of empirical findings are definitely needed to establish robustness for such OO productivity metrics. A drawback of OO metrics is that there are no conversion rules to lines of code metrics and to function point metrics. As such, comparisons between OO projects described by OO metrics and projects outside the OO paradigm cannot be made. According to Jones (2002), function point metrics works well with OO projects. Among the clients of the Software Productivity Research, Inc. (SPR), those who are interested in comparing OO productivity and quality level to procedural projects all use function point metrics (Jones, 2002). The function point could eventually be the link between OO and non-OO metrics. Because there are variations in the function and responsibility of classes and methods, there are studies that started to use the number of function points as a weighting factor when measuring the number of classes and methods.

Finally, as a side note, regardless of whether it is classes per PM for OO projects or LOC per PY and function points per PM for procedural languages, these productivity metrics are two dimensional: output and effort. The productivity concept in software, especially at the project level, however, is three-dimensional: output (size or function of deliverables), effort, and time. This is because the tradeoff between time and effort is not linear, and therefore the dimension of time must be addressed. If quality is included as yet another variable, the productivity concept would be four-dimensional. Assuming quality is held constant or quality criteria can be established as part of the requirements for the deliverable, we can avoid the confusion of mixing productivity and quality, and productivity remains a three-dimensional concept. As shown in Figure 12.2, if one holds any of the two dimensions constant, a change in the third dimension is a statement of productivity. For example, if effort (resources) and development time are fixed, then the more output (function) a project produces, the more productive is the project team. Likewise, if resources and output (required functions) are fixed, then the faster the team delivers, the more productive it is.

It appears then that the two-dimensional metrics are really not adequate to measure software productivity. Based on a large body of empirical data, Putnam and Myers (1992) derived the software productivity index (PI), which takes all three

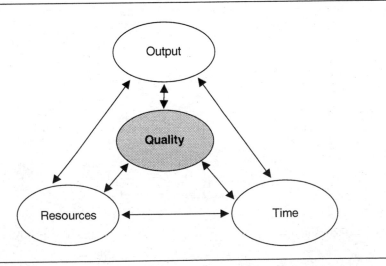

FIGURE 12.2
Dimensions of the Productivity Concept

dimensions of productivity into account. For the output dimension, the PI equation still uses LOC and therefore the index is subject to all shortcomings associated with LOC, which are well documented in the literature (Jones, 1986, 1991, 1993, 2000). The index is still more robust comparing to the two-dimensional metrics because (1) it includes time in its calculation, (2) there is a coefficient in the formula to calibrate for the effects of project size, and (3) after the calculation is done based on the equation, a categorization process is used to translate the raw number of productivity parameters (which is a huge number) to the final productivity index (PI), and therefore the impact of the variations in LOC data is reduced. Putnam and associates also provided the values of PI by types of software based on a large body of empirical data on industry projects. Therefore, the calculated PI value of a project can be compared to the industry average according to type of software.

For procedural programming, function point productivity metrics are regarded as better than the LOC-based productivity metrics. However, the time dimension still needs to be addressed. This is the same case for the OO productivity metrics. Applying Putnam's PI approach to the function point and OO metrics will likely produce better and more adequate productivity metrics. This, however, requires more research with a large body of empirical data in order to establish appropriate equations that are equivalent to the LOC-based PI equation.

12.4 Quality and Quality Management Metrics

In procedural programming, quality is measured by defects per thousand LOC (KLOC), defects per function point, mean time to failure, and many other metrics and models such as those discussed in several previous chapters. The corresponding measure for defects per KLOC and defects per function point in OO is defects per class. In search of empirical data related to OO defect rates, we noted that data about OO quality is even more rare than productivity data. Table 12.7 shows the data that we tracked for some of the projects we discuss in this chapter.

Testing defect rates for these projects ranged from 0.21 defects per class to 0.69 per class and from 2.6 defects per KLOC (new and changed code) to 8.2 defects per KLOC. In our long history of defect tracking, defect rates during testing when the products were under development ranges from 4 defects per KLOC to about 9 defects per KLOC for procedural programming. The defect rates of these OO projects compare favorably with our history. With one year in the field, the defect rates of these products ranged from 0.01 defects per class to 0.05 defects per class and from 0.05 defects per KLOC to 0.78 defects per KLOC. Again, these figures, except the defects/KLOC for Project B, compare well with our history.

With regard to quality management, the OO design and complexity metrics can be used to flag the classes with potential problems for special attention, as is the

TABLE 12.7
Testing Defect Rate and Field Defect Rates for Some OO Projects

	Project B (C++)	Project C (C++)	Project D (Smalltalk)	Project F (Smalltalk)
Testing Defect Rate				
Defects/Class	0.21	0.82	0.27	0.69
Defects/KLOC	3.1	8.2	2.6	5.9
Field Defect Rate (1 Year After Delivery)				
Defects/Class	0.05	na	0.04	0.01
Defects/KLOC	0.78	na	0.41	0.05

practice at the NASA SATC. It appears that researchers have started focusing on the empirical validation of the proposed metrics and relating those metrics to managerial variables. This is certainly the right direction to strengthen the practical values of OO metrics. In terms of metrics and models for in-process quality management when the project is under development, we contend that most of the metrics discussed in this book are relevant to OO projects, for example, defect removal effectiveness, the inspection self-assessment checklist (Table 9.1), the software reliability growth models (Chapters 8 and 9), and the many metrics for testing (Chapter 10). Based on our experience, the metrics for testing apply equally well to OO projects. We recommend the following:

- [ ] Test progress S curve
- [ ] Testing defect arrivals over time
- [ ] Testing defect backlog over time
- [ ] Number of critical problems over time
- [ ] Number of system crashes and hangs over time as a measure of system stability
- [ ] The effort/outcome paradigm for interpreting in-process metrics and for in-process quality management

Furthermore, for some simple OO metrics discussed in this chapter, when we put them into the context of in-process tracking and analysis (for example, trend charts), they can be very useful in-process metrics for project and quality management. We illustrate this point below with the examples of a small project.

Project MMD was a small, independent project developed in Smalltalk with OO methodology and iterative development process over a period of 19 weeks (Hanks, 1998). The software provided functions to drive multimedia devices (e.g., audio and video equipment) and contained 40 classes with about 3,200 lines of code. The team consisted of four members—two developers for analysis, design, and coding, and two testers for testing, tracking, and other tasks required for the product to be ready to ship. With good in-process tracking and clear understanding of roles and responsibilities, the team conducted weekly status meetings to keep the project moving. Throughout the development process, four major iterations were completed. Figure 12.3 shows the trends of several design and code metrics over time. They all met the threshold values recommended by Lorenz (1993). Figure 12.4 shows the number of classes and classes discarded over time (i.e., metric number 11 in Table 12.1). The trend charts reflect the several iterations and the fact that iterative development process was used.

Figure 12.5 shows the relationship between defect arrivals and testing time, with a fitted curve based on the delayed S reliability growth model. This curve fitting confirms the applicability of reliability growth models to data from OO projects. In fact, we contend that this match may be even better than data from procedural software projects, because in OO environment, with the class structure, the more difficult bugs tend to be detected and "flushed" out earlier in the testing process.

Finally, if we use this project as another data point for productivity estimates, with 40 classes and 76 person-weeks (4 x 19 weeks) and assuming 4.33 person-weeks

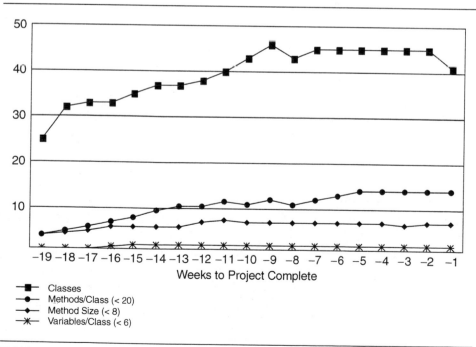

FIGURE 12.3

Trends of Several OO Metrics

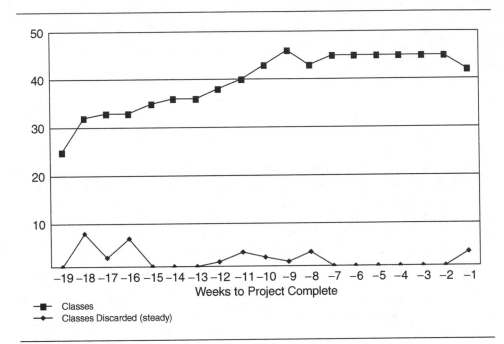

FIGURE 12.4
Class Statistics over Time

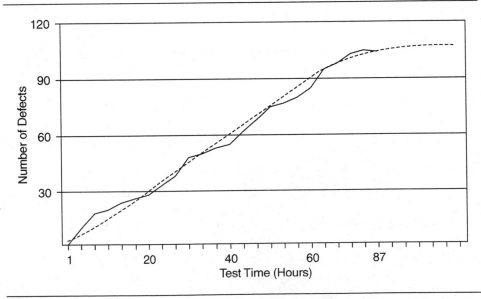

FIGURE 12.5
OO Testing Defect Arrivals Follow the Pattern of a Software Reliability
Growth Model

per person-month (PM), we get 2.3 classes per PM. This number falls between the numbers for the framework-related projects (1.2 and 1.9 classes per PM) and the mature systems software projects (about 4 classes per PM).

12.5 Lessons Learned from OO Projects

At IBM Rochester, the deployment of OO technology in software development began in the early 1990s. More than ten years later, numerous projects are now developed with this technology. We conducted assessments of selected projects throughout the past decade and the following is a summary of lessons learned. Organizations with OO deployment experience may have made similar observations or learned additional lessons.

Education and Skills Level

To transition from structural design and procedural programming to OO design and programming, it is crucial to allow time for the learning curve. Formal classroom education is needed. A curriculum customized to the organization or specific projects and timely delivery are major considerations in a training program. The most effective curriculum spreads out class time with on-the-job training. Consultants or trainers should be industry experts or experienced in-house experts with full-time training jobs, so that classroom education as well as consulting and trouble shooting when the project is under way can be provided. The education should include the entire design and development life cycle (requirements, analysis, design, coding, and testing) and not focus only on language and programming. Based on experience, it takes six months to complete OO skills training based on the model that classroom education is spread out with on-the-job training: three months in calendar time to complete initial training followed by three months of advanced training. After training, it takes three months to become capable, that is, to acquire the working knowledge to do OO design and development. It takes another nine to twelve months to become proficient in OO technology, provided that the developers have been working on a project.

Like any software projects, domain-specific knowledge and skills and software engineering skills are equally important. For OO software engineering, if we dichotomize domain knowledge and OO skills and cross-tabulate the two variables, we get the four skills categories shown in Figure 12.6.

For developers who are not experienced in OO skills and domain knowledge (e.g., a banking application software, or an operating system architecture and design), the progression in skills would be from category I to II to IV. For experienced developers with rich domain-specific knowledge who are transitioning to OO technology, the transition path would be from category III to IV. For an OO development project, at any phase in the development process, there should be OO experts (category IV

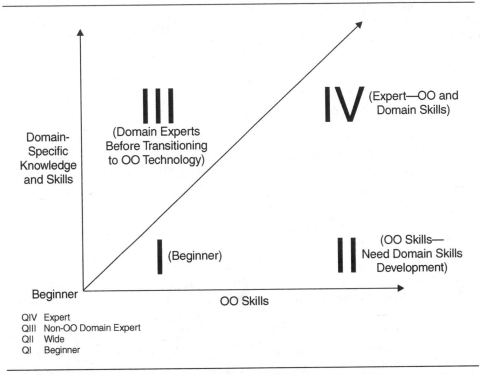

FIGURE 12.6
Domain Knowledge and OO Skills Typology

skills) leading the projects and providing on-the-job guidance to those who are less experienced. The composition of skills categories and the percentage of OO experts can vary across the development cycle. The percentage of OO skills over the phases of the development cycle can be distributed as shown in Figure 12.7 so that the project has enough OO experts to enhance its success, and at the same time has the capacity for skills development. In the figure, the line curve approximates the staffing curve of a project, and the phases are characterized by different distribution of the analysis, design, code, and test (ADCT) activities.

Tools and Development Environment

A consistent process architecture in an organization is important so each new project does not require reinvention of the wheel. Consistency is also the basis for systematic improvements. If at all possible, use a mature tool set and a stable development environment, and have peer support for the language that is being used. Many good tools exist in the industry. But the robustness of the tools and the integration of tools to

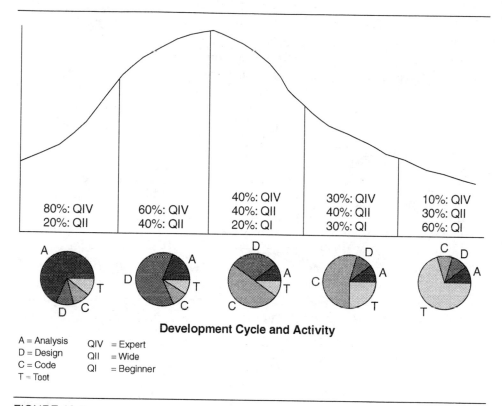

80%: QIV	60%: QIV	40%: QIV	30%: QIV	10%: QIV
20%: QII	40%: QII	40%: QII	40%: QII	30%: QII
		20%: QI	30%: QI	60%: QI

Development Cycle and Activity

A = Analysis   QIV = Expert
D = Design   QII = Wide
C = Code   QI = Beginner
T = Toot

FIGURE 12.7
Skill Requirements for the Development Cycle

provide cohesive development environments are even more important. Tools and development environment are as important as the languages and specific OO methods to be used for the project. Developing your own tools should be considered only as a last resort. At the same time, it is very advantageous if the development team knows its compiler well because changes may be needed for performance tuning.

Project Management

Good project management is ever more important due to the iterative nature of the OO development process. We recommend monthly goals or mini-milestones be set with the project schedule, and explicit and frequent checkpoints be conducted. The use of metrics to show the status and trends of the project progress, such as those shown in Figures 12.3 through 12.5, enhances the focus of the team. As illustrated in the example illustrated with these figures, metrics are applicable to large projects as well as small ones. The measurements should be decided at the outset and the team should ensure that everyone knows the measurements and that measurements are collected regularly. Status reporting is another area that must be watched because developers might regard status reporting as dead time. It is not rare that teams disclose the information that they are going to fail to meet a target only when they have actually failed.

Inevitably, some large software projects involve multiteam and multilocation development. Our experience suggests that, because of the iterative nature of the OO process, such projects require more coordination and better communication than projects using the conventional approach.

Directly related to the iterative nature of the OO development process are two major items on the top of the project management list: (1) beware of analysis and design without code—the so called analysis/paralysis phenomenon, and (2) beware of prototypes that never end. Prototypes play an important role in OO development and are often used in building a fully functional user interface or in showing a proof of feasibility of the project. Seeing is believing; prototypes usually command high visibility from customers, project managers, and particularly executives of the organization. However, there is a big gap between the completion of prototypes and the completion of the design and development of the project. To fill the gap, rigorous work on the overall architecture, design (internal as well as external), scaling, and implementation needs to happen. Technical leaders need to provide the leadership to bridge the gap and project management needs to plan and drive the necessary activities and milestones after successful prototypes were achieved. We have seen OO projects that kept on prototyping and iterating, that mistook the success of prototypes as success of the project, and that significantly underestimated the design and development work after prototypes and therefore failed to meet product delivery targets. Warning signs include hearing conversation among developers like the following: "What have you been up to in the past several months?" "I have been working on our prototype project."

Reuse

Good reusable classes are hard to build. To encourage reuse, some projects purchased libraries of reusable classes, some projects created internal programs (e.g., a reuse council), and some projects took both approaches. But they resulted in only a slight increase in reuse, and there were few submissions to the reuse program. This was a clear contrast to the original anticipation associated with the OO technology and process. This low level of reuse is consistent with the findings in the literature (Kemerer, 1999) with regard to inheritance and reuse.

Our lesson learned is that OO technology is not automatically equal to code reuse. To have tangible results, the team has to design for it, and must continually work at it. Class reuse issues may not even be able to be adequately addressed at the project level. From the perspective of product development, there is an inherent conflict of interest between development cycle time and the building of reusable classes. It is more effective to have a reuse strategy in place at the organization level so that issues related to the management system, interproject coordination, libraries for reusable classes, possible incentive program, and so on, can be dealt with on a long-term basis.

Performance

Performance is a major concern in most, if not all, OO projects during development, especially new projects. It is not uncommon that initial measures of performance cause serious distress. We did see projects fail due to performance problems. Performance problems can be attributed to several factors related to experience and technology:

- ☐ An inexperienced team may be overzealous in class creation, leading to over-modularization.
- ☐ Dynamic memory allocations may not be used appropriately.
- ☐ OO compiler technology may not yet be optimized for performance.

With regard to the compiler factor, its contribution to performance problems should be lesser now than in the early days of OO technology. Although the compiler technology has improved, it remains a concern to OO development experts. A recent assessment of an OO project that had to be rewritten due to performance problems confirms that compiler optimization (or the lack thereof) remains a critical factor.

On the positive side, our experience indicates that performance tuning in OO structure is not too difficult to achieve, especially if it is done early. In most cases, performance problems were overcome when the project was complete. The lesson with regard to performance: It is a concern to be taken seriously, and early performance measurement and tuning are crucial.

Quality and Development Practices

Assessments by developers were that in OO development, bugs are easier to find and fix. Our data also indicate that more often than not, defect rates for OO projects are indeed lower during the testing phases as well as when the products are in the field. The data on OO quality for a few projects that were discussed earlier in this chapter do support these observations. Type checking abilities of OO compilers, the practice of object coherence checking, the class structure in OO designs, the focus on analysis and design in the OO development process, and design tools are among the many positive factors for quality.

Recommendations for Small Organizations

Like the complexity metrics discussed in Chapter 11, design and complexity metrics for OO projects are most effectively practiced by small teams. For large projects, the chief architect is responsible for the overall system design and oversees the different pieces of the system fitting together. For detailed design and implementation, usually the small teams own the specific subsystems and components. The examples discussed in the chapter include large, medium, and small projects.

To collect data and for precise assessment of these metrics, OO counting tools are needed. Such tools are usually part of the design and development environment tools suite. In the case that metrics counting tools are not available, the teams can still practice the recommended rules of thumb with regard to the essential design and common metrics. OO developers would agree that metric values for their project (e.g., methods per class, depth of inheritance tree, number of children, number of classes, and methods thrown away along the development cycle) can be easily tracked without a metrics counting tool, especially for small projects. Indeed, developers could tell the approximate values of these metrics during their development activities. Metrics such as average method size, lines of code per class, average number of instance variables per class, and number of times class is reused will need counting tools to provide data. Metrics such as weighted methods per class, coupling between object classes, response for a class, and lack of cohesion on methods may require further operational definitions by language and special counting tools.

To practice effective metrics, the team doesn't have to use a large number of metrics. The MMD project discussed in the chapter (Figures 12.3 through 12.5) is a perfect example. A small team of four persons with a development cycle of 19 weeks for a project of 40 classes and about 3,200 lines of code, the example demonstrates the value of metrics in the development process. It also shows that when used in the in-process context via trend charting, simple metrics can be very useful.

Finally, with regard to metrics for testing and for in-process quality management, I want to reiterate that the metrics for procedural programming also applies to OO projects, for examples, metrics such as design reviews scoring checklist, test progress S curve, testing defect arrival pattern, test effectiveness, and many others discussed in this book.

Summary

This chapter discusses design and complexity metrics, productivity metrics, and metrics for measuring quality and for in-process tracking and management for OO projects. On design and complexity metrics, it highlights the Lorenz metrics and the CK metrics suite. We found the rules of thumb for some of Lorenz's metrics useful for interpreting actual project data. We also provide actual project data in the discussions and attempt to put the metrics and the threshold values into proper context. With regard to productivity, we put the stakes in the ground by showing the productivity numbers of several types of OO class. Certainly a lot more empirical data has to be accumulated before consistent guidelines for OO productivity can be derived. But starting the process is important. We also show examples of simple OO metrics for in-process project and quality management. We assert that in addition to specific OO metrics, many metrics and models for quality management while the project is under development discussed here, are as applicable to OO projects as to conventional projects.

In the last section we offer the lessons learned from OO development projects with respect to education, training and OO skills, tools and development environment, project management, reuse, performance, and quality.

References

1. Babsiya, J., and C. G. Davis, "A Hierarchical Model for Object-Oriented Design Quality Assessment,"*IEEE Transactions on Software Engineering*, Vol. 28, No. 1, January 2002, pp. 4–17.
2. Basili, V .R., L. C. Briand, and W. L. Melo, "A Validation of Object-Oriented Design Metrics as Quality Indicators," *IEEE Transactions on Software Engineering*, Vol. 22, No. 10, October 1996, pp. 751–761.
3. Briand, L., "Measurement and Quality Modeling of OO Systems," paper presented at The Sixth International Symposium on Software Metrics, Boca Raton, Florida, November 4–6, 1999.
4. Card, D., and B. Scalzo, "Measurement for Object-Oriented Software Projects," paper presented at The Sixth International Symposium on Software Metrics, Boca Raton, Florida, November 4–6, 1999.
5. Chidamber, S. R., and C. F. Kemerer, "A Metrics Suite for Object-Oriented Design," *IEEE Transactions on Software Engineering*, Vol. 20, 1994, pp. 476-493.
6. Chidamber, S. R., D. P. Darcy, and C. F. Kemerer, "Managerial Use of Metrics for Object-Oriented Software: An Exploratory Analysis," Katz Graduate School of Business Working paper no. 750, University of Pittsburgh, Pittsburgh, PA, December 1997.
7. De Champeaux, D., *Object-Oriented Development Process and Metrics*, Upper Saddle River, N. J.: Prentice Hall, 1997.
8. Hanks, B., "Metrics for OO Software Development," IBM internal technical paper, 1998.
9. Hamilton, J., *Object-Oriented Programming for AS/400 Programmers, An Introduction with Examples in C++*, Loveland, Colo.: Duke Press.
10. Hendeson-Selles, B., *Object-Oriented Metrics, Measures of Complexity*, Englewood Cliffs, N. J.: PTR Prentice-Hall, 1996.
11. IBM Object-Oriented Technology Council, "IBM Object-Oriented Metrics," IBM internal technical paper, February 2, 1993.
12. Jacobson, J., G. Booch, and J. Rumbaugh, *The Unified Software Development Process*, Reading, Mass.: Addison-Wesley, 1999.
13. Jones, C., *Programming Productivity*, New York: McGraw-Hill, 1986.
14. Jones, C., *Applied Software Measurement, Assuring Productivity and Quality*, New York: McGraw-Hill, 1991.

15. Jones, C., *Software Productivity and Quality Today: The Worldwide Perspective,* Carlsbad, Calif.: IS Management Group, 1993.

16. Jones, C., *Software Assessments, Benchmarks, and Best Practices,* Boston: Addison-Wesley, 2000.

17. Jones, Capers, Personal communications, February 2002.

18. Kemerer, C. F., "Metrics for Object-Oriented Software: A Retrospective," paper presented at The Sixth International Symposium on Software Metrics, Boca Raton, Florida, November 4–6, 1999.

19. Li, W., and S. Henry, "Object-Oriented Metrics That Predict Maintainability," *Journal of Systems and Software,* Vol. 23, pp. 111–122, 1993.

20. Lorenz, M., *Object-Oriented Software Development: A Practical Guide,* Englewood Cliffs, N. J.: PTR Prentice Hall, 1993.

21. Lorenz, M., and J. Kidd, *Object-Oriented Software Metrics, A Practical Guide,* Englewood Cliffs, N. J.: PTR Prentice-Hall, 1994.

22. McGregor, J. D., and D. A. Sykes, *A Practical Guide to Testing Object-Oriented Software,* Boston: Addison-Wesley, 2001.

23. Morris, K. L., Metrics for Object-Oriented Software Development Environments, Master's Thesis, M.I.T. Sloan School of Management, 1989.

24. Putnam, L. H., and W. Myers, *Measures for Excellence: Reliable Software on Time, Within Budget,* Englewood Cliffs, N. J. : Prentice-Hall, 1992.

25. Rosenberg, L., R. Stapko, and A. Gallo, "Applying Object-Oriented Metrics," paper presented at The Sixth International Symposium on Software Metrics, Boca Raton, Florida, November 4–6, 1999.

26. West, M. IBM Object-Oriented Technology Council metrics focal point, personal communication, 1999.

13

Availability Metrics

Imagine you are in the middle of a stock transaction on the Internet and then the application hangs for more than half an hour. Or, it is Friday morning and you are running your quarter-end financial report, which is due Monday, and your system crashes and stays down for 96 hours. Or, you are doing a business transaction on a well-known web site and the server supporting it crashes, rendering the site unavailable for a prolonged time. Scenarios such as these are far more frequent than desirable and are incurring costs and decreasing productivity.

The following was from a financial news posted on the Netscape Web site not long ago:

> Nasdaq will extend trading for one hour today, to 5 P.M. EDT, after a network problem forced the electronic stock market to temporarily suspend trading through the SelectNet and Small Order Execution System, or SOES.
>
> Today marked the second day in a row and the third time this month that the Nasdaq has had problems with its execution system.

In this Internet age of network computing, one of the most critical quality attributes is system and network availability, along with reliability and security. Requirements for high availability by mission-critical operations have existed since society became reliant on computer technologies. In the Internet age, software code is distributed across networks and businesses increasingly share data, a lack of system

359

availability is significantly increasing adverse impacts. In this chapter we discuss the definition and measurements of system availability, possible approaches to collecting customer's outage data, and the ways to use customer's data and availability metrics to drive improvement of the product.

13.1 Definition and Measurements of System Availability

Intuitively, system availability means the system is operational when you have work to do. The system is not down due to problems or other unplanned interruptions. In measurement terms, system availability means that the system is available for use as a percentage of scheduled uptime. The key elements of this definition include:

- ☐ The frequency of system outages within the time frame for the calculation
- ☐ The duration of outages
- ☐ Scheduled uptime

The frequency of outages is a direct reliability statement. The duration of outages reflects the severity of the outages. It is also related to the recovery strategies, service responsiveness, and maintainability of the system. Scheduled uptime is a statement of the customer's business requirements of system availability. It could range from 5 x 8 (5 days a weeks, 8 hours a day) to 7 x 24 (7 days a week, 24 hours a day) or 365 x 24 (365 days a year, 24 hours a day). Excluding scheduled maintenance, the 7 x 24 shops require continuous system availability. In today's business computing environments, many businesses are 7 x 24 shops as far as system availability is concerned.

The inverse measurement of system availability is the amount of down time per system per time period (for example, per year). If scheduled up-time is known or is a constant (for example, for the 7 x 24 businesses), given the value of one measurement, the other can be derived. Table 1 shows some examples of system availability and hours in down time per system per year.

The 99.999% availability, also referred to as the "five 9s" availability, is the ultimate industry goal and is often used in marketing materials by server vendors. With regard to measurement data, a study of customer installations by the consulting firm Gartner Group (1998) reported that a server platform actually achieved availability of 99.998% (10 minutes downtime per year) via clustering solutions. For a single system, availability of that same server platform was at 99.90%. There were servers at 99.98% and 99.94% availability also. At the low end, there was a PC server platform with availability below 97.5%, which is a poor level in availability measurements. These are all known server platforms in the industry.

TABLE 13.1
Examples of System Availability and Downtime per System per Year

System Availability (%) (24 x 365 basis)	Downtime per System per Year
99.999	5.3 minutes
99.99	52.6 minutes
99.95	4.4 hours
99.90	8.8 hours
99.8	17.5 hours
99.7	26.3 hours
99.5	43.8 hours
99.0	87.6 hours
98.5	131.4 hours
98.0	175.2 hours
97.5	219.0 hours

Business applications at major corporations require high levels of software quality and overall system availability. Servers with system availability less than 99.9%, which is the threshold value for high availability, may not be adequate to support critical operations. As reported in *Business Week* ("Software Hell," 1999), at the New York Clearing House (NYCH), about $1.2 trillion in electronic interbank payments are cleared each day by two Unisys Corporation mainframe computer systems. The software was developed for operations that must not fail and the code is virtually bug-free. For the seven years prior to the *Business Week* report, NYCH had clocked just 0.01% downtime. In other words, its system availability was 99.99%. This kind of high-level availability is a necessity because if one of these systems is down for a day, its ramifications are enormous and banks consider it a major international incident. The same report indicated NYCH also has some PC servers that it uses mostly for simple communications programs. These systems were another story with regard to reliability and availability in that they crashed regularly and there was a paucity of tools for diagnosing and fixing problems.

In a study of cost of server ownership in enterprise relations management (ERM) customer sites, the consulting firm IDC (2001) compared the availability of three server platforms, which we relabeled as platforms A, B, and C for this discussion. The availability of these three categories of servers for ERM solutions are 99.98%, 99.67%, and 99.90%, respectively. Since system availability has a direct impact on user productivity, IDC called the availability-related metrics productivity metrics. Table 13.2 shows a summary of these metrics. For details, see the original IDC report.

TABLE 13.2
Availability-Related Productivity Metrics for Three Server Platforms for ERM Solutions

User Productivity	Platform A Solution	Platform B Solution	Platform C Solution
Unplanned Downtime Hours per Month	0.24	2.7	1
Percent of Internal Users Affected	42	63	53
Unplanned User Downtime (Hours per Year/100 Users)	1,235	20,250	6,344
Availability (%)	99.98	99.67	99.9

From IDC white paper, "Server Cost of Ownership in ERM Customer Sites: A Total Cost of Ownership Study," by Jean S. Bozman and Randy Perry. Copyright © 2001, IDC, a market intelligence research firm. Reprinted with permission.

System availability or platform availability is a combination of hardware and software. The relationship between system availability and component availability is an "AND" relationship, not an "OR" relationship. To achieve a certain level of system availability, the availability of the components has to be higher. For example, if the availability of a system's software is 99.95% and that of the hardware is 99.99%, then the system availability is 99.94% (99.99% x 99.95%).

13.2 Reliability, Availability, and Defect Rate

In Chapter 1 we discussed software quality attributes such as capability, usability, performance, reliability, install, maintainability, documentation, and availability (CUPRIMDA) and their interrelations. Reliability and availability certainly support each other. Indeed, among the pair-relationships of quality attributes, this pair is much more strongly related than others. Without a reliable product, high availability cannot be achieved.

The operational definition of *reliability* is mean time to failure (MTTF). For the exponential distribution, the failure rate (or better called the instantaneous failure rate) (λ) is constant and MTTF is an inverse of it. As an example, suppose a company manufactures resistors that are known to have an exponential failure rate of 0.15% per 1,000 hours. The MTTF for these resistors is thus the inverse of .15%/1000 hours (or 0.0000015), which is 666,667 hours.

The F in MTTF for reliability evaluation refers to all failures. For availability measurement of computer systems, the more severe forms of failure (i.e., the crashes and hangs that cause outages) are the events of interest. Mean time to system outage, a reliability concept and similar to MTTF calculation-wise, is a common availability measurement. As an example, if a set of systems has an average of 1.6 outages per system per year, the mean time to outage will be the inverse of 1.6 system-year, which is 0.625 years.

As discussed earlier, in addition to the frequency of outages, the duration of outage is a key element of measuring availability. This element is related to the mean time to repair (MTTR) or mean time to recovery (average downtime) measurement. To complete the example in the last paragraph, suppose the average downtime per outage for a set of customers was 1.5 hours, the average downtime per system per year was 2.3 hours, and the total scheduled uptime for the systems was 445,870 hours, the system availability would be 99.97%.

Because of the element of outage duration, the concept of availability is different from reliability in several aspects. First, availability is more customer-oriented. With the same frequencies of failures or outages, the longer the system is down, the more pain the customer will experience. Second, to reduce outage duration, other factors such as diagnostic and debugging tools, service and fix responsiveness, and system backup/recovery strategies play important roles. Third, high reliability and excellent intrinsic product quality are necessary for high availability, but may not be sufficient. To achieve high availability and to neutralize the impact of outages often requires broader strategies such as clustering solutions and predictive warning services. Indeed, to achieve high availability at the 99.99% (52.6 minutes of downtime per year) or 99.999% level (5.2 minutes of downtime per year), it would be impossible without clustering or heavy redundancy and support by a premium service agreement. Predictive warning service is a comprehensive set of services that locally and electronically monitor an array of system events. It is designed to notify the customer and the vendor (service provider) of possible system failures before they occur. In recent years several vendors began offering this kind of premium service as a result of the paramount importance of system availability to critical business operations.

Over the years, many technologies in hardware and software have been and are being developed and implemented to improve product reliability and system availability. Some of these technologies are:

- Redundant array of inexpensive disks (RAID)
- Mirroring
- Battery backup
- Redundant write cache
- Continuously powered main storage
- Concurrent maintenance
- Concurrent release upgrade
- Concurrent apply of fix package
- Save/restore parallelism
- Reboot/IPL (initial program load) speed

☐ Independent auxiliary storage pools (I-ASP)
☐ Logical partitioning
☐ Clustering
☐ Remote cluster nodes
☐ Remote maintenance

Where data breakout is available, of the outages affecting system availability, software normally accounts for a larger proportion than hardware. As the *Business Week* report (1999) indicates, a number of infamous Web site and server outages were due to software problems. Software development is also labor intensive and there is no commonly recognized software reliability standard in the industry.

Both reliability (MTTF) and defect rate are measures of intrinsic product quality. But they are not related in terms of operational definitions; that is, MTTF and defects per KLOC or function point are not mathematically related. In the software engineering literature, the two subjects are decoupled. The only relationship between defect levels and ranges of MTTF values reported in the literature (that we are aware of) are by Jones (1991) based on his empirical study several decades ago. Table 13.3 shows the corresponding values for the two parameters.

Jones's data was gathered from various testing phases, from unit test to system test runs, of a systems software project. Size of the project is a key variable because it could provide crude links between defects per KLOC and total number of defects, and therefore possibly to the volume of defects and frequency of failures. But this information was not reported. However, this relationship is very useful because it is based on empirical data on systems software. This area clearly needs more research with a large amount of empirical studies.

TABLE 13.3
Association Between Defect Levels and MTTF Values

Defects per KLOC	MTTF
More than 30	Less than 2 minutes
20–30	4–15 minutes
10–20	5–60 minutes
5–10	1–4 hours
2–5	4–24 hours
1–2	24–160 hours
Less than 1	Indefinite

Source: From *Applied Software Measurement: Assuring Productivity and Quality,* by Capers Jones (Table on MTTF Values, p. 282). Copyright © 1991. Reprinted by permission of The McGraw-Hill Companies, Inc., New York.

The same *Business Week* report ("Software Hell," 1999) indicates that according to the U.S. Defense Department and the Software Engineering Institute (SEI) at Carnegie Mellon University, there are typically 5 to 15 flaws per KLOC in typical commercial software. About a decade ago, based on a sample study of U.S. and Japanese software projects by noted software developers in both countries, Cusumano (1991) estimated that the failure rate per KLOC during the first 12 months after delivery was 4.44 in the United States and 1.96 in Japan. Cusumano's sample included projects in the areas of data processing, scientific, systems software, telecommunications, and embedded/real time systems. Based on extensive project assessments and benchmark studies, Jones (2001) estimates the typical defect rate of software organizations at SEI CMM level 1 to be 7.38 defects per KLOC (0.92 defects per function point), and those at SEI CMM level 3 to be 1.30 defects per KLOC (0.16 defects per function point). For the defect rates per function point for all CMM levels, see Jones (2000) or Chapter 6 in which we discuss Jones's findings. Per IBM customers in Canada, this writer was told that the average defect rate of software in Canada a few years ago, based on a survey, was 3.7 defects per KLOC. Without detailed operational definitions, it is difficult to draw meaningful conclusions on the level of defect rate or failure rate in the software industry with a certain degree of confidence. The combination of these estimates and Jones's relation between defect level and reliability, however, explains why there are so many infamous software crashes in the news. Even though we take these estimates as "order of magnitude" estimates and allow large error margins, it is crystal clear that the level of quality for typical software is far from adequate to meet the availability requirements of businesses and safety-critical operations. Of course, this view is shared by many and has been expressed in various publications and media (e.g., "State of Software Quality," *Information Week*, 2001).

Based on our experience and assessment of available industry data, for system platforms to have high availability (99.9+%), the defect rate for large operating systems has to be at or below 0.01 defect per KLOC per year in the field. In other words, the defect rate has to be at or beyond the 5.5 sigma level. For new function development, the defect rate has to be substantially below 1 defect per thousand new and changed source instructions (KCSI). This last statistic seems to correlate with Jones's finding (last row in Table 13.3). To achieve good product quality and high system availability, it is highly recommended that in-process reliability or outage metrics be used, and internal targets be set and achieved during the development of software. Before the product is shipped, its field quality performance (defect rate or frequency of failures) should be estimated based on the in-process metrics. For examples of such in-process metrics, refer to the discussions in Chapters 9 and 10; for defect removal effectiveness during the development process, refer to Chapter 6; for projection and estimation of field quality performance, refer to Chapters 7 and 8.

In addition to reducing the defect rate, any improvements that can lead to a reduction in the duration of downtime (or MTTR) contribute to availability. In software, such improvements include, but are not limited to, the following features:

☐ Product configuration
☐ Ease of install and uninstall
☐ Performance, especially the speed of IPL (initial program load) or reboot
☐ Error logs
☐ Internal trace features
☐ Clear and unique messages
☐ Other problem determination capabilities of the software

13.3 Collecting Customer Outage Data for Quality Improvement

How does one collect customer outage data to determine the availability level of one's product (be it software, hardware, or a server computer system including hardware and software) and use the data to drive quality improvement? There are at least three approaches: collect the data directly from a small core set of customers, collect the data via your normal service process, and conduct special customer surveys.

Collecting outage data directly from customers is recommended only for a small number of customers. Otherwise, it would not be cost-effective and the chance of success would be low. Such customers normally are key customers and system availability is particularly important to them. The customers' willingness to track outage data accurately is a critical factor because this is a joint effort. Examples of data collection forms are shown in Figures 13.1 and 13.2. The forms gather two types of information: the demographics of each system (Figure 13.1) and the detailed information and action of each outage (Figure 13.2). These forms and data collection can also be implemented in a Web site.

The raw data gathered via the two forms is sufficient to derive the following indicators:

☐ Scheduled hours of operations (uptime)
☐ Equivalent system years of operations
☐ Total hours of downtime
☐ System availability
☐ Average outages per system per year
☐ Average downtime (hours) per system per year
☐ Average time (hours) per outage

System	System Name	System Description	Model and Processor Feature	Machine Serial Number	Version Release	Scheduled Hours Of System Availability This Month	Unscheduled Outages– Total Number This Month	Unscheduled Outages– Total Hours This Month
	Example	Production database, back-end OptiConnect System	530-2162	12345	V1R1	31 days × 24 hours/day = 744 hours (minus any scheduled downtime)	1	3.5
1								
2								
3								
4								
5								

FIGURE 13.1
A Tracking Form for System Demographics and Outage Summary

System Name	Date	Time	Problem Number (PMR)	Description or Cause of Outage	Type	Total Downtime	Resolution or Action Taken
Example	3/1/97	01:00 PM	12345	System hung —SRC xxxxxxxx	O software O hardware	3.5 hours	RE-IPLed, AF xxxxxxx oper xxxxxxx appli
1					O software O hardware		
2					O software O hardware		
3					O software O hardware		
4					O software O hardware		
5					O software O hardware		
6					O software O hardware		
7					O software O hardware		
8					O software O hardware		
9					O software O hardware		
10					O software O hardware		

FIGURE 13.2
A Tracking Form for Outage Specifics

The value of these metrics can be estimated every month or every quarter, depending on the amount of data available (i.e., sufficient number of equivalent system years of operations for each period). Trends of these metrics can be formed and monitored, and correlated with the timing of new releases of the product, or special improvement actions.

With more data, one can analyze the causes of outages, identify the problem components of the system, and take systematic improvement actions. Note that in the form in Figure 13.2, the problem management record (PMR) number should be used to link the outage incident to the customer problem record in the normal service process. Therefore, in-depth data analysis can be performed to yield insights for continual improvement.

Figure 13.3 shows a hypothetical example of the contribution of software components to the unavailability of a software system. In this case, component X of the system accounted for the most outages and downtime. This is likely an indication of poor intrinsic product quality. On the other hand, component Y accounts for only two incidents but the total downtime caused by these two outages are significant. This may be due to issues related to problem determination or inefficiencies involved in developing and delivering fixes. Effective improvement actions should be guided by these metrics and results from causal analyses.

The second way to obtain customer outage data is via the normal service process. When a customer experiences a problem and calls the support center, a call record or problem management record (PMR) is created. A simple screening procedure (e.g., via a couple of standard questions) can be established with the call record process to identify the outage-related customer calls. The total number of licenses of the product in a given time period can be used as a denominator. The rate of outage-related customer problem calls normalized to the number of license data can then be used to form some indicator of product outage rate in the field. Because this data is from the service problem management records, all information gathered via the service process is available for in-depth analysis.

Figure 13.4 shows an example of the outage incidence rate (per 1000 systems per year) for several releases of a software system over time, expressed as months after the delivery of the releases. None of the releases has complete data over the 48-month time span. Collectively, the incidence curves show a well-known pattern of the exponential distribution. Due to the fluctuations related to small numbers in the first several months after delivery, initially we wondered whether the pattern would follow a Rayleigh model or an exponential model. But with more data points from the last three releases, the exponential model became more convincing and was confirmed by a statistical goodness-of-fit test.

We note that outage data from the service process is related to the frequencies of outages and their causes. However, the outage duration data is usually not available because it would require a two-pass process that is expensive to implement—

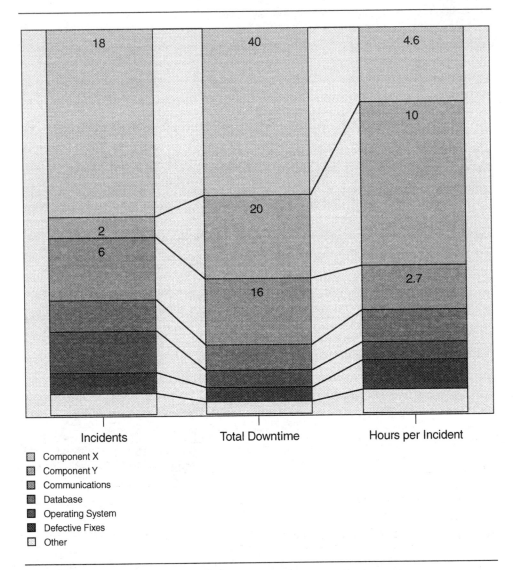

FIGURE 13.3
Incidents of Outage, Total Downtime, and Hour per Incident by Software Component

following up with the customers and requesting duration data when the problem is resolved. Because of this, the metric derived from this data (such as the example in Figure 13.4) pertains more to the reliability concept instead of the system availability. Nonetheless, it is also an availability measurement because the numerator data is outages. The delineation between reliability and availability in this case becomes blurred.

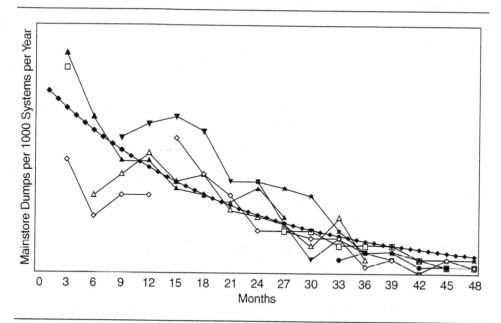

FIGURE 13.4

Software High-Impact Outage Rate and Exponential Model

The third approach to collecting customer outage information is through special customer surveys, which have several advantages. First, through sampling designs, one can get a representative and sufficiently large sample of one's entire customer set. Second, the survey can cover related topics in addition to outage information per se, such as customers' maintenance practices, scheduled downtime, scheduled uptime, satisfaction with system availability, and specific elements that contribute to system availability. Responses from these related topics can provide useful information for the product vendor with regard to its improvement strategies and customer relationship management. Third, surveys are cost-effective. On the other hand, a major drawback of the survey approach is that the accuracy of the quantitative outage data is not likely as good as that of the previous approaches. If the customers didn't have regular outage tracking in place, their responses might be based on recollection and approximation. Another limitation is that survey data is not adequate for root cause analysis because it is not meant to provide in-depth information of specific outage incidents.

Our experience is that special customer surveys can provide useful information for the overall big picture and this approach is complementary to the other approaches. For example, a representative survey showed that the customers' profile of scheduled uptime (number of hours per week) for a software system is as follows:

- [ ] 40 hours: 11%
- [ ] 41–80 hours: 17%
- [ ] 81–120 hours: 8%
- [ ] 121–160 hours: 11%
- [ ] 168 hours (24 x 7): 53%

It is obvious from this profile that the customers of this software would demand high availability. When this data is analyzed together with other variables such as satisfaction with system availability, maintenance strategy, type of business, types of operations the software is used for, and potential of future purchases, the information will be tremendously useful for the product vendor's improvement plans.

13.4 In-process Metrics for Outage and Availability

To improve product reliability and availability, sound architecture and good designs are key. Root causes and lessons learned from customer outages in the field can be used to improve the design points for the next release of the product. In terms of in-process metrics when the product is under development, however, we don't recommend premature tracking of outages and availability during the early phases of testing. Such tracking should be done during the product-level testing or during the final system test phase in a customerlike environment. During early phases of testing, the defect arrival volume is high and the objective is to flush out the functional defects before the system stabilizes. Tracking and focus at these phases should be on testing progress, defect arrivals, and defect backlog. When the system is achieving good stability, normally during the final phase of testing, metrics for tracking system availability become meaningful. In Chapter 10, we discuss and recommend several metrics that measure outages and availability: number and trend of system crashes and hangs, CPU utilization, and Mean Time to unplanned IPL (initial program load, or reboot). While some metrics may require tools, resources, and a well-established tracking system, tracking the system crashes and hangs can be done by paper and pencil, and can be implemented easily by small teams.

For projects that have a beta program, we recommend tracking customer outages in beta, especially those customers who migrated their production runs to the new release. The same focus as the field outages should be applied to these outages during the beta program. Outages during the beta program can also be used as a predictive indicator of the system outages and availability in the field after the product is shipped. The difference is that during beta, there are still chances to take improvement actions before the product is made available to the entire customer population. We have experience in tracking system crashes during customer beta for several years. Due to small numbers, we haven't established a parametric correlation between beta outages and field outages yet. But using nonparametric (rank-order) correlation methods and comparing releases, we did see a positive correlation between the two—the more crashes during beta, the more outages and less system availability in the field.

Summary

In this chapter we discuss the definition and measurements of system availability. System availability is perhaps one of the most important quality attributes in the modern era of Internet and network computing. We reference a couple of industry studies to show the status of system availability. We explore the relationships among reliability, availability, and the traditional defect level measurement in software development. The concept and measurement of availability is broader than reliability and defect level. It encompasses intrinsic product quality (reliability or defect level), customer impact, and recovery and maintenance strategies. System availability is a customer-oriented concept and measure.

It is clear that the current quality of typical software is far from adequate in meeting the requirements of high availability by businesses and the society.

There are several ways to collect customer outage data for quality improvement: direct customer input, data from the service process, and special customer surveys. Root cause analyses of customers' outages and a process similar to the defect prevention process (discussed in Chapter 2), are highly recommended as key elements of an outage reduction plan. Quality improvement from this process should include both corrective actions for the current problems and preventive actions for long-term outage reduction.

Finally, to complete the closed-loop process in our discussions, we cite several in-process metrics that are pertinent to outage and availability. We highly recommend that the tracking of system crashes and hangs during the final test phase be adopted by all projects. This is a simple and critical metric and can be implemented in different ways, ranging from complicated automated tracking to paper and pencil, by large as well as small teams.

References

1. Gross N., M. Stepanek, and O. Port, "Software Hell," *Business Week,* December 6, 1999.
2. Cusumano, M., *Japan's Software Factories,* New York: Oxford University Press, 1991.
3. Gartner Group, "Platform Availability Data: Can You Spare a Minute?" Gartner Group Research Note, October 29, 1998.
4. IDC, "Server Cost of Ownership in ERM Customer Sites: A Total Cost of Ownership Study," An IDC white paper (Analysts: Jean S. Bozman and Randy Perry), August 2001.
5. "The State of Software Quality," *Information Week,* May 21, 2001.

6. Jones, C., *Applied Software Measurement: Assuring Productivity and Quality,* New York: McGraw-Hill, 1991.

7. Jones, C., "Measuring Software Process Improvement, Version 8," Boston: Software Productivity Research, March 6, 2001.

8. Wolstenholme, L., *Reliability Modeling: A Statistical Approach,* Boca Raton, Fla. Chapman & Hall/CRC, 1999.

14

Measuring and Analyzing
Customer Satisfaction

Customer satisfaction is the ultimate validation of quality. Product quality and customer satisfaction together form the total meaning of quality. Indeed, what differentiates total quality management (TQM) from the sole focus on product quality in traditional quality engineering is that TQM is aimed at long-term business success by linking quality with customer satisfaction. In this modern-day quality era, enhancing customer satisfaction is the bottom line of business success. With ever-increasing market competition, customer focus is the only way to retain the customer base and to expand market share. Studies show that it is five times more costly to recruit a new customer than it is to keep an old customer, and that dissatisfied customers tell 7 to 20 people about their experiences, while satisfied customers tell only 3 to 5.

As a result of TQM, more and more companies are conducting surveys to measure their customers' satisfaction. In this chapter we discuss customer satisfaction surveys and the analysis of survey data. As an example, we describe an analysis of the relationship between overall customer satisfaction and satisfaction with specific attributes for a software product. In the last section we discuss the question of how good is good enough.

14.1 Customer Satisfaction Surveys

There are various ways to obtain customer feedback with regard to their satisfaction levels with the product(s) and the company. For example, telephone follow-up regarding a customer's satisfaction at a regular time after the purchase is a frequent practice by many companies. Other sources include customer complaint data, direct customer visits, customer advisory councils, user conferences, and the like. To obtain representative and comprehensive data, however, the time-honored approach is to conduct customer satisfaction surveys that are representative of the entire customer base.

14.1.1 Methods of Survey Data Collection

There are three common methods to gather survey data: face-to-face interviews, telephone interviews, and mailed questionnaires (self-administered). The personal interview method requires the interviewer to ask questions based on a prestructured questionnaire and to record the answers. The primary advantage of this method is the high degree of validity of the data. Specifically, the interviewer can note specific reactions and eliminate misunderstandings about the questions being asked. The major limitations are costs and factors concerning the interviewer. If not adequately trained, the interviewer may deviate from the required protocol, thus introducing biases into the data. If the interviewer cannot maintain neutrality, any statement, movement, or even facial expression by the interviewer could affect the response. Errors in recording the responses could also lead to erroneous results.

Telephone interviews are less expensive than face-to-face interviews. Different from personal interviews, telephone interviews can be monitored by the research team to ensure that the specified interview procedure is followed. The computer-aided approach can further reduce costs and increase efficiency. Telephone interviews should be kept short and impersonal to maintain the interest of the respondent. The limitations of this method are the lack of direct observation, the lack of using exhibits for explanation, and the limited group of potential respondents—those who can be reached by telephone.

The mailed questionnaire method does not require interviewers and is therefore less expensive. However, this savings is usually at the expense of response rates. Low response rates can introduce biases to the data because if the respondents are different from the nonrespondents, the sample will not be representative of the population. Nonresponse can be a problem in any method of surveys, but the mailed questionnaire method usually has the lowest rate of response. For this method, extreme caution should be used when analyzing data and generalizing the results. Moreover, the questionnaire must be carefully constructed, validated, and pretested before final use. Questionnaire development requires professional knowledge and experience and should be dealt with accordingly. Texts on survey research methods provide useful guidelines and observations (e.g., Babbie, 1986).

Figure 14.1 shows the advantages and disadvantages of the three survey methods with regard to a number of attributes.

14.1.2 Sampling Methods

When the customer base is large, it is too costly to survey all customers. Estimating the satisfaction level of the entire customer population through a representative sample is more efficient. To obtain representative samples, scientific probability sampling methods must be used. There are four basic types of probability sampling: simple random sampling, systematic sampling, stratified sampling, and cluster sampling.

If a sample of size n is drawn from a population in such a way that every possible sample of size n has the same chance of being selected, the sampling procedure is called simple random sampling. The sample thus obtained is called a simple random sample (Mendenhall et al., 1971). Simple random sampling is often mistaken as convenient sampling or accidental sampling for which the investigator just "randomly" and conveniently selects individuals he or she happens to come across. The latter is not a probability sample. To take a simple random sample, each individual in the population must be listed once and only once. Then some mechanical procedure (such as using a random number table or using a random number-generating computer program) is used to draw the sample. To avoid repeated drawing of one

Type of Survey	Cost	Sampling	Response Rate	Speed	Flexibility	Observations	Length of Interview	Exhibits	Validity
In Person	– –	+ –	+ –	+ –	+ +	+ +	+	+	+ +
Phone	+	+	+ +	+	+	–	–	–	+
Mail	+ +	–	– –	–	–	–	+	+ –	–

– = Disadvantage (– – = Worst)
+ = Advantage (+ + = Best)
+ – = Could be an Advantage or a Disadvantage

FIGURE 14.1
Advantages and Disadvantages of Three Survey Methods

individual, it is usually more convenient to sample without replacement. Notice that on each successive draw the probability of an individual being selected increases slightly because there are fewer and fewer individuals left unselected from the population. If, on any given draw, the probabilities are equal of all remaining individuals being selected, then we have a simple random sample.

Systematic sampling is often used interchangeably with simple random sampling. Instead of using a table of random numbers, in systematic sampling one simply goes down a list taking every kth individual, starting with a randomly selected case among the first k individuals. (k is the ratio between the size of the population and the size of the sample to be drawn. In other words, $1/k$ is the sampling fraction.) For example, if we wanted to draw a sample of 500 customers from a population of 20,000, then k is 40. Starting with a random number between 1 and 40 (say, 23), then we would draw every fortieth on the list (63, 103, 143, . . .).

Systematic sampling is simpler than random sampling if a list is extremely long or a large sample is to be drawn. However, there are two types of situations in which systematic sampling may introduce biases: (1) The entries on the list may have been ordered so that a trend occurs and (2) the list may possess some cyclical characteristic that coincides with the k value. For example, if the individuals have been listed according to rank and salary and the purpose of the survey is to estimate the average salary, then two systematic samples with different random starts will produce systematic differences in the sample means. As another example for bias (2), suppose in a housing development every twelfth dwelling unit is a corner unit. If the sampling fraction happens to be $1/12$ ($k = 12$), then one could obtain a sample either with all corner units or no corner units depending on the random start. This sample could be biased. Therefore, the ordering of a list should be examined before applying systematic sampling. Fortunately, neither type of problem occurs frequently in practice, and once discovered, it can be dealt with accordingly.

In a stratified sample, we first classify individuals into nonoverlapping groups, called *strata,* and then select simple random samples from each stratum. The strata are usually based on important variables pertaining to the parameter of interest. For example, customers with complex network systems may have a set of satisfaction criteria for software products that is very different from those who have standalone systems and simple applications. Therefore, a stratified sample should include customer type as a stratification variable.

Stratified sampling, when properly designed, is more efficient than simple random sampling and systematic sampling. Stratified samples can be designed to yield greater accuracy for the same cost, or for the same accuracy with less cost. By means of stratification we ensure that individuals in each stratum are well represented in the sample. In the simplest design, one can take a simple random sample within each stratum. The sampling fractions in each stratum may be equal (proportional stratified sampling) or different (disproportional stratified sampling). If the goal is to compare subpopulations of different sizes, it may be desirable to use disproportional stratified sampling. To yield the maximum efficiency for a sample design, the following guidelines for sample size allocation can be used: Make the sampling fraction for each stratum directly proportional to the standard deviation within the stratum and inversely proportional to the square root of the cost of each case in the stratum.

In stratified sampling we sample within each stratum. Sometimes it is advantageous to divide the population into a large number of groups, called *clusters,* and to sample among the clusters. A cluster sample is a simple random sample in which each sampling unit is a cluster of elements. Usually geographical units such as cities, districts, schools, or work plants are used as units for cluster sampling. Cluster sampling is generally less efficient than simple random sampling, but it is much more cost effective. The purpose is to select clusters as heterogeneous as possible but which are small enough to cut down on expenses such as travel costs involved in personal interviews. For example, if a company has many branch offices throughout the country and an in-depth face-to-face interview with a sample of its customers is desired, then a cluster sample using branch offices as clusters (of customers) may be the best sampling approach.

For any survey, the sampling design is of utmost importance in obtaining unbiased, representative data. If the design is poor, then despite its size, chances are the sample will yield biased results. There are plenty of real-life examples in the literature with regard to the successes and failures of sampling. The *Literary Digest* story is perhaps the most well known. The *Literary Digest,* a popular magazine in the 1930s, had established a reputation for successfully predicting winners of presidential elections on the basis of "straw polls." In 1936 the *Digest's* history of successes came to a halt when it predicted a 3-to-2 victory for the Republican nominee, Governor Alf Landon, over the incumbent Franklin Roosevelt. As it turned out, Roosevelt won by a landslide, carrying 62% of the popular votes and 46 of the 48 states. The magazine suspended publication shortly after the election.

For the prediction, the *Digest* chose a sample of ten million persons originally selected from telephone listings and from the list of its subscribers. Despite the huge sample, the prediction was in error because the sample was not representative of the voting population. In the 1930s more Republicans than Democrats had telephones. Furthermore, the response rate was very low, about 20% to 25%. Therefore, the responses obtained from the poll and used for the prediction were not representative of those who voted (Bryson, 1976).

14.1.3 Sample Size

How large a sample is sufficient? The answer to this question depends on the confidence level we want and the margin of error we can tolerate. The higher the level of confidence we want from the sample estimate, and the smaller the error margin, the larger the sample we need, and vice versa. For each probability sampling method, specific formulas are available for calculating sample size, some of which (such as that for cluster sampling) are quite complicated. The following formula is for the sample size required to estimate a population proportion (e.g., percent satisfied) based on simple random sampling:

$$n = \frac{N_x Z^2 \times p(1-p)}{NB^2 + \left[Z^2 \times p(1-p)\right]}$$

where
N = population size
Z = Z statistic from normal distribution:
        for 80% confidence level, $Z = 1.28$
        for 85% confidence level, $Z = 1.45$
        for 90% confidence level, $Z = 1.65$
        for 95% confidence level, $Z = 1.96$
p = estimated satisfaction level
B = margin of error

A common misconception with regard to sample size is that the size of a sample must be a certain percentage of the population in order to be representative; in fact, the power of a sample depends on its absolute size. Regardless of the size of its population, the larger the sample the smaller its standard deviation will become and

Expected Satisfaction	80% Confidence		85% Confidence		90% Confidence		95% Confidence	
	+/- 5%	+/- 3%	+/- 5%	+/- 3%	+/- 5%	+/- 3%	+/- 5%	+/- 3%
80%	104	283	133	360	171	462	240	639
85%	83	227	106	289	137	371	192	516
90%	59	161	75	206	97	265	136	370
95%	31	86	40	110	51	142	72	199

FIGURE 14.2
Examples of Sample Size (for 10,000 customers) in Relation to Confidence Level and Error Margin

therefore the estimate will be more stable. When the sample size is up to a few thousands, it gives satisfactory results for many purposes, even if the population is extremely large. For example, sample sizes of national fertility surveys (representing all women of childbearing age for the entire nation) in many countries are in the range of 3,000 to 5,000.

Figure 14.2 illustrates the sample sizes for 10,000 customers for various levels of confidence with both 5% and 3% margins of error. Note that the required sample size decreases as the customer satisfaction level increases. This is because the larger the p value, the smaller its variance, $p(1 - p) = pq$. When an estimate for the satisfaction level is not available, using a value of 50% ($p = 0.5$) will yield the largest sample size that is needed because pq is largest when $p = q$.

14.2 Analyzing Satisfaction Data

The five-point satisfaction scale (very satisfied, satisfied, neutral, dissatisfied, and very dissatisfied) is often used in customer satisfaction surveys. The data are usually summarized in terms of percent satisfied. In presentation, run charts or bar charts to show the trend of percent satisfied are often used. We recommend that confidence intervals be formed for the data points so that the margins of error of the sample estimates can be observed immediately (Figure 14.3).

Traditionally, the 95% confidence level is used for forming confidence intervals and the 5% probability (p value) is used for significance testing. This p value means that if the true difference is not significant, the chance we wrongly conclude that the difference is significant is 5%. Therefore, if a difference is statistically significant at the 5% level, it is indeed very significant. When analyzing customer satisfaction, it is not necessary to stick to the traditional significance level. If the purpose is to be more sensitive in detecting changes in customers' satisfaction levels, or to trigger actions when a significant difference is observed, then the 5% level is not sensitive enough. Based on our experience, a p value as high as 20%, or a confidence level of 80%, is still reasonable—sensitive enough to detect a substantial difference, yet not giving false alarms when the difference is trivial.

Although percent satisfied is perhaps the most used metric, some companies, such as IBM, choose to monitor the inverse, the percent nonsatisfied. Nonsatisfied includes the neutral, dissatisfied, and very dissatisfied in the five-point scale. The rationale to use percent nonsatisfied is to focus on areas that need improvement. This is especially the case when the value of percent satisfied is quite high. Figure 12.3 in Chapter 12 shows an example of IBM Rochester's percent nonsatisfied in terms of CUPRIMDA (capability, usability, performance, reliability, installability, maintainability, documentation/information, and availability) categories and overall satisfaction.

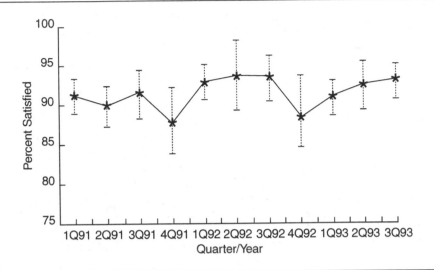

FIGURE 14.3
Quarterly Trend of Percent Satisfied with a Hypothetical Product

14.2.1 Specific Attributes and Overall Satisfaction

The major advantage of monitoring customer satisfaction with specific attributes of the software, in addition to overall satisfaction, is that such data provide specific information for improvement. The profile of customer satisfaction with those attributes (e.g., CUPRIMDA) indicates the areas of strength and weakness of the software product. One easy mistake in customer satisfaction analysis, however, is to equate the areas of weakness with the priority of improvement, and to increase investment to improve those areas. For instance, if a product has low satisfaction with documentation (D) and high satisfaction with reliability (R), that does not mean that there is no need to continually improve the product's reliability and that the first priority of the development team is to improve documentation. Reliability may be the very reason the customers decide to buy this product and that customers may expect even further improvement. On the other hand, customers may not like the product's documentation but may find it tolerable given other considerations. To answer the question on priority of improvement, therefore, the subject must be looked at in the broader context of overall customer satisfaction with the product. Specifically, the correlations of the satisfaction levels of specific attributes with overall satisfaction need to be examined. After all, it is the overall satisfaction level that the software developer aims to maximize; it is the overall satisfaction level that affects the customer's purchase decision.

Here we describe an example of analyzing the relationship between satisfaction level with specific attributes and overall satisfaction for a hypothetical product. For this product, data are available on the UPRIMD parameters and on availability (A). The purpose of the analysis is to determine the priority for improvement by assessing the extent to which each of the UPRIMD-A parameters affects overall customer satisfaction. The sample size for this analysis is 3,658. Satisfaction is measured by the five-point scale ranging from very dissatisfied (1) to very satisfied (5).

To achieve the objectives, we attempted two statistical approaches: least-squares multiple regression and logistic regression. In both approaches overall customer satisfaction is the dependent variable, and satisfaction levels with UPRIMD-A are the independent variables. The purpose is to assess the correlations between each specific attribute and overall satisfaction simultaneously. For the ordinary regression approach, we use the original five-point scale. The scale is an ordinal variable and data obtained from it represent a truncated continuous distribution. Sensitivity research in the literature, however, indicates that if the sample size is large (such as in our case), violation of the interval scale and the assumption of Gaussian distribution results in very small bias. In other words, the use of ordinary regression is quite robust for the ordinal scale with large samples.

For the logistic regression approach, we classified the five-point scale into a dichotomous variable: very satisfied and satisfied (4 and 5) versus nonsatisfied (1, 2, and 3). Categories 4 and 5 were recoded as 1 and categories 1, 2, and 3 were recoded as 0. The dependent variable, therefore, is the odds ratio of satisfied and very satisfied versus nonsatisfied. The odds ratio is a measurement of association that has been widely used for categorical data analysis. In our application it approximates how much more likely customers will be positive in overall satisfaction if they were satisfied with specific UPRIMD-A parameters versus if they were not. For instance, let customers who were satisfied with the performance of the system form a group and those not satisfied with the performance form another group. Then an odds ratio of 2 indicates that the overall satisfaction occurs twice as often among the first group of customers (satisfied with the performance of the system) than the second group. The logistic model in our analysis, therefore, is as follows:

$$\log\left(\frac{sat + v.\ sat}{v.\ dis + dis + neut}\right) = \beta_0 + \beta_1 x_1 + \ldots + \beta_k x_k + e$$

The correlation matrix, means, and standard deviations are shown in Table 14.1. Two types of means are shown: the five-point scale and the 0–1 scale. Means for the latter reflect the percent satisfaction level (e.g., overall satisfaction is 85.5% and satisfaction with reliability is 93.8%). Among the parameters, availability and reliability have the highest satisfaction levels, whereas documentation and installability have the lowest.

TABLE 14.1
Correlation Matrix, Means, and Standard Deviations

	Overall	U	P	R	I	M	D	A
Overall								
U—usability	.61							
P—performance	.43	.46						
R—reliability	.63	.56	.42					
I—installability	.51	.57	.39	.47				
M—maintainability	.40	.39	.31	.40	.38			
D—documentation	.45	.51	.34	.44	.45	.35		
A—availability	.39	.39	.52	.46	.32	.28	.31	
Mean	4.20	4.18	4.35	4.41	3.98	4.15	3.97	4.57
Standard Deviation	.75	.78	.75	.66	.90	.82	.89	.64
% SAT	85.50	84.10	91.10	93.80	75.30	82.90	73.30	94.50

As expected, there is moderate correlation among the UPRIMD-A parameters. Usability with reliability, installability, and documentation, and performance with availability are the more notable ones. In relation to overall satisfaction, reliability, usability, and installability have the highest correlations.

Results of the multiple regression analysis are summarized in Table 14.2. As indicated by the p values, all parameters are significant at the 0.0001 level except the availability parameter. The total variation of overall customer satisfaction explained by the seven parameters is 52.6%. In terms of relative importance, reliability, usability, and installability are the highest, as indicated by the t value. This finding is consistent with what we observed from the simple correlation coefficients in Table 14.1. Reliability being the most significant variable implies that although customers are quite satisfied with the software's reliability (93.8%), reliability is still the most determining factor for achieving overall customer satisfaction. In other words, further reliability improvement is still demanded. For usability and installability, the current low and moderate levels of satisfaction, together with the significance finding, really pinpoint the need for drastic improvement.

More interesting observations can be made on documentation and availability. Although being the lowest satisfied parameter, intriguingly, documentation's influence on overall satisfaction is not strong. This may be because customers have become more tolerant with documentation problems. Indeed, data from software systems within and outside IBM often indicate that documentation/information usually receive the lowest ratings among specific dimensions of a software product. This does not mean that one doesn't have to improve documentation; it means that documentation is not as sensitive as other variables when measuring its effects on the

TABLE 14.2
Results of Multiple Regression Analysis

Variable	Regression Coefficient (Beta)	t value	Significance Level (p Value)
R—reliability	.391	21.4	.0001
U—usability	.247	15.2	.0001
I—installability	.091	7.0	.0001
P—performance	.070	4.6	.0001
M—maintainability	.067	5.4	.0001
D—documentation	.056	4.5	.0001
A—availability	.022	1.2	.22 (not significant)

overall satisfaction of the software. Nonetheless, it still is a significant variable and should be improved.

Availability is the least significant factor. On the other hand, it has the highest satisfaction level (94.5%, average 4.57 in the five-point scale).

Results of the logistic regression model are shown in Table 14.3. The most striking observation is that the significance of availability in affecting customer satisfaction is in vivid contrast to findings from the ordinary regression analysis, as just discussed. Now availability ranks third, after reliability and usability, in affecting overall satisfaction. The difference observed from the two models lies in the difference in the scaling of the dependent and independent variables in the two approaches. Combining the two findings, we interpret the data as follows:

☐ Availability is not very important in influencing the average shift in overall customer satisfaction from one level to the next (from dissatisfied to neutral, from neural to satisfied, etc.).
☐ However, availability is very important in affecting whether customers are satisfied versus nonsatisfied.
☐ Therefore, availability is a sensitive factor in customer satisfaction and should be improved despite its level of high satisfaction.

Because the dependent variable of the logistic regression model (satisfied versus nonsatisfied) is more appropriate for our purpose, we use the results of the logistic model for the rest of our example.

The odds ratios indicate the relative importance of the UPRIMD-A variables in the logistics model. That all ratios are greater than 1 means that each UPRIMD-A variable has a positive impact on overall satisfaction, the dependent variables. Among them, reliability has the largest odds ratio, 14.4. So the likelihood of overall

TABLE 14.3
Results of Logistic Regression Analysis

Variable	Regression Coefficient (Beta)	Chi Square	Significance Level (p Value)	Odds Ratio
R—reliability	1.216	138.6	<.0001	11.4
U—usability	.701	88.4	<.0001	4.1
A—availability	.481	16.6	<.0001	2.6
I—installability	.410	33.2	<.0001	2.3
M—maintainability	.376	26.2	<.0001	2.1
P—performance	.321	14.3	.0002	1.9
D—documentation	.164	5.3	.02	1.4

satisfaction is much higher for customers who are satisfied with reliability than for those who aren't. On the other hand, documentation has the lowest odds ratio, 1.4. This indicates that the impact of documentation on overall satisfaction is not very strong, but there is still a positive effect.

Table 14.4 presents the probabilities for customers being satisfied depending on whether or not they are satisfied with the UPRIMD-A parameters. These conditional probabilities are derived from the earlier logistic regression model. When customers are satisfied with all seven parameters, chances are they are 96.32% satisfied with the overall software product. From row 2 through row 8, we show the probabilities that customers will be satisfied with the software when they are not satisfied with one of the seven UPRIMD-A parameters, one at a time. The drop in probabilities in row 2 through row 8 compared with row 1 indicates how important that particular parameter is to indicate whether customers are satisfied. Reliability (row 6), usability (row 8), and availability (row 2), in that order, again, are the most sensitive parameters. Data in rows 9 through 16 show the reverse view of rows 1 through 8: the probabilities that customers will be satisfied with the software when they are satisfied with one of the seven parameters, one at a time. This exercise, in fact, is a confirmation of the odds ratios in Table 14.3.

By now we have a good understanding of how important each UPRIMD-A variable is in terms of affecting overall customer satisfaction in the example. Now let us come back to the initial question of how to determine the priority of improvement among the specific quality attributes. We propose the following method:

1. Determine the order of significance of each quality attribute on overall satisfaction by statistical modeling (such as the regression model and the logistic model in the example).

TABLE 14.4
Conditional Probabilities

Row	P(Y=1/X)	U	P	R	I	M	D	A	Frequency
1	.9632	1	1	1	1	1	1	1	1632
2	.9187	1	1	1	1	1	1	0	14
3	.9552	1	1	1	1	1	0	1	267
4	.9331	1	1	1	1	0	1	1	155
5	.9287	1	1	1	0	1	1	1	212
6	.7223	1	1	0	1	1	1	1	12
7	.9397	1	0	1	1	1	1	1	42
8	.8792	0	1	1	1	1	1	1	47
9	.0189	0	0	0	0	0	0	0	20
10	.0480	0	0	0	0	0	0	1	8
11	.0260	0	0	0	0	0	1	0	2
12	.0392	0	0	0	0	1	0	0	9
13	.0132	0	0	0	1	0	0	0	1
14	.1796	0	0	1	0	0	0	0	12
15	.0353	0	1	0	0	0	0	0	4
16	—	1	1	0	0	0	0	0	0

Y = 1: satisfied, Y = 0: nonsatisfied; X: the UPRIMDA vector

2. Plot the coefficient of each attribute from the model (Y-axis) against its satisfaction level (X-axis).
3. Use the plot to determine priority by
   □ going from top to bottom, and
   □ going from left to right, if the coefficients of importance have the same values.

To illustrate this method based on our example, Figure 14.4 plots the estimated logistic regression coefficients against the satisfaction level of the variable. The Y-axis represents the beta values and the X-axis represents the satisfaction level. From the plot, the order of priority for improvement is very clear: reliability, usability, availability, installability, maintainability, performance, and documentation. As this example illustrates, it is useful to use multiple methods (including scales) to analyze customer satisfaction data—so as to understand better the relationships hidden beneath the data. This is exemplified by our seemingly contradictory findings on availability from ordinary regression and logistic regression models.

Our example focuses on the relationships between specific quality attributes and overall customer satisfaction. There are many other meaningful questions that our example does not address. For example, what are the relationships among the

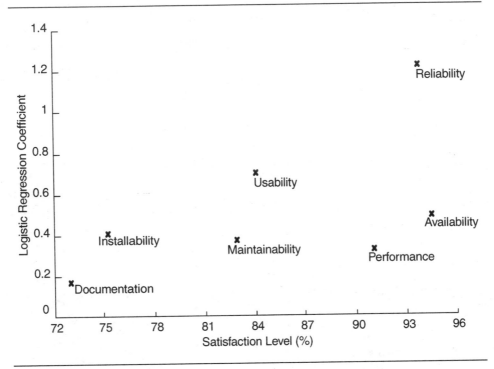

FIGURE 14.4
Logistic Regression Coefficients versus Satisfaction Level

specific quality attributes (e.g., CUPRIMDA) in a cause-and-effect manner? What variables other than specific quality attributes, affect overall customer satisfaction? For instance, in our regression analysis, the R^2 is 52.8%. What are the factors that may explain the rest of the variations in overall satisfaction? Given the current level of overall customer satisfaction, what does it take to improve one percentage point (in terms of CUPRIMD-A and other factors)?

To seek answers to such questions, apparently a multitude of techniques is needed for analysis. Regardless of the analysis to be performed, it is always beneficial to consider issues in measurement theory, such as those discussed in Chapter 3, whenever possible.

14.3 Satisfaction with Company

Thus far our discussion on customer satisfaction has been product oriented—satisfaction with the overall software and with specific attributes. A broader scope of the subject deals with customers' overall satisfaction with the company. This broad definition of customer satisfaction includes a spectrum of variables in addition to the quality of the products. For instance, in their study of the customers' view model with regard to IBM Rochester, Hoisington and associates (Hoisington et al., 1993; Naumann and Hoisington, 2001) found that customers' overall satisfaction and loyalty is attributed to a set of common attributes of the company (as perceived by the customers) and satisfaction levels with specific dimensions of the entire company. The common attributes include ease of doing business with, partnership, responsiveness, knowledge of customer's business, and the company's being customer driven. The key dimensions of satisfaction about the company include technical solutions, support and service, marketing, administration, delivery, and company image. The dimension of technical solutions includes product quality attributes. In the following, we list several attributes under each dimension:

- ☐ *Technical solutions:* quality/reliability, availability, ease of use, pricing, installation, new technology
- ☐ *Support and service:* flexible, accessible, product knowledge
- ☐ *Marketing:* solution, central point of contact, information
- ☐ *Administration:* purchasing procedure, billing procedure, warranty expiration notification
- ☐ *Delivery:* on time, accurate, postdelivery process
- ☐ *Company image:* technology leader, financial stability, executives image

It is remarkable that in Hoisington's customer view model, company image is one of the dimensions of customer satisfaction. Whether this finding holds true in other cases remains to be seen. However, this finding illustrates the importance of both a company's actual performance and how it is perceived with regard to customer satisfaction.

It is apparent that customer satisfaction at both the company level and the product level needs to be analyzed and managed. Knowledge about the former enables a company to take a comprehensive approach to total quality management; knowledge about the latter provides specific clues for product improvements.

Yet another type of analysis centers on why customers choose a company's products over other companies', and vice versa. This kind of analysis requires information that is not available from regular customer satisfaction surveys, be they product level or company level. It requires data about customers' decision making for purchases and requires responses from those who are not the company's current customers as well as those who are. This type of analysis, albeit difficult to conduct, is worthwhile because it deals directly with the issue of gaining new customers to expand the customer base.

14.4 How Good Is Good Enough?

How much customer satisfaction is good enough? Of course, the long-term goal should be 100%—total customer satisfaction. However, there are specific business questions that need better answers. Should my company invest $2,000,000 to improve satisfaction from 85% to 90%? Given that my company's customer satisfaction is at 95%, should I invest another million dollars to improve it or should I do this later?

The key to answering questions such as these lies in the relationship between customer satisfaction and market share. The basic assumption is that satisfied customers continue to purchase products from the same company and dissatisfied customers will buy from other companies. Therefore, as long as market competition exists, customer satisfaction is key to customer loyalty. Even if a company has no direct competitors, customers may purchase substitute products if they are dissatisfied with that company's products. Even in monopoly markets, customer dissatisfaction encourages the development and emergence of competition. Studies and actual cases in business have lent strong support to this assumption.

Assuming that satisfied customers will remain customers of the company, Babich (1992) studied the "how good is good enough" question based on a simplified model of customer satisfaction and market share that contains only three companies: A, B, and C. Therefore, when customers are dissatisfied with company A, they choose company B or C, and so forth. Babich further assumed that the distribution of dissatisfied customers among the alternative suppliers is in proportion to the suppliers' current market share. Babich then determined the algorithm for the market shares of the three companies at time $t + 1$ as follows:

$$A_{t+1} = A_t(1-x) + B_t y\left[A_t/(A_t + C_t)\right] + C_t z\left[A_t/(A_t + B_t)\right]$$
$$+ G\left[A_t/(A_t + B_t + C_t)\right]$$

$$B_{t+1} = B_t(1-y) + A_t x\left[B_t/(B_t + C_t)\right] + C_t z\left[(B_t/A_t + B_t)\right]$$
$$+ G\left[B_t/(A_t + B_t + C_t)\right]$$

$$C_{t+1} = C_t(1-z) + A_t x\left[C_t/(B_t + C_t)\right] + B_t y\left[C_t/(A_t + C_t)\right]$$
$$+ G\left[C_t/(A_t + B_t + C_t)\right]$$

where:
A = number of A customers
B = number of B customers
C = number of C customers
G = number of new customers to market

x = dissatisfaction level with A products
y = dissatisfaction level with B products
z = dissatisfaction level with C products
t = time

Based on this model, Babich computed the market shares of the three companies assuming satisfaction levels of 95%, 91%, and 90% for A, B, and C, respectively, over a number of time periods. The calculations also assume equal initial market share. As shown in Figure 14.5 (A), after 12 time periods the 95% satisfaction prod-

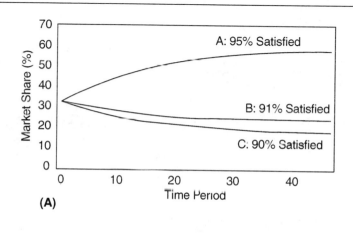

(A)

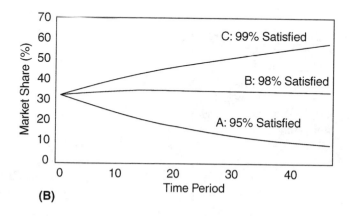

(B)

FIGURE 14.5
Satisfaction Levels and Market Share

From "Customer Satisfaction: How Good Is Good Enough?" by Pete Babich. *Quality Progress*, December 1992. Copyright © 1992 American Society for Quality. Reprinted with permission.

uct (company A) would basically own the market. However, had the satisfaction levels of companies B and C been 98% and 99%, respectively, and company A's satisfaction level remained at 95%, company A's product would have had less than 10% market share in 24 time periods, as shown in Figure 14.5(B).

From Babich's simple model and examples, the answer to the "how good is good enough" is obvious: You have to be better than your competitors. Therefore, it is important to measure not only one's customer satisfaction level, but also the satisfaction level of one's competitors. Indeed, many companies have been doing exactly that.

Finally, we emphasize that measuring and analyzing customer satisfaction is but one element of customer satisfaction management. A good customer satisfaction management process must form a closed loop of measurement, analysis, and actions. While it is not the intent of this chapter to cover the customer satisfaction management process, we recommend that such a process cover at least the following elements:

- ☐ Measure and monitor the overall customer satisfaction over time, one's own as well as key competitors'.
- ☐ Perform analyses on specific satisfaction dimensions, quality attributes of the products and their strengths, weaknesses, prioritization, and other relevant issues.
- ☐ Perform root cause analysis to identify inhibitors for each dimension and attribute.
- ☐ Set satisfaction targets (overall and specific) by taking competitors' satisfaction levels into consideration.
- ☐ Formulate and implement action plans based on the above.

Recommendations for Small Organizations

Total quality management (TQM) literature recommends three key elements of a good customer satisfaction management program: a postpurchase call back program, a complaint management process, and a customer satisfaction survey program. Although in this chapter we focus on the last element, many companies practice all three elements. Implementing any of the programs requires resources. Our view of the order of importance of the three elements is that complaint management is the most important, followed by postpurchase call back, and then overall satisfaction surveys. The first two are immediate and important to customer's transaction experience, and the last one is for systematic quality and business improvement.

Besides measuring customer satisfaction, perhaps more relevant to software engineers is the roles customers can play in software development. Development teams should leverage the benefits of customer involvement for better quality and customer satisfaction. Following are some scenarios of customer involvement that a team can leverage throughout the software development process. With the exception of large-scale customer beta programs, these processes and programs can be implemented by large and small organizations. For small organizations that don't have a customer focus program in place, I strongly recommend integrating one or more of these practices into their development process.

• *Requirements:* Good requirements-gathering and analysis techniques always involve the users closely. For long-term product strategy, customer advisory councils usually provide good directions. For Extreme Programming (XP), customer involvement is regarded as so important that an onsite customer is part of the development team and is responsible for domain expertise and acceptance testing. For object-oriented processes in general, the role of use cases in requirements analysis is another illustration of the importance of user involvement.

• *Design:* The prototyping approach is a good way to get customers' feedback and to ensure that the product satisfies requirements. In recent years, some companies use the term *user-centered design (UCD)* to signify the heavy user involvement in their design process.

• *Functional verification test (FVT):* Customer testing can start early, when FVT is near completion. This early customer testing is not a beta program, and is called a hackers' invitational or customer invitational program. A selected small number of customer experts who know the product well are invited to the vendor's development laboratory to test the new function and to attempt to break the system.

• *Customerlike testing:* Unit tests and functional verification tests are normally for functional defect removal. For product-level testing or system testing, which are normally conducted by an independent test team, many software organizations adopt a customerlike testing strategy. The testing environments and the test scenarios simulate customer operations, and therefore offer the chance to find latent defects that are likely to be encountered by customers.

• *Internal Beta*, or eating one's own cooking: When product development is about complete, and independent testing about to start, the development organization can put the product into production mode running its own business operations. This strategy puts the development team into the customer's shoes and can really motivates the team's quality focus.

• *Customer beta:* This is a broad-based customer validation program. It usually starts when final testing is about done and before the product is released to the market. The product has to be at a fairly good quality level at this stage. The main purpose is to get customer validation and feedback for further improvement. Customer beta programs should not be used as an extended development phase as a major activity for defect removals.

• *Special inbound customer testing:* Unlike the broad-based beta programs, this strategy is to invite a small set of one's core customers to the development laboratory to test applications before releasing the product to the market. This approach focuses on depth, and is relevant for a small set of customers who depend on the software for their mission-critical business applications.

14.5 Summary

Various methods are available to gauge customer satisfaction, the most common of which is to conduct representative sampling surveys. The three major methods of survey data collection are face-to-face interview, telephone interview, and mailed questionnaire. Each method has its advantages and disadvantages. To obtain representative samples, scientific probability sampling methods must be used. There are four basic types of probability sampling: simple random sampling, systematic sampling, stratified sampling, and cluster sampling.

Given a probability sample, the larger the sample size, the smaller the sampling error. A common misconception with regard to sample size is that it must be a certain percentage of the population in order to be representative; in fact, the power of a sample depends on its absolute size. However, the sample must be a scientific (probability) sample. If the sample is drawn unscientifically, then even a huge size does not guarantee its representativeness. There are many real-life examples of huge and unrepresentative samples, which are results of unscientific design.

When analyzing and presenting customer satifaction survey data, the confidence interval and margin of error must be included. Furthermore, good analysis is paramount in transforming data into useful information and knowledge. In satisfaction surveys, satisfaction with specific quality attributes of a product are often queried, in addition to overall satisfaction. However, attributes with the lowest levels of satisfaction should not automatically be accorded the highest priority for improvement and additional investment. To answer the priority question, the subject must be looked at in the broader context of customers' overall satisfaction with the product; the correlations of the satisfaction levels of specific attributes with overall satisfaction need to be examined; and the improvement actions should aim to maximize overall satisfaction.

Beyond satisfaction with a product, customers' satisfaction with the company should be analyzed. A customer view model at the company level often entails improvement actions in areas in addition to product improvement, such as marketing, order process, delivery, support, and so forth. As a simple market-share model illustrates in this chapter, one must be better than one's competitors in overall customer satisfaction in order to retain customer loyalty and to expand market share.

References

1. Babbie, E., *The Practice of Social Research*, Belmont, Calif.: Wadsworth, 1986.
2. Babich, P., "Customer Satisfaction: How Good Is Good Enough?" *Quality Progress*, December 1992, pp. 65–67.
3. Bryson, M. C., "The Literary Digest Poll: Making of a Statistical Myth," *The American Statistician*, Vol. 30, No. 4, November 1976, pp. 184–185.

4. Feigenbaum, A. V., "The Power Behind Consumer Buying and Productivity," *Quality Progress,* April, 2002, pp. 49–50.

5. George, S., "Bull or Bear?" *Quality Progress,* April 2002, pp. 32–39.

6. Hoisington, S., T. H. Huang, T. Suther, and T. Cousins, "Customer View of Ideal Business Machine Enterprise (Part I—Methodology and Results)," Technical Report TR 07.2010, IBM Rochester, Minn., January 1993.

7. Hosmer, D. W., and L. Stanley, *Applied Logistic Regression,* New York: John Wiley & Sons, 1989.

8. Mendenhall, W., L. Ott, and R. L. Scheaffer, *Elementary Survey Sampling,* Belmont, Calif.: Duxbury Press, 1971.

9. Naumann, E., and S. H. Hoisington, *Customer Centered Six Sigma, Linking Customers, Process Improvement, and Financial Results,* Milwaukee, Wisc.: ASQ Quality Press, 2001.

10. Taormina, T., "From Quality to Business Success," *Quality Progress,* April 2002, pp. 40–48.

15

Conducting In-Process Quality Assessments

How do you determine if your product development is on track to satisfy its quality objectives? How do you ferret out the current and upcoming risks to your product's quality? Will the product meet customers' quality expectations? Development teams, project managers, and especially the quality professional(s) on the project team need to ask these questions routinely while their product is under development so timely actions can be applied.

In this chapter[1], we present a four-step process of in-process quality assessment: preparation, evaluation, summarization, and recommendations. A distinction between a quality assessment and a quality audit should be noted. A quality audit, as recognized in current industry literature (e.g., an ISO 9000 registration audit), compares actual practices to the defined process or standard. A quality assessment is concerned with what is occurring, what will be the likely results, and what needs to occur to correct discrepancies between the expected results and the desired results. A quality assessment is concerned with the quality status of the project rather than the state of process practices although there is likely correlation among the two. To achieve an

---

1. This chapter is a revision of the paper "A Quality Assessment Process for Products Under Development" by Diane Manlove and Stephen H. Kan, which was presented at the Ninth International Conference on Practical Software Quality Techniques (PSQT 2001 North), St. Paul, Minnesota, October 9–10, 2001.

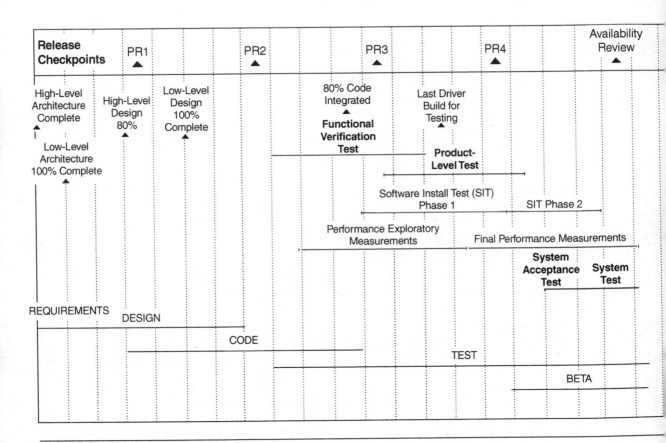

FIGURE 15.1
A Sample Schedule Showing Project Checkpoints

effective quality assessment, the development process, the environment, and the project plan must be well understood.

A quality assessment can be conducted by an independent team or by the quality professionals who are part of the project team. In-process quality assessment should be an integral part of project management. It should be conducted several times during the development cycle for medium and large projects. Figure 15.1 shows a combination of a simplified software project schedule, a high-level view of a development process, and a set of project management checkpoint reviews. The project checkpoint reviews, denoted PR1 through PR4, are the top row in the figure. For software projects with a development cycle time of one year or longer, it is not unusual to have four or five project checkpoint reviews. For rapid development projects that involve multiple teams and have a development cycle time of six months or shorter, it is preferable to have two or three checkpoint reviews. For small-team projects, formal project checkpoint reviews may not be necessary because the normal project management activities would be adequate to evaluate the overall health of the project. Project checkpoint reviews cover all aspects of the project such as schedule, function, quality, cost, and the overall readiness of the plans to support the delivery of the product. A candid assessment of the in-process quality status of the project should be an integral part of these checkpoint reviews; the following discussions of quality assessment are based on this scenario.

15.1 The Preparation Phase

The first phase of a quality assessment is the preparation phase. One must first understand the development process and the key activities and milestones of the project schedule, then identify where the project is relative to the phase of that development process and the project schedule. Medium and large software projects normally have many components with varying schedules under the rubric of overall system schedules. The majority of them, however, should be in the same phase at a given time.

15.1.1 What Data Should I Look At?

For projects with an iterative development process, the macro level of product development would contain phases such as analysis, design, code, test, and customer validation although at the micro level, selected components may still be going through the iterative cycles near the back end of the project schedule.

For each macro phase of the development process and project schedule, there is a set of data, both quantitative and qualitative, that gauges the development progress, helps to surface problems, and can provide a predictive indication of final product quality. Previous chapters contain many examples of phase-specific metrics and data.

In general, fewer data and metrics are available in the early phases of the development cycle. Those very early indicators are also less representative of final product quality than those at the back end of the development cycle. For example, the frequency of system crashes and hangs during the system test phase indicates better how the product will perform in the field than the number of defects found during unit testing. This does not mean quality assessments at the early cycles of the project are less important. One needs to make sure that the project is on track at every major phase in order to achieve the desirable final outcome. For example, positive indicators from the requirements and design phases mean that the stability and predictability of the back end of the development process will be better.

Suppose we are conducting a quality assessment for Project Checkpoint Review 1 (PR1) in the project depicted by Figure 15.1. The data to be gathered and assessed would be related to requirements and design such as progress of design complete, coverage and effectiveness indicators of design reviews, and so on. If one is conducting an assessment for PR2, then indicators pertaining to the status of coding activities and code integration into the system library, and builds and releases of drivers for testing will be pertinent. It is important to plan ahead the indicators, metrics, and information you intend to rely on for your assessment at various checkpoints. If you have a metrics program in place and have been tracking the necessary data on an ongoing basis, conducting quality assessments will be much easier. However, if you are starting from scratch at this point, don't despair. There are always data, information, and observations available that one can gather and analyze even when a metrics program is not in place. This is also a good time to start such a program and to demonstrate the value-added of the tracking system and the metrics.

15.1.2 Don't Overlook Qualitative Data

The preceding discussion implies quantitative data. *Qualitative* data is equally important, and at times even more so. We gather much of our qualitative data through one-on-one interviews or small group discussions. Information gathered via formal meetings such as the presentations from functional development teams are useful but usually need in-depth follow-up. We first determine *who* we want to talk to, then we prepare a list of *what* questions we want to ask. To determine the "who," think about the following:

- ☐ Whose input is key at this stage?
- ☐ Which people are the most knowledgeable about what's happening at this stage?
- ☐ Am I including people from a variety of areas (developers, testers, support groups) to give me a balanced view?

Checkpoint/ Development Phase	Common Quality Parameters	Examples of Project-Specific Parameters
PR1—Early design phase	Schedule feasibility Resources roll-off from the prior project Requirements clarification indicator Initial design progress	System risk assessment Line item prioritization Line item–level risk assessment
PR2—Usually at the code and unit test phases	Design status Estimated inspection defect removal effectiveness Code integration and drivers FVT S curve—planned, attempted, actual Defect arrivals—actual to plan Defect backlog—actual to plan	Test plan effectiveness indicators Indicators from test planning
PR3—Usually during Function Verification Test (FVT)	Plan churn FVT S curve—planned, attempted, actual Defect arrivals—release-to-release or to plan Defect backlog—release-to-release or to plan	National Language Version Testing indicators Solution testing indicators Translation verification test indicators Install test indicators Performance test and measurements
PR4 or Product Availability Checkpoint—usually in system test and beta phases	System test progress System stability Critical problems Defect arrivals Defect backlog Estimated overall defect removal effectiveness	CPU utilization System crashes and hangs Mean time to unplanned IPL (initial program load, or reboot) Install test Information development status Serviceability/upgrade test Internal beta Beta feedback/indicators

FIGURE 15.2
Quality Indicators by Checkpoint and Development Phase

To develop the list of questions, use both specific and open-ended questions. Open-ended questions are often the most useful. Here are some examples:

- ☐ Where are we?
- ☐ What's the outlook?
- ☐ Where are the weak areas?
- ☐ What are the risks?
- ☐ Are there any mitigation plans? What are they?
- ☐ How does this project compare to past projects in your assessment?

This last question helps to put the person's comments into perspective. Asking people to compare the current release to a specific past release puts all qualitative data into a similar frame of reference. During the preparation phase, we determine which past release or releases would be best for such comparison. For organizations without historical data for comparison or analysis of metric levels and trends, quality assessment planning may not be easy. For quality indicators that are well practiced in the industry (e.g., defect removal efficiency), targets can be based on industry benchmarks and best practices (Jones, 2000).

Figure 15.2 shows a list of quality indicators for quality assessment at various project checkpoints. The list includes both quantitative and qualitative indicators.

15.2 The Evaluation Phase

You figured out which data are important to look at and now you are ready to analyze and evaluate them. This is when one can apply all possible data analysis and statistical techniques to extract the messages within it.

15.2.1 Quantitative Data

For quantitative analysis tools such as control charts, trend charts, histograms, pareto diagrams, and scatter diagrams or statistical techniques ranging from simple tabulation analysis to sophisticated multivariate methods are all fair game. It is our experience that simple techniques can be very powerful and most of the time sophisticated statistical techniques are unnecessary. The key point is to garner useful information from the data. As discussed in previous chapters, we found that using the effort/outcome paradigm is particularly useful in assessing in-process metrics. Of course, the data gathered must include both effort indicators and outcome indicators in order to apply this approach, and this should be a consideration in the planning and preparation phase. At the least, from raw data to useful information, some meaningful comparisons with relevant baseline, plan, or a previous similar product need to take place.

When analyzing the data, it is always good practice to pay particular attention to anything unusual. Good questions to ask in such situations are, "What more can I learn about this?" and "How can I put this into perspective?" Figures 15.3, 15.4, and 15.5 include examples of data that bear further investigation. In Figure 15.3, Team A was significantly behind plan in its functional test and Component X had not even started its testing. In Figure 15.4, the defect arrival pattern of the current project differed from that for previous comparable projects. Was the higher defects volume in the early part of the defect curve due to more effective testing and better progress? Was the testing effectiveness and progress about the same as previous project at this point in the development cycle? In Figure 15.5, the test plan S-curve shows an unusual and potentially unachievable pattern.

15.2.2 Qualitative Data

For the qualitative evaluation, information from the interviews and open-ended probing can be classified, grouped, and correlated with existing knowledge and findings from quantitative analyses. The strongest proponents of quantitative methods argue that without metrics, an assessment is just another opinion. While quantitative data is important, our experience indicates that effective quality assessments are characteristically based on cross validation of findings and observations of both quantitative data and qualitative evaluation. Expert opinions also carry special weight. To that regard, the assessor should be equipped with acute observations to delineate whether the input he or she is getting is true expert opinion or opinion clouded by other factors. For example, opinions of the quality of the project may be optimistic by the

	% Attempted of Plan	% Successful of Plan	% Attempted of Total	% Successful of Total
Total	100.3	94.87	26.93	25.47
Team A	71.55	70.56	19.72	19.52
Team B	91.96	87.65	33.48	31.91
Team C	93.48	90.73	43.85	42.56
.... Etc.				
Component X	0	0	0	0

FIGURE 15.3

Data on Functional Tests that Beg for Further Investigation

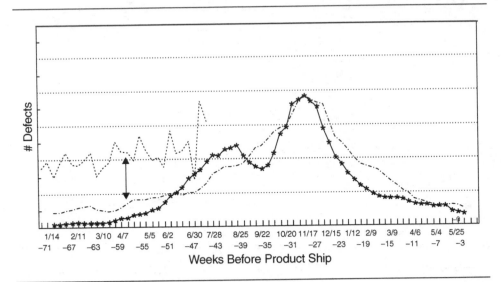

FIGURE 15.4
A Defect Arrival Pattern that Deviates from Historical Data

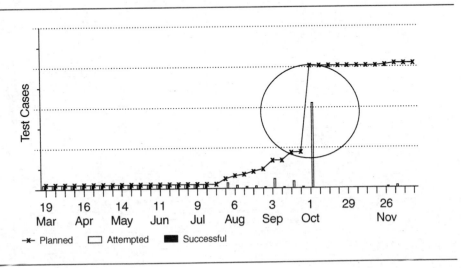

FIGURE 15.5
A Test Plan S Curve Showing an Unusual Pattern

development manager and pessimistic by the testing manager. It is not uncommon that at project checkpoint review meetings, the status of the project goes from excellent to poor, or vice versa, in just a few moments depending on the order of presentations by the development, support, testing, and service groups.

15.2.3 Evaluation Criteria

Evaluation of qualitative data is based on expert judgment and cross validation. For quantitative indicators, you may want to use predetermined criteria to ensure consistency. The following are sample criteria for evaluation of quantitative indicators:

☐ Green = actual within (<=) 5% behind or better than plan (model or a comparable previous project)

☐ Yellow = actual is between 5% and (<=) 15% behind plan (model or a comparable previous project)

☐ Red = actual is greater than 15% behind plan (model or a comparable previous project)

☐ For some indicators, specific considerations apply. For example, for testing defect arrivals, higher is better at earlier phases. After peaking, lower is better if testing effort is not compromised.

The following are sample criteria for a qualitative indicator (plan change):

☐ Green = no or small amount of plan changes after the commitment checkpoint of the project. No additional risks involved.

☐ Yellow = some amount of plan changes after the commitment checkpoint of the project, but not on critical line items of the project. Risks identified and assessed, and plans in place to mitigate and control risks.

☐ Red = plan changes on critical line items that took place after the project commitment checkpoint put the project at high risk. Assumptions at the commitment checkpoint are no longer valid.

The following shows sample criteria for an indicator that may require both qualitative and quantitative evaluation (design status):

☐ Green = no major design issues; design review status within (<=) 5% behind or ahead of plan.

☐ Yellow = design issues identified and plans being put in place to resolve, or design review status between 5% and (<=) 15% behind plan.

☐ Red = critical, project-gating design issues identified with no plans to resolve, or design reviews behind plan greater than 15%.

15.3 The Summarization Phase

This is the time to pull it all together. A good beginning is to look for recurring themes in the qualitative and quantitative data. For example, if a test expert comments that the testers seem to be finding a lot of problems in a certain component, and that component shows up in a pareto analysis as well, this is a good indication of a problem area.

15.3.1 Summarization Strategy

In summarizing the key issues and concerns, a quick analysis of the potential impacts of the identified problem areas can help rank the issues properly. For instance, the discovery of several low-severity problems in one area might not be a major concern, but a potential installation problem that customers will run into first thing when they install the product could be a very big deal. To put the information into perspective, one might compare a potential problem to a similar problem that occurred with a competitor's product or a discovery in a past beta test. Furthermore, in summarizing data, don't forget to identify what's done *right*. This information can be every bit as useful as the problem areas. If an incremental improvement in one component's code inspection process that resulted in nearly problem-free testing for that component during functional test, this could potentially provide a major breakthrough for the quality improvement effort of the entire team.

We found the format in Table 15.1 useful for summarizing and displaying the results. Each row shows a different quality parameter, listed in the first column. We often include key findings from the metrics or comments and information from interviews in the "observations" column. The final column shows an assessment for each parameter. At each interview, we ask for a "thumbs up" or "thumbs down" of the project compared with a previous similar project, and an overall assessment with regard to the project's quality goals. However, it's the assessor's overall equalizing judgment that goes on the final assessment, as shown in the table.

Table 15.1 shows only a sample of the parameters and their assessment summary. The set of parameters for a quality assessment should include all pertinent attributes of the project's quality objectives and development activities associated with those attributes. Some of the parameters may be phase-specific and others applicable for most of the development cycle. (See Figure 15.2 for a list of parameters.)

15.3.2 The Overall Assessment

In each assessment we provide an overall assessment as the "bottom line." The overall assessment should be developed with regard to the quality, function, and schedule objectives. In other words, "What is the likelihood that the product will meet quality

TABLE 15.1
Example Format for Summarizing Data

Indicator	Observations	Assessment
Design reviews	100% complete, earlier than comparison project relative to months to product ship date	Green
Code inspections	95% complete; tracking close to plan	Green
Function integration (to system library)	92% of function integrated by Driver Y; code integration and driver build (used for formal testing) executing to plan	Green
Function verification test	Test progress tracking close to a comparison project, but is 6% behind plan; concern with a critical item (EY) being late; risk mitigation plans in place	Yellow
Test defect arrivals	Tracking close to a comparison project; concern with delayed defect arrivals because of the late start of testing of item EY	Yellow
Test defect backlog	Good early focus; expect level to grow as arrivals peak, but currently below plan	Yellow
Install testing	98% of planned test cases attempted, and 95% successful; 60% into test cycle	Green
Late change	Late changes for tuning and scaling and for preventing performance degradation; plans to mitigate the impact of system stability not yet in place	Red
System test	Concern with availability of a key hardware product for the test environment to fully function	NA (too early)

objectives with the current content and schedule?" The overall assessment should be an integrated element in the project risk management process.

It is important to develop criteria for each level of the scale that you can clearly communicate along with your final assessment. It is useful to develop criteria that can be used over time and across multiple assessments. The following is an example of an overall quality assessment scale.

- ☐ Red = high probability of not meeting product quality goals or customer quality expectations
- ☐ Yellow = moderate risk of not meeting product quality goals or customer quality expectations
- ☐ Green = likely to meet product quality goals and satisfy customer quality expectations

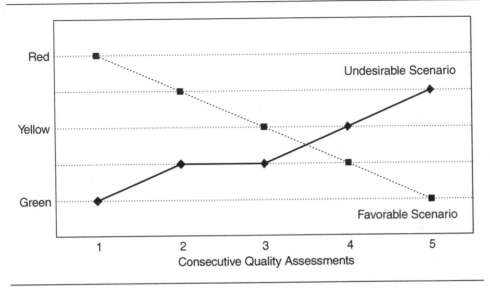

FIGURE 15.6
Scenarios of Quality Assessment Ratings of a Project over Time

Figure 15.6 displays potential quality assessment ratings over the project check-point reviews for two scenarios. Apparently the scenario of steadily declining assessment rating (from red to green) is more favorable. This trend might occur when a company is developing a cutting-edge product. In any project, the risks and unknowns could be very high early on, resulting in an overall assessment of "Red." Ideally, as the project progresses, the risks are addressed and problems resolved, thus improving the product's potential for meeting quality objectives.

The second scenario is undesirable not only because the final rating is poor, but also because the ratings worsen over time and initial ratings suggest low risk. While it is entirely possible for a project risk to increase (loss of key personnel would be one example), one should examine early positive ratings closely. It can be difficult to identify risks early in a project, but failure to do so can result in false positive ratings. In the early phases of a project, there are few concrete indicators, much less quantitative metrics, and it is human to assume no news is good news. The challenge to the quality professionals who conduct quality assessments is to make use of all fuzzy information and murky indicators to come up with a candid assessment.

15.4 Recommendations and Risk Mitigation

Recommendations are really part of the assessment summary, not a separate phase in the assessment process, but they are so important we put them in a separate section.

Developing recommendations is probably the most challenging part of the assessment, but it can also be the most beneficial part for the project.

There is no magic formula for developing recommendations. Just as the problems you identify will probably be unique for every assessment you do, so will the solutions and recommendations. However, reviewing good project management and risk mitigation techniques is useful for developing recommendations. A good understanding of the findings of software assessments and best practices in the industry will be helpful (for example, see Jones, 2000). Can dependency management help to resolve the potential for late test completion that you identified? Is more detailed planning required to successfully implement a new beta program? Can resources be shared across component teams of the project? If you are the project manager assessing the quality status of your project, this is the time to put your project manager hat back on. If you are the quality expert on the project team who is responsible for quality assessments, at this phase you need to think like a project manager.

Identification of risks and risk management is an important aspect of any assessment. It is akin to making a recommendation on a project checkpoint and is useful in determining the impact, consequences, or probable outcome of findings. Risk mitigation techniques include containing, reducing, or eliminating the risk. Table 15.2 shows risk management strategies as defined by the Project Management Institute,

TABLE 15.2
Risk Mitigation Strategies

Strategy	Definition	Example
Contain	Minimize the occurrence of effect of the risk.	Establish and enforce a checklist for code integration (into the system library) to minimize problems during the driver build process.
Contingency	Create an action plan in case the risk occurs.	Develop an incentive program for additional defect removal at "development complete" that involves testers, developers, and service specialists who have good customer perspectives in the event that defect arrival during the system test phase is higher than desirable (an indication of more latent defects in the product).
Transfer	Transfer all or part of the risk to another party.	
Ignore/ accept	Accept the consequences if the risk occurs.	
Avoid	Avoid the risk as in □ Use a different type of process. □ Eliminate the feature.	Identify functions that can be removed if schedule pressures occur.

along with several examples. Brainstorming ideas for each type of strategy can help you to surface a viable solution to a risk or problem.

15.5 Summary

In-process quality assessments help you understand if your project is on target to meet its quality objectives. Good assessments require good planning, analysis, evaluation, summarization, and recommendations. Quality assessments should be integrated in the project risk management process. This chapter discusses a four-step process of in-process quality assessment. Here are a few final thoughts regarding quality assessments.

Be sure to retain a copy of quality assessments for your records. A thorough quality assessment package provides data that can be useful references in future assessments. It can also help to provide a frame of reference, particularly for determining overall assessment ratings. For future quality assessments of the same project (i.e., assessments at later checkpoints), it is a good idea to review prior assessments to identify if past problems were addressed and what actions were effective.

It is good practice to record lessons learned for future assessments to avoid repeating unsatisfactory actions and to streamline the process. Right after you complete an assessment is a good time to make plans to start tracking for future products, the data that you wish you would have had for this assessment. It is also a good time to consider what data you'll need for future assessments of the current project. When a project is launched, the first document to be reviewed should be the list of lessons learned from previous projects.

Finally, the quality of a quality assessment depends on three factors: the assessment method and process; the information, integrity and quality of the data used for the assessment; and the assessor. We have discussed a simple process that is based on our experience with numerous assessments and which we believe is robust. We emphasize the importance of making use of all pertinent indicators, quantitative and qualitative, with cross-validation. The quality and integrity of the data can never be overstated. The assessor can be experienced or inexperienced. Regardless of the assessor's experience, the worst assessment is perhaps one that is done mechanically via some kind of checklist approach without adequate support of actual data, specific information, and in-depth probing and analysis. It is the assessor's responsibility to make sure that the undertaking of a Quality Assessment is entirely different from the practice of "passive checking of conformance to rules" (Gunter, 1998). Once findings are determined, recommendations should be made and risks assessed and managed.

References

1. Gunter, B., "Farewell Fusillade: An Unvarnished Opinion on the State of the Quality Profession," *Quality Progress,* April 1998, pp. 111–119.
2. Jones, C., "Critical Problems in Software Measurement," Burlington, Mass.: Software Productivity Research, 1992.
3. Jones, C., *Assessment and Control of Software Risks,* Englewood Cliffs, N. J.: Yourdon Press, 1994.
4. Jones, C., *Applied Software Measurement, Assuring Productivity and Quality,* 2nd ed., New York: McGraw-Hill, 1997.
5. Jones, C., *Software Assessments, Benchmarks, and Best Practices,* Boston: Addison-Wesley, 2000.
6. Mills, C. A., *The Quality Audit,* Milwaukee, Wisc.: McGraw-Hill, 1989.
7. PMI., *A Guide to Project Management Body of Knowledge,* Newton Square, PA: Project Management Institute, 1996.

16

Conducting Software Project Assessments

In this chapter we discuss how to conduct software project assessments.[1] The *scope of a project assessment* includes the end to end methodologies for the development and management of the project. *Development methodologies* refer to the development process from requirements and specifications, to design, code, integration and driver build, testing, and early customer programs (when applicable), tools and development environment, sizing and schedule development, dependency management, and overall project management. The level and scope of concern here is different from the discussions in the last chapter in which the focus of interest was to determine a project's in-process quality status and whether it is on track to achieve its quality objectives. Here we are concerned with the overall development effectiveness and efficiency, and improvement opportunities. In-process quality assessments are key activities of the project quality management effort and conducted by members of the project team. Project assessments are invariably conducted by people external to the project team. A project assessment can be conducted when the project is under development or when it is complete. Usually, a project assessment is triggered by

---

1. An earlier version of this chapter was presented by Stephan H. Kan and Diane Manlove at the Tenth International Conference on Practical Software Quality Techniques (PSQT 2002 North), St. Paul, Minnesota, September 10–11, 2002.

some unfavorable field results, with the intent to improve a follow-on release or another project by the same team.

Software assessments, which originated from the need for improvement in the software industry, started in the 1960s and 1970s as informal assessments. Since then software assessments have evolved into formal software process assessments based on the maturity concept and standard questionnaires. In recent years, they have become a fast growing subindustry. Arguably, the standard assessment approaches all gear toward the organization level as the assessment unit. At the same time, in software development organizations, managers continue to ask the original question: How do I improve my project or how do I perform my next project better. Conducting project assessments for their organization is still the bona fide responsibility of software quality professionals. Peer reviews of projects are also common in software development organizations. The assessment unit of these project assessments, by definition, is at the project level. These kinds of project assessments, not organizational-level process assessments, are the subject of this chapter. The interest is on assessing a specific project for immediate improvement actions or for a small number of projects for identifying best practices. We propose a systematic approach for conducting software project assessments.

16.1 Audit and Assessment

It is important to recognize the difference between an audit and an assessment (Zahran, 1997). The IEEE's definition (IEEE-STD-610) of an audit is as follows:

> An independent examination of a work product or set of work products to assess compliance with specifications, standards, contractual agreements, or other criteria.

According to ISO documents (ISO 9000-3), the concepts of certification and audit are defined as follows:

> Certification, or third-party assessment (referred to as registration in some countries), is carried out by an independent organization against a particular standard.

The outcome of an audit is in compliance or not in compliance, or pass or fail. Humphrey's view is that "a software process assessment is not an audit but a review of a software organization to advise its management and professionals on how they can improve their operation" (Humphrey, 1989, p. 149). Zahran (1997, p. 149) provides a comprehensive definition of a software process assessment and its objectives according to the maturity framework:

A software process assessment is a disciplined examination of the software processes used by an organization, based on a process model. The objective is to determine the maturity level of those processes, as measured against a process improvement road map. The result should identify and characterize current practices, identifying areas of strengths and weaknesses, and the ability of current practices to control or avoid significant causes of poor (software) quality, cost, and schedule. The assessment findings can also be used as indicators of the capability of those processes to achieve the quality, cost, and schedule goals of software development with a high degree of predictability. (p. 149)

Depending on who plays the key role in an assessment, a software assessment (or audit) can be a self-assessment (or first-party assessment), a second-party assessment, or a third-party assessment. A self-assessment is performed internally by an organization's own personnel. A second-party or third-party assessment is performed by an external party. The assessing party can be the second party (e.g., a company hires an external assessment team, or a company is being assessed by a customer) or the third party (e.g., a supplier is being assessed by a third party to verify its ability to enter contracts with a customer).

In the SEI (Software Engineering Institute at Carnegie Mellon University) terminology, a distinction is made between software process assessments and software capability evaluations because the two differ in motivation, objective, outcome, and ownership of the results. Software capability evaluations are used by the Department of Defense (DoD) and other major customers for selection and monitoring of software contractors or for assessing the risks associated with the procurement of a given product. The results are known to DoD or the initiator of the evaluation, and no member of the organization being evaluated is on the evaluation team. They are conducted in a more audit-oriented environment. Software process assessments, in contrast, are performed in an open, collaborative environment. They are for the use of the organization to improve its software process, and results are confidential to the organization. The organization being assessed must have members on the assessment team (Zahran, 1997). With the move to the Standard CMMI[sm] Appraisal Method for Process Improvement (SCAMPI[sm]) by SEI, this distinction is going away (Software Engineering Institute, 2000). The same assessment method will be used both for internal improvement and external source selection.

16.2 Software Process Maturity Assessment and Software Project Assessment

The scope of a software process assessment can cover all processes in the organization, a selected subset of the software processes, or a specific project. For most process assessments that are based on the maturity concept, the target unit of analysis and rating is normally at the organizational level. In fact, most of the standard-based process assessment approaches are invariably based on the concept of process maturity. This is the case for the SEI (Software Engineering Institute at Carnegie Mellon University) capability maturity model (CMM), the SPR (Software Productivity Research, Inc.) approach, the Trillium model (a CMM-based model developed by a consortium of telecommunications companies, headed by Bell Canada), as well as the recently developed BOOTSTRAP methodology (the result of a European Community project) and the ISO/IEC 15504 draft standard (Zahran, 1997).

When the assessment target is the organization, the results of a process assessment may differ, even on successive applications of the same method. Paulk and colleagues (1995) explain the two reasons for the different results. First, the organization being investigated must be determined. For a large company, several definitions of *organization* are possible and therefore the actual scope of appraisal may differ in successive assessments. Second, even in what appears to be the same organization, the sample of projects selected to represent the organization may affect the scope and outcome. This project sampling effect can be substantial for large organizations with a variety of projects.

When the target unit of assessment is at the project level, the potential problems associated with organizational-level assessments just discussed are not relevant. The ambiguities and vagueness with regard to assessment results do not exist. Furthermore, some process dimensions of a standard process assessment method may not apply to a specific project. On the other hand, a software project assessment should include all meaningful factors that contribute to the success or failure of the project. It should not be limited by established dimensions of a given process maturity model. One should assess not only the processes of the project, but also the degree of implementation and their effectiveness as substantiated by project data. Project assessments address "hows" and "whys" with sufficient depth, in addition to the "whats." Therefore, exploratory and in-depth probing are key characteristics of software project assessments. In this regard, the standard questionnaires used by the maturity assessment models may not be sufficient. It is well known that the standard questionnaires address the "whats" but not the "hows" by design so that each organization can optimize its own approach to process maturity. Because of this inherent limitation of standard questionnaires, standard-based process assessment models also rely on other data gathering methods such as document reviews and extensive interviewing.

In addition to the difference in the unit of analysis, the very concept of process maturity may not be applicable to the project level. What matters is the success or failure of the project, as measured in field performance and development effectiveness and efficiency. If the projects achieve measurable improvement, whether or not a certain set of process activities is being practiced, or a certain maturity level is achieved, is not relevant. If a project fails, the remedial actions have to aim directly at the causes of failure. Process maturity becomes relevant when an organization intends to embark on an overall long-term improvement strategy. Even then, the additional value derived from the implementation of additional process elements needs to be monitored and verified at the project level.

Software project assessments, informal or formal, must be independent assessments in order to be objective. The assessment team may be in the same organization but must be under a different management chain from the project team. It may come from a different division of the company, it could be an external team, or it could be a combination of internal personnel and external consultants.

The necessity of and demand for project assessments exist regardless of whether the organization is pursuing a long-term process maturity improvement strategy. Within an organization of a specific maturity level, there are always variations among projects with regard to the state of practices of development methodologies, how they are implemented and why, and their correlation with the project outcome. The two types of assessment can be complementary: the process maturity assessments for overall improvement strategy for the organization and specific project assessments to drive immediate and specific improvement actions at the project level. With customization and a shift in the assessment focus (unit of analysis), standard process assessment methods might be applied to project assessments. For small organizations with a few projects, the distinction between a process maturity assessment and a project assessment may be blurred.

16.3 Software Process Assessment Cycle

According to Paulk and colleagues (1995), the CMM-based assessment approach uses a six-step cycle. The first step is to select a team. The members of the team should be professionals knowledgeable in software engineering and management. In the second step, the representatives of the site to be appraised complete the standard process maturity questionnaire. Then the assessment team performs an analysis of the questionnaire responses and identifies areas that warrant further exploration according to the CMM key process areas. The fourth step is for the assessment team to conduct a site visit to gain an understanding of the software process followed by the site. At the end of the site visit comes step 5, when the assessment team produces a list of findings that identifies the strengths and weakness of the organization's software process. Finally, the assessment team prepares a key process area (KPA) profile analysis and presents the results to the appropriate audience.

The SEI also developed and published the CMM-Based Appraisal for Internal Process Improvement (CBA IPI) (Dunaway and Masters, 1996). The data collected for CBA IPI is based on key process areas of the CMM as well as non-CMM issues. For an assessment to be considered a CBA IPI, the assessment must meet minimum requirements concerning (1) the assessment team, (2) the assessment plan, (3) data collection, (4) data validation, (5) the rating, and (6) the reporting of assessment results. For example, the assessment team must be led by an authorized SEI Lead Assessor. The team shall consist of between 4 and 10 team members. At least one team member must be from the organization being assessed, and all team members must complete the SEI's Introduction to the CMM course (or its equivalent) and the SEI's CBA IPI team training course. Team members must also meet some selection guidelines. With regard to data collection, the CBA IPI relies on four methods: the standard maturity questionnaire, individual and group interviews, document reviews, and feedback from the review of the draft findings with the assessment participants.

The Standard CMMI Assessment Method for Process Improvement (SCAMPI), developed to satisfy the CMMI model requirements (Software Engineering Institute, 2000), is more stringent than CBA IPI. Both the CBA IPI and the SCAMPI consist of three phases: plan and preparation, conducting the assessment onsite, and reporting results. The activities for the plan and preparation phase include:

- ☐ Identify assessment scope.
- ☐ Develop the assessment plan.
- ☐ Prepare and train the assessment team.
- ☐ Make a brief assessment of participants.
- ☐ Administer the CMMI Appraisal Questionnaire.
- ☐ Examine Questionnaire responses.
- ☐ Conduct initial document review.

The activities for the onsite assessment phase include:

- ☐ Conduct an opening meeting.
- ☐ Conduct interviews.
- ☐ Consolidate information.
- ☐ Prepare presentation of draft findings.
- ☐ Present draft findings.
- ☐ Consolidate, rate, and prepare final findings.

The activities of the reporting results phase include:

- ☐ Present final findings.
- ☐ Conduct executive session.
- ☐ Wrap up the assessment.

The description of the CBA IPI and the SCAMPI assessment cycle appears to be more elaborate. Its resemblance to the assessment approach outlined by Paulk and colleagues in 1995 remains obvious.

The SPR assessment process involves similar steps (Jones, 1994). The initial step is an assessment kickoff session (1), followed by project data collection (2), and then individual project analysis (3). A parallel track is to conduct management interviews (4). The two tracks then merge for benchmark comparison, aggregate analysis, and interpretation (5). The final phase is measurement report and improvement opportunities (6). Data collection and interviews are based on the structured SPR

TABLE 16.1

Zahran's Generic Phases and Main Activities of Software Process Assessment

Phase	Sub-phase	Main activities
Preassessment	Preplanning	Understanding of business context and justification, objectives, and constraints Securing sponsorship and commitment
Assessment	Planning	Selection of assessment approach Selection of improvement road map Definition of assessment boundaries Selection of assessment team Launching the assessment Training the assessment team Planning fact gathering, fact analysis and reporting activities
	Fact gathering	Selecting a fact gathering approach (e.g., questionnaire, interviews, and group discussion) Defining the target interviewees Distributing and collecting questionnaire responses Conducting the interviews
	Fact analysis	Analysis of questionnaire responses Analysis of facts gathered in the interviews Analysis of the evidence gathered Collective analysis of the data gathered Calibration of the findings against the road map Identifying strengths and weaknesses and areas of improvement
	Reporting	Documenting the findings: strengths and weaknesses Documenting the recommendations
Postassessment	Action plan for process improvement	Implementing the process improvement actions Managing and monitoring the process improvement plan

From *Software Process Improvement, Practical Guidelines for Business Success,* by Sami Zahran (Table 8.3, p. 161). © 1998 Addison-Wesley Longman. Reprinted by permission of Pearson Education, Inc.

assessment questionnaire. The SPR assessment approach uses multiple models and does not assume the same process steps and activities for all types of software.

While each assessment approach has its unique characteristics, a common schema should apply to all. Zahran (1997) developed a generic cycle of process assessment that includes four phases: planning, fact finding, fact analysis, and reporting. Besides the assessment cycle per se, a preassessment and preplanning phase and a postassessment and process improvement plan phase are in Zahran's generic cycle. The main activities of the phases are shown in Table 16.1.

The generic phases and the main activities within each phase serve as a useful overall framework for assessment projects. Zahran also successfully mapped the current process assessment approaches into this framework, including the CMM, the Trillium model, the BOOTSTRAP methodology, and the ISO/IEC 15504 draft standard for software process assessment. In the next sections when we discuss our method for software project assessments, we will refer to the main activities in this framework as appropriate.

16.4 A Proposed Software Project Assessment Method

We propose a software project assessment method as shown in Figure 16.1, which is based on our project assessment experience over the past many years. We will discuss each phase with some details, but first there are several characteristics of this method that may be different from other assessment approaches:

- ☐ It is project based.
- ☐ There are two phases of facts gathering and the phase of a complete project review precedes other methods of data collection. Because the focus is on the project, it is important to understand the complete project history and end-to-end processes from the project team's perspective before imposing a questionnaire on the team.
- ☐ This method does not rely on a standard questionnaire. There may be a questionnaire in place from previous assessments, or some repository of pertinent questions maintained by the process group of the organization. There may be no questionnaire in place and an initial set of questions needs to be developed in the preparation phase. In either case, customization of the questionnaire after a complete project review is crucial so that each and every question is relevant.
- ☐ Observations, analysis, and possible recommendations are part of an ongoing process beginning at the start of the assessment project. With each additional phase and input, the ongoing analysis and observations are being refuted, confirmed, or refined. This is an iterative process.
- ☐ The direct input by the project team/development team with regard to strengths and weaknesses and recommendations for improvement is important, as reflected in steps 3 through 6, although the final assessment still rests on the assessment team's shoulders.

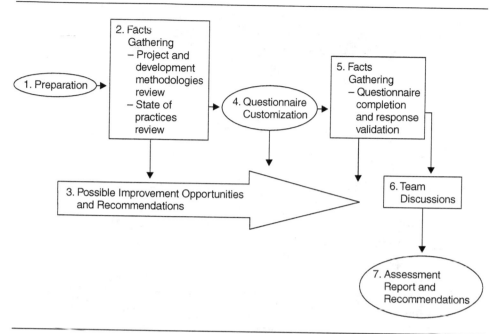

FIGURE 16.1
A Proposed Software Project Assessment Method

16.4.1 Preparation Phase

The preparation phase includes all planning and preparation. For an assessment team external to the organization whose project is to be assessed, a good understanding of the business context and justification, objectives, and commitment is important. Since most of the project assessments are done by personnel within the organization, or from a separate division of a company, this is normally not needed. In this phase, a request for basic project data should be made. General information on the type of software, size, functions, field performance, skills and experience of the development team, organizational structure, development process, and language used is important for the assessment team to start formulating some frames of reference for the assessment. This data doesn't have to be specific and precise and should be readily available from the project team. If there is no questionnaire from a previous similar project, the assessment team should start developing a battery of questions based on the basic project data. These questions can be revised and finalized when the facts gathering phase I is completed.

For overall planning, we recommend the assessment be run as a project with all applicable project management practices. It is important to put in place a project plan that covers all key phases and activities of the assessment. For internal assessments, a very important practice at the preparation phase is to obtain a project charter from the sponsor and commitment from the management team of the project being assessed. The project charter establishes the scope of the assessment and the authority of the assessment team. It should be one page or shorter and probably is best drafted by the assessment leader and signed and communicated by the sponsor executive.

Another easily neglected activity in the preparation phase is a project closeout plan. Good project management calls for planning for the closeout on day 1 of the project. A closeout plan in this case may include the kind of reports or presentations that will be delivered by the assessment team, the audience, and the format.

16.4.2 Facts Gathering Phase 1

The first phase of facts gathering involves detailed review of all aspects of the project from the project team's perspective. The format of this phase may be a series of project team's descriptions or presentations. In the assessment team's request for information, at least the following areas should be covered:

- ☐ Project description and basic project data (size, functions, schedule, key dates and milestones)
- ☐ Project and development team information (team size, skills, and experience)
- ☐ Project progress, development timeline, and project deliverables
- ☐ End-to-end development process from requirements to testing to product ship
- ☐ Sizing and schedule development, staffing
- ☐ Development environment and library system
- ☐ Tools and specific methodologies
- ☐ Project outcome or current project status
- ☐ Use of metrics, quantitative data, and indicators
- ☐ Project management practices
- ☐ Any aspects of the project that the project team deems important

The assessment team's role in this phase is to gather as much information as possible and gain a good understanding of the project. Therefore, the members should be in a listening mode and should not ask questions that may mislead the project team. Establishing the whats and hows of the project are the top priority, and sometimes it is necessary to get into the whys via probing techniques. For example, the project may have implemented a joint test phase between the development group and the independent test team to improve the test effectiveness of the project, and to make sure that the project meets the entry criteria of the system verification test (SVT) phase. This is a "what" of the actual project practices. The joint test phase was implemented at the end of the functional verification test (FVT) and before SVT start during the SVT acceptance test activities. Independent test team members and developers were paired for major component areas. The possible gaps between the FVT and the SVT plans were being tested. The testing environment was a network of testing systems maintained by the independent group for SVT test. To increase the chances for latent defects to surface, the test systems were stressed by running a set of performance workloads in the background. This test phase was implemented because meeting SVT entrance criteria on time had been a problem in the past, and due to the formal hand-off between FVT and SVT, it was felt that there was room for improvement with regard to the communication between developers and independent testers. The project team thinks that this joint test practice contributed significantly to the success of the project because a number of additional defects were found before SVT (as supported by metrics), SVT entrance criteria were met on time, the testers and developers learned from each other and improved their communications as a result, and the test added only minimum time to the testing schedule so it didn't negatively affect the project completion date. These are the "hows" and "whys" of the actual implementation. During the project review, the project team may describe this practice briefly. It is up to the assessment team to ask the right questions to get the details with regard to hows and whys.

At the end of a project review, critical success factors or major reasons for failure should be discussed. These factors may also include sociological factors of software development, which are important (Curtis et al., 2001; DeMarco and Lister, 1999; Jones, 1994, 2000). For the entire review process, the assessment team's detailed note-taking is important. If the assessment team consists of more than one person and the project review lasts more than one day, discussions and exchange of thoughts among the assessment team members is always a good practice.

16.4.3 Questionnaire Customization and Finalization

Now that the assessment team has gained a good understanding of the project, the next step is to customize and finalize the questionnaire for formal data collection. The assumption here is that a questionnaire is in place. It may be from a previous assessment project, developed over time from the assessment team's experience, from a repository of questions maintained by the software engineering process group (SEPG) of the organization, or from a prior customization of a standard questionnaire of a software process assessment method. If this is not the case, then initial questionnaire construction should be a major activity in the preparation phase, as previously mentioned.

Note that in peer reviews (versus an assessment that is chartered by an executive sponsor), a formal questionnaire is not always used.

There are several important considerations in the construction and finalization of a questionnaire. First, if the questionnaire is a customized version of a standard questionnaire from one of the formal process assessment methods (e.g., CMM, SPR, and ISO software process assessment guidelines), it must be able to elicit more specific information. The standard questionnaires related to process maturity assessment usually are at a higher level than is desirable at the project level. For example, the following are the first three questions of the Peer Reviews key process activity (KPA) in the CMM maturity questionnaire (Zubrow et al., 1994).

1. Are peer reviews planned? (Yes, No, Does Not Apply, Don't Know)
2. Are actions associated with defects that are identified during peer reviews tracked until they are resolved?
3. Does the project follow a written organizational policy for performing peer reviews?

The following two questions related to peer design reviews were used in some project assessments we conducted:

1. What is the most common form of design reviews for this project?
   □ Formal review meeting with moderators, reviewers, and defect tracking, and issue resolution and rework completion are part of the completion criteria
   □ Formal review but issue resolution is up to the owner
   □ Informal review by experts of related areas
   □ Codevelper (codesigner) informal review
   □ Other ..... please specify
2. To what extent were design reviews of the project conducted? (Please mark the appropriate cell in each row in the table)

	All Design Work Done Rigorously	All Major Pieces of Design Items	Selected Items Based on Criteria (e.g., Error Recovery)	Design Reviews Were Occasionally Done	Not Done
Original design					
Design changes/ rework					

The differences between the two set of questions are obvious: One focuses on process maturity and organizational policy and the other focuses on specific project practices and degree of execution.

Second, a major objective of a project assessment is to identify the gaps and therefore opportunities for improvement. To elicit input from the project team, the vignette-question approach in questionnaire design can be used with regard to importance of activities in the development process. Specifically, the vignette questions include a question on the state of practice for the specific activity by the project and another question on the project team's assessment of the importance of that activity. The three following questions provide an example of this approach:

1. Are there entry/exit criteria used for the independent system verification test phase?
   If yes,   (a) please provide a brief description.
              (b) how is the criteria used and enforced?
2. Per your experience and assessment, how important is this practice (entry/exit criteria for SVT) to the success of the project?
   □ Very important
   □ Important
   □ Somewhat important
   □ Not sure
3. If your assessment in question 2 is "very important" or "important" and your project's actual practice did not match the level of importance, what were the reasons for the disparity (e.g., obstacles, constraints, process, culture)? Please explain.

Third, it is wise to ask for the team's direct input on strengths and weaknesses of the project's practices in each major area of the development process (e.g., design, code, test, and project management). The following are the two common questions we used in every questionnaire at the end of each section of questions. *Caution:* These questions should not be asked before a description of the overall project practices are completed (by the project team) and understood (by the assessment team), otherwise the project team will be led prematurely to a self-evaluative mode. In this assessment method, there are two phases of facts gathering and asking these questions at the second phase is part of the design of the method.

1. Is there any practice(s) by your project with regard to testing that you consider to be a strength and that should be considered for implementation by other projects? If so, please describe and explain.
2. If you were to do this project all over again, what would you do differently with regard to testing and why?

The Appendix in this book shows a questionnaire that we have used as a base for customization for many software project assessments.

16.4.4 Facts Gathering Phase 2

In this phase, the questionnaire is administered to the project team including development managers, the project manager, and technical leads. The respondents complete the questionnaire separately. All sections of the questionnaire may not apply to all respondents. The responses are then analyzed by the assessment team and validated via a session with the project team. Conflicts of responses among the respondents and between information from the project review and the questionnaire responses should be discussed and resolved. The assessment team can also take up any topic for further probing. At the second half of the session, a brainstorming session on strengths and weaknesses, what's done right, what's done wrong, and what would the project team have done differently is highly recommended.

16.4.5 Possible Improvement Opportunities and Recommendations

As Figure 16.1 depicts, this phase runs parallel with other phases, starting from the preparation phase and ending with the final assessment report phase. Assessing the project's strengths and weakness and providing recommendations for improvement constitute the purpose of a project assessment. Because the quality of the observations and recommendations is critical, this activity should not be done mechanically. To accomplish this important task, the assessment team can draw on three sources of information:

1. *Findings from the literature.* For example, Jones (1994, 1995, 2000) provides an excellent summary of the risks and pitfalls of software projects, and benchmarks and best practices by types of software, based on the SPR's experiences in software assessment. Another example is the assessment results from the CMM-based assessments published by the SEI. A familiarity with the frameworks and findings in the assessment literature enhances the breadth of the assessment team's framework for development of recommendations. Of course, you cannot use the findings in the literature for recommendations unless they are pertinent to the project being assessed. Those findings are great references, however, so the big-picture view will be maintained while combing through the tremendous amount of project-specific information. Based on Jones's findings (2002), the most significant factors associated with success and failure are the following:

Successful projects
- Effective project planning
- Effective project cost estimating
- Effective project measurements
- Effective project milestone tracking
- Effective project quality control
- Effective project change management
- Effective development processes
- Effective communications
- Capable project managers
- Capable technical personnel
- Significant use of specialists
- Substantial volume of reusable materials

Failing projects

- Inadequate project planning
- Inadequate cost estimating
- Inadequate measurements
- Inadequate milestone tracking
- Inadequate quality control
- Ineffective change control
- Ineffective development processes
- Ineffective communications
- Ineffective project managers
- Inexperienced technical personnel
- Generalists rather than specialists
- Little or no reuse of technical material

2. *Experience:* The assessment team's experience and findings from previous project assessments are essential. What works and what doesn't, for what types of projects, under what kind of environment, organization, and culture? This experience-based knowledge is extremely valuable. This factor is especially important for internal project assessments. When sufficient findings from various projects in one organization are accumulated, patterns of successes and failure may emerge. This is related to the concept of the experience factory discussed by Basili (1995).

3. *Direct input from the project team.* As discussed earlier in the chapter, we recommend placing direct questions in the questionnaire on strengths and weakness, and what the team would do differently. Direct input from the team provides an insider's view and at the same time implies feasibility of the suggested improvement opportunities. Many consultants and assessors know well that in-depth observations and good recommendations often come from the project team itself. Of course, the assessment team must evaluate the input and decide whether or not, and what part of, the project team's input will become their recommendations.

Jones's findings highlight the importance of good project management and project management methods such as estimating, measurements, and tracking and control. Sizing and schedule development without the support of metrics and experience from previous projects can lead to overcommitment and therefore project failure. This can happen even in well-established development organizations.

When developing improvement recommendations, feasibility of implementation in the organization's environment should be considered. In this regard, the assessment team should think like a project manager, software development managers, and team leaders. At the same time, recommendations for strategic improvements that may pose challenges to the team should not be overlooked. In this regard, the assessment team should think like the strategist of the organization. In other words, there should be two sets of recommendations and the assessment team ought to wear two hats when developing the recommendations. In either case, recommendations should be based on facts and analysis and should never be coverage-checklist type items.

As an example, the following segment of recommendations is extracted from a project assessment report that we were involved with. This segment addresses the intersite communication of a cross-site development project.

> It was not apparent as to whether there were trust issues between the two development teams. However, given that the two teams have never worked together on the same project and the different environments at the two sites, there is bound to be at least some level of unfamiliarity if not a lack of trust. The following techniques could be employed to address these issues.
>
> □ Nothing can replace face-to-face interaction. If the budget allows it, make time for the Leadership Team (managers, technical leads, project leads) to get together for face-to-face interaction. A quarterly "Leadership Summit" can be useful to review the results of the last 90 days and establish goals for the next 90 days. The social interaction during and after these meetings is as important as the technical content of meetings.
>
> □ A close alternative to travel and face-to-face meetings is the use of video conferencing. Find a way to make video conference equipment available to your teams and encourage its use. While it is quite easy to be distracted with mail or other duties while on a teleconference call, it is much more difficult to get away with it on a video conference. Seeing one another as points are raised in a meeting allows for a measure of nonverbal communication to take place. In addition, the cameras can be focused on the white boards to hold chalk talks or discuss design issues.
>
> □ A simple thing that can be done to enhance cross-site communications is to place a picture board at each site with pictures of all team members.
>
> □ Stress the importance of a single, cross-site team in all area communications and make sure the Leadership Team has completely bought into and is promoting this concept. Ensure processes, decisions, and communications are based on technical merit without unwarranted division by site. One simple example is that the use of site-specific distribution lists may promote communications divided between the sites. We recommend the leadership team work to abolish use of these lists and establish distribution lists based on the needs and tasks of the project.

16.4.6 Team Discussions of Assessment Results and Recommendations

In this phase, the assessment team discusses its findings and draft recommendations with the project team and obtains its feedback before the final report is completed. The two teams may not be in total agreement, and it is important that the assessment team make such a declaration before the session takes place. Nonetheless, this phase is important because it serves as a validation mechanism and increases the buy-in of the project team.

16.4.7 Assessment Report

The format of the report may vary (a summary presentation, a final written report, or both) but a formal meeting to present the report is highly recommended. With regard to content, at least the following topics should be covered:

- ☐ Project information and basic project data
- ☐ The assessment approach
- ☐ Brief descriptions and observations of the project's practices (development process, project management, etc.)
- ☐ Strengths and weaknesses, and if appropriate, gap analysis
- ☐ Critical success factors or major project pitfalls
- ☐ What the project team would do differently (improvements from the project team's perspective)
- ☐ Recommendations

Tables 16.2 through 16.4 show report topics for three real assessed projects so you can relate the outcome to the points discussed earlier (for example, those on questionnaire construction). All three assessed projects were based on similar versions of the questionnaire in the Appendix. Project X is the software that supports the service processor of a computer system, Project Y is the microcode that supports a new hardware processor of a server, and Project Z is the software system that supports a family of disk storage subsystem products. The subsystem integrates hundreds of disk drives through a storage controller that provides redundant arrays of inexpensive disks (RAID), disk caching, devices emulation, and host attachment functions.

Table 16.2 shows the basic project data for the three projects. Table 16.3 summarizes the state of practices of key development and project management activities throughout the development cycle, and the project team's self-assessment of the importance of the specific practices. For most cells, the vignette of 'state of practice' and 'importance assessment' is shown. A gap exists where the importance assessment is Important or Very Important but the state of practice is No, Seldom, Occasionally, or Not Done.

The most gaps were identified for Project X, in the areas of requirements and reviews, specifications, design document in place to guide implementation, design reviews, effective sizing and bottom-up schedule development, major checkpoint reviews, staging and code drop plans, and in-process metrics.

For Project Y, gaps were in the areas of design document, design reviews, effective sizing and bottom-up schedule development, and in-process metrics. For Project

Z , the gaps were in the project management areas such as sizing and bottom-up schedule development as they related to the planning process and project assumptions. Development/unit test was also identified as a key gap as related to the Cleanroom software process used for the project. The Cleanroom software process focuses on specifications, design and design verification, and mathematical proof of program correctness. For testing, it focuses on statistical testing as it relates to customers' operations profiles (Mills et al., 1987). However, the process does not focus on program debug and does not include a development unit test phase (i.e., from coding directly to independent test). Furthermore, questions on scalability (e.g., large and complex projects with many interdependencies) and the feasibility of implementations of customer operations profiles were raised by critics of the process. For Project Z, the use of this development process was a top-down decision, and faulty productivity and quality assumptions related to this process were used in schedule development.

Table 16.4 shows the project team's improvement plan as a result of the iterative emphasis of the assessment method. Note that the project team's own improvement ideas or plan are separate from the final recommendations by the assessment team, although the latter can include or reference the former.

TABLE 16.2
Basic Project Data for Projects X, Y, and Z

	Project X	Project Y	Project Z
Size (KLOC)			
• Total	228	4000	1625
• New and changed	78	100	690
Team size	10.5	35	225
Development cycle time (mo)			
• Design to GA	30	18	38
• Design to development test complete	23	17	29
Team experience	Inexperienced 70% <2 yr	Very experienced 70% >5 yr some >15 yr	Very experienced 80% >5 yr
Cross-site development	Y	Y	Y
Cross-product brand development	Y	N	Y
Development environ/library	CMVC	PDL, Team Connect	AIX CMVC DEV2000
Project complexity (self-rated 10 pts)	7	8	10

TABLE 16.3
State of Practice, Importance Assessment, and Gap Analysis
for Projects X, Y, and Z

Project Activity	Project X	Project Y	Project Z
Requirements reviews	**-Seldom** **-Very important**	-Always -Very important	-Always -Very important
Develop specifications	**-Seldom** **-Very important**	-Usually -Very important	-Always -Very important
Design documents in place	**-No** **-Very important**	**-No** **-Very important**	-Yes -Very important
Design reviews	**-Not done** **-Very important**	**-Occasionally** **-Very important**	-Major pieces -Very important
Coding standard/ guidelines	-No	-Yes	-Yes
Unit test	-Yes - ad hoc	-Yes	-No
Simulation test/environment	**-No** **-Very important**	-Yes -Very important	**-No** **-Important**
Process to address code integration quality and driver stability	-Yes -Very important	-Yes -Very important	-Yes -Very important
Driver build interval	-Weekly – >Biweekly	-Biweekly with fix support	-1 – 3 days
Entry/exit Criteria for independent test	-Yes -Very important	-Yes -Very important	-Yes -Important
Change control process for fix integration	-Yes -Very important	-Yes -Very important	-Yes -Important
Microcode project manager in place	-Yes (midway through project)	-No	-No
Role of effective project management	-Very important	-Important	-Important
Effective sizing and bottom-up schedule development	**-No** **-Very important**	**-No** **-Important**	**-No** **-Very important**
Staging and code drop plans	**-No** **-Very important**	-Yes -Very important	-Yes -Important
Major checkpoint reviews	**-No** **-Very important**	-No Somewhat important	-Yes -Very important
In-process metrics	**-No (started** **midway)** **-Very important**	**-No** **-Very important**	-Yes -Somewhat important

TABLE 16.4
Project Teams' Improvement Plans Resulting from Assessment
of Projects X, Y, and Z

Project	Improvement Plan
Project X	
Requirements and specifications:	Freeze external requirements by a specific date. Create an overall specifications document before heading into the design phase for the components. Force requirements and specifications ownership early in the development cycle.
Design, code, and reviews:	Eliminate most/all shortcuts in design and code to get to and through bring-up. The code that goes into bring-up is the basis for shipping to customers and many times it is not the base that was desired to be working on. Establish project-specific development milestones and work to those instead of only the higher-level system mile-stones.
Code integration and driver build:	Increase focus on unit test for code integration quality, document unit test plans.
Test:	Establish entry/exit criteria for test and then adhere to them.
Project management (planning, schedule, dependency management, metrics):	Staff a project manager from the beginning. Have dependency management mapped to a specific site, and minimize cross-site dependency.
Tools and methodologies:	Use a more industry-standard toolset. Deploy the mobile toolset recently available on Thinkpad. Establish a skills workgroup to address the skills and education of the team.
Project Y	
Requirements and specifications:	Focus more on design flexibility and considerations that could deal with changing requirements.
Design, code, and reviews:	Conduct a more detailed design review for changes to the system structure.
Test:	Better communications between test groups, make sure enough understanding by the test groups that are in different locations.
Project management (planning, schedule, dependency management, metrics):	Implement microcode project manager(s) for coordination of deliverables in combination with hardware deliverables.
Tools and methodologies:	Force the parallel development of test enhancement for regression test whenever new functions are developed.

TABLE 16.4 *(continued)*

Project	Improvement Plan
Project Z	
Requirements and specifications:	Link requirements and specifications with schedule and review schedule assumptions.
Design, code, and reviews:	Document what types of white box testing need to be done to verify design points.
Project Management (planning, schedule, dependency management, metrics):	Strong focus on project management, scheduling, staffing, and commitments. Periodically review schedule assumptions and assess impact as assumptions become invalid.

16.4.8 Summary

Table 16.6 summarizes the essential points discussed under each phase of the proposed software project assessment method.

TABLE 16.6
Essential Activities and Considerations by Phase of a Proposed Software Project Assessment Method

Phase	Essential Activities and Considerations	Phase — continued
(1) Preparation	- As appropriate - Gain understanding of business context and justification, objectives and constraints. - Establish assessment project plan. - Establish project charter and secure commitment. - Request basic project data. - Develop an initial set of questions based on information available thus far, or use an existing. questionnaire. - Establish assessment project closeout plan.	(3) Phase 3 - possible improvement opportunities and recommendations. - Review findings and improvement frameworks in the literature.
(2) Facts gathering — phase 1	- Build a detailed project review from the project team's perspective. - Focus on whats and hows; at times on whys via probing.	- Formulate ideas at the end of project review.

TABLE 16.6 Essential Activities and Considerations by Phase of a Proposed
Software Project Assessment Method *(continued)*

Phase	Essential Activities and Considerations	Phase — continued
(4) Questionnaire customization	- Customize to project being assessed. - Use vignette-question approach for gap analysis. - Define strengths and weaknesses. - Gather team's improvement ideas.	- Design questionnaire to include questions on improvements from the project team.
(5) Facts gathering — phase 2	- Administer questionnaire to project personnel. - Validate responses. - Triangulate across respondents and with information gathered from Phase 1. - Brainstorm project strengths and weaknesses; ask what the project team would have done differently.	- Formulate whole list of recommendations - actions for immediate improvements and for strategic directions.
(6) Team discussions and feedback	- Review with project team assessment results and draft recommendations.	- Finalize recommendations.
(7) Reporting and closeout	- Complete final report including recommendations - Meet with assessment executive sponsor and management of assessed project.	

16.5 Summary

Software project assessments are different from software process assessments that are based on the process maturity framework. While process maturity assessments are more applicable to the organization level and are important for long-term improvement, specific project assessments are crucial to drive experience-based improvement. Process maturity assessments focus on the whats, and coverage and maturity level of key process activities and practices. Project assessments focus on the whats, hows, and whys of specific practices of the target project(s) and address the issue of improvement from the development team's perspective. The two approaches are complementary.

A seven-step project assessment method, which was derived from experience, is proposed. Effective assessment and quality recommendations depend on three factors: the assessment approach; the experience and quality of the assessment team; and the quality, depth, and breadth of project data and information. The proposed method does not rely on a standard questionnaire to collect data and responses, or use a maturity framework to derive recommendations. The two-phase approach for fact finding in the method enhances the accuracy and depth of relevant project information and data. This method stresses the importance of quality professionals or peer development leaders who have deep understanding of the organization's cultures and practices. It puts the project team back in the assessment process and therefore enhances the relevance and buy-in of the recommendations.

References

1. Basili, V. R., "Software Development: A Paradigm for the Future," Proceedings 13th International Computer Software and Applications Conference (COMPSAC), Keynote Address, Orlando, Fla., September 1989.
2. Basili, V. R., "Software Measurement Workshop," University of Maryland, 1995.
3. Curtis, B., W. E. Hefley, S. A. Miller (eds.), *People Capability Maturity Model*, Reading, Mass.: Addison-Wesley, 2001.
4. DeMarco, T., and T. R. Lister, *Peopleware: Productive Projects and Teams*, 2nd ed., New York: Dorset House, 1999.
5. Dunaway, D. K., and S. Masters, "CMM^{SM}-Based Appraisal for Internal Process Improvement (CBA IPI): Method Description," Carnegie Mellon University Software Engineering Institute, CMU/SEI-96-TR-007, April 1996.
6. Humphrey, W. S., *Managing the Software Process*, Reading, Mass.: Addison-Wesley, 1989.
7. Jones, C., *Assessment and Control of Software Risks*, Englewood Cliffs, N. J.: Yourdon Press, 1994.
8. Jones, C., *Patterns of Software System Failure and Success*, Boston: International Thomson Computer Press, 1995.
9. Jones, C., *Software Assessments, Benchmarks, and Best Practices*, Boston: Addison-Wesley, 2000.
10. Jones, C., Personal communications, February 2002.
11. Mills, H. D., M. Dyer, and R. C. Linger, "Cleanroom Software Engineering," *IEEE Software*, September 1987, pp. 19–24.
12. Paulk, M. C., C. V. Weber, B. Curtis, and M. B. Chrissis, *The Capability Maturity Model: Guidelines for Improving the Software Process*, Reading, Mass.: Addison-Wesley, 1995.
13. Software Engineering Institute, "Standard CMMI^{SM} Assessment Method for Process Improvement: Method Description, Version 1.0," CMMI Product Development Team, Carnegie Mellon University, CMU/SEI-2000-TR-009, October 2000.
14. Software Engineering Institute, "Capability Maturity Model Integration (CMMI), Version 1.1, CMMI for Systems Engineering and Software Engineering (CMMI-SE/SW, V1.1)," Continuous Representation, Carnegie Mellon University, CMU/SEI-2002-TR-001, December 2001a.

15. Software Engineering Institute, "Capability Maturity Model Integration (CMMI), Version 1.1, CMMI for Systems Engineering and Software Engineering (CMMI-SE/SW, V1.1), Staged Representation," Carnegie Mellon University, CMU/SEI-2002-TR-002, December 2001b.

16. Zahran, S., *Software Process Improvement, Practical Guidelines for Business Success,* Reading, Mass.: Addison-Wesley, 1997.

17. Zubrow, D., W. Hayes, J. Siegel, and D. Goldenson, "Maturity Questionnaire," Software Engineering Institute Special Report, CMU/SEI-94-SR-7, June 1994.

17

Dos and Don'ts of Software Process Improvement

Patrick O'Toole

This chapter provides an overview of CMMI-based process maturity measures and describes how maturity and capability levels are determined. It sheds insight into some practices that may heighten the probability of success for an improvement program, and others that may lead to a less desirable outcome.[1]

Many organizations perceive a correlation between the quality of their software processes and the quality of their resulting products and services. This holds true both for software development organizations and the software products they produce, as well as software support organizations and the software they maintain. A number of these organizations use a model-based approach, such as the Capability Maturity

---

1. From *Dos and Don'ts of Software Process Improvement,* by Patrick O'Toole. © 2002, Process Assessment, Consulting & Training. Reprinted by permission. All rights reserved.

Pat O'Toole is a Principal Consultant at Process Assessment, Consulting & Training (PACT) where he provides a variety of services to his process improvement clients. Pat is one of the most active SEI authorized CBA IPI and SCAMPI lead assessors, and has led assessments spanning all maturity levels, including the largest and most complex Level 5 assessment conducted to date. He is a candidate lead assessor for the People-CMM, and is an SEI transition partner for the Introduction to CMMI course.

Model for Software (CMM) or Capability Maturity Model Integration (CMMI), to guide and measure their process improvement efforts.[2]

Unfortunately, many well-intentioned organizations fail to achieve their stated improvement goals. In many organizations, the goal is stated in terms of attaining a CMMI level, rather than in terms linked directly to project performance. Process maturity is a laudable goal—provided it leads to improved project performance aligned with the organization's business objectives.

17.1 Measuring Process Maturity

Using the CMMI, an organization can plan and execute a process improvement strategy based on industry best practices and a proven approach. The staged representation of the CMMI provides five levels of process maturity:

Maturity level 1: Initial

Maturity level 2: Managed

Maturity level 3: Defined

Maturity level 4: Quantitatively Managed

Maturity level 5: Optimizing

In the staged representation, maturity levels 2 and higher consist of a series of process areas that form evolutionary plateaus of process improvement and performance. For example, the maturity level 2 process areas are:

1. Requirements Management
2. Project Planning
3. Project Monitoring and Control
4. Supplier Agreement Management
5. Measurement and Analysis
6. Process and Product Quality Assurance
7. Configuration Management

The determination of an organization's maturity level is accomplished by conducting a formal assessment such as the CMM-Based Appraisal for Internal Process Improvement (CBA IPI), Software Capability Evaluation (SCE), or Standard CMMI Appraisal Method for Process Improvement.

The Standard CMMI Appraisal Method for Process Improvement (SCAMPI) is designed to provide benchmark quality ratings relative to Capability Maturity

---

2. Capability Maturity Model® and CMM® are registered in the U.S. Patent and Trademark Office; CMM[SM] Integration and SCAMPI[SM] are service marks of Carnegie Mellon University.

Model Integration (CMMI) models. It is applicable to a wide range of appraisal usage models, including both internal process improvement and external capability determinations. SCAMPI satisfies all of the Appraisal Requirements for CMMI (ARC) requirements for a Class A appraisal method and can support the conduct of ISO/IEC 15504 assessments.

SCAMPI v1.1 enables a sponsor to do the following:

1. Gain insight into an organization's engineering capability by identifying the strengths and weaknesses of its current processes.
2. Relate these strengths and weaknesses to the CMMI model.
3. Prioritize improvement plans.
4. Focus on improvements (correct weaknesses that generate risks) that are most beneficial to the organization given its current level of organizational maturity or process capabilities.
5. Derive capability level ratings as well as a maturity level rating.
6. Identify development/acquisition risks relative to capability/maturity determinations.[3]

When conducting a SCAMPI, a lead assessor authorized by the Software Engineering Institute (SEI) at Carnegie Mellon University works with a trained assessment team to gather and examine objective evidence and relate it to the CMMI. Data is gathered from questionnaires, organizational and project documents, interviews with organizational personnel, and presentations.

Based on the evidence, observations are written for each CMMI practice in the scope of the assessment. The ultimate objective for data gathering at the practice level is to characterize the extent to which each practice, or a satisfactory alternative practice, is implemented in the organization, and how well that implementation supports the associated process area goal. As data gathering continues, evidence is captured at the project or group level and then aggregated to the organizational level. After sufficient evidence has been obtained and evaluated, the assessment team characterizes organization-level implementation for each practice in the scope of the assessment according to this scale:

1. Fully implemented
2. Largely implemented
3. Partially implemented
4. Not implemented

After the assessment team has characterized the implementation status of each practice, preliminary findings are generated. The preliminary findings are presented

3. Standard CMMI Appraisal Method for Process Improvement (SCAMPI), Version 1.1: Method Definition

to the interview participants such that the findings can be confirmed or countermanding evidence can be gathered. Separate presentation sessions may be conducted for managers, project managers, and practitioners in order to encourage open communication, and thereby gather data with higher integrity.

Presentations of the preliminary findings are typically the assessment's last activity in the data-gathering phase prior to rating process area goals and determining the maturity level. Using the data gathered throughout the assessment, the team exercises professional judgment in determining whether the goals associated with each process area are satisfied. The goal ratings determine the organization's maturity level. The organization's maturity level is the highest level at which all goals are satisfied, and all goals at lower levels are also satisfied. In other words, in order for an organization to achieve CMMI maturity level 3, the organization must have satisfied all of the goals associated with the level 2 and level 3 process areas.

17.2 Measuring Process Capability

When measuring process capability, the CMMI "continuous representation" is used. In the continuous representation, each process area is assigned a capability level as follows:

Capability Level 0: Incomplete
Capability Level 1: Performed
Capability Level 2: Managed
Capability Level 3: Defined
Capability Level 4: Quantitatively Managed
Capability Level 5: Optimizing

In the CMMI continuous representation, capability level profiles are used to depict the list of process areas and their corresponding capability levels. Achievement profiles represent the current state and target profiles represent the desired state. The SCAMPI assessment method is also used for formal determination of an organization's achievement capability level profile.

17.3 Staged versus Continuous—Debating Religion

The CMMI includes two representations, staged and continuous, due largely to the model's legacy. The CMMI model is founded on source models that employed *either* the staged representation (software engineering) or the continuous representation (systems engineering). Rather than risk alienating members from either engineering discipline, the authors of the CMMI decided to provide both representations.

Early adopters of the CMMI tend to favor the representation inherited from their legacy model. The CMMI's continuous representation has taken most software engineering groups out of their comfort zones. It's new to them, it's different from what they're used to, and therefore they perceive it as wrong/bad/evil. Besides, it has a level 0 and everybody knows that *real* models start at level 1!

Not too terribly long after completing the Intro to CMMI course, a process improvement consultant found herself in the midst of a battle between a Software Engineering Process Group (SEPG) and its process improvement sponsor. The SEPG was very much in favor of the continuous representation, because the members perceived it gave them more flexibility in implementing improvements as well as a more granular means of planning and tracking their progress. The sponsor, who wanted to use the tried-and-true staged representation, brought the consultant in for one day to arbitrate a peaceful resolution to this lingering conflict.

After spending a few hours with the SEPG to gain a better understanding of that perspective, the consultant met individually with the sponsor. They talked for an hour before lunch, and it was pretty obvious that the sponsor was adamant about using the staged representation. Based on the consultant's experience (as well as her personal comfort) with the CMM for Software, she tended to agree with the sponsor. Now all she had to do was figure out how to ease the SEPG into the "correct" way of thinking.

Over lunch, the sponsor was bragging about his daughter, gloating that she had achieved a 3.8 grade point average in her freshman year at an Ivy League school. "It's funny," the consultant mused, "using a 'staged GPA representation' she would only be a 3." His jaw tightened as he pondered the remark. "It's worse than that," the sponsor finally admitted, "to date she has received nine A's and one C, so she'd only be a 2." The remainder of the lunchtime conversation focused on how to implement the continuous representation throughout the sponsor's organization!

17.4 Measuring Levels Is Not Enough

As indicated, most organizations that follow a model-based approach to process improvement designate a process improvement team, typically called the Software Engineering Process Group (SEPG), to spearhead the effort. Working under the auspices of a senior management sponsor, the SEPG is responsible for documenting, deploying, and improving the processes suggested by the corresponding model.

Imagine that six months ago your senior management directed your SEPG to achieve CMMI maturity level 2 within a year. As an SEPG member, you have invested extensive (some might say "excessive") time and effort generating all the required policies, procedures, templates, measures, checklists, and training materials, but you are now having trouble getting the development projects to pilot and adopt any of these new process components.

Being a reasonable, proactive change agent, you solicit your sponsor's assistance. The sponsor eloquently reminds project personnel how important it is to reach their target maturity level and urges them to be more open to helping the organization achieve this distinctive honor. The sponsor instructs software quality assurance personnel to be more aggressive in explaining the value of all this new process stuff and in identifying process deviants. But nothing really changes; the process assets continue to gather dust and the SEPG's frustration continues to mount.

Why are the project teams being so difficult and how can the SEPG achieve maturity level 2 if they don't get with the program? Why aren't they helping the SEPG to be successful?

But wait a minute . . . why is the organization doing process improvement? They're not *really* doing it to "achieve CMMI maturity level 2"; they're doing it to *improve*. They shouldn't be forcing the projects to grunt through a pile of administrivia to accommodate the CMMI; they should be employing process aspirin to relieve project pain. Perhaps they can exploit the CMMI to help the projects achieve greater success!

Let's check this hypothesis by determining which of two possible results would be preferred:

A. The organization is assessed at CMMI maturity level 2, but the projects achieve no measurable improvement; or
B. The projects achieve measurable improvement, but never achieve CMMI maturity level 2.

Unless there are compelling business reasons to reach a particular CMMI level (i.e., your customers will not allow you to bid on work unless you have been assessed at maturity level 2), if your answer is A, you've probably been in the "quality" organization too long!

On the other hand, if the SEPG continues to help the projects succeed, its value will be recognized and the group will overcome much of the natural resistance to change. In addition, if the projects continue to demonstrate sustainable improvement, the CMMI level will ultimately come. Remember that using the CMMI is merely one tactic to achieve a higher-level (no pun intended) business strategy through the execution of successful projects.

The CMMI maturity level is intended to be a leading indicator of the organization's process capability, but the real value of process improvement is in running more successful projects. The organization shouldn't merely measure the CMMI maturity level; it should also monitor the additional value derived from the implementation of these improved process elements.

Many organizations use the acronym SPI to mean "Software Process Improvement." The organization should consider keeping the SEPG focused properly by changing the meaning of "SPI" to Software *Project* Improvement and establishing the SEPG's motto as: "If we are not helping the projects achieve measurable improvement, we are failing!" The projects do not exist to help the SEPG achieve success, but rather the other way around.

One of the critical steps in beginning (and continuing) with a CMMI assessment is to develop a process capability baseline, which serves as the basis for determining what to improve and to assess progress along the way. These desired outcomes might include:

- ☐ Delivered quality
- ☐ Productivity
- ☐ Schedule
- ☐ Reduced overtime
- ☐ Defect injection rate
- ☐ Defect discovery rate
- ☐ In-process defect removal efficiency
- ☐ Defect distribution

17.5 Establishing the Alignment Principle

Project managers often tell their customers, "Faster, better, or cheaper—pick two." What they mean, of course, is that if the customer demands a high-quality product in the shortest amount of time, they reserve the right to tell her how much it will cost. Conversely, if the customer prefers a low-cost product in the shortest amount of time, it may have quality problems (typically referred to as "undocumented features"). The point is that the solution can be constrained in only two of the three dimensions—there must be at least one independent variable.

The "alignment principle" requires you as an SEPG member, to take this concept a step farther. You need to tell senior management, "faster, better, or cheaper—pick *one*." Since senior management has funding and firing authority over the SEPG, however, you may want to ask questions like:

- ☐ What is the business imperative in our marketplace?
- ☐ What gives us a competitive edge in the minds of our customers?
- ☐ Why do our potential customers keep buying our competitor's products?

It seems fairly obvious that if your firm manufactures pacemakers, quality is the attribute to be maximized. Such an organization will quickly conclude that it would be willing to sacrifice a bit of time and cost to reduce the number of field-reported defects—especially those reported by the relatives of their late customers.

But what about your company? How would your senior managers answer if the question were posed to them? The response to this question is the most important piece of planning data for the process improvement program, because it is the foundation of the alignment principle. It is imperative that senior management, not the SEPG, establish this. The alignment principle is the strategic business imperative that will be supported by the tactical implementation of improved process elements. Strategic decisions are the responsibility of senior management; tactical plans are generated and executed by organizational personnel based on those decisions.

Suppose senior management has just informed you that quality, defined by field-reported defects, is the most important competitive dimension in the minds of your customers. So now it's time to craft the alignment principle. Continuing with the pacemaker example, we may establish an alignment principle something like: "Achieve an annual, sustainable 20% reduction in field-reported defects without degrading current levels of cost, schedule, and functional variance."

Now you know what it means when you say that the SEPG is going to help the projects achieve greater success, and the project teams now know what's most important to senior management. When the SEPG pilots a new process element that demonstrates a measurable reduction in defects, the projects will be anxious to deploy and adopt this enhancement. Rather than force projects to use process elements in which they perceive little value, the Alignment Principle guides the SEPG to provide services that demonstrate measurable benefit. In this manner, the SEPG and the projects are aligned.

17.6 Take Time Getting Faster

Maturity level 2 in the CMMI is called "Managed," but even maturity level 1 organizations "manage" their projects. For instance, many maturity level 1 projects manage to target project completion on the earliest date with a nonzero probability of success. The thinking is that if everyone works 60+ hours per week, and nobody gets sick or takes weekends or holidays off, the project might just manage to finish on time.

And now your senior management has proclaimed that the overarching goal of the process improvement program is to reduce cycle time. They are not being unreasonable—it's hard to deny that for many software-intensive products the primary competitive dimension is time to market. Customers, whether internal or external, are always clambering to get new products and features in an ever-decreasing time frame. But as a member of the SEPG you fear that this edict simply gives the project teams an excuse to circumvent existing processes and standards in order to get the job done any way they see fit.

Customers apply schedule pressure as part of a "ritualistic dance." They get project managers to commit to delivering in twelve months in the desperate hope that they will receive the full product in fifteen months, or alternatively, that they will get 60% of the core functionality by the committed date. The project manager knows it, the customer knows it, and yet the charade plays out release after release. It's just like budgeting's ritualistic dance—if you need $5M for your project you request $7.5M, knowing that one-third of the budget will be cut back during the approval cycle. We all know the tune and the dance continues!

So what do the customers *really* want? They want to believe! Customers want to know that when you commit to delivering a product on March 31 that it will be available for implementation on April 1 (an appropriate date?). Although they claim they want the software faster, they really want it more reliably.

As much as the customers want to believe, the software development staff wants to be believed. They would like their managers to leave their professional integrity intact by accepting and even defending their estimates. They would like senior management to understand and mitigate the devastating effects of golf course commitments and uncontrolled scope creep. They would like their customers to realize that it is in their mutual best interest to plan and execute projects in a disciplined manner. Finally, they would like to see their spouses and children more often than Sunday evenings!

Rather than establish a goal of finishing projects *faster*, the organization would be better served initially with the goal of estimating and executing projects more *reliably*. To achieve this goal, the organization must

1. gather and analyze historical data to develop and calibrate estimation models,
2. codify good engineering and project management practices that lead to more reliable results,
3. establish the means to control the projects' requirements and configuration baselines, and
4. enjoy the strong support of leadership in achieving this goal.

Disciplined planning and execution significantly reduce the variability of project results. They also establish a solid foundation for getting projects done faster, the organization's ultimate goal. Since you are unlikely to achieve sustainable cycle time reductions without first achieving reasonably reliable results, follow Steven Covey's advice and "put first things first." The SEPG's challenge is to convince senior management that generating more reliable estimates is a necessary prerequisite to reducing cycle time—and that once customers believe and estimation credibility has been established, the tune of the ritualistic dance will be altered forever.

17.7 Keep It Simple — or Face Decomplexification

A friend of mine flies all the time. Whenever he boards a plane, he sneaks a peak into the cockpit to see what the crew is up to. He says he feels a sense of comfort when he sees the captain filling out the preflight checklist. This simple act tells him that the pilot's objectives are similar to his own—making sure this bird can

- ☐ get off the ground safely,
- ☐ fly all the way to their destination, and
- ☐ get back down—preferably in a controlled manner.

That is, the captain fills out the preflight checklist because he/she wants to live as much as the passengers do. On the other hand, imagine how nervous my friend might be if his glance in the cockpit found the captain reading the operator's manual!

As they board, the passengers' working assumption is that the pilot knows how to fly the plane. The pilot simply uses the preflight checklist to ensure that the plane is fit for use, and to lower the probability that critical safety precautions are inadvertently overlooked.

So why is it that your organization's multivolume set of software process documentation gets less use than a preflight checklist? Are you not working on important projects that would make internal headlines if they "crashed and burned?" Is the project team not entrusted with planning the project at the outset, performing project activities throughout, and ultimately delivering products to your customers, preferably in working order? Have you really committed the full process to memory so that you know the processes that you execute once every three months better than those a pilot executes three or four times a day?

One reason that process documentation remains on the shelf is that its authors have a different working assumption about project personnel than passengers have about pilots. Authors of such documentation typically assume that the project personnel do not know how to plan, manage, or fulfill their project responsibilities.

But let's face facts; when the process was written, your people probably didn't have all the requisite skills to perform their project responsibilities using the newly defined process. So naturally the documentation was written to fulfill this need. However, just imagine how thick the preflight checklist would be if it were written such that any passenger would be able to fly a modern commercial airliner. (And imagine how quickly you would bolt from the plane if they asked the person sitting next to you to proceed to the cockpit to try!)

Lack of skills is a transient issue that should be addressed by training. Your organization should provide ample skill-building interventions to train novices, to address skill deficiencies, and to introduce major process changes. But it is unrealistic to expect experienced project personnel to need or use the same detailed instructions required by the novice. Is it any surprise, then, that your process documentation remains on the shelf unopened if 90% of its bulk is dedicated to such mundane tasks?

So, differentiate between training material and process documentation. For students, training material is typically a single-use asset—they use it in the classroom and then stick it on the shelf. In contrast, process documentation should serve as a ready reference guide for the process executor. Like a preflight checklist, it should focus on the vital process elements that lower the probability that critical steps will be overlooked. Like the airline's preflight checklists, software process documentation should be continuously reviewed to assess its effectiveness and improved to allow better control and software quality.

17.8 Measuring the Value of Process Improvement

Oscar Wilde said, "Nowadays, people know the cost of everything and the value of nothing." Unfortunately this is often true for organizations focusing on process improvement. Most organizations can tell you their process improvement budget for the year and how much they have spent to date, but few can relate hard data regarding the benefits they've derived from that investment.

When asked about the benefits, management is likely to tell you things like: "Projects seem to be running a lot smoother now." "We don't seem to have as many late projects as we used to." "Customers seem to be happier with the quality of the products that we're producing." "We've achieved CMMI maturity level 3, so we know we're doing well!" If a process capability baseline was established before the project began, you should be able to demonstrate improvements in the list of desired outcomes.

Soft, qualitative data is comforting, but it is not likely to sustain the improvement program through the next budgeting cycle, let alone the next economic downturn. When times get tough, programs that cannot support the benefits they provide with hard data are likely to be thanked for their contribution as their people are redeployed to work on "real" projects that can.

So how does an SEPG go about measuring the benefits derived from process improvement? Clearly the alignment principle provides some guidance in this regard. Using the sample alignment principle, the organization must measure:

- ☐ Field-reported defects
- ☐ Cost variance
- ☐ Schedule variance
- ☐ Functional variance

The success (or lack thereof) of the process improvement program can be determined objectively by comparing the results of the projects with those proclaimed in the alignment principle. An SEPG that can demonstrate sustainable benefit in quantifiable terms is much more likely to have the opportunity to repeat this success.

To further establish the "measurement mentality" for process improvement, the SEPG should be encouraged (or is it "expected?") to hypothesize the value of each improvement in measurable terms prior to piloting it on a real project. The pilot should be conducted in such a way that it confirms or denies the realization of the hypothesized value, and deployment decisions should be based on this objective analysis. Deploying the process element as is, modifying the process element and running additional pilots, or abandoning the proposed changes are likely outcomes of such postpilot analyses. Remember that pilots are simply data-gathering activities; a successful pilot is one that contributes to organizational knowledge, not necessarily one that demonstrates a proposed process change is ready to be inflicted on all projects.

17.9 Measuring Process Adoption

As the hypothesized value of new process elements is proved by pilot projects, the SEPG should prepare for broad deployment and subsequent implementation. Many organizations make the process elements available via the Web and expect that the projects will simply start using them. This Field of Dreams approach ("if you build it, they will come") is intuitively appealing to the SEPG, but rarely proves to be an effective or efficient means of changing people's behavior.

Other organizations follow a strategy similar to that employed for their software packages. These organizations package multiple new or modified process elements into periodic "process releases," and accompany each release with release notes, testimonial data from the pilot projects, process training, internal consultation, and a great deal of fanfare. Typically, these process releases are made one to four times per year. This approach provides sufficient process stability and ensures that project personnel aren't constantly struggling to figure out what *today's* process is.

Regardless of the deployment approach, as new process elements are released, the SEPG should monitor the project adoption rate—the rate at which the new process elements are being adopted by the project teams. The primary question addressed by measuring the adoption rate is: How many of the projects that *should* be using these new elements *are* using them?

The SEPG should seek to apply process improvement concepts to its own processes ("physician, heal thyself"), one of which is the deployment process. In an effort to provide better services in the future, the SEPG should ask a series of secondary questions related to the adoption rate such as:

- ☐ Why are some projects resisting adoption of the new elements?
- ☐ Is this resistance based on inadvertent side effects that weren't experienced on the pilot projects?
- ☐ Should there be additional support mechanisms to assist behavioral change and project adoption?
- ☐ Should there be tailoring guidelines that reduce the administrative overhead of these new process elements when implemented in small projects?
- ☐ How much effort is being invested in supporting the adoption of these new elements?"

The data derived from the answers to such questions can be analyzed to accelerate the adoption of the current process release as well as to enhance the means of releasing new process elements in the future.

17.10 Measuring Process Compliance

Organizations that are using the CMM or CMMI to guide their process improvement activities have typically established a Software Quality Assurance (SQA) group. SQA is responsible for verifying that project activities and work products conform to the project's designated processes, procedures, standards, and requirements. SQA conducts audits and reviews on various aspects of the project work and reports the results.

SQA groups generally establish checklists of items to be verified. The checklist for verifying that a peer review was conducted properly may include items such as:

- ☐ Was a qualified peer review moderator designated for the review?
- ☐ Did the review team have the appropriate skills to review the work product adequately?
- ☐ Was the work product to be reviewed published at least three days in advance of the review meeting?
- ☐ Did the moderator verify that at least 80% of the invited reviewers participated in the review?
- ☐ Did the scribe note the preparation time on the peer review data sheet?
- ☐ Did the moderator verify that the reviewers were adequately prepared for the review?
- ☐ Did the scribe note the defects, their location in the work product, and the responsible person on the peer review data sheet?
- ☐ Was the peer review data entered into the peer review database?
- ☐ Were the defects resolved?
- ☐ Did the moderator (or designee) verify the resolution of the defects?

Verifying and measuring compliance can identify:

☐ Areas where compliance to the process is degrading

☐ Process steps in which additional training or coaching is necessary

☐ Process elements that may warrant additional tailoring guidelines (or replacement)

☐ Elements of the process that are deemed administratively burdensome

☐ Areas where tool support may be beneficial

Project personnel are rarely noncompliant just to be belligerent. Unless this is a relatively new and therefore unproved process element, noncompliance usually indicates a change in the work pattern from that which was in place when the process element was introduced. Monitoring process compliance trends can detect shifts in project behavior and can result in initiation of corrective action in a timely manner.

If the SEPG established a process capability baseline, process results at each step should be verified against these desired outcomes. This will help keep management informed and engaged based upon expectations that were established when the project was first begun. It will also serve as a means to maintain commitment and focus to the project.

17.11 Celebrate the Journey, Not Just the Destination

A few weeks before the Twin Cities Marathon, a local running club traditionally hosts a 20-mile training run followed immediately by a potluck lunch. To get runners of varying skill to finish around the same time, they have the slower runners start out at 8 A.M., the medium runners at 8:30 A.M., and the fast runners at 9 A.M.

A couple of years ago, I participated in the run and went out with the medium runners. At mile 17, I happened across a 285-pound "runner," who was lumbering along at a pace slower than most people walk. He was breathing heavily (no pun intended), sweating profusely, and looking as though he was about to pass out. I was convinced that it was only the thought of the pending feast that kept him moving at all!

My first concern was medical, "Are you all right?" I asked. "I'm doing OK," he replied, "but I'm sure glad I started out at 6:30." After he assured me that he was going to make it, I promised to save him a plate of grub, bid him a fond farewell, and left him to ponder Newton's first law of motion.

The run ended at an elementary school where we used the cafeteria for our luncheon. The "moving mountain" was the primary topic of conversation as the returning runners loaded up their plates and took their seats. "How could a runner allow himself to get into such bad shape?" was the question of the hour. "No 'real runner' would ever allow himself to fall apart like that."

With lunch just about over, the first runner to set out became the last to finish. As promised, I had saved him some food, and so I brought it to the table where he had plopped down with a sense of self-satisfaction. A few members of the running club are newspaper reporters; they joined us at the table, each carrying another plate of food for our beleaguered colleague. The questions started slowly but the pace picked up as his story unfolded.

It turns out that about a year prior, Bill had tipped the scale at 400 pounds and decided right then to turn his life around. His friends scoffed when he made a public commitment to run a marathon. After consulting a sports doctor, he started off slowly, but still managed to drop over 100 pounds in the next 11 months. With only three weeks to go he was still hoping to run the full 26.2 miles within the six-hour time limit—and darned if he didn't do it! Bill's miraculous feat was featured in *Runner's World* magazine—an experience that most of us "real runners" will probably never enjoy. OK, to the moral of the story . . .

At every SEPG conference there is at least one presentation entitled something like "How We Achieved Level 2 in Three Months." These sessions are jammed with hopeful newbies praying for the miracle of instantaneous success. They could probably learn more from talking to Bill, the marathoner. First, they could learn that "one data point does not a trend make." They shouldn't judge the distance the presenters have traveled by only seeing them cross the finish line. After all, the presenters can run a 100 yard dash quicker than your organization can run a marathon.

They could also learn that you really can set aggressive goals and achieve them. But, more important, they could reflect on the fact that even if Bill had not successfully completed the marathon that year, he had still dropped 100 pounds and was a better man for it. Bill's life didn't miraculously improve because he ran a marathon; his life improved because he worked out every day for 11 months.

Don't waste time looking for the easy path; start improving your projects' performance one day at a time and you will be successful, whether or not you ever achieve level 2. As an anonymous marathoner said, "The miracle isn't that I finished... the miracle is that I had the courage to start." So take that first step—and enjoy the journey!

17.12 Summary

An assessment using the CMMI model is a significant undertaking, and the journey to the next level may take a long time to accomplish. Therefore, it is essential to sustain management commitment along the way. Process measurements and progress against desired outcomes should be communicated to management on a regular basis to avoid having process improvement fall off the management radar screen.

References

1. Paulk, M.C., C. V. Weber, B. Curtis, and M. B. Chrissis, *The Capability and Maturity Model: Guidelines for Improving the Software Process.* Reading, Mass.: Addison-Wesley, 1995.
2. Software Engineering Institute, Capability Maturity Model Integration (CMMI), Version 1.1, CMMI for Systems Engineering and Software Engineering (CMMI-SE/SW, V1.1), Continuous Representation, Carnegie Mellon University, CMU/SEI-2002-TR-001, December 2001.
3. Software Engineering Institute, Capability Maturity Model Integration (CMMI), Version 1.1, CMMI for Systems Engineering and Software Engineering (CMMI-SE/SW, V1.1), Staged Representation, Carnegie Mellon University, CMU/SEI-2002-TR-002, December 2001.

18

Using Function Point Metrics to Measure Software Process Improvements

Capers Jones

Software cost overruns, schedule delays, and poor quality have been endemic in the software industry for more than 50 years.

Since the incorporation of the Software Engineering Institute (SEI) in 1984, it has often been asserted that companies or projects that use state-of-the-art development processes and advanced tool suites can create software applications faster and with fewer risks of failure than traditional methods.

Are these assertions true? For software process improvement, there has been comparatively little solid, empirical data published on four important topics:

1. What does it cost to improve software processes?
2. How long does it take to see tangible improvements if processes do improve?

3.   What kind of value results from process improvements in terms of
     □ Fewer failures?
     □ Higher productivity and quality?
     □ Shorter schedules?
     □ Higher user satisfaction?
4.   Fewer lawsuits for breach of contract?

Colleagues at Software Productivity Research (SPR) and I have examined data from more than 10,000 software projects between 1984 and today. Our methodology includes standardized questionnaires for gathering both qualitative and quantitative information. A discussion of this methodology is outside the scope of this chapter. For information on how the data were collected, refer to Jones (1996, 2000).

We have examined software projects at all five levels of the SEI capability maturity model (CMM). We have also examined many projects that do not use the SEI CMM. (Refer to Paulk et al., 1995 for a discussion of the CMM.) Some of our findings have been published in a number of books that address the economic and quality aspects of software process improvement. (Jones 1994, 1996, 1997, 1998, and 2000). The examined data come primarily from our clients, which consist of about 600 companies and government agencies.

Among our clients, software process improvements do not occur in random patterns. When the patterns used by the best overall companies are examined, it can be seen that the initial activity is a formal process assessment and a baseline, followed by a six-stage improvement program in a specific order:

Stage 0: Software Process Assessment, Baseline, and Benchmark

Stage 1: Focus on Management Technologies

Stage 2: Focus on Software Processes and Methodologies

Stage 3: Focus on New Tools and Approaches

Stage 4: Focus on Infrastructure and Specialization

Stage 5: Focus on Reusability

Stage 6: Focus on Industry Leadership

Note that the assessment itself does not improve anything, so it is outside the six numbered improvement stages. A software process assessment is analogous to a medical diagnostic study. A diagnostic study does not cure any illness, but provides physicians with the information necessary to plan effective therapies.

These six stages provide a structure for software improvement strategies. However, each company is different and therefore the specifics of each company's improvement strategy must match its local culture and particular needs. Other authors also discuss various strategies for software process improvement (Grady 1997).

18.1 Software Process Improvement Sequences

The six stages along the path to process improvements usually occur in the same sequence from company to company. The sequence is based on practical considerations. For example, software managers have to produce the cost justifications for investments, so they need to be fully aware of the impacts of the latter stages. Unless project management excellence is achieved first, it is not likely that the latter stages will even occur. Let us consider the initial assessment and baseline stages, and then examine each of the six improvement stages in turn.

18.1.1 Stage 0: Software Process Assessment and Baseline

The first, or 0, stage is numbered so that it is outside the set of six improvement phases. There is a practical reason for this. Neither an assessment nor a baseline, by itself, causes tangible improvement. Some companies forget this important point and more or less stop doing anything after the initial assessment and baseline.

A successful software process improvement begins with a formal process assessment and the establishment of a quantitative baseline of current productivity and quality levels. The *assessment* is like a medical diagnosis to find all of the strengths and weaknesses associated with software. The *baseline* is to provide a firm quantitative basis for productivity, schedules, costs, quality, and user satisfaction in order to judge future rates of improvement.

Software process assessments are often performed by consulting groups licensed to use the methodology developed by the Software Engineering Institute (SEI). However, other assessment methods are available as well. Assessments are concerned primarily with qualitative information such as the presence or absence of a quality assurance function.

In addition to qualitative assessment information, it is also useful to record quantitative baseline data. A baseline is a snapshot of the organization's productivity levels, quality levels, schedules, and costs at the time of the assessment. The baseline data serve to demonstrate future progress. Function point metrics are widely used for baseline data collection, because they cover such a wide range of activities.

Many companies also commission quantitative benchmarks to judge their performance against similar companies in the same industry, such as banking, insurance, telecommunications, defense, or whatever. A benchmark is a formal comparison of software methods and quantitative results against those of similar organizations. External benchmarks are often performed by third-party consulting groups such as Compass Group, David Consulting Group, Gartner Group, the International Function Point Users Group, Meta Group, Howard Rubin Associates, and Software Productivity Research. These companies have large collections of software data from many companies and industries.

Assessments, baselines, and benchmarks are all valuable and are synergistic. Assessments alone lack the quantification of initial quality and productivity levels needed to judge improvements later. A quantitative baseline is a prerequisite for serious process improvements, since the cost justification for the initial investments have to be proved by comparing results against the baseline. External benchmarks against other companies are an optional but useful adjunct to software process improvement tasks.

Since it is likely that the quantitative data will be collected using function point metrics. A short discussion of function point metrics may be useful. Function point metrics were developed by A. J. Albrecht and colleagues at IBM in the mid 1970s (Albrecht 1979). The function point metric was placed in the public domain by IBM in 1978, and responsibility for function point counting rules was taken over by a non-profit organization in 1984. The organization responsible for defining function point counting rules is the International Function Point Users Group (IFPUG). (Refer to the IFPUG Web site (*http://www.IFPUG.org*) for additional information.) A new primer on function point analysis was recently published by Herron and Garmus (2001), who are officers in the IFPUG organization).

Function points are derived from the external aspects of software applications. Five external attributes are enumerated: inputs, outputs, inquiries, logical files, and interfaces. Because the counting rules are complex, accurate counting of function points is normally carried out by specialists who have passed a certification exam administered by the IFPUG organization.

Compared to lines of code, or LOC, metrics function points offer some significant advantages for baselines and benchmarks. Because coding is only part of the work of building software, LOC metrics have not been useful for measuring the volume of specifications, the contributions of project management, or the defects found in requirements and design documents. Further, LOC metrics tend to behave erratically from language to language. Indeed, for some languages such as Visual Basic, there are no effective LOC counting rules.

Because function point metrics can measure all software activities (i.e., requirements, design, coding, testing, documentation, management, etc.), they have become the de facto standard for software baselines and benchmarks. This is not to say that function point metrics have no problems of their own. But for collecting quantitative data from software projects, function points offer such significant advantages to LOC metrics that most of the published software benchmark data uses function point metrics. Let us now consider what happens after the assessment, baseline, and benchmark data are collected.

18.1.2 Stage 1: Focus on Management Technologies

Because software project management is a weak link on software projects, the first improvement stage concentrates on bringing managers up to speed on critical technologies such as planning, sizing, cost estimating, milestone tracking, quality and productivity measurement, risk analysis, and value analysis. It is necessary to begin with managers, because they are the ones who need to calculate the returns on investment that will occur later. They also have to collect the data to demonstrate progress. Unless managers are trained and equipped for their roles, it is not likely that progress will be significant.

18.1.3 Stage 2: Focus on Software Processes and Methodologies

The second stage concentrates on improved approaches for dealing with requirements, design, development, and quality control. Since tools support processes, rather than the other way around, new development processes need to be selected and deployed before investments in tools occur.

Some of the proved processes deployed in this stage include joint application design (JAD), any of several formal design methods such as Warnier-Orr, Yourdon, Merise, the Unified Modeling Language (UML), and several others. Formal design and code inspections and formal change management procedures are also selected and deployed during this stage.

18.1.4 Stage 3: Focus on New Tools and Approaches

As improved software processes begin to be deployed it is appropriate to acquire new tools and to explore advanced or new technologies. It is also the time to explore difficult technologies with steep learning curves such as client-server methods and the object-oriented paradigm. Jumping prematurely into client-server projects, or moving too quickly toward object-oriented analysis and design, usually means trouble because poorly trained practitioners are seldom successful. The first-time failure rate of new technologies is alarmingly high. Therefore, careful selection of new technologies and thorough training of personnel in the selected technologies are prerequisites to successful deployment of new technology.

Some of the kinds of tools acquired during this stage might include configuration control tools, code complexity analysis tools, test case monitors, analysis and design tools, and perhaps advanced language tools for Java or very high-level programming languages.

18.1.5 Stage 4: Focus on Infrastructure and Specialization

To reach the top plateau of software excellence, it is necessary to have a top-notch organizational structure as well as excellent tools and methods.

The infrastructure stage deals with organization and specialization, and begins to move toward establishment of specialized teams for handling critical activities. It has long been known that specialists can outperform generalists in a number of key software tasks. Some of the tasks where specialists excel include testing, maintenance, integration, configuration control, technical writing, and quality assurance. Policies on continuing education are important too during this stage.

In addition to better development processes and better tool suites, industry leaders are usually characterized by better organizational structures and more specialists than average companies, and much better than laggards.

18.1.6 Stage 5: Focus on Reusability

Reusability has the best return on investment of any software technology, but effective reuse is surprisingly difficult. For a general discussion of software reuse, refer to Jacobsen et al. (1997).

If software quality control is not at state-of-the-art levels, then reuse will include errors that cause costs to go up instead of down. Also, reuse includes much more than just code. In fact, an effective software reuse program should include a minimum of six reusable artifacts:

1. Reusable requirements
2. Reusable designs and specifications
3. Reusable source code
4. Reusable user documents
5. Reusable test plans
6. Reusable test cases and test scripts

If only source code is reused, the return on investment will be marginal. Optimal benefits occur only when reusability spans all major deliverable items.

18.1.7 Stage 6: Focus on Industry Leadership

Organizations that go all the way to the sixth stage are usually the leaders in their respective industries. These organizations are the kind that would be found at level 5 on the SEI capability maturity model (CMM). These organizations may be in a position to acquire competitors. They can almost always outperform their competitors in all phases of software development and maintenance work unless the competitors are also at the top.

Industry leadership is a coveted goal that many companies strive to achieve, but few do. Among the attributes of industry leadership that are visible to outside consultants, the following twelve factors stand out:

- ☐ Effective project management tool suites
- ☐ Effective software development tool suites
- ☐ Effective quality assurance and testing tool suites

☐ Effective software processes and methods
☐ Effective organizational structures
☐ Effective management teams
☐ Effective technical teams with substantial specialization
☐ High morale among the software staff
☐ High user-satisfaction levels as noted by customer surveys
☐ High regard by top corporate management
☐ High regard by industry analysts
☐ High regard by competitive organizations

No company examined so far has been excellent in every attribute of software success, but the leaders are superior in many attributes.

Let us examine the costs, timing, and anticipated results of software process improvement activities as noted among our clients engaged in process improvement activities.

18.2 Process Improvement Economics

Although this report contains general industry data, each company needs to create an individualized plan and budget for its improvement strategy. Table 18.1 presents information based on the size of companies in terms of software personnel. The cost data in Table 18.1 is expressed in terms of "cost per capita" or the approximate costs for each employee in software departments. The cost elements include training, consulting fees, capital equipment, software licenses, and improvements in office conditions.

TABLE 18.1
Process Improvement Expenses per Capita

Stage	Meaning	Small Staff (< 100)	Medium Staff (< 1,000)	Large Staff (< 10,000)	Giant Staff (> 10,000)	Average
0	Assessment	$100	$125	$150	$250	$156
1	Management	1,500	2,500	3,500	5,000	3,125
2	Process	1,500	2,500	3,000	4,500	2,875
3	Tools	3,000	6,000	5,000	10,000	6,000
4	Infrastructure	1,000	1,500	3,000	6,500	3,000
5	Reuse	500	2,500	4,500	6,000	3,375
6	Industry leadership	1,500	2,000	3,000	4,500	2,750
Total expenses		$9,100	$17,125	$22,150	$36,750	$21,281

The sizes in Table 18.1 refer to the software populations, and divide organizations into four rough size domains: fewer than 100 software personnel, fewer than 1,000 personnel, fewer than 10,000 personnel, and more than 10,000 which implies giant software organizations such as IBM, Accenture Consulting, and Electronic Data Systems (EDS), all of which have more than 50,000 software personnel corporatewide.

As Table 18.1 shows, software process assessments are fairly inexpensive. But improving software processes and tool suites after a software process assessment can be very expensive indeed.

It sometimes happens that the expenses of process improvement would be high enough so that companies prefer to bring in an outsource vendor. This option is used most often by companies that are below average. If a company is far behind similar companies, then turning over software development and maintenance to an outside company that already uses state-of-the-art processes and tool suites may make good business sense.

Another important topic is the time it will take to move through each stage of the process improvement sequence. Table 18.2 illustrates the approximate number of calendar months devoted to moving from stage to stage. Smaller companies can move much more rapidly than large corporations and government agencies. Large companies often have entrenched bureaucracies with many levels of approval. Thus, change in large companies is often slow and sometimes very slow.

For large companies process improvement is of necessity a multiyear undertaking. Corporations and government agencies seldom move quickly, even if everyone

TABLE 18.2
Process Improvement Stages in Calendar Months

Stage	Meaning	Small Staff (< 100)	Medium Staff (< 1,000)	Large Staff (< 10,000)	Giant Staff (> 10,000)	Average
0	Assessment	2.00	2.00	3.00	4.00	2.75
1	Management	3.00	6.00	9.00	12.00	7.50
2	Process	4.00	6.00	9.00	15.00	8.50
3	Tools	4.00	6.00	9.00	12.00	7.75
4	Infrastructure	3.00	4.00	9.00	12.00	7.00
5	Reuse	4.00	6.00	12.00	16.00	9.50
6	Industry leadership	6.00	8.00	9.00	12.00	8.75
Sum (worst case)		26.00	38.00	60.00	83.00	51.75
Overlap (best case)		16.90	26.60	43.20	61.42	33.64

is moving in the same direction. When there is polarization of opinion or political opposition, progress can be very slow or nonexistent.

An important question is, what kind of value or return on investment will occur from software process improvements? Table 18.3 shows only the approximate improvements for schedules, costs, and quality (here defined as software defect levels). The results are expressed as percentage improvements compared to the initial baseline at the start of the improvement process.

The best projects in the best companies can deploy software with only about 5% of the latent defects of similar projects in lagging companies. Productivity rates are higher by more than 300%, and schedules are only about one-fourth as long. These notable differences can be used to justify investments in software process improvement activities.

As can be seen from this rough analysis, the maximum benefits do not occur until stage 5, when full software reusability programs are implemented. Since reusability has the best return and greatest results, our clients often ask why it is not the first stage.

The reason that software reuse is delayed until stage 5 is that a successful reusability program depends on mastering software quality. Effective software quality control implies deploying a host of precursor technologies such as formal inspections, formal test plans, formal quality assurance groups, and formal development processes. Unless software quality is at state-of-the-art levels, any attempt to reuse materials can be hazardous. Reusing materials that contain serious errors will result in longer schedules and higher costs than having no reusable artifacts.

TABLE 18.3
Improvements in Software Defect Levels, Productivity, and Schedules

Stage	Meaning	Delivered Defects (%)	Development Productivity (%)	Development Schedule (%)
0	Assessment	0.00	0.00	0.00
1	Management	−10.00	10.00	−12.00
2	Process	−50.00	30.00	−17.00
3	Tools	−10.00	25.00	−12.00
4	Infrastructure	−5.00	10.00	−5.00
5	Reuse	−85.00	70.00	−50.00
6	Industry leadership	−5.00	50.00	−5.00
	Total	−95.00	365.00	−75.00

18.3 Measuring Process Improvements at Activity Levels

For measuring process improvements over time, gross measures of entire projects are not granular enough to be effective. We have learned that it is necessary to get down to the level of specific activities in order for process improvements to become visible and measurable.

Activity-based costs can highlight the activities that process improvements benefit, and also illustrate activities where no tangible benefits are noted. This kind of analysis is not be possible using only project-level data. Software benchmarking companies have found that function point metrics are superior to the older LOC metrics for measuring activity-based costs and schedules. The reason is that function points can measure noncoding activities such as requirements, design, documentation, and management.

We use the function point metrics defined by IFPUG. The current standard for function points published by IFPUG is version 4.1, which is used here. For a general introduction to the topic of function point analysis, refer to Dreger (1989) or to Garmus and Herron (1995).

Note that while IFPUG function points are the most widely used metric in the United States and Western Europe, other forms of function point metric are in use too. For example, in the United Kingdom a function point metric called Mark II function points are very common. For a discussion of the Mark II function points, refer to Symons (1991).

Table 18.4 illustrates a hypothetical project of 1,000 function points (roughly 125,000 C source statements). The organization producing this application would be a typical civilian organization at CMM level 1. Level 1 organizations are not very sophisticated in software development approaches. Thus, level 1 organizations often have missed schedules, cost overruns, and poor-quality products.

The most obvious characteristic of CMM level 1 organizations is that testing is both the most expensive and the most time-consuming activity. The root cause of this phenomenon is that CMM level 1 organizations usually have excessive defect levels and are deficient in two key quality factors: defect prevention and pretest reviews and inspections.

By contrast, Table 18.5 illustrates exactly the same size and kind of software project. However, Table 18.5 shows the results that have been noted in somewhat more mature level 3 organizations on the Software Engineering Institute capability maturity model scale. For the level 3 organization, testing has diminished significantly in terms of both timing and costs. This is because defect prevention methods have improved and pretest design reviews and code inspections have both been strengthened.

TABLE 18.4
Example of Activity-Based Cost Analysis for SEI CMM Level 1

Application class	Systems software
Programming language(s)	C
Size in function points (FP)[a]	1,000
Size in lines of code (LOC)[b]	125,000
Work hours per month	132
Average monthly salary (burdened)[c]	$7,500

Activity	Work Hours per FP	Staff[d]	Effort (Person Months)[e]	Schedule (Months)[f]	Costs by Activity	Percent of Costs
Requirements	1.20	2.00	9.09	4.55	$ 68,182	4%
Design	2.93	3.33	22.22	6.67	166,667	11
Design reviews	0.38	4.00	2.86	0.71	21,429	1
Coding	7.76	6.67	58.82	8.82	441,176	29
Code inspections	0.53	8.00	4.00	0.50	30,000	2
Testing	8.25	6.67	62.50	9.38	468,750	31
Quality assurance	1.32	1.00	10.00	10.00	75,000	5
Documentation	1.10	1.00	8.33	8.33	62,500	4
Management	3.57	1.00	27.03	27.03	202,703	13
Totals	27.04	6.33	204.85	32.35	$1,536,406	100%
FP per month	4.88					
LOC per month	610					
Cost per FP	$1,536.41					
Cost per LOC	$12.29					

a. FP = function points per IFPUG Counting Practices Manual 4.1.
b. LOC = lines of noncommentary code.
c. Burdened = basic compensation and overhead costs.
d. Staff = number of workers assigned to major activities. Decimal values indicate some part-time personnel.
e. Person month = 22 workdays of 8 hours each.
f. Calendar months.

As Table 18.6 shows, a side-by-side analysis of the costs indicates an overall reduction of about 20% between the level 1 and level 3 versions, but the activity costs illustrate that most of the savings occur during the testing phase.

Indeed, the costs of inspections are higher, rather than lower, for the CMM level 3 version. Also, some costs such as those for user documentation are the same in both scenarios. Activity-based cost analysis allows a detailed scrutiny of differences

TABLE 18.5
Example of Activity-Based Cost Analysis for SEI CMM Level 3

Application class	Systems software	
Programming language(s)	C	
Size in function points (FP)[a]	1,000	
Size in lines of code (LOC)[b]	125,000	
Work hours per month	132	
Average monthly salary (burdened)[c]	$7,500	

Activity	Work Hours per FP	Staff[d]	Effort (Person Months)[e]	Schedule (Months)[f]	Costs by Activity	Percent of Costs
Requirements	1.06	2.00	8.00	4.00	$ 60,000	5%
Design	2.64	3.33	20.00	6.00	150,000	12
Design reviews	0.88	4.00	6.67	1.67	50,000	4
Coding	6.00	6.67	45.45	6.82	340,909	28
Code inspections	1.06	8.00	8.00	1.00	60,000	5
Testing	3.30	6.67	25.00	3.75	187,500	15
Quality assurance	2.20	1.00	16.67	16.67	125,000	10
Documentation	1.10	1.00	8.33	8.33	62,500	5
Management	3.30	1.00	25.00	25.00	$187,500	15
Totals	21.53	6.33	163.12	25.76	$1,223,409	100%
FP per month	6.13					
LOC per month	766					
Cost per FP	$1,223.41					
Cost per LOC	$9.79					

a. FP = function points per IFPUG Counting Practices Manual 4.1.
b. LOC = lines of noncommentary code.
c. Burdened = basic compensation and overhead costs.
d. Staff = number of workers assigned to major activities. Decimal values indicate some part-time personnel.
e. Person month = 22 workdays of 8 hours each.
f. Calendar months.

between processes, and opens up a way to perform rather sophisticated cost and schedule models which cannot be done using coarser project-level data.

If we turn now to quality, the results of improving both defect prevention and defect removal approaches in the level 3 example causes a very significant reduction in delivered defects. In turn, the reduced numbers of defects allow shorter and more cost-effective development cycles. When projects run late, it often happens that problems escape notice until testing begins. When major defects are found during testing,

TABLE 18.6
Side-by-Side Comparison of Activity-Based Costs

Application class	Systems software
Programming language(s)	C
Size in function points (FP)[a]	1,000
Size in lines of code (LOC)[b]	125,000
Work hours per month	132
Average monthly salary (burdened)[c]	$7,500

Activity	SEI CMM Level 1	SEI CMM Level 3	Variance in Costs	Variance Percent
Requirements	$68,182	$60,000	-$8,182	-12.00
Design	166,667	$150,000	-16,667	-10.00
Design reviews	21,429	$50,000	28,571	133.33
Coding	441,176	$340,909	-100,267	-22.73
Code inspections	30,000	60,000	30,000	100.00
Testing	468,750	$187,500	-281,250	-60.00
Quality assurance	75,000	125,000	50,000	66.67
Documentation	62,500	62,500	0	0.00
Management	202,703	187,500	-15,203	-7.50
Totals	$1,536,406	$1,223,409	-$312,997	-20.37%
Cost per FP	$1,536.41	$1,223.41	-$313.00	-20.37%
Cost per LOC	$12.29	$9.79	-$2.50	-20.37%

a. FP = function points per IFPUG Counting Practices Manual 4.1.
b. LOC = lines of noncommentary code.
c. Burdened = basic compensation and overhead costs.

it is too late to bring the project back under control. The goal is to prevent defects or eliminate them before testing gets under way.

Table 18.7 illustrates the differences in defect potentials, defect removal efficiency levels, and delivered defects of the two cases. As can be seen, a combination of defect prevention and defect removal can yield significant reductions in delivered defect levels. Because finding and fixing defects is the most costly and time-consuming activity for software, projects that are successful in preventing defects or removing them via inspections will achieve shorter schedules and higher productivity as well as better quality.

If software process improvement is to become a mainstream technology it is important to demonstrate exactly what is being improved, and by how much.

Activity-based cost analysis illustrates that process improvement does not create a homogenous improvement of every activity equally. Improvements tend to be very

TABLE 18.7
SEI CMM Level 1 and Level 3 Defect Differences

Level	Potential Defects[a]	Removal Efficiency[b] (%)	Delivered Defects	Defects per Function Point[c]	Defects per KLOC[d]
SEI Level 1	6150	85.01%	922	0.92	7.38
SEI Level 3	3500	95.34	163	0.16	1.30

a. Effects likely to be encountered from the start of requirements through at least one year of customer use.
b. Percentage of potential defects found before delivery of the software to customers.
c. Function points per IFPUG Counting Practices Manual 4.1.
d. KLOC = one thousand lines of code.

significant for key activities such as testing but scarcely visible for other activities such as user documentation.

Indeed, for a number of important activities such as design and code inspections and quality assurance work, the costs will be higher for more mature organizations at level 3 on the CMM than for those at level 1 on the CMM.

18.4 Summary

Software process improvement is an important research topic, and should continue to grow in importance well into the twenty-first century. However, some software technologies have a shorter lifetime. Unless tangible results can be achieved and demonstrated, interest in the process improvement technology will quickly wane.

The data presented here are approximate and have a high margin of error. Further, software projects range in size from fewer than 100 function points to more than 100,000 function points. The examples used here centered on 1,000 function points, and the data should not be used for significantly larger or smaller projects. Only levels 1 and 3 on the CMM scale are illustrated. Thus every company should create its own data using its own assessment and baseline studies and not depend upon external sources such as this report.

Function point metrics provide useful and interesting insights into the economics of software, and into the domain of software process improvement in particular. The older LOC metric was not a good choice for exploring software process improvement. LOC metrics were especially troublesome for the noncoding phases such as requirements and design phases.

For large software projects of more than 10,000 function points, the noncoding activities comprise more than 50% of the effort. The activities that can be studied using lines of code metrics comprise less than 30% of the total effort devoted to large systems, as illustrated by the two examples in this article.

Function point metrics are not perfect, but they are leading to new and useful discoveries that extend beyond those made with the older lines of code metrics. Success in exploring the impact of software process improvements is a sign that the function point metric is a useful one. However, the real goal of such studies is to understand the economics of software.

References

1. Albrecht, A., "Measuring Application Development Productivity," *Proceedings of the Joint Share/Guide/IBM Application Development Symposium,* Monterey, California, April 1979.
2. Dreger, B., *Function Point Analysis,* Englewood Cliffs, N. J.: Prentice Hall, 1989.
3. Garmus, D., and Herron, D., *Measuring the Software Process: A Practical Guide to Functional Measurement,* Englewood Cliffs, N. J.: Prentice-Hall, 1995.
4. Garmus, D., and Herron, D., *Function Point Analysis,* Boston, Mass.: Addison Wesley Longman, 2001.
5. Grady, R. B., *Successful Process Improvement,* Upper Saddle River, N. J.: Prentice-Hall PTR, 1997.
6. IFPUG Counting Practices Manual, Release 4.1, International Function Point Users Group, Westerville, Ohio: April 1999.
7. Jacobsen, I., M. Griss, and P. Jonsson, *Software Reuse: Architecture, Process, and Organization for Business Success,* Reading, Mass.: Addison Wesley Longman, 1997.
8. Jones, C., *Assessment and Control of Software Risks,* Englewood Cliffs, N. J.: Prentice-Hall, 1994.
9. Jones, C., *Patterns of Software System Failure and Success,* Boston, Mass.: International Thomson Computer Press, 1995.
10. Jones, C., *Applied Software Measurement,* 2nd ed., New York: McGraw Hill, 1996.
11. Jones, C., *Software Quality: Analysis and Guidelines for Success,* Boston, Mass.: International Thomson Computer Press, 1997.
12. Jones, C., *Estimating Software Costs,* New York: McGraw Hill, 1998.
13. Jones, C., *Software Assessments, Benchmarks, and Best Practices,* Reading, Mass.: Addison Wesley Longman, 2000.
14. Paulk, M., V Charles, B. Curtis, and M. Chrissis, *The Capability Maturity Model – Guidelines for Improving the Software Process,* Reading, Mass.: Addison Wesley, 1995.
15. Symons, C. R., *Software Sizing and Estimating—Mk II FPA (Function Point Analysis),* Chichester, England: John Wiley & Sons, 1991.

19

Concluding Remarks

The previous eighteen chapters cover a spectrum of topics on the theme of metrics and models in software quality engineering. Beginning with the definition of software quality and the need to measure and drive improvement via metrics and models, we surveyed the major existing software development process models, examined the fundamentals in measurement theory, provided an overview of major software quality metrics that cover the entire software life cycle, and looked into the application of techniques from traditional quality engineering (e.g., as the seven basic quality tools) in software development. Then we examined the concept of defect removal effectiveness, which is central to software development, and its measurements. We then discussed and presented two categories of model in software quality engineering: reliability models for quality projection and estimation, and quality management models. We discussed in-process metrics supporting the models. We illustrated with examples the effort/outcome model in interpreting in-process metrics and in managing in-process quality. We then discussed the third category of models—the complexity metrics and models. We discussed metrics for objected-oriented projects from both perspectives of design and complexity metrics and quality management metrics. Our focus then moved on to the fourth category of metrics and model—the customer view of quality. We discussed the availability and outage metrics and the measurement and analysis of customer satisfaction.

This coverage of the entire spectrum of metrics and models—from quality models, product quality metrics, and in-process metrics, to customer-oriented metrics and customer satisfaction measurements—provided a direct link to discussions of the definition of quality and total quality management (TQM). Then we discussed in-process quality assessment (Chapter 15), proposed a software project assessment method (Chapter 16), offered practical advice on the dos and don'ts of software process improvement (Chapter 17), and analyzed and examined the quantitative results of software process improvement (Chapter 18). These four chapters close the loop to the earlier discussions on the software process models, the process assessment frameworks, and the premise that quality, metrics and models, process, and process improvement are all closely related. Throughout the discussions, many examples were presented. The purpose here has been to establish and illustrate a framework for the application of software quality metrics and models.

In this final chapter we discuss several observations with regard to software measurements in general and software quality metrics and models in particular, and offer a perspective on the future role of measurement in software engineering.

19.1 Data Quality Control

Few would argue that software measurement is critical and necessary to provide a scientific basis for software engineering. What is measured is improved. For software development to be a true engineering discipline, measurement must be an integral part of the practice. For measurements, metrics, and models to be useful, the data quality must be good. Unfortunately, software data are often error-prone (as discussed in Chapter 4). In our view, the data quality issue is a big obstacle to wide acceptance of software measurement in practice. It is perhaps even more important than the techniques of metrics and models per se. It is the most basic element on which the techniques of metrics and models in software engineering can build. Garbage in, garbage out; without adequate accuracy and reliability of the raw data, the value added from metrics, models, and analysis will diminish. Therefore, strong focus should be placed on the quality of the data in the collection and analysis process. Data collection and project tracking must encompass validation as an integral element. Any analysis and modeling work should assess the validity and reliability of the data and its potential impact on the findings (as discussed in Chapter 3).

Note that the data quality problem goes far beyond software development; it appears to permeate the entire information technology and data processing industry. The accuracy of data in many databases is surprisingly low; error rates of roughly 10% are not uncommon (Huh et al., 1992). In addition to accuracy, the most pertinent issues in data quality appear to be completeness, consistency, and currency. Furthermore, the magnitude of the problem often multiplies when databases are combined and when organizations update or replace applications. These problems usually result in unhappy customers, useless reports, and financial loss. In a survey conducted by *Information Week* (Wilson, 1992), 70% of the responding information system (IS) managers said their business processes had been interrupted at least once by bad data. The most common causes were inaccurate entry, 32%; incomplete entry, 24%; error in data collection, 21%; and system design error, 15%. Information technology has permeated every facet of the institutions of modern society, so the impact of poor-quality data is enormous. In recent years, the data quality in many business and public databases does not seem to have improved. However, because data mining as a way of improving business has been receiving attention, this could be a starting point of data quality improvement in the business world. Business requirements could become a driving force for the improvement.

In the fields of quality and software engineering, experts have noticed the implications of poor data quality and have started making efforts toward improvements. For instance, back in 1992, at the International Software Quality Exchange conference (ISQE, 1992), which was organized by the Juran Institute, members of the panel on prospective methods for improving data quality discussed their experiences with some data quality improvement methods. The proposed approaches included:

- ☐ Engineering (or reengineering) the data collection process and entry processes for data quality
- ☐ Human factors in data collection and manipulation for data quality
- ☐ Establishing joint information systems and process designs for data quality
- ☐ Data editing, error localization, and imputation techniques
- ☐ Sampling and inspection methods
- ☐ Data tracking—follow a random sample of records through the process to trace the root sources of error in the data collection and reporting process

Emerging trends are encouraging for those who are concerned with data quality and the practice of metrics and measurements in software engineering. First, more experts have started addressing the data quality issues and providing advice with regard to the data collection process, measurement specifications and procedures, and data validation methods at conferences and in publications. Second, the practice of metrics and measurements appears to have been gaining a wide acceptance by development teams and organizations in their software engineering efforts. More usage and analyses of data will certainly drive improvements in data quality and enhance the focus on data validation as a key element of the data collection and analysis process.

Of course, in the practice of software metrics and measurement, data quality control is just a starting point. The process hinges on translating raw data into information and then into knowledge that can lead to effective actions and results.

Raw data —> Information —> Knowledge —> Actions —> Results

To translate raw data into meaningful information, we need metrics and models. To translate information into knowledge, we need analysis of the metrics and models in the context of the team's experience. To formulate effective actions, we further need analysis and information on cause-and-effect relationships and good decisions. To support action implementation and to evaluate the results, we again need data, measurements, metrics, and models.

19.2 Getting Started with a Software Metrics Program

Once a development organization begins collecting software data, there is a tendency for overcollection and underanalysis. The amount of data collected and the number of metrics need not be overwhelming. It is more important that the information extracted from the data be accurate and useful. Indeed, a large volume of data may lead to low data quality and casual analysis, instead of serious study. It may also incur a sizable cost on the project and a burden on the development team. As discussed earlier, to transform raw data into meaningful information, and to turn information into knowledge, analysis is the key. Analysis and its result, understanding and knowledge, drive improvement, which is the payback of the measurement approach. Therefore, it is essential for a measurement program to be analysis driven instead of data driven.

By "analysis driven" I mean the data to be collected and the metrics used should be determined by the models we use for development (such as models for development process, quality management, and reliability assessment) and the analysis we intend to perform. Associated with the analysis-driven approach, a key to operating a successful metrics program is knowing what to expect from each metric. In this regard, measurement paradigms such as Basili's Goal/Question/Metrics (GQM) approach prove to be useful (Basili, 1989, 1995). In Chapters 1 and 4 we briefly discussed the GQM approach and gave examples of implementation. To establish effective in-process metrics, I recommend the effort/outcome model, which was discussed in Chapters 8 and 9.

Metrics and measurements must progress and mature with the development process of the organization. If the development process is in the initial stage of the maturity spectrum, a heavy focus on metrics may be counterproductive. For example, if there is no formal integration control process, tracking integration defects will not be meaningful; if there is no formal inspection or verification, collecting defect data at the front end provides no help.

Suppose we draw a line on a piece of paper to represent the software life cycle, from the start of the development process to the maintenance phase, and put a mark on the line at about two-thirds from the start (and one-third from the end) to represent the product delivery date. Then the starting metrics in general ought to center around the product delivery phase. Then work backward into the development process to establish in-process metrics, and work forward to track the quality performance in the field. Usually field quality metrics are easier to establish and track because they are normally a part of the support and service process. Establishing and implementing effective in-process metrics are more challenging.

As an example, suppose we are to begin a simple metrics program with only three metrics. I would highly recommend these metrics be the size of the product, the number of defects found during the final phase of testing, and the number of defects found in the field (or other reliability measures). Assuming that the data collection process put in place ensures high accuracy and reliability, then here are a few examples of what can be done from these pieces of data:

- ☐ Calculate the product defect rate (per specified time frame) (A).
- ☐ Calculate the test defect rate (B).
- ☐ Determine a desirable goal for A, and monitor the performance of the products developed by the organization.
- ☐ Monitor B for the products in the same way as A.
- ☐ Assess the correlation between A and B when at least several data points become available.
- ☐ If a correlation is found between A and B, then form the metric of testing effectiveness (final phase), (B/A) x 100%. Or one can derive a simple regression model predicting A from B (a simple static reliability model).
- ☐ Use the B/A metric to set the test defect removal target for new projects, given a predetermined goal for the product defect rate.
- ☐ Monitor and use a control chart for the B/A metrics for all products to determine the process capability of the test defect removal of the organization's development process.

This simple example illustrates that good use of simple data can be quite beneficial. Of course, in real life we would not stop at the B/A metrics. To improve the B/A value, a host of questions and metrics will naturally arise: Is the test coverage improving? How can we improve the test suite to maximize test defect removal effectiveness? Is a test-focused defect removal strategy good for us? What alternative methods would make us more cost effective in removing defects? The point is that for metrics programs to be successful, it is important to make good use of small amounts of data, then build on the proven metrics in order to maximize the benefits of quantitative software quality engineering. As more metrics are used and more data collected, they should progress in reverse direction of the development process—from the end product to the back end of the process, then to the front end of the process. Metrics and data are usually more clear-cut at the back end and more difficult to define and collect in the front end.

For small teams, I have recommended, in various chapters, a couple of quality management models and a small set of metrics, including the metrics in the preceding example. These metrics can be implemented easily, and for some that require tools and statistical expertise for implementation, I provided quick and easy alternatives. Regardless of small and large teams, I recommend the following to jump-start a metrics program:

- ☐ Start the metrics practice at the project level, not at the process level or the organizational level. Select one or more projects to get started.
- ☐ Integrate the use of metrics as part of the project quality management process, which in turn, is a key element of the project management process. For small projects, especially when the project lead is interested in metrics and measurement, the ideal situation is for the project lead to do the metrics himself or herself, with support from the project team. For larger projects, a member of the project team can lead the measurement process. In either case, the practice of metrics and measurement has to be part of the project management activities, not a separate activity.
- ☐ Most importantly, determine and select a very small number of metrics (for example, two or three) that are important to the project and start the tracking and reporting based on the existing infrastructure. The existing infrastructure may not be adequate to provide precise tracking. Even with rudimentary tracking and basic tools (e.g., 1-2-3 spreadsheet, pencil and paper), it is essential to get the practice started. As discussed in various chapters, many of the metrics can indeed be implemented via basic project management tools and software that are widely available.
- ☐ Always make use of the visual element of the metrics, measurements, and models. The availability and prevalent use of graphic and presentation software makes it easy to show the project's status via metrics and measurement, to maintain the team's interest, and to incorporate metrics in project management activities.

For long-term success at the organizational level, it is important to secure management commitment and to establish a data tracking system, which includes processes and tools. The point is that to jump-start a metrics program, it is essential to get started at the project level and to establish the relevance of some specific metrics to the success of the projects as soon as possible. A continual project-level focus is necessary for the continual success of a metrics program.

In addition to a tracking system, tools, and process, investment is also required to establish metrics expertise. When the development organization is small, data collection and analysis can be done by managers and project leaders. In large organizations, full-time metrics professionals are warranted for a successful program. I recommend that organizations with more than 100 members have at least one full-time metrics person. The metrics personnel design the metrics that support the organization's quality goals, design and implement the data collection and validation system, oversee the data collection, ensure data quality, analyze data, provide feedback to the development team, and engineer improvements in the development process. They can also provide training and support to the project teams. Or, for large projects they can be members of the project management team responsible for driving metrics, analysis, and quality into the mainstream of project management. The best candidates for a software metrics team are perhaps the members with training and experience in statistics (or related fields), software engineering, and quality. Large organizations can even form a metrics council, which could be called the software engineering metrics group (SEMG), to provide overall direction and consultations to specific projects. To be effective, the group's success must be measured by the success of specific projects that it is associated with, not by its high-level definition and process work. In other words, metrics and process definition should not be separated from implementation.

Developers play a key role in providing data. Experience indicates that it is essential that developers understand how the data are to be used. They need to know the relationship between the data they collect and the issues to be solved. Such an understanding enhances cooperation and, hence, the accuracy and completeness of the data. Of course, the best situations are those in which the metrics can be used by the developers themselves. Unless the data are collected automatically without human intervention, the development team's willingness and cooperation is the most important factor in determining data quality

When the process is mature enough, the best approach is to incorporate software data collection with the project management and the configuration management process, preferably supported by automated tools. In contrast, analysis should never be fully automated. It is helpful to use tools for analysis. However, the analyst ought to retain intellectual control of the process, the sources of the data, the techniques involved, the meaning of each piece of the data within the context of the product, development process, environment, and the outcome. This is the part of software quality engineering that the human mind cannot relegate. I have seen examples of funny outcomes of analysis, and of failures of metrics practices when the analysts lost control over the automated analysis process.

19.3 Software Quality Engineering Modeling

Software quality engineering, in particular software quality modeling, is a relatively new field for research and application. In this book we discuss four types of software quality models: reliability and projection models, quality management models, complexity metrics and models, and customer-oriented metrics, measurements, and models. A list of the models follows.

☐ Reliability and projection models
  ▫ Rayleigh model
  ▫ Exponential model
  ▫ Weibull distribution with different shape parameters
  ▫ Reliability growth models that were developed specifically for software
  ▫ The polynomial regression models for defect arrivals and backlog projections
☐ Quality management models
  ▫ The Rayleigh model framework for quality management The phase-based defect removal model and defect removal effectiveness
  ▫ The code integration pattern metric or heuristic model
  ▫ The defect arrival (PTR) nonparametric (heuristic) model
  ▫ The polynomial regression models for defect arrivals and backlog projections
  ▫ Use of reliability models to set targets for the current project
  ▫ The models for spreading the total projected field defects over time for maintenance planning (heuristic or using the reliability models)
  ▫ Statistical models on customer satisfaction analysis
  ▫ The effort/outcome model for establishing in-process metrics and for assessing in-process quality status
  ▫ Other tools, metrics, and techniques
☐ Complexity metrics and models
  ▫ Analysis and statistical models linking complexity metrics, syntactic constructs, structure metrics, and other variables to quality
  ▫ Analysis and statistical models linking the object-oriented design and complexity metrics to quality and managerial variables
☐ Customer-oriented metrics, measurements, and models
  ▫ System availability and outage metrics
  ▫ Methods and models to measure and analyze customer satisfaction

There is a tremendous amount of literature on customer satisfaction. The scope of customer satisfaction research and analysis goes beyond the discipline of software engineering. Therefore, in the following discussions, we confine our attention to the first three types of model.

Of the first three types of model, reliability and projection models are more advanced than the other two. Quality management models are perhaps still in their early maturity phase. It is safe to say that in spite of a good deal of progress in the past decade, none of the three types of models has reached the mature stage. The need for improvement will surely intensify in the future as software plays an increasingly critical role in modern society and quality has been brought to the center of the development process. Software projects need to be developed in a much more effective way with much better quality.

Note that the three types of model are developed and studied by different groups of professionals. Software reliability models are developed by reliability experts who were trained in mathematics, statistics, and operations research; complexity models and metrics are studied by computer scientists. The different origins explain why the former tends to take a black-box approach (monitoring and describing the behavior of the software from an external viewpoint) and the latter tends to take a white-box approach (looking into the internal relationships revolving around the central issue of complexity). Quality management models emerged from the practical needs of managing software development projects and draw on principles and knowledge in the field of quality engineering (traditionally being practiced in manufacturing and production operations). For software quality engineering to become mature, an interdisciplinary effort to combine and merge the various approaches is needed. A systematic body of knowledge in software quality engineering should encompass seamless links among the internal structure of design and implementation, the external behavior of the software system, and the logistics and management of the development project.

From the standpoint of the software industry, perhaps the most urgent challenge is to bridge the gap between state of the art and state of practice. On the one hand, better training in software engineering in general, and metrics and models in particular, needs to be incorporated into the curriculum for computer science and software engineering. Some universities and colleges are taking the lead in this regard; however, much more needs to be done and at a faster pace. Developers need not become experts in measurement theory, failure analysis, or other statistical techniques. However, they need to understand the quality principles, the impact of various development practices on the software's quality and reliability, and the findings accumulated over the years in terms of effective software engineering. Now that software is playing a more and more significant role in all institutions of our society, such training is very important. Indeed, the impact of poor software quality has been the subject of news headlines.

On the other hand, this gap poses a challenge for academicians and researchers in metrics and modeling. Many models, especially the reliability models, are expressed in sophisticated mathematical notations and formulas that are difficult to understand. To facilitate practices by the software industry, models, concepts, and algorithms for implementation need to be communicated to the software community (managers, software engineers, designers, testers, quality professionals) in their language. The model assumptions need to be clarified; the robustness of the model needs to be investigated and presented when some assumptions are not met; and much more applied research using industry data needs to be done.

With regard to the state of the art in reliability models, it appears that the fault count models give more satisfactory results than the time between failures models. In addition, the fault count models are usually used for commercial projects where the estimation precision required is not as stringent. In contrast, for safety-critical systems, precise and accurate predictions of the time of the next software failure is necessary. Thus, the time between failures software reliability models are largely unsuccessful. Furthermore, the validity of reliability models depends on the size of the software. The models are suitable for large-size software; small-size software may make some models nonsensical. For small projects, sometimes it is better to use simple methods such as the test effectiveness example (simple ratio method) discussed in the previous section, or a simple regression model.

A common feature of the existing software reliability models is the probability assumption. Researchers have challenged this assumption in software reliability (Cai et al., 1991). For the probability assumption to hold, three conditions must be satisfied: (1) The event is defined precisely, (2) a large number of samples is available, and (3) sample data must be repetitive in the probability sense. Cai and associates (1991) observed that software reliability behavior is fuzzy in nature and cannot be precisely defined: Reliability is workload dependent; test case execution and applications of various testing strategies are time variant; software complexity is defined in a number of ways; human intervention in the testing/debugging process is extremely complex; failure data are sometimes hard to specify; and so forth.

Furthermore, software is unique; a software debugging process is never replicated. Therefore, Cai and associates contend that the probability assumption is not met and that is why software reliability models are largely unsuccessful. They strongly advise that fuzzy software reliability models, based on fuzzy set methodologies, be developed and used. Hopefully, this line of reasoning will shed light on the research of software reliability models.

Another technology that could be valuable in quality modeling and projection is the reemerging neural network computing technology. Based loosely on biological neural networks, a neural network computer system consists of many simple processors and many adaptive connections between the processors. Through inputs and outputs, the network learns mapping of inputs to outputs by performing mathematical functions and adjusting weight values. Once trained, the network can produce good outputs given new inputs. Different from expert systems, which are expertise based (i.e., from a set of inference rules), neural networks are data based. Neural network systems can be thought of as pattern recognition machines, which are especially useful where fuzzy logic is important. In the past decade, applications of neural networks have begun in areas such as diagnosis, forecasting, inventory control, risk analysis, process control, scheduling, and so forth. Several neural network program products are also available in the commercial market.

For software quality and reliability, neural networks could be used to link various in-process indicators to the field performance of the final product. As such, neural networks can be regarded as machines for automatic empirical modeling. However, as mentioned, to use this approach, large samples with good quality data must be available. Therefore, it seems that until measurements become engrained in practice, the software industry may not be able to take good advantage of this technology. When neural network systems are in use, quality engineers or process experts must also retain intellectual control of the models produced by the networks, discern spurious relationships from the genuine ones, interpret the results, and, based on the results, plan for improvements.

In the meantime, for a software development organization to choose its models, the criteria for model evaluation discussed in Chapters 7 through 12 can serve as guidelines. Moreover, experience indicates that it is of utmost importance to establish the empirical validity of the models based on historical data relative to the organization and its development process. Once the empirical validity of the models is established, the chance for satisfactory results is significantly enhanced. At times, calibration of the model or the projection may be needed. Furthermore, it is good practice to use more than one model. For reliability assessment, cross-model reliability can be examined. In fact, research in reliability growth models indicates that combining the results of individual models may give more accurate predictions (Lyu and Nikora, 1992). For quality management, the multiple-model approach can increase the likelihood of achieving the criteria of timeliness of indication, scope of coverage, and capability.

Empirical validity may become the common ground to bridge the different modeling approaches and a promising path for the advancement of software quality engineering modeling. *Empirical validity* refers to situations in which the predictive validity and the capability (usefulness) of the model is supported by empirical data of the organization, or the models are based on theoretical underpinnings *and* empirical relationships derived from the organization's history. Good models ought to have theoretical backings and at the same time should be relevant to actual experience. Many of the quality management models we discussed are substantiated by empirical validity, and some of them were developed based on our experience with commercial projects. For complexity and design metrics, the relationships are based on empirical statistical models (e.g., multiple regressions). There is also a recognition that the direction of complexity metrics research (including the object-oriented metrics) is to conduct more empirical validation studies, and to correlate these metrics to the managerial variables (e.g., quality improvement, productivity, project management).

In software reliability modeling, it is long recognized that some models sometimes give good results, some are almost universally awful, and none can be trusted to be accurate at all times. I contend that the reason behind this phenomenon is empirical validity, or the lack of it. Note that empirical validity may vary across organizations, processes, and types of software. It is therefore important for an organization to pick and choose the right models to use. Recent software reliability research on the Bayesian approach (Fenton and Neil, 1999; Neil et al., 2000) and on improving reliability prediction by incorporating information from a similar project (Xie et al., 1999; Xie and Hong, 1998) indicates that empirical validity is receiving attention among software reliability researchers.

Finally, in our discussions of the quality management models, there is the Rayleigh model, or a discrete phase-based model as the overall framework of the entire development process. Within this framework, we discussed specific models and metrics to cover the major phases of development. Our objective is to build links among these models and metrics so the project's quality can be engineered from the early stages. Because not all of these models are "parametric," we again rely on the heuristic linkages. Figure 19.1 shows an example of the linkages among the code integration pattern, the test plan S curve, and the testing defect arrival model. Based on the empirical relationships observed among the several patterns, once the planned code integration pattern is available, which is early in the development cycle, we would be able to determine the position of the test S curve and the testing defect arrival model in the time line in terms of number of weeks prior to product ship. An early outlook of the quality of the project can then be derived: the higher the intersecting point between the projected defect arrival curve and the vertical line at product ship, the worse the quality of the project will be, and vice versa. Then the team can engineer improvement actions throughout the development cycle to improve the quality outlook. When the project progresses along the development cycle and more

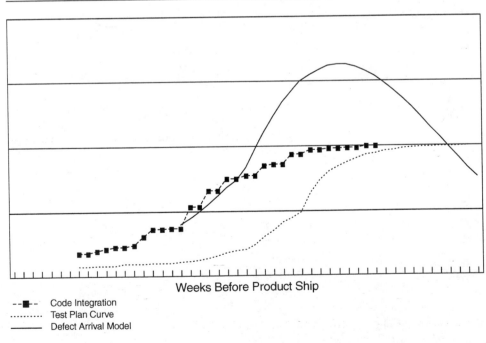

Weeks Before Product Ship

--■-- Code Integration
.... Test Plan Curve
——— Defect Arrival Model

FIGURE 19.1
Linkages Among Several Models and Metrics for Early Quality Planning

information becomes available, the models and their linkages can be updated periodically. For examples:

- [ ] When design and code development are being completed, their quality can be assessed via the design reviews/code inspections in-process metrics or data from the inspection scoring checklist. If the quality of the design and code is assessed to be better than the baseline project, then the area under the projected testing defect arrival curve can be adjusted to be smaller, and vice versa.
- [ ] When the actual code integration takes place over time, the pattern may shift and so may the testing pattern and the defect arrival pattern.
- [ ] The actual test progress status again will affect the defect arrival pattern.

19.4 Statistical Process Control in Software Development

For manufacturing production, the use of control charts is synonymous to statistical process control (SPC) or statistical quality control (SQC). In Chapter 5 we discussed the differences between software development and manufacturing processes. The use of control charts in software development, while helpful, is far from achieving SPC because of the many reasons discussed. The most important reason is that there is no established correlation between the mean and control limits of a control chart (of some in-process parameter) and the level of end-product quality, so the meaning of process capability is not established. The quality of the delivered software is also affected by many factors. It is not meaningful to use a control chart for the final product quality either because when the data are available, the software development is complete. It is not possible to effect changes at that time. In manufacturing production the unit of analysis is parts, and the production process is an ongoing, real-time process. A certain process mean and control limits are associated with a specific quality level (e.g., defective parts per million). When the process is out of control, the samples or the parts involved are excluded from the final deliverables.

It appears that control charts in software are a tool for enhancing consistency and stability with regard to process implementation. With ingenuity and meaningful application, control charting can eventually be used as a high-level process control for product quality at the organizational level—see the discussion on control-charting defect removal effectiveness in Chapter 5. The use of control charts is more appropriate at the process and organizational levels, and for the maintenance phase, rather than at the project level during the development process.

At the project level, software development appears to be far more complex and dynamic than the scenarios that control charts describe—the dynamics of design and development (versus production), the phases of a development process, the life-cycle concepts, the S curve patterns, the complexities involving predictive validity, the effort and outcome nature of in-process metrics, and so forth. One needs to employ a variety of tools, methods, and techniques, together with effective project management, in order to achieve the state of statistical quality control, in the general meaning of the term. We contend that the metrics, models, methods, and techniques discussed in this book, of which control chart is one, are what is needed to achieve SPC or SQC in software development. We need an overall defect model (or models) or defect removal strategy for the overall plan. We need phase-based parameters and specific models to relate the results of the implementation status at various development phases to the end-product quality outlook. We need models with theoretical backings and at the same time with relevance to actual experience of the organization. We need various metrics and measurements to support the models. We need to employ the effort/outcome model to make sure that we are reading the in-process quality status of the project right. We need comparisons to baselines, or projection models, to derive the quality outlook of the product when it is delivered.

The metrics and models ought to be able to relate in-process characteristics to end-product quality. Control charts and other quality control tools can be used to enhance the chance the model parameter values can be achieved. For example, if the model sets a certain in-process-escape-rate target (e.g., Figure 9.19 in Chapter 9) for the product, control charts can be used to identify the components or the inspections that are out of the control limits. Without a good overall model, the use of control charts may become a piecemeal approach. When a project meets the in-process targets according to the metrics and models used, and at the end achieves the end-product quality goal, then we can say it is under statistical process control, in the relaxed sense of the term.

The preceding statements are confined to the narrow meaning of quality control. In a broader sense, other parameters such as schedule, resource, and cost should be included. To achieve the broader meaning of quality control, good planning and project management, effective development process, effective use of metrics and models, and all key factors related to process, people, and technology have to function together well.

Finally, with regard to the use of statistical methods in software development, I offer my observations with respect to test of significance, or forming confidence intervals. First, in software development, we found that the testing for differences between two patterns (e.g., between a defect arrival curve during system test and a target curve, or between two code integration patterns) is useful and I recommend the Kolmogorov-Smirnov test (Rohatgi, 1984). Second, the traditional practices of forming 95% confidence intervals and using the 5% probability ($\alpha = 0.05$) for rejecting the null hypothesis in tests of significance deserve a closer look. Our experience indicates that the 95% confidence intervals are often too wide to be useful (even when other factors such as the multiple common causes in control charting are accounted for). Using the 5% probability as the basis for significance tests, we seldom found statistically significant differences, even when the situations warranted additional actions and would cause measurable differences in the end-product's quality level.

In tests of statistical significance, a null hypothesis and an alternative hypothesis are involved. The alternative hypothesis is normally the research hypothesis and the null hypothesis usually assumes there is no difference (between the two items being tested). The rationale is to use some probability level as the criterion for accepting or rejecting the null hypothesis, and therefore supporting or refuting the alternative hypothesis (research hypothesis). If the null hypothesis is true and it is rejected via the test, then we commit an error. The rejection of a true null hypothesis is called a type I error, α. If the null hypothesis is false but we failed to reject it via the test, then we also commit an error. The acceptance of a false null hypothesis is called a type II error, β. When α is set at the 0.05 level, we are saying that we are accepting a 5% type I error—if there is no difference in the items being compared, 5 out of 100 times we say there is a difference. The calculation of type II error, and the subject of the power of the test are more complicated. But in general, the smaller type I error, the larger the type II error, and the weaker the power of the test in detecting meaningful differences. In other words, using a smaller α value in significance tests will reduce false alarms, but at the same time, the probability in detecting true difference will decrease.

Therefore, the use of a certain α criteria in tests for significance is relative. When the null hypothesis (of no difference) is accepted, the situation merits careful thought. A nonsignificant result does not prove that the null hypothesis is correct—merely that the data do not give adequate grounds for rejecting it. In setting the α level for significance tests, the consequences of wrongly assuming the null hypothesis to be correct should also be weighed. For example, an assumption that two medications have the same frequency of side effects may not be critical if the side effects are minor temporary annoyances. If these side effects can be fatal, it is a different matter. In software development, a false alarm probably means that additional improvement actions will be taken. Failing to detect a meaningful difference in the in-process indicators, on the other hand, may result in less than desirable quality in the field. In our experience, many situations warrant alerts even when a nonsignificant result is obtained using $\alpha = 0.05$. As a result, we have used the .1 and .15 α levels in our applications as warranted by the specific situations. Our recommendation is not to rely solely on the traditional criteria for conducting significance tests, forming confidence intervals, or setting control limits. It is always beneficial to use empirical experience (e.g., what level of deterioration in the in-process indicators will cause a measurable difference in field quality) to substantiate or to adjust those criteria. For those who challenged the probability assumption of software reliability models, such as the argument discussed in the last section, control limits, confidence intervals, and significance tests that are based on probability distribution would not even be meaningful.

19.5 Measurement and the Future

Measurement is becoming more important and gaining acceptance in software development. In this modern-day quality era, customers demand complex software solutions of high quality. To ensure effective development, software development organizations must gain control over the entire development process. Measurement is the key to achieving such control and to making software development a true engineering discipline. Without effective use of measurements, progress in the tasks of planning and controlling software development will remain slow and will not be systematic.

Various software engineering techniques have emerged in the past decades: CASE tools, formal methods, software fault tolerance, object technology, new development processes, and the like. Software developers are faced with an enormous choice of methods, tools, and standards to improve productivity and quality. Relatively, there is little quantitative data and objective evaluation of various methods in software engineering. There is an urgent need for proper measurements to quantify the benefits and costs of these competing technologies. Such evaluations will help the software engineering discipline grow and mature. Progress will be made at adopting innovations that work well, and discarding or improving those that do not. Likewise, proposed process improvement practices must be tested and, substantiated or refuted via empirical studies. Software project assessments and process assessments ought to gather quantitative data on quality and productivity parameters and evaluate the link between process practices and measurable improvements.

The "state of the art" in measurements needs to be continually refined and improved, including all kinds of metrics and models that are discussed: software reliability models, quality management models and metrics, complexity metrics and models, and customer-oriented metrics and measurement. Good measurements must be based on sound theoretical underpinnings and empirical validity. Empirical validation is the key for natural selection and for these measurements to improve and mature. It may be the common ground for the different types of metrics and models that are developed by different groups of professionals.

To make their metrics program successful, development organizations ought to place strong focus on the data tracking system, the data quality, and the training and experience of the personnel involved. The quality of measurement practice plays a pivotal role in determining whether software measurement will become engrained in the state of practice in software engineering.

There are certainly encouraging signs on all these fronts.

References

1. Abraham, B., and J. Ledolter, *Statistical Methods for Forecasting,* New York: John Wiley & Sons, 1983.
2. Basili, V. R., "Software Development: A Paradigm for the Future," *Proceedings of the 13th International Computer Software and Applications Conference (COMPSAC),* Keynote Address, Orlando, Fla., September 1989.
3. Brackett, M. H., *Data Resource Quality: Turning Bad Habits into Good Practices,* Boston: Addison-Wesley, 2000.
4. Briand, L. C., B. Freimut, and F. Vollei, "Assessing the Cost-Effectiveness of Inceptions by Combining Project Data and Expert Opinion," *Proceedings of the 11th International Symposium on Software Reliability Engineering,* San Jose, California, October 8–11, 2000.
5. Burr, A., and M. Owen, *Statistical Methods for Software Quality: Using Metrics to Control Process and Product Quality,* London and New York: International Thomson Computer Press, 1996.
6. Cai, K. Y., C. Y. Wen, and M. L. Zhang, "A Critical Review on Software Reliability Modeling," *Reliability Engineering and System Safety,* Vol. 32, 1991.
7. Curtis, B., "Quantitative Process Management and Process Capability Baselines," SEPG 2002 QM Tutorial, Phoenix, Arizona, SEPG 2002, February 18–21.
8. Fenton, N., "How Effective Are Software Engineering Methods?" *Journal of Systems Software,* Vol. 22, 1993.
9. Fenton, N. E., and S. L. Pfleeger, *Software Metrics: A Rigorous Approach,* 2nd ed., London and Boston: International Thomson Computer Press, 1997.
10. Fenton, N., and M. Neil, "A Critique of Software Defect Prediction Research," *IEEE Transaction on Software Engineering,* Vol. 25, No. 5, 1999.
11. Gilb, T., "Optimizing Software Engineering Specification Quality Control Processes (Inspections)" SPIN Team Leader Course, Washington, D. C. SPIN Chapter, June 15–18, 1999.
12. Grady, R. B., and D. L. Caswell, *Software Metrics: Establishing a Company-Wide Program,* Englewood Cliffs, N. J.: Prentice-Hall, 1986.
13. Gunter, B., "Farewell Fusillade: An Unvarnished Opinion on the State of the Quality Profession," *Quality Progress,* April 1998.
14. Hetzel, B., *Making Software Measurement Work: Building an Effective Measurement Program,* Boston: QED Publishing Group, 1993.
15. Huang, K.T., Y. W. Lee, and R. Y. Wang, *Quality Information and Knowledge,* Upper Saddle River, N. J.: Prentice-Hall PTR, 1999.
16. Huh, Y. U., R. W. Pautke, and T. C. Redman, "Data Quality Control," *ISQE 92 Conference Proceedings,* Wilton, Conn.: Juran Institute, 1992.
17. Hong, G. Y., "Present and Future of Software Reliability Engineering," *QC Focus,* No. 35, January/February, 1998.
18. ISQE, "Session 7A Data Quality," *ISQE 92 Conference Proceedings,* Wilton, Conn.: Juran Institute, 1992.
19. Jones, C., *Programming Productivity,* New York: McGraw-Hill, 1986.
20. Jones, C., "Critical Problems in Software Measurement," Burlington, Mass.: Software Productivity Research, 1992.
21. Jones, C., *Assessment and Control of Software Risks,* Englewood Cliffs, N. J.: Yourdon Press, 1994.

22. Jones, C., *Applied Software Measurement, Assuring Productivity and Quality,* 2nd ed., New York: McGraw-Hill, 1997.

23. Jones, C., *Software Assessments, Benchmarks, and Best Practices,* Boston: Addison-Wesley, 2000.

24. Layman, B., B. Curtis, J. Puffer, and C. Webet,"Solving the Challenge of Quantitative Management, Section 4: Problems in the Use of Control Charts," SEPG 2002 QM Tutorial, Phoenix, Arizona, February 18–21, 2002.

25. Lipke, W., "Statistical Process Control of Project Performance," *CrossTalk, The Journal of Defense Software Engineering,* Vol. 15, No. 3, March 2002.

26. Loshin, D., *Enterprise Knowledge Management: The Data Quality Approach,* San Diego, Calif.: Academic Press, 2001.

27. Lyu, M. R., and A. Nikora, "Applying Reliability Models More Effectively," *IEEE Software,* July 1992.

28. McGarry, J., D. Card, C. Jones, B. Layman, E. Clark, J. Dean, and F. Hall, *Practical Software Measurement, Objective Information for Decision Makers,* Boston: Addison-Wesley, 2001.

29. Montgomery, D. C., *Introduction to Statistical Quality Control,* New York: John Wiley & Sons, 1985.

30. Naumann, E., and S. H. Hoisington, *Customer Centered Six Sigma, Linking Customers, Process Improvement, and Financial Results,* Milwaukee, Wisc.: ASQ Quality Press, 2001.

31. Neil, M., N. E. Fenton, and L. Nielsen, "Building Large-Scale Bayesian Networks," *The Knowledge Engineering Review,* Vol. 15, No. 3, 2000.

32. Neufelder, A. M., "How to Measure the Impact of Specific Development Practices on Fielded Defect Density," *Proceedings of the 11th International Symposium on Software Reliability Engineering,* San Jose, Calif., October 8–11, 2000.

33. Redman, T. C., *Data Quality: The Field Guide,* Boston: Digital Press, 2001.

34. Rohatgi, V. K., *Statistical Inference,* New York: John Wiley & Sons, 1984.

35. Snedecor, G. W., and W. G. Cochran, *Statistical Methods,* 7th ed., Ames, Iowa: The Iowa State University Press, 1980.

36. Software Productivity Research, *Quality and Productivity of the SEI CMM,* Burlington, Mass.: Software Productivity Research, 1994.

37. Wilson, L., "Devil in Your Data," *Information Week,* August 31, 1992.

38. Xie, M., and G. Y. Hong, "A Study of the Sensitivity of Software Release Time," *The Journal of Systems and Software,* Vol. 44, 1998.

39. Xie, M., G. Y. Hong, and C. Wohlin "Software Reliability Prediction Incorporating Information from a Similar Project," *The Journal of Systems and Software,* Vol. 49, 1999.

40. Xie, M., and G. Y. Hong, "Software Reliability Modeling and Analysis," chapter in *Handbook of Statistics 20: Advances in Reliability,* N. Balakrishnan and C. R. Rao, eds., New York: Elsevier Science, 2002.

Appendix

A Project Assessment Questionnaire

There are no right or wrong answers to these questions, the purpose of these questions is to ascertain an accurate view of the past and current development processes, methodologies, and practices used for your project.

A. Project and Development Team Information

1. Name of project: _____

   (a) Please provide a brief description of the project and product.

   (b) Names and roles of respondent(s) to this questionnaire:

2. Size of project (lines of code, function points, or other units):

   VA Java code?

   DB-related code?

   Other (C, C++, etc.)

3. Delivery dates for key functions (or target delivery dates) including original dates and any reset dates: _____

_____

4. Current stage of the project if not already shipped (e.g., functional test almost complete, in final test phase, product/release in beta, etc.):

5. (a) Does/did the project involve cross-site or cross-lab development?

   (b) If yes, what site(s) and lab(s)?

   (c) Is there a cross-lab development process available?

   (d) At what organizational level are cross-site/cross-team development implemented (e.g., 1st line level, 2nd line/functional level, etc.)?

6. (a) Did the design point of the project serve to satisfy multiple users or constituencies?

   (b) Was the project implemented on an open/common platform (e.g., Intel, PowerPC, Linux, Window, FreeBSD)?

       Please specify:

7. On a scale of 1 to 10 (10 being the most complex), how would you rate the complexity of the project based on your experience and knowledge of similar types of software projects?

8. Development cycle time (equate ship date with final delivery in an iterative model):

   (a) From design start to ship: _____ months

   (b) From design start to bring-up: _____ months

   (c) From bring-up to code integration complete (all coding done): _____ months

   (d) From code integration complete to internal customer use (all development tests complete) of the product: _____ months

   (e) From development test complete to GA: _____ months

9. Development team information (please provide estimates if exact numbers are not available):

   (a) Total size of team of the entire project: _____

   (b) Number of VA Java programmers spending 100% of time on project: _____

   (c) Number of VA Java programmers spending less than 100% of time on project: _____

   (d) Number of database programmers spending 100% of time on project _____

   (e) Number of database programmers spending less than 100% of time on project _____

   (f) Number of other programmers _____ (specify skills)

   (g) Distribution of team members by education background (percent):

Computer science	_____ %
Computer engineering	_____ %
Others (please specify)	_____ %
_____	_____ %

   Total 100.0% (N = total number of members)

   (h) Approximate annual turnover rate of team members: _____

10. How would you describe the skills and experience levels of this team (e.g., years with tools experience, very experienced team, large percent of new hires, etc.)?

    (a) Are there sufficient skilled technical leaders/developers in the organization to lead and support the whole team?

(b) If possible, please give percent distribution estimates with regard to years of industry software development experience:

< 2 years   _____ %

2–5 years   _____ %

> 5 years   _____ %

TOTAL   100.0%

B. Requirements and Specifications

11. To what extent did the development team review the requirements before they were incorporated into the project. (Please mark the appropriate cell for each row in the table)

	Always	Usually	Sometimes	Seldom	Never
Functional requirements					
Performance requirements					
Reliability/availability/ serviceability (RAS) requirements					
Usability requirements					
Web Publishing/ID requirements					

(a) Per your experience and assessment, how important is this practice (requirements review) to the success of tools projects? (Please mark the appropriate cell for each row in the table.)

	Very Important	Important	Somewhat Important	Not Sure
Functional requirements				
Performance requirements				
Reliability/availability/ serviceability (RAS) requirements				
Usability requirements				
Web Publishing/ID requirements				

12. Specifications were developed based on the requirements and used as the basis for project planning, design and development, testing, and related activities.

   a. Always

   b. Usually

   c. Sometimes

   d. Seldom

   e. Never

   (a) Per your experience and assessment, how important is this practice (specifications and requirements to guide overall project implementation) to the success of this project?

      a. Very important

      b. Important

      c. Somewhat important

      d. Not sure

   (b) If your assessment of the above is "very important" or "important" and your project's actual practice didn't match the level of importance, what were the reasons for the disparity (e.g., obstacles, constraints, process, culture, experiences, etc.)?

13. How did your project deal with (a) late requirements and (b) requirements changes? Please elaborate.

Project Strengths and Weaknesses with Regard to Section B

(B1) Is there any practice(s) by your project with regard to requirements and specifications that you consider a strength and that should be considered for implementation by other projects? If so, please describe and explain.

(B2) If you were to do this project all over again, what would you do differently with regard to requirements and specifications, and why?

C. Design, Code and Reviews/Inspections

14. To what extent did the design work of the project take the following into account? (Please mark the appropriate cells.)

	Largest Extent Possible	Important Consideration	Sometimes	Seldom	Don't Know
(a) Design for extensibility					
(b) Design for performance					
(c) Design for reliability/ availability/ serviceability (RAS)					
(d) Design for usability					
(e) Design for debugability					
(f) Design for maintainability					
(g) Design for testability					
(h) Design with modularity (component structure) to allow for component ownership and future enhancements					

15. Was there an overall high-level design document in place for the project as overall guidelines for implementation and for common understanding across teams and individuals?

   a. Yes

   b. No

   (a) Per your experience and assessment, how important is this practice (overall design document) to the success of this project?

      a. Very important

b. Important

c. Somewhat important

d. Not sure

16. To what extent were design reviews of the project conducted? (Please mark the appropriate cell in each row in the table.)

	All Design Work Done Rigorously	All Major Pieces of Design Items	Selected Items Based on Criteria (e.g., Error Recovery)	Design Reviews Were Occasionally Done	Not Done
Original design					
Design changes/ rework					

(a) Per your experience and assessment, how important is this practice (design review/verification) to the success of this project?

a. Very important

b. Important

c. Somewhat important

d. Not sure

(b) If your assessment in question 16(a) is "very important" or "important" and your project's actual practice didn't match the level of importance, what were the reasons for the disparity (e.g.,obstacles, constraints, process, culture, experiences, etc.)?

17. What is the most common form of design reviews for this project?

a. Formal review meeting with moderators, reviewers/inspectors, and defect tracking—issues resolution and rework completion as part of the completion criteria

b. Formal review but issue resolution is up to the owner

c. Informal review by experts of related areas

d. Codeveloper (codesigner) informal review

e. Other.....(Please specify.)

18. In your development process, are there an entry/exit criteria for major development phases?

    (a) If yes to question 18, is the review process related to the entry/exit criteria of process phases (e.g., is the successful completion of design reviews part of exit criteria of the design phase)?

    (b) If yes to question 18a, how effectively are the criteria followed/enforced?

        a. Very effectively

        b. Effectively

        c. Somewhat effectively

        d. Not effectively

    (c) If yes to question 18, if entrance/exit criteria were not met, what did you do?

    (d) Per your experience and assessment, how important is this practice (successful design review as part of exit criteria for the design phase) to the success of this project?

        a. Very important

        b. Important

        c. Somewhat important

        d. Not sure

    (e) If your assessment in question 18d is "very important" or "important" and your project's actual practice didn't match the level of importance, what were the reasons for the disparity (e.g., obstacles, constraints, process, culture, experiences, etc.)?

19. Were any coding standards used?

    If yes, please briefly describe.

20. To what extent did the code implementation of the project take the following factors into account? (Please mark the appropriate cell for each row in the table.)

	Largest Extent Possible	Important Consideration	Sometimes	Seldom	Don't Know
Code for extendibility					
Code for performance					
Code for debugability					
Code for reliability/ availability/ serviceability (RAS)					
Code for usability					
Code for maintainability					

21. To what extent were code reviews/inspections conducted? (Please mark the appropriate cell for each row in the table.)

	Rigorously 100% of the Code	Major Pieces of Code	Selected Items Based on Criteria (e.g., Error Recovery Code)	Occasionally Done	Not Done
Original code implementation					
After significant rework/changes					
Final (or near final) code implementation					

(a) Per your experience and assessment, how important is this practice (code reviews and inspections) to the success of this project?

    a. Very important

    b. Important

    c. Somewhat important

    d. Not sure

(b) If your assessment in question 21(a) is "very important" or "important" and your project's actual practice didn't match the level of importance, what were the reasons for the disparity (e.g., obstacles, constraints, process, culture, experiences, etc.)?

Project Strengths and Weaknesses with Regard to Section C

(C1) Is there any practice(s) by your project with regard to design, code, and reviews/inspections that you consider a strength and that should be considered for implementation by other projects? If so, please describe and explain.

(C2) If you were to do this project all over again, what would you do differently with regard to design, code, and reviews/inspections, and why?

D. Code Integration and Driver Build

22. Was code integration dependency (e.g., with client software, with database, with information development, with other software, with other organizations or even with other sites) a concern for this project?

    a. Yes

    b. No

(a) If yes to question 22, please briefly describe **how** such dependencies were managed from a code integration/driver build point of view for this project and **what** (tools, process, etc.) was used.

(b) Per your experience and assessment, how important is this practice (code integration dependency management) to the success of this project?

    a. Very important

    b. Important

    c. Somewhat important

    d. Not sure

(c) If your assessment in question 22b is "very important" or "important" and your project's actual practice didn't match the level of importance, what were the reasons for the disparity (e.g., obstacles, constraints, process, culture, experiences, etc.)?

23. With regard to the integration and build process, how do you control part integration?

(a) In a cross-site development environment, how is the part integration handled from an organizational point of view? Is there an owning organization responsible for part integration?

(b) If yes to question 23(a), how is the development group involved in the integration/bring-up task?

24. Please briefly describe your process, if any, in enhancing code integration quality and driver stability.

(a) Per your experience and assessment, how important is this practice (code integration control, action/process on integration quality and driver stability) to the success of this project?

    a. Very important

    b. Important

    c. Somewhat important

    d. Not sure

(b) If your assessment in question 24(a) is "very important" or "important" and your project's actual practice didn't match the level of importance, what were the reasons for the disparity (e.g., obstacles, constraints, process, culture, experiences, etc.)?

25. What is your driver build cycle (e.g., daily, weekly, biweekly, monthly, flexible— build when ready, etc.)? Please provide your observations on your build cycle as it relates to your project progress (schedule and quality). If it varied throughout the project, please describe how this was handled through the different phases (i.e., early function delivery and bring-up, vs. fix-only mode, etc.).

Project Strengths and Weaknesses with Regard to Section D

(D1) Is there any practice(s) by your project with regard to code integration and driver build that you consider a strength and that should be considered for implementation by other projects? If so, please describe and explain.

(D2) If you were to do this project all over again, what would you do differently with regard to code integration and driver build, and why?

E. Test

26. Was there a test plan in place for this project at the functional (development test) and overall project level (including independent test team)? Who initiated the test plan? (Please fill in the cells in the table.)

	Test Plan in Place (Yes/No)	Who Initiated	Who Executed
Development Test			
Overall Project			

27. What types of test/test phases (unit, simulation test, functional, regression, independent test group, etc.) were conducted for this project? Please specify and give a brief explanation of each.

(a) Please elaborate on your error recovery or "bad path" testing.

(b) Please elaborate on your regression testing.

28. Was test coverage/code coverage measurement implemented?
    If yes, for which test(s), and who does it?

29. Are entry/exit criteria used for the major test phases/types?
    If yes, (a) please provide a brief description.

    (b) How are the criteria used or enforced?

    (a) Per your experience and assessment, how important is this practice
        (entry/exit criteria for major tests) to the success of this project?
        a. Very important
        b. Important
        c. Somewhat important
        d. Not sure

    (b) If your assessment in question 29a is "very important" or "important" and
        your project's actual practice didn't match the level of importance, what were
        the reasons for the disparity (e.g., obstacles, constraints, process, culture,
        experiences, etc.)?

30. Is there a change control process in place for integrating fixes?
    a. Yes (please briefly describe)
    b. No

(a) If yes, how effectively in your assessment is the process being implemented?

  a. Very effectively

  b. Effectively

  c. Somewhat effectively

  d. Not effectively

(b) Per your experience and assessment, how important is this practice (change control for defect fixes) to the success of this project?

  a. Very important

  b. Important

  c. Somewhat important

  d. Not sure

(c) If your assessment in question 30b is "very important" or "important" and your project's actual practice/effectiveness didn't match the level of importance, what were the reasons for the disparity (e.g., obstacles, constraints, process, culture, experiences, etc.)?

Project Strengths and Weaknesses with Regard to Section E

(E1) Is there any practice(s) by your project with regard to testing that you consider a strength and that should be considered for implementation by other projects? If so, please describe and explain.

(E2) If you were to do this project all over again, what would you do differently with regard to testing, and why?

F. Project Management

  31. Was there a dedicated project manager for this project?

  (a) How would you describe the role of project management for this project?

    a. Project management was basically done by line management.

b. There was a project coordinator—coordinating activities and reporting status across development teams and line managers.

c. There was a project manager but major project decisions were progress-driven by line management.

d. The project manager, together with line management, was responsible for the success of the project. The project manager drove progress (e.g., dependency, schedule, quality) of the project and improvements across teams and line management areas.

e. Other.....(Please specify/describe.)

(b) Per your experience and assessment, how important is this practice (effective role of project management) to the success of this project?

a. Very important

b. Important

c. Somewhat important

d. Not sure

(c) If your assessment in question 31(b) is "very important" or "important" and your project's actual practice didn't match the level of importance, what were the reasons for the disparity (e.g., obstacles, constraints, process, culture, experiences, etc.)?

32. How were sizing estimates of the project (specifically the amount of design and development work) derived?

33. How was the development schedule developed for this project? Please provide a brief statement (e.g., top-down [GA date mandated], bottom-up, bottom-up and top-down converged with proper experiences and history, based on sizing estimates, etc.).

(a) Per your experience and assessment, how important is this practice (effective sizing and schedule development process based on skills and experiences) to the success of this project?

a. Very important

b. Important

c. Somewhat important

d. Not sure

(b) If your assessment in question 33(a) is "very important" or "important" and your project's actual practice didn't match the level of importance, what were the reasons for the disparity (e.g., obstacles, constraints, process, culture, experiences, etc.)?

34. Was a staged delivery/code drop plan developed early based on priorities and dependencies and executed?

  a. Yes, please briefly describe.

  b. No, please briefly describe.

  (a) Per your experience and assessment, how important is this practice (good staging and code drop plan) to the success of this project?

      a. Very important

      b. Important

      c. Somewhat important

      d. Not sure

  (b) If your assessment in question 34a is "very important" or "important" and your project's actual practice didn't match the level of importance, what were the reasons for the disparity (e.g., obstacles, constraints, process, culture, experiences, etc.)?

35. Does this project have to satisfy multiple constituents or diverse users?

    If yes, (a) how was work prioritized?

    (b) How was workload distribution determined?

    (c) How was conflict resolved?

36. If this is a cross-site development project (Question 5), please briefly describe how cross-site dependency was managed.

37. Under what level of management were major dependencies for deliverables managed?

    a. Under the same development manager

    b. Under the same functional manager

    c. Across functional areas but under the same development directors

    d. Coordination across development directors

    e. Under the same project executive

    f. Other... Please describe.

38. What were the major obstacles, if any, to effective team communications for your project?

39. Were major checkpoint reviews conducted at various stages of the project throughout the development cycle?

    a. Yes

    b. No

    (a) If yes to question 39, please describe the major checkpoint review deliverables.

    (b) If yes to question 39, how effective in your view were those checkpoint reviews? Please briefly explain.

        a. Very effective

        b. Effective

        c. Somewhat effective

        d. Not effective

(c) Per your experience and assessment, how important is this practice (effective checkpoint process) to the success of this project?

   a. Very important

   b. Important

   c. Somewhat important

   d. Not sure

(d) If your assessment in question 39(c) is "very important" or "important" and your project's actual practice didn't match the level of importance, what were the reasons for the disparity (e.g., obstacles, constraints, process, culture, experiences, etc.)?

Project Strengths and Weaknesses with Regard to Section F

(F1) Is there any practice(s) by your project with regard to project management that you consider a strength and that should be considered for implementation by other projects? If so, please describe and explain.

(F2) If you were to do this project all over again, what would you do differently with regard to project management, and why?

G. Metrics, Measurements, Analysis

40. Were any in-process metrics used to manage the progress (schedule and quality) of the project (e.g., function delivery tracking, problem backlog tracking, test plan execution, etc.)?

   a. Yes

   b. No

   (a) If yes, please specify/describe where applicable.

      (1) Metric(s) used at the front end of the development cycle (i.e., up to code integration)

      (2) Metric(s) used for driver stability

      (3) Metric(s) used during testing with targets/baselines for comparisons

      (4) Others (simulation measurement, test coverage/code coverage measurement, etc.)—Please specify.

(b) Per your experience and assessment, how important is this practice (good metrics for schedule and quality management) to the success of this project?

   a. Very important

   b. Important

   c. Somewhat important

   d. Not sure

(c) If your assessment in question 40(b) is "very important" or "important" and your project's actual practice didn't match the level of importance, what were the reasons for the disparity (e.g., obstacles, constraints, process, culture, experiences, etc.)?

41. Was there any defect cause analysis (e.g., problem components, Pareto analysis) which resulted in improvement/corrective actions during the development of the project?

   If yes, please describe briefly.

Project Strengths and Weaknesses with Regard to Section G

(G1) Is there any practice(s) by your project with regard to metrics, measurements, and analysis you consider a strength and that should be considered for implementation by other projects? If so, please describe and explain.

(G2) If you were to do this project all over again, what would you do differently with regard to metrics, measurements, and analysis, and why?

H. Development Environment/Library

42. Please name and describe briefly your development environment/platform(s) and source code library system(s).

43. To what extent was the entire team familiar with the operational, build, and support environment?

44. Was your current development environment or any part of it a hindrance in any way? What changes might enhance the development process for quality, efficiency, or ease-of-use? Please provide specifics.

Project Strengths and Weaknesses with Regard to Section H

(H1) Is there any practice(s) by your project with regard to development environment/library system that you consider a strength and that should be considered for implementation by other projects? If so, please describe and explain.

(H2) If there is any development environment/library system that per your assessment is the best for tools development, please describe and explain.

(H3) If you were to do this project all over again, what would you do differently with regard to development environment/library system, and why?

I. Tools/Methodologies

45. In what language(s) was the code for the project written?

46. Was the project developed with

    a. object-oriented methodology?

    b. procedural methods?

47. Are multiple environments required in order to fully test the project? If so, please describe.

48. Are any kind of simulation test environments available? Please describe.

(a) If yes to question 48, how important is this to the success of tools projects?

    a. Very important

    b. Important

    c. Somewhat important

    d. Not sure

49. Please describe briefly any tools that were used for each of the following areas:

    (a) Design

    (b) Debug

    (c) Test—code coverage

    (d) Test—automation/stress

    (e) Other. Please explain.

50. What was the learning curve of the development team to become proficient in using the above tools and the development environment/library discussed earlier? Please provide information if any specific education is needed.

Project Strengths and Weaknesses with Regard to Section I

(I1) Is there any practice(s) by your project with regard to tools and methodologies you consider a strength and that should be considered for implementation by other projects? If so, please describe and explain.

(I2) If any tools and methodologies that per your assessment are the best for the type of projects similar to this project, please describe and explain.

(I3) If you were to do this project all over again, what would you do differently with regard to tools and methodologies?

J. Project Outcome Assessment

51. Please provide a candid assessment of the schedule achievement (vs. original schedule) of the project. Please provide any pertinent information as appropriate (e.g., adherence to original schedule, meeting/not meeting GA date, meeting/not meeting interim checkpoints, any schedule reset, any function cutback/increase, unrealistic schedule to begin with, etc.).

52. Please provide a candid assessment of the quality outcome of the project. Please provide any pertinent information as appropriate (e.g., in-process indicators, test defect volumes/rates, field quality indicators, customer feedback, customer satisfaction measurements, customer critical situations, any existing analysis and presentations. Please attach files or documents, etc.).

53. How would you rate the overall success of the project (schedule, quality, costs, meeting commitments, etc.)?

    a. Very successful

    b. Successful

    c. Somewhat successful

    d. Not satisfactory

K. Comments

Please provide any comments, observations, insights with regard to your project specifically or tools projects in general.

Index

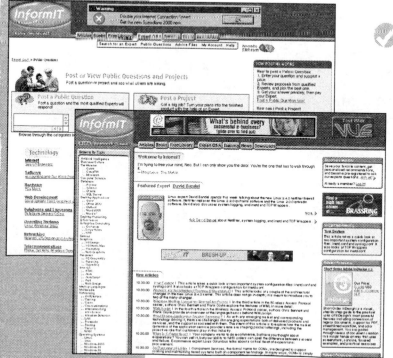